# The Backyard Bird Lover's
# FIELD GUIDE

# The Backyard Bird Lover's

## FIELD GUIDE

### Secrets to Attracting, Identifying, and Enjoying Birds of Your Region

## SALLY ROTH

RODALE

Rodale books may be purchased for business or promotional use or for special sales. For information, please write to:
Special Markets Department, Rodale Inc., 733 Third Avenue, New York, NY 10017

Printed in the United States of America
Rodale Inc. makes every effort to use acid-free ♾, recycled paper ♻.

Book design by Christina Gaugler
Illustrations by Neil Gower

**Library of Congress Cataloging-in-Publication Data**

Roth, Sally.
    The backyard bird lover's field guide : secrets to attracting, identifying, and enjoying birds of your region / Sally Roth.
        p.    cm.
    Includes bibliographical references and index.
    ISBN-13 978-1-59486-603-6 hardcover
    ISBN-10 1-59486-603-1 hardcover
    ISBN-13 978-1-59486-602-9 paperback
    ISBN-10 1-59486-602-3 paperback
    1. Birds—United States—Identification.    I. Title.
QL682.R68   2007
598.07'23473—dc22                                                                                                2007015222

**Distributed to the trade by Holtzbrinck Publishers**

2   4   6   8   10   9   7   5   3   1   hardcover
2   4   6   8   10   9   7   5   3   1   paperback

We inspire and enable people to improve their lives and the world around them

For more of our products visit **rodalestore.com** or call 800-848-4735

*For Gretel and David, with love*

# CONTENTS

## Chapter Seven: Birds of the Northeast....121

## Chapter Eight: Birds of the Far North....147

## Chapter Nine: Birds of the Southeast and South....175

# ACKNOWLEDGMENTS

Writing a book reminds me of growing a garden. Without the sun and rain, without the wiggly earthworms and the wrens, without the seeds and the nurturing, a garden wouldn't look like much.

Thanks to senior editor Karen Bolesta for guiding this book from the first sprout of an idea to the full-flowering result you now hold in your hands. Just as important, Karen, thanks for always being ready to lend a supportive ear, whether I was whining about work or about the eddies of my personal life.

Weeding and arranging makes a garden look its best, and an editor does the same for a book. Anne Halpin White, a birder herself, is the kind of astute and good-natured editor that writers usually only dream of. She edited my words with grace and good humor, even when the schedule was at its tightest—right at Christmastime! Thanks, Anne, for keeping me laughing. A whole sackful from Santa Claus can't compare with the gift of your work on this book.

As any gardener knows, watching for pests is part of the process. On a book, copyeditors are the last line of defense. They notice every little spot where a missing comma or misplaced phrase might give a reader pause. Senior project editor Nancy Bailey and copy editor Claire McCrea did a great job of polishing the details and alerting me to places where my typing fingers raced too far ahead of my brain, where readers might be left scratching their heads and wondering, "What does she mean?"

Have you ever noticed how a summer shower refreshes the garden? Kris Kennedy, the best naturalist I've ever met, kept me inspired by sharing the joy of nature both afield and in conversation. He generously contributed his own knowledge of western birds, and he tirelessly researched the latest science to make sure my observations were in keeping with the experts. Sometimes that wasn't the case, which led to spirited discussions about discrepancies between what real live bird-watchers see for themselves and the historical "facts" in literature that sometime turn out to be only repeated lore. In those cases, I relied on my own observations instead of those of the experts. I may not have a string of initials following my name, but after a lifetime of watching birds, I trust my own eyes.

Beauty is one of the big reasons we love our gardens, and it's just as important in a book. A big thank you to associate art director Christina Gaugler, who prettied up these pages with an eye toward the aesthetic. That's quite a trick, when you consider that the pages also have to be readable and inviting. Thanks, Chris, for your artistic design—any chance you can work on my wardrobe next? Photo editor Robin Hepler added more beauty to these pages with her careful selection of photos. For the bird profiles, she managed to find photos that show each bird in detail, but also give a glimpse into their personalities. Thanks to layout designer Faith Hague, who grappled with the tough task of finding room for all of my observations, anecdotes, and fun facts on each bird profile page. And finally, thanks to artist Neil Gower for his beautiful map illustrations.

Of course, without somebody to share the thrill of those first ripe tomatoes or sweet-scented roses, a garden isn't nearly as much fun. My most heartfelt thanks goes to you, the backyard bird lover. Writing with you in mind makes me feel like we're looking at birds together, telling stories and sharing observations. I hope you feel that way, too.

# INTRODUCTION

I was exploring the Cascade Mountains with a naturalist friend one fine fall day when we stopped to better admire the fantastic draperies of old-man's beard lichen decorating the firs. The gray lichen hung down 3 feet or more, backlit by the sun low in the sky and swaying with the slightest breath of wind.

The lichen was beautiful but was instantly upstaged as soon as my friend asked, "What's that bird?"

It's unusual for us not to announce a bird by name: Usually we say "Junco," or "Pileated," or "Varied thrush," not "What's that bird?" So I hurriedly focused my binoculars on the small bird perched quietly on a bare branch in the treetop.

"Owl!" I exclaimed, recognizing the bigger than usual head and neckless look. "Saw-whet? Pygmy?" I'm not nearly as good at identifying owls as I am at identifying songbirds in the Northwest region where I live. All I was sure of was that this was one of the small owl species.

"Not a saw-whet," my friend said with surety. "Pygmy. Look at that tail."

Meanwhile, I was scrabbling through my Sibley field guide, flipping through pages as fast as I could while trying to keep one eye on the bird.

"Northern pygmy owl," I confirmed, finding the match for our small, long-tailed bird.

We went back to looking, quietly commenting on the details—the speckled back, the boldly striped breast, the white-freckled face. Even with the sun behind it, we could make out enough markings to be certain of the ID.

The 7-inch owl stayed put, occasionally turning its head to look at us. I pulled out the book again. "Largely diurnal," I read, and right then, the bird took off. Leaving his treetop perch, he sailed downward across the dirt road, swooping upward at the end to a new perch just a few feet from the ground, exactly like a varied thrush, a common bird in these forested hills, might do.

"Wow, he looked just like a thrush flying," I said. "Wonder how many times I've seen one and thought 'thrush'?"

We never got another look at the owl, which stayed hidden among the dense branches. But ever since, I've looked longer and harder at any bird I've seen, just in case it's a 7-inch owl instead of a songbird.

It was Jim Brett, curator emeritus of Hawk Mountain Sanctuary in eastern Pennsylvania, who first gave me the same advice. I'd grown lazy about identifying the many hawks that approached the lookout at the sanctuary, dropping my binoculars as soon as I had a fix on which raptor I was seeing—which I usually did by recognizing its silhouette alone, while the bird was still at a distance.

"Keep looking as long as you can see the bird," Jim advised the watchers at the lookout. Sometimes a bird identified as a red-tailed hawk might turn out to be an eagle;

sometimes a Cooper's hawk might actually be a peregrine falcon. Only by keeping sight of the bird in binoculars until an unmistakable and unique feature was noted could anyone be absolutely, positively sure of the identification.

I've taken Jim's advice to heart. Even after years of watching birds, I can still be fooled: A flock of white-throated sparrows might have a golden-crowned in their midst. A hummingbird in dim light might be a black-chinned, not an Anna's. And a varied thrush might really be a northern pygmy owl.

Most times, though, identifying a bird at a glance doesn't require so much attention to detail. Most birds are so unique in their looks and habits that it's easy to ID them with just one quick look.

I bet you're already good at identifying some of the birds in your backyard. Mourning dove? Junco? Hummingbird? White-throated sparrow? American goldfinch (well, at least the male)? Chances are, you have 'em nailed.

You already know how those birds look and act, and where the likeliest places are that you'll see them. So when you spot one of these birds, your brain comes up with the right name as if by magic.

It's not magic, but experience, that puts those names on the tip of our tongue. We unconsciously add up every bit of information we're seeing, sift through it lightning-fast, and presto! Those big, grayish tan birds with the long pointy tails, the ones that are quietly nibbling seeds below the feeder—why, they have to be mourning doves. How do we know? We've recognized their appearance, we know that's their usual place in our yard, we've heard their cooing, and we probably have even registered that they usually show up in pairs or small groups.

In Part One of this book, you'll discover general tips and tricks of bird identification—methods and suggestions that will help you become a better bird-watcher. In Part Two, you'll meet the beautiful birds that keep life interesting in every part of the country. You'll find a "First Impression," the instant information that's a huge clue to pinpointing a species, as well as the finer points that you can also use to narrow it down. And, since I couldn't stop there, you'll also learn about each species' home life and habits, and how to make that bird happy in your own yard.

Learning how to identify what you're looking at only increases the fun of watching birds. As you learn their names, you'll be paying more attention to their fascinating behavior. You'll feel a stronger connection, whether the birds are at your feeder or singing in your tree. And you'll be looking forward to the next visitor that wings its way into your backyard. I wonder what it will be?

# IDENTIFYING BIRDS

How can you figure out who's who among birds when typical field guides show hundreds of pictures that take forever to sort out?

Welcome to bird identification, Sally-style.

In *The Backyard Bird Lover's Field Guide*, I've kept it simple. Instead of sifting through hundreds of "slim chance" birds, you'll find a much more manageable flock—the *most likely backyard birds* in your own geographic region.

You'll learn more about my quick-and-easy approach in Part Two of this book. Go ahead, turn to your region and see what's in store. I'll wait.

Then come back to Part One to discover how identifying birds can bring you health, happiness, and, well, not wealth, I'm sorry to say, but how about a lifetime of delight?

# Chapter One

# Why Birds?

One of my favorite things in nature is lichens, especially those flat, round patches that decorate rocks. The idea that anything would grow on a rock, turning sunlight into food and very slowly disintegrating that rock, just boggles my mind. So does the incredibly slow growth rate of some lichens, which spread outward so infinitesimally that you can't tell the difference 5 years later.

Finding a lichen I haven't seen before is as big a thrill to me as finding a new seashell on the beach. But finding someone to share that thrill with used to be a little trickier. Now that lichen appreciators can find each other on the Internet, I have others to share my finds with. Still, it's a very small group of enthusiasts.

Thankfully, my other obsessions have a much wider appeal. I have plenty of folks to talk about flowers or butterflies with. And birds? They're the hottest topic of all. In the past 10 years, the birding scene has exploded. Today, more than 50 million of us take part—that's one out of every five people in the United States!

Whether we fill a feeder or take a trip to a hummingbird hot spot, we have plenty of company. Birding is bigger than gardening. Bigger than hunting and fishing combined. I know, I can hardly believe it either. But the "birding industry"—the suppliers of seed, feeders, and all other products or services related to our favorite pastime—assures us it's true.

**It's easy to get hooked on birds—just fill a feeder and watch who comes to dinner. Millions of us, of all ages, share the thrill.**

3

Most of us participate in our own back-yards, so it's no wonder the pastime tends to fly under the radar. Maybe we should all take up wearing lime green porkpie hats, so we could spot each other.

Speaking of dorky hats, remember when bird-watchers used to be a joke? Cartoons often featured a bunch of folks peering through binoculars, with a mocking punch line aimed at the earnest group.

All you had to do was say, "Yellow-bellied flycatcher," to make your friends burst out laughing.

Okay, so "yellow-bellied flycatcher" still sounds funny. And a bunch of people staring through binocs at the same spot is incongruous enough to cause a giggle (unless you're wondering, "Hey, what are they looking at?").

But nobody's laughing at bird-watchers

## Oohing and Aahing

No matter how different we are, we all seem to agree on what's beautiful, what's endearing, or what's repulsive.

Sure, some of those reactions are dictated by culture, and they may change with the times. (Remember when mauve looked good?)

But other things seem to affect us at a visceral level.

Think about a Fourth of July fireworks show, when one of those huge, arching gold fountains rains down overhead. The whole crowd exclaims "Ooh!" in unison.

Beautiful scenery? We agree on that, too. We put it on puzzle boxes and calendars and the picture over the sofa, and we travel to see it. (Hint: It's not a strip mall or a freeway.)

A puppy, colt, lamb, curly-haired toddler? Say "Aww," everyone.

As for gross, there's no need to go into details. We all know what makes us say "Eew!"

I'm convinced that these emotional reactions we seem to share are a big reason why birds have such wide appeal. We simply enjoy watching them as they go about their lives.

Lots of birds fall into the cute or pretty category. Chickadees and fuzzy-headed young birds at our feeder get an involuntary "Aww." Goldfinches, magpies, jays, and other colorful characters make us sit up and take notice. And, like that finale at the fireworks, bluebirds, buntings, tanagers, orioles, and a flock of cardinals in winter are so beautiful, we just have to say "Ooh."

**Chickadees are so irresistibly cute that they sell everything from sweatshirts to coffee mugs. Live birds are even better!**

anymore, not since we've become an industry all by ourselves.

How big an industry?

Hang onto that seed scoop: Birding brings in $25 billion a year. Yessir, all those bags of seed sure add up. Not to mention the fancy feeders and binoculars and ecotours to Costa Rica.

So just what is it about birds? Why not, say, rocks? Or lizards? Or, for that matter, lichens? Let's take a look.

## A PERFECT FIT

Rocks and lizards definitely have their fans. But they miss out on wide appeal for a few simple reasons.

A crystal of clear quartz or a bit of smooth veined turquoise is beautiful to look at. For a few minutes. But no matter how long you watch them, rocks don't do very much. They don't change, unless you have a way longer life expectancy than the rest of us.

Besides, hunting for special rocks is not something you want to share with anyone outside a small, close circle. Rock hounds generally keep quiet about their best finds, instead of letting others in on the discovery. (Anytime you want to share that favorite opal digging spot with me, just give a holler!)

Lizards . . . well, let's just say that for many people, they're an acquired taste. Scales just can't compare to pretty feathers. Lizards aren't often seen basking in the backyard in many areas, either.

Sure, cute little chameleons had a run of popularity there for a while. But most folks never cross the line into putting out a feeder for Gila monsters or raising chickens to tempt a 6-foot iguana.

Birds, on the other hand, have built-in appeal.

Alert and active, bright-eyed birds are a pleasure to watch. They communicate with each other, by song and calls. They're everywhere, in plain sight. And there's no ick factor, like there is with lizards. As a bird-loving friend used to say, "What's not to like?"

Plus, despite that $25 billion figure, you don't have to spend a cent to enjoy them. They're singing right in your own backyard.

## Convenience Counts

If your garage is bursting at the seams with tennis racquets, mountain bikes, and all the other apparatus of your outdoor pursuits, you'll appreciate the simplicity of bird-watching.

All you really need are the birds, and they're everywhere.

And maybe a pair of binoculars. Oh, and a metal can for storing seed. But that's it. Unless you want to make your own feeders and houses. Then you'll need a corner for that workbench.

## The Birth of Birdfeeders

When the movie *The Graduate* came out in 1967, I was a young teen. I left the theater with a serious crush on Dustin Hoffman. But what I should have paid attention to was the single word of advice he got from an older man in the movie: "Plastics," the fellow said, as if imparting the wisdom of the ages.

You know, maybe it was.

If I'd followed that advice and bought stock in plastics companies way back then, well, let's just say I wouldn't be shopping for cheap deals on sunflower seed.

Speaking of sunflower seed, I'm convinced that the hobby of bird-watching owes much of its amazing growth to plastic. Plastic feeders, to be exact. Red barn–shaped feeders, if we want to narrow it down even further. They were cheap. They were cute, in a country-folksy kind of way. And all of a sudden, in the early 1970s, they were for sale everywhere.

If you remember *The Graduate* (in movie theaters—DVDs don't count!), you probably also remember those feeders. They weren't particularly elegant, but they brought in birds.

That's why I say the boom in bird-watching began with plastic: Feeders could be mass-produced, instead of being sawed and hammered together one at a time. They could carry a tempting low price, just right for that impulse buy near the checkout.

Of course, if you bought a bird feeder, you needed some seed to put in it. Presto, another branch of the industry was born.

Then came another juggernaut: the introduction of the hummingbird nectar feeder, with parts molded from—take a wild guess—yep, plastic. Perky-Pet of Colorado, branching out from its pet-supplies line, made one of the first models. Although another company came up with an earlier model way back in 1950, it was Perky-Pet's reasonably priced and widely available feeder that really started the wave, sometime in the 1970s. The hummingbird feeder was an instant hit because, like the red barn feeder, it worked. Word started to spread, as friends and neighbors enthused about their birds.

Early entrepreneurs started packaging new seed mixes and new seeds. Thistle seed, now called nyjer or niger, arrived on the scene, and soon so did the tube feeders to hold it.

Droll Yankee, Inc., made the first tube feeders in the early 1970s. They were built to last but carried a hefty price tag. Still, once you saw their perches stacked with goldfinches, you wanted one yourself. A Droll Yankee tube feeder in your yard conveyed instant status among those in the know.

Imitations soon arrived, many made from—you guessed it—plastic. Now everyone could have goldfinches!

Success builds on itself. As their feeders attracted birds, folks wanted more—more birds, different birds, more feeders, more foods.

The industry was happy to oblige. Although it stayed relatively small for years, by 1984 birdseed alone was bringing in a cool half-billion bucks. Only 8 years later (1992),

A basin of fresh water is basic to a bird-friendly yard, as this goldfinch attests.

more than $2 billion in birdseed was flying off the shelves.

Yep. Shoulda bought plastics.

## Come a Little Bit Closer

Birds are abundant across the country. We don't need to travel to where the birds are. We can just stay home and let them come to us.

Every neighborhood has its birds. No matter where you live, you can just step out the door—or look out a window—and you'll soon see some birds to watch.

You won't have any problem finding a robin to look at. Some birds are perfectly happy to hop about out in the open where we can plainly see them.

Other birds, though, tend to stick to the bushes or trees instead of parading around on the lawn. It takes a lot of patience to get a good look at a chickadee, for instance. Like a lot of birds, chickadees are always on the move, swinging from one branch to another or flitting away before you get a good look.

That's why most of us soon set up a feeder. A tempting tray or tube of seed, plus a block of suet, will quickly coax birds into easy view. Even if they dash in and out at the feeder, we'll still get a better look than if they were in a tree.

Add a birdbath or a fountain, and birds will have another reason to come a little closer. In late winter, you can nail up birdhouses to attract a family. Come spring, you can set out bits of string, cotton, wool, and other materials to entice nesting birds.

Besides putting out food and water and nesting materials for birds, we have another sneaky way to bring them into better view.

## Have a Seat

I do a lot of my backyard bird-watching from my sitting spots—a bench under the apple tree, a couple of old wooden chairs out front, the edge of the porch, the back steps. And whenever I go out looking for birds, I spend way more time leaning against a tree or sitting on a comfy rock than I do scrambling through brush or hiking the trails.

Birds are easy to scare, and they'll take cover or slip away if they see an unusual motion or an intruder. But when birds think you're just part of the scenery, you'll get to see more birds, and more interesting behavior.

I could blame my aging joints for my habit of sitting, but really, it's because the bird-watching is better when I'm sitting still. Once I get settled, it takes just a few minutes for the birds to return to their normal activities all around me.

There aren't many outdoor pursuits in which sitting still is a valuable skill. Those of us with creaky knees are grateful!

**Watching birds is a great excuse, er, reason, to spend more time sitting in your garden. A young friend adds to the fun.**

Put a pair of binoculars to your eyes, and you'll be able to see the faintest stripe at a sparrow's eye, or the color of its beak.

Binoculars aren't strictly necessary, especially if your feeder is near your window. But they do make it easier to see details. And they're indispensable when you branch out beyond the feeder to the fields.

### The Other Side of the Fence

It's human nature to want what we don't have. No matter how great the birds are in your own backyard, you'll still find yourself lingering over pictures of birds from other areas.

Maybe it's an indigo bunting you long to see at your feeder, or a bluebird that's your Holy Grail. "Oh, if only we had (bird *x*)," you sigh.

I do it, too.

Just a few days after an out-of-town guest had marveled at the Bullock's orioles and black-headed grosbeaks in my backyard—birds I see every day in summer—I found myself pining for a bird I couldn't have.

I was chatting with a radio show host in southeast Texas, reminiscing about the cypress swamps and the grasslands down there in Big Thicket land.

"Say hi to those cattle egrets for me," I said. "I sure do miss them."

"Cattle egrets? You mean white cowbirds? You miss *them*?"

"Absolutely," I said. "We don't have them up here in the Pacific Northwest."

He couldn't believe it. These small heron relatives are so common down there, no one gives them a second thought. They're just part of the scenery in any cow pasture, totally taken for granted. To a northwesterner, though, they're a bird to yearn for.

That's why you'll find tons of mouth-watering ads in any birding magazine for trips to exotic places—like Costa Rica, Mexico … and New Jersey. Come see sandhill cranes dancing in Wisconsin. Whooping cranes in Texas. Hummingbirds in Arizona, wood warblers in Michigan, hawks in New Jersey. It all sounds so tempting, like living a *National Geographic* magazine article.

Whenever I start feeling deprived by not being able to travel to see special birds, I remind myself of the way "the grass is always greener" syndrome works.

If I lived in the North Woods, where wood warblers are a dime a dozen, I'd be lusting after hummingbirds in Arizona.

And if I had a house in the canyon in Arizona and went through gallons of sugar water a day, I'd probably have the ad for that wood warbler trip taped to my refrigerator.

Whenever I start to feel the grass is greener in other backyards, I remind myself of the first time I saw a Steller's jay. Or an Anna's hummingbird. Or any of the other birds that make birding in the Northwest so special. (Especially if you live somewhere else!)

**Steller's jay is a common sight in the West.**

## Something Different Every Day

The more you watch birds, the more you'll see—and hear. You'll learn their songs and their plumages. You'll note behavior differences and personality types.

Every day brings something new. And just when you think you have a bird figured out, it'll do something that takes you totally by surprise.

### The Changing Scene

Whenever I see the first small flock of red-winged blackbirds getting together, I feel a twinge of melancholy. The beginning of flocking behavior, in blackbirds, grackles, starlings, or swallows, means the end of summer. No more long lazy evenings on the deck. Shorter days. And soon the rainy season once again.

As you spend more time watching birds, you'll realize that they follow a yearly pattern in their lives that's timed to the cycle of the seasons. The pattern is just as predictable as a maple flaming red in October.

Here's a quick preview of what you can expect.

◆ Spring will bring incredible migrants stopping by, calling you out the door with unusual songs or thrilling you with a flash of exotic color. Indigo buntings, rose-breasted grosbeaks, tanagers—anything can happen!

◆ Summer slows feeder traffic, because birds are nesting and natural food is at its peak. Now's the time to look for parents carrying food to nests. Add mealworms to your birds' menu, too, to attract the takeout trade.

◆ Late summer brings fledglings to the feeder with their parents. Watch for many birds to take on new colors now, too, as they shift into quieter plumage for fall and winter. Birdsong fades away after nesting; no more dawn chorus.

◆ In late summer to early fall, you'll notice some birds beginning to hang out in small flocks. Some, such as grackles, blackbirds, or starlings, may stick around in flocks that can grow to enormous numbers. Others, such as flickers, robins, and finches, will move along on migration.

◆ Fall means saying goodbye to some favorites, like wrens and tanagers, and hello to other birds passing through or returning for winter. If you live in a mild winter area, you'll be greeting birds that summered up north, like bluebirds and catbirds.

◆ Late fall and winter will be a busy time at your feeder, with dozens of birds hoping for a handout every day.

◆ Some species are reliable friends that you see year-round—jays, house finches, song sparrows, and a handful of others. They're the foundation of your backyard bird club, the charter members who stick around.

### Pleasures of the Ordinary

When you watch birds, you never know what you're going to see.

But you *can* count on seeing something interesting.

Some days are "Oh wow!" days. Maybe a storm has blown an oddball bird off course, right into your yard. Maybe a migrating flock has decided to have breakfast in your bushes. Maybe the titmice have brought their fuzzy-headed babies to the peanut-butter feeder.

More often you'll just share "ordinary life" with your birds. Could be you'll happen to notice a cardinal collecting twigs for its nest, or you'll see a song sparrow pulling dead grass from your *Miscanthus* clump for its nest. Maybe you'll see a robin filling its beak with mud at the place where your hose is hooked up. Or a blue jay splashing in your birdbath.

That's the best thing about watching birds. Even the most ordinary bird activities are fascinating to see.

### Continuing Education

I learn plenty just by watching birds, but sometimes I get scientific and devise an experiment.

A few years back, I put a pair of orioles to the test. I'd been putting out white strings for them to use in the nest they were building. Sometimes the strings got into a tangle, but I noticed the orioles always managed to get the snarl undone.

Ah, but how clever were they at knots?

First, I tied a tempting piece of string to the branch with a single over-and-under knot, like you do when tying your shoes.

No challenge at all. The male oriole instantly pulled it free.

Okay, double knot. That took him a little longer, but he got that one pretty quick, too.

Triple? Hmm, now he looked confused. After a few minutes he gave up, and the female arrived. She was baffled at first. Then she carefully peered at the knots, her head cocked to one side like she was thinking hard. With a flurry of short, quick jerks at seemingly random spots on the knot, she managed to work it free.

Four knots was too hard a task. Neither bird could tug them loose. Finally, they began shredding the ends of the string and pulling out individual fibers.

Fast-forward 15 years to a new pair of orioles on the other side of the country. It's May of last year, I have just moved to a new place, and I'm wondering how my pair of Bullock's orioles in Washington State compares to its Baltimore relatives back East?

I put out string. One knot, nothing to it.

Two knots: Hey, what's this? The female looks suspiciously toward the house, as if she knows I'm playing a trick on her. But she works it out and triumphantly carries off the string.

Three knots. Uh-oh. No can do. Much chattering, much tugging, no luck.

After two days, I clipped the now very tight knot, loosened the string, and stopped making their lives difficult.

"You know, they sure are pretty, but these

**Want a Bullock's or Baltimore oriole? Try a nectar feeder with perches.**

orioles aren't as smart as my old ones," I announced to a friend, as we watched the birds drink sugar water from the feeder they visited every morning.

Oh, aren't they?

"Someone's at the door," called the same friend from the kitchen a few days later, "and he has a complaint."

"What? Where?" I asked, not seeing anyone outside the full-length glass door.

My friend pointed to the floor of the deck, just outside the door. There stood the male oriole, on tiptoe, pecking at the glass. "I think he's trying to tell you something."

The nectar feeder was empty.

Hmm. Intelligence test, indeed.

Wonder how fast the last people who lived here figured that out?

## 50 YEARS OF ENTERTAINMENT

Maybe I'm just easily amused, but I've been watching birds for 50-some years, oops, I mean 39, and it hasn't lost its thrill one bit.

I love being out in the yard on an April morning at the peak of migration, when all my old friends—the vireos, the warblers, the tanagers—are singing "We're back! We're back!"

But the plain old feeder can also keep me entertained for way longer than seems likely. An hour can slip by like nothing when there's a crew of chickadees, nuthatches, and jays coming and going on a winter day. Even house sparrows and starlings are fun to watch.

Not only does watching birds cure boredom, it's also good for your blood pressure. Researchers discovered years ago that feeder-watching takes your mind off your cares and woes, and lowers heart rate and blood pressure.

You can pick up this lifelong hobby at any age. No matter how old you are, or how young you are, birds are fascinating to see.

Watching birds is even more fun when you share it with someone, because you both get to share the thrill of your discoveries. Family and friends—of any age—will love having coffee with the chickadees or spying on the hummingbirds at the hostas.

There's even more good news: You can be a birder on any kind of budget. The only must is a working pair of eyes or ears. Everything else is optional!

## Get Equipped

How much did you say that last set of golf clubs cost you? And the bag and shoes? The balls? The little hats for your clubs? Oh, and let's not forget the greens fees.

Or maybe you'd rather run the numbers on mountain biking? Skiing? Fishing?

Face it. Whatever we want to play outside costs money these days. Serious money.

Except birding.

When it comes to watching birds, you don't need the right shoes, the right clothes, the right *anything*.

People have watched and listened to birds for thousands of years using nothing more than their own eyes and ears.

All you need is an interest—you already have that, or you wouldn't be reading this—and a pair of binoculars. And if you're on a Ramen noodles budget, you can hold off on the binocs.

Oh, sure, there are all kinds of high-power spotting scopes and hiking boots and birdcall CDs and other accessories. Somehow, though, I've managed to get to know hundreds of birds without ever owning a $200 pair of waterproof boots or a $2,000 pair of binoculars (though I admit I did drool over a pair of real Irish tweed trousers for a while).

Besides, I think we ought to rough it a bit now and then. I'm not talking about collecting dew for drinking water. But I do think we can survive occasional wet feet. Not to mention you'll be starting out in your own backyard—where dry socks are just a few steps away.

As for those two-grand binoculars? Somehow they keep getting pushed to the bottom of the wish list. Though if you want to put in a good word for me with Santa Claus, that'd be great!

## Expand Your Vision

Even the cheapest pair of binoculars, those

## Numbers Game

My first binoculars were 7 × 35 powered, one of the standard specs in the world of binoculars.

The first number tells you how much magnification you're getting—the larger the number, the bigger the bird will appear in the binoculars.

In this case, not double or triple or even quadruple your normal vision, but septuple! (I've been waiting for years to use that word.) Seven times better than your natural eyesight: What birder could resist?

Eventually, I moved on to 10-power (decuple!) binoculars, which give me eyesight 10 times better than my own.

Before you rush out and buy the biggest first number you can find, consider this shaky problem. Binoculars will also magnify every tremor and quiver from your hands (better skip that second cup of coffee), the wind, or the vibration of your car if you're in an idling vehicle.

More magnification, more blurring. It's easy to get a good image at 7- or even 8-power. At 10-power, you'll need very steady hands; for 12-power binoculars, better have

ice water in your veins. Or high-tech image-stabilizing binocs. Advanced birders often invest in a spotting scope, a telescope that may let you count the scales on that fish a far-off heron is eating.

For backyard bird-watching, 7- or 8-power binoculars will be all you need, unless your "yard" runs to acres.

The second number (35, in the case of those 7 × 35s) is the size in millimeters of the objective lenses, the lenses at the bottom of the binoculars, farthest from your eyes. The bigger the lens, the more light it can admit. So what you see will look brighter, and the color and details of the image—that'd be the birdie—will be easier to make out.

Naturally, there's a trade-off. A bigger objective lens means a heavier pair of binoculars. If you did all of your bird-watching in a shady woods, it might be worth building up your neck muscles so you could lug around a pair with 100-mm lenses. But we usually look at birds in a variety of places, from bright sun to shade. Most birders find that 35 mm or 50 mm lenses work well for them.

$29.99 jobs you can find at any discount store, are a big improvement over unaided eyes. You'll be amazed at the details you can see with them.

When I got my first pair of binoculars, I figured I'd only be using them when I was away from home, to look at birds I didn't know very well. After all, I already was so familiar with my feeder birds that I could recognize them across the yard without binoculars.

Then, one day, I picked up the binocs and took a look at the feeder crowd. It was a revelation. Those white-throated sparrows I knew so well—some of them had a bright yellow patch by their beaks that I'd never noticed with my naked eyes. The woodpeckers had pointy tail feathers as stiff as wire, something I hadn't seen. And bird feet! Those tiny black chickadee toes were simply remarkable. With the binoculars, I could even see the remains of the previous meal on the cardinal's big beak: purple pokeberries, by the looks of it.

When a batch of kinglets came through a few days later, I really appreciated my powerful new "eyes." Instead of sneaking up on the birds as they moved from one tree to another, all I had to do was stand back, lift the binoculars, and look for the little clues that told me which kind of kinglet I was looking at. White bars on the wings and a striped head, hah, that was the golden-crowned. Plainer bird with wide-eyed look—finally I got a clear view at that tiny patch of red on a ruby-crowned's head.

Choosing binoculars is a lot trickier than buying birdseed. What brand? What magnification? Full size or compact? A week's salary or less than a tank of gas? And what if you wear glasses?

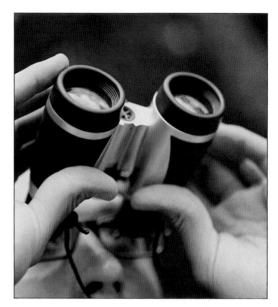

**You won't need Popeye's arms to watch birds with lightweight compact binoculars.**

You can get as educated as you like, but choosing binoculars still boils down to one question: Are they right for you?

- If the binoculars are too heavy to hold comfortably, it doesn't matter how great their lenses are—quivering muscles will make it all blurry anyway. So choose a pair that you can comfortably hold up to your eyes for minutes (possibly many minutes!) at a time.

- Do the eyepieces adjust to fit the width between your eyes? I've borrowed some that couldn't be closed up enough to fit my not-all-that-close-set eyes.

- If you wear glasses, pull up or twist open the eyecups and try using the binoculars with your glasses on. Comfy?

- Play with the focus knob or wheel. Does it work smoothly and quickly? Is it in easy reach? Does the focus change with a small adjustment, or do you need to turn and turn? You'll be using that wheel a lot when you're looking at birds, so it should be swift, sure, and easy.

- A crisp, clear view is the goal. If the binoculars give you a double image, a wavy spot, an odd colored outline or halo, or streaks of color at the edges of the field of view, or if the view seems distorted in some way, put them back and move on to the next pair.

- Binoculars are status symbols among some birders. Zeiss and Leica, a couple of old-school brands, still get a lot of respect. But the scene is changing rapidly as new manufacturers and models come on the market.

- "Try before you buy" used to be the rule. These days, many folks buy from online or mail-order sources. Wherever you shop, check for a warranty and a reasonable return policy, in case there's a defect in your new binoculars. They should work perfectly from the start.

Some experts tell you to buy the best binoculars you can afford for your first pair. But why should you drop a few hundred bucks on binoculars—or a couple thousand—before you have some experience using binoculars, so that you know which features are important to you?

Binoculars last a long time, unless they've spent a lot of time in the school of hard knocks. I've tried out military-surplus binoculars from World War II and found the image still crisp and bright.

That's why I suggest you start with a perfectly adequate pair of reasonably priced binoculars, which you can buy for less than $50. After you've used them for a while, you'll know which bells and whistles you're hankering for. Then you can invest in a lifetime pair.

How do you decide which kind to buy? Experts' picks and test groups that published their findings in birding magazines used to be the way to go. They're still helpful. But there are so many kinds of binoculars out there that these occasional reviews are always just a sampling.

"What about model ABC," I find myself wondering, "and where's model XYZ?"

On the Internet, that's where. For the first time, we can get an idea of how a particular model works in the real world, by reading users' reviews. Just Google "binocular ratings" to find a vast selection of frank opinions on binoculars of all makes, models, and prices. I often use Amazon.com user reviews for particular models to help me make my decision, too.

### Binocular Breakthroughs

Not very long ago, binoculars were big, clunky, metal things that weighed on your neck like a ton of bricks.

Today, you can pick up a pair of compact plastic binoculars small enough to slip in a pocket and light enough that you'll forget they're around your neck. (And you can still get hefty, bigger ones if you prefer.)

Not only have binoculars been downsized, they've also acquired a couple of features that seem like magic: a zoom feature, and a method for practically eliminating vibration in high-power binocs.

**Zoom binoculars.** Zoom binoculars have something like a zoom lens on a camera: After you zero in on the bird, you can

# COMPARING PRICES

You can be a bird-watcher on any budget. The items you might buy to draw in birds for close-up viewing are available at all kinds of prices. Here's how your shopping list might change, depending on how much chicken scratch you can spare.

| PINCHING PENNIES | IN MODERATION | SKY'S THE LIMIT |
|---|---|---|
| **Platform feeder** | | |
| Wooden tray homemade from scrap wood. Free | Woodlink Platform Feeder, hanging or pole mounted. Simple wood tray with metal screen bottom. $28.95, www.bestnest.com | Savannah Estate Feeder, white cast resin, plantation-porch motif with fluted pillars, detailed balustrade, and verdigris copper roof, weighs 25 lbs. $485, www.abirdsworld.com |
| **Suet feeder** | | |
| Wire suet cage. Plastic-covered wire with latching top and chain for hanging. $3.99, discount store | Squirrel-Proof Suet Haven, wire cage of suet within larger wire cage to exclude squirrels. $23.95, www.duncraft.com | Antique-copper-finish suet feeder with decorative design of two nuthatches on a branch. $29.95, www.bestnest.com |
| **Tube feeder** | | |
| Nyjer sock. Plump woven fabric tube already filled with seed for birds to pull through weave. 2 for $4.95, discount store | Droll Yankee Armored Thistle Feeder, tube protected from hungry squirrels by metal bands, with metal feeding ports. $34.99, www.bestnest.com | Royal Masterpiece tube feeder within Victorian-style metal birdcage. $124.95, www.duncraft.com |
| **Birdbath** | | |
| Clay plant saucer. $3, discount store | Concrete pedestal-style birdbath. $50, garden center or discount store | Mini Two-Level Cascade Kit, two shallow pools with small waterfall. $180, www.duncraft.com |
| **Nesting box** | | |
| Homemade bluebird house from free plans on www.daycreek.com, made from single cedar fence board. $2.50 | Eastern Bluebird House, natural wood with 1½" entrance hole and predator-proof extension. $29.95, www.duncraft.com | The Colonial Home, white hand-painted wood with tall, steep, wood-shingled roof with pineapple finial. $349.95, www.abirdsworld.com |
| **Binoculars** | | |
| Bushnell Nature View 8 × 40 binoculars. $39, www.amazon.com | Audubon Vector 8 × 42 binoculars. $129.99, www.amazon.com | Leica Ultravid 8 × 42 Rubber Armored Binoculars. $1,695, www.amazon.com |
| **TOTAL COST** | | |
| $53.44 | $297.83 | $2,864.85 |

make it look bigger in your binocs by zooming in on it.

If you come across binoculars described as, say, 8–12 × 40, you're looking at zoom binocs. With a flick of your finger, that bird in your binoculars will zoom from 8 times bigger to as much as 12 times bigger. It's a nifty feature when you want to check out a fine point or get a better look at a faraway bird.

**Image stabilization.** Of course we want the most magnification we can get in binoculars. But there's a glitch—the more the image is magnified, the more that tiny tremble of your hands is bumped up, too.

Ta-da! Technology to the rescue!

Canon and Nikon have introduced binoculars that, at the touch of a button, automatically compensate for your shaky grip.

Image Stabilization (IS) is in its infancy, but it's already making a big splash in the

**Zero in for a better view with binoculars that have a built-in zoom lens.**

birding world. A push of a button stabilizes the image you're looking at, eliminating any blurriness from your trembling hands or a stiff breeze. No more straining to make out a blurry picture, or guessing at a too-small image with lower-power lenses.

With this feature, anyone can use 10-, 12-, even 15-power binoculars and see a crystal clear image of a faraway bird. You can even use binoculars in a moving car, something that used to be impossible. (Try this trick only when you're a passenger!)

I think of IS as sort of like the anti-skip feature on a CD player, which smooths out any jolts to the player so that the music keeps coming through without a hitch. Same deal with this binocular feature: It smooths over any shakiness so that all you see is a constantly steady image. That's huge news for birders.

If it works as well as it's said to, seems like standard high-power binocs may soon be left in the dust (hmm, could that mean bargain closeout sales?). It's hard to stick up for costly classics when this innovation supplies super magnification without blur, in a smaller, lighter pair of binoculars for less money.

So far, only Canon and Nikon offer the feature, using the same technology that's available in their digital cameras. Canon uses the name IS for its method, while Nikon calls its version StabilEyes VR (vibration reduction).

Whatever you call it, it's apparently a wonder. It allows you to look through very high-power lenses, without any of the blurring that would normally occur.

The reviews make my mouth water, but I plan to wait a year or two for the technology to become more established (i.e., cheaper!) before I give it a try.

Besides, my old binocs still work just fine.

If you too can talk yourself out of the latest and greatest, you can find lots of good binoculars for $50 or less. They'll give you years of satisfying use. Move up to $100, and you have even more choices.

If you're looking for a real buy, or if you need to outfit a family, you can find perfectly usable binoculars on eBay for as little as $10, shipping included. You can't beat that!

Well, not unless you happen to hit the right garage sale. Like the one I heard about years ago, when I was watching migrating hawks at a birding hot spot.

It was a friendly, competitive group, and I was getting some good-natured ribbing about the El Cheapos I had slung around my neck. After a while, one of the birders, an out-of-state fellow, proudly offered me a look through his fine binoculars.

Instant surge of envy. They were of legendary quality, with lenses that made mine seem like I was looking through the bottom of a drinking glass.

"Very nice," I said, handing them back before I got too attached.

"Guess what I paid for them," he said.

"Uh, a lot?" seemed a safe answer. They were easily worth a cool $1,000.

I can't remember whether they were Leica or Zeiss, but I do know he was pleased as punch to have found them at a garage sale for—sitting down?—a quarter. Yep, 25 cents.

"Wow, guess the seller didn't know what they were," I said.

"Nope," he chuckled, "not at all. She was a widow getting rid of her husband's stuff. Said she was trying to raise the money to go live with her daughter. Even apologized for not having one of the lens caps."

"Did you tell her?" I asked, hoping he would say he tucked a hundred-dollar bill into her hand.

He gave me an "Are you crazy?" look and pointedly turned his back.

I went back to scanning the sky. Suddenly, my $25 binoculars felt just fine.

Watching Mr. Birder unlock his luxury car a while later, I thought about all the quarters it takes to add up to $1,000.

Guess what? You don't need fancy binoculars to recognize a weasel.

### Hitting the Books

The tall bookcase beside my desk is entirely filled with books on identifying birds. Some are tiny, made for children some 60 years ago, with charming drawings and old-fashioned text.

Others are so heavy they could serve as doorstops: *Birds of Ohio,* for instance, totals 671 pages. It's a 1903 edition, dedicated to the author's "first-born son," who's pictured in a short dress and a wide hat, standing in what appear to be his father's big lace-up boots.

You wouldn't lug this one along outside, but you could use it to identify the birds you've seen by comparing them to the book's color photographs of dead, stuffed birds in "lifelike" poses.

As in other old books, the bird descriptions are long and painstaking, practically feather-by-feather. It seems a bit excessive, until you

# The One That Started It All

There's still a little space left on my shelf of field guides, because someday, right after I get those Leicas, I plan to pick up the 1934 first edition of the book that started the whole wave of modern birding: *A Field Guide to the Birds: Giving Field Marks of All Species Found in Eastern North America* by Roger Tory Peterson.

That original book sells for about $3,500 today, but back in 1934, Peterson was lucky to get it published at all.

America was still sunk in the Depression when young naturalist Roger tried to sell his thin little bird book to publishers. With so many people down on their luck, the audience seemed slim. Luckily, Houghton Mifflin Company took a chance on a first printing of 2,000 copies.

Birders had never seen anything like it.

It had hardly any words at all, just a simple drawing of each bird, with—and here's the biggest innovation of all—small arrows pointing to distinguishing features that set the bird apart from its fellows.

To those who were accustomed to pondering paragraphs of feather-by-feather descriptions, in which the most noticeable characteristics were buried in the verbiage, Peterson's book was a revelation.

Now, for the first time, *you could identify birds at a glance.*

That first edition sold out in 1 week.

More than 7 million copies of Peterson's guide, with various revisions, have ended up in birders' hands over the years.

The book has changed over the years. It now has color and more lifelike drawings. But the little arrows are still there, helping you sort out a robin from a towhee, a tree sparrow from a field sparrow.

Battered copies of old Peterson's guides often turn up at library sales, garage sales, and auctions. It's fun to look at them and see how the guide has changed over the years—and how well the older editions still hold up.

**A scrub jay checks to make sure this field guide shows him on his good side. Look for a book with "field mark" arrows for fast ID.**

realize that the person writing that description was looking at a dead bird: "Birding" was done with a gun back in the old days, so there was plenty of time to examine and describe the resulting specimens at leisure.

Here, take a look at this description from the book:

*Adult male:* Head black, interrupted by white of chin and white with black stripes of throat; eyelids and a supraloral spot white [*Getting anywhere yet?*]; tail blackish with white terminal spots on inner webs of outer pair of rectrices; wings dusky except on external edges; remaining upper parts grayish slate below [*Guesses, anyone? Anyone?*]; breast, sides, upper belly and lining of wings cinnamon-rufous [*Aha! Now you've got it! It's Robin Redbreast—but we're not done yet ...* ]; lower belly and crissum white, touched irregularly with slate; bill yellow with blackish tip; feet blackish with yellowish soles [*Ah, yes, those yellowish soles! A dead giveaway!*]."

I love to page through my old books, but the books I use most often are collected on a shelf in easy reach. These are the field guides—bird books that are small enough to carry in your pocket when you're out in the field. Eastern birds, western birds, birds of the Pacific Coast, birds of Texas, waterbirds, seabirds—they're all here.

You'll definitely want a comprehensive field guide for your own collection, so you can learn more about the birds you're seeing with those new binoculars. Choosing a field guide is a lot like picking out binoculars: Buy the one that feels right to you. To test-drive a field guide, see how easy it is to find a few of the birds that you already know—without using the index. How fast can you find a Canada goose, pigeon, robin, chickadee, woodpecker, sparrow, and hummingbird? That will give you an idea of how easy (or how frustrating) it is to use that particular book.

Check out Recommended Reading, starting on page 309, for a few of my favorites, which you might want to start with.

# Chapter Two

# Why ID?

Learning the names of our backyard birds is really about learning to notice things. Watching birds is the gateway to a whole new way of seeing. Now we're slowing down and really looking at those birds and what they're doing, instead of giving them just a glance and never really "seeing" them.

## A CLOSER CONNECTION

Here's a revealing little quiz: Which of your neighbors do you feel closer to: the ones you've met by name or those whose names you don't know?

Funny, isn't it, how knowing someone's name automatically makes you feel more connected to him or her. It seems to give us permission to get to know each other on a deeper level, instead of staying at arm's length.

When I moved to a small town in Washington State, I quickly became a regular at the little grocery store in town. I'd chitchat with the owner about the weather as he rang up my dog food or chocolate bar. Neither of us quite met the other's eye, although we were pleasant to each other.

After a few weeks of this, I finally stuck my hand out, looked him full in the face, and said, "I'm Sally, by the way."

"Tony," he answered, with a warm handshake.

Since then, I've noticed a definite change in the atmosphere when I go into the store. Now I feel as if there's a friend-to-be on the other side of the counter, no matter how gradually we get to know each other.

It works the same way with birds.

You can pass over a bunch of small brown birds with a casual glance, just like you'd nod to a neighbor you've never met.

Or you can take a closer look, and say "good morning" to the song sparrow, the chipping sparrow, the white-throated sparrow—and, look, there's a fox sparrow; he must be on his way north for nesting. Instantly, you feel as if you've just greeted four friends.

## Friends with Feathers

Once you know their names, birds aren't just birds anymore. They're on their way to becoming friends.

Watching your feeder will be more fun when you can put a name to each visitor. I even say it out loud sometimes: "Oh, good morning, chickadees! Hiya, juncos. Howya doin' today, Mr. Towhee?"

Figuring out the names is just the first step to a deeper appreciation of birds. Once you start paying attention to your backyard birds, you'll be amazed at all the things you notice.

Oh, look—it's your friend Mr. Cardinal with his goldfinch and house finch breakfast buddies. Knowing the names makes backyard birds into personal pals.

All you have to do is focus on whatever bird happens to be handy.

Your own eyes are fine if the bird is nearby, but binoculars can make things a lot more interesting.

It doesn't matter what kind of bird you're watching—a robin, a sparrow, a cardinal. Even a plain old starling is fascinating to watch and wonder about.

Once you start really looking at birds, you'll wonder about all kinds of things. Why is that finch crouching and fluttering its wings like it's begging? What is that starling stabbing at in the lawn? Is that chickadee carrying a feather in its beak?

All those whys, whats, and hows are the beginning of a lifetime of learning.

## LEARNING FROM NATURE

My son David figured out one of the big secrets to a happy life long before he graduated from college. In fact, I think he was about 6 or 7 years old at the time.

He was completely fascinated by ants then and had just shown me how he could tell the difference between ants that were arriving at the hummingbird feeder (their bellies were black) and ants that were departing the feeder (their bellies were so full of sugar water, they looked like tiny transparent bubbles).

"If I just have something alive to watch," he commented, "I never get bored."

"Isn't it great," I agreed. "And there's always something to watch, no matter where you are."

"And then you can wonder about why. Like why is this ant carrying this stick?"

David asked. "Why isn't he getting sugar water? Fun to think about."

"Sure is," I said. "Let's watch to see what he does next. Maybe that'll tell you why."

Watching what a creature does next may not give us the entire solution—but it's likely to supply the next piece of the puzzle. Meanwhile, without even realizing it, we have a whole new interest.

Anything that we pay attention to becomes more special to us. That's why learning to identify birds will give you a closer connection to them. It will make you feel more connected to nature, too.

What I love best is that no special lessons or practice sessions are called for. All we have to do is open our eyes.

## The Worldwide Web

All apologies to the Internet, but it's Mother Nature who should hold the patent on this "worldwide web" thing.

**Save the spotted owl? Not without saving flying squirrels, lichens, fungi, and trees.**

Every living thing is part of that master plan, from microscopic bacteria and ants to grand old redwoods and African elephants. They're all connected.

Tracking these connections is as much fun as reading a good detective story.

Spotted owls are a hot topic in the Pacific Northwest, where the presence of this endangered species has saved many a stand of grand old trees from the chainsaw. But the owls are just one small strand in an interconnected web that also draws in lichens, fungi, and flying squirrels.

One lichen in the Douglas-fir forests of the Northwest goes by the descriptive name of "tree hair" or "brown beard lichen." It looks like it would fit right in with ZZ Top.

In winter, flying squirrels that live high in the towering trees rely on this lichen for their main food.

In summer, the flying squirrels switch to eating underground fungi (perhaps you've had a taste of truffles yourself?).

Simple enough, so far.

After dining, flying squirrels travel through the forest, depositing spores from those fungi wherever they happen to leave their droppings.

When those spores germinate, the quickly emerging "roots," or *mycelia*, hook up with the roots of trees in a *mycorrhizal association* that benefits the tree in a big way.

No sign of owls yet. But here's where the gee-whiz part comes in:

The tree that those mycelia are helping to nourish provides a home to hundreds, maybe thousands, of creatures. Including—ta-da!—brown beard lichen, flying squirrels, and spotted owls.

Just goes to show how much of the web of life we're still learning about.

Here's some more nature lore to learn from birds.

- Why do birds migrate? Birds that depend on insects depart when the weather turns cold in fall. Birds that eat mostly seeds are usually with us year-round.

- Why does the feeder get busy before a storm? You'll notice a big rush at your feeders when a winter storm is on the way. The birds are stocking up because there's likely to be a cold night ahead, and snow or ice will make it harder to find food.

- How do birds know a storm is coming? Birds are sensitive to air pressure changes that herald an approaching storm. Birds stop calling and disappear when severe summer weather approaches. But as soon as the worst has passed, they'll sing the all-clear.

- Why do birds come around when you cut the grass? Mowing the lawn stirs up insects. If you have a large, open lawn, watch for swallows or martins to swoop in for an airborne feast. Small yard? Wrens, robins, and blackbirds will happily check out the pickings your mower leaves behind.

- Why do birds wait until summer to nest? Nesting season is perfectly timed to the peak of caterpillar season. When caterpillars are super-abundant, bird nests are filled with hungry nestlings.

What's an ideal meal to stuff into those gaping beaks? Nice plump caterpillars!

- Where did that little bunch of sunflower seedlings come from? Thank your jays. These birds have a habit of burying the nuts and seeds they carry off from your feeder or from natural sources. Supposedly they come back to eat them later, but I've noticed that they overlook way more than they recollect. You don't suppose they might be planting more food on purpose? I wonder.

- Why do birds sometimes act so agitated? They're passing the word when a strolling cat or other danger is around. Birds don't have an enviable position in the ol' food chain. Eggs, nestlings, adults—every stage of bird life is yummy to some toothed, clawed, or slithery creature. Repeated, insistent chirps are a big clue that a possible bird eater is on the prowl.

**Those volunteer sunflower seedlings that pop up all over your yard have been planted by jays. Watch a jay when it leaves your feeder, and you may see it planting the seeds.**

Without that tree, there'd be no brown beard lichen for the flying squirrels to eat in winter.

Without the brown beard lichen, there'd be no flying squirrels.

Without the flying squirrels, the tree couldn't hook up with mycelia to bring it nutrients.

Without the flying squirrels, the spotted owl would go hungry.

That's a particularly nifty part of the web. But once you start noticing birds, you'll uncover all kinds of connections, including many simpler ones.

Take goldfinches, for example. You'll discover they nest later than nearly all other birds, waiting until midsummer before they start a family. Midsummer also happens to be when weedy thistles in fields and along roadsides begin to go to seed, their lavender flowers turning to silky tufts.

What do goldfinches line their nests with? Thistledown.

Who eats thistle seed, and drops undigested seeds to start new plants? Goldfinches.

Flickers and ants are another fun duo to watch. Flickers are big, brown woodpeckers that eat mostly ants and also "bathe" in anthills, to get rid of some of the pests that plague them. Sometimes they take an ant in their beak and smear it over their body to deter pests. Or they may perform "passive anting," in which the bird droops its wings over an anthill, fluffs itself up, and lets the ants crawl through its feathers to find lice and other tiny tidbits.

By the way, ever wonder why flickers are brown instead of the more usual black and white? I figure it's because they spend so much time on the ground, eating ants. A brown back blends in better against bare ground; hawks overhead and other predators nearby have a harder time spotting the bird when it's busy anting.

Every day, our backyard birds have something new to teach us. All we have to do is watch. And wonder.

## EYES WIDE OPEN

Sooner or later it's going to hit you—you'll realize what you've been missing all these years, simply by not taking notice.

There's no need to feel bad; we all do it. Give yourself a big pat on the back instead. Your eyes are now open!

You never know which bird is going to give the wake-up call, but when it happens, you'll know it.

For me, it was a starling, a bird I'd taken for granted until the day I really *saw* one, and

**The first meadowlark you see may seem like a rare bird, until you realize you just haven't noticed them before.**

# Would You Like That Rare?

Back in the 1970s, "consciousness-raising" was the buzzword. If you became aware of some injustice or other, you'd start noticing that behavior everywhere. Groups held sessions on various topics to help people open their eyes to what was going on around them.

You don't need group therapy for this one. Anything that has a personal connection to you can raise your consciousness.

Just ask any woman who's ever been pregnant. I bet nearly all of us have commented, "Have you noticed how many pregnant women there are these days?"

Or maybe you've bought a new car. Suddenly, you see a lot more of those cars on the highway.

Is it because there are more of those expectant mothers or those cars?

Nope. It's because you're now noticing them. Pregnancy or that kind of car now means something to you.

I see this very human quirk all the time in bird-watchers, too. Friends and family, and sometimes total strangers, often share their bird sightings with me.

I can't tell you how many times one of them has asked, "That must be a rare bird, isn't it?"

Or a variation: "They must be rare around here, aren't they?"

I've done the same thing myself (embarrassing details follow in Chapter 5). So I know that it can be pretty embarrassing to find out that the bird you just saw for the very first time—that "rare" bird—is as common as crabgrass.

"Just watch," I often tell these folks, "Now that you've seen it, you're going to start noticing it all over the place!"

**Expecting? Suddenly you'll notice that lots of other women seem to be, too.**

noticed the creamy stars sprinkled over its iridescent feathers. Wow! If I'd been missing that with starlings, what else was I missing?

For a country friend of mine, it was a meadowlark that opened her eyes. Betty had lived on a farm her whole life. She'd raised 13 kids, fed cows, cut and baled hay, and cultivated acres of corn.

One early spring day we were driving down the long dirt lane to her house, past the barn and fields she'd spent time in nearly every day of her life, when I happened to see a meadowlark leave the field and alight on a fence post along the road.

I slowed to a stop and handed Betty my battered binoculars.

"These aren't the best," I apologized, "but see if you can get a look at that bird on the post. Just twist that ring in the middle to make 'em focus."

After some fumbling and complaining, I heard her suddenly draw in her breath.

"Ooh," she said, "what in the world is *that*?"

"A meadowlark."

"Now that must be a really rare bird," she said.

Mr. Meadowlark sure looked like a prize, with his big butter yellow chest and bold black necklace. But in these fields, meadowlarks were a dime a dozen.

"Sure is beautiful, isn't he," I said, avoiding the issue.

Betty wouldn't let me off the hook. "But rare, right? All these years, I've never seen one."

"Um, not often seen, anyway," I waffled, "unless you're looking for them."

Her sharp eyes pinned me down. "So they're all over the place, then?"

"Watch the field for a minute," I suggested. "There! See that bird that just flew up? Looks dumpy like a starling, but has white edges on its stubby tail? That's a meadowlark."

We spent the next half-hour or so getting acquainted with the meadowlarks in the field.

As a hardworking farm woman, Betty had never happened to take notice of the birds around her. Her attention had been focused on animals and her own brood, not to mention constant worry about the crops.

Now she had the luxury of being able to spend time looking at birds, and she was instantly hooked. Feeders and birdhouses soon filled the yard around her little house.

When I stopped by at Christmas, Betty hurried me to the feeder window. A multi-

tude of cardinals at the trays and in the snowy bushes made the scene look like a Christmas card.

But the picture-perfect cardinals weren't what Betty wanted to show me.

"Just wait," she said. "Oh good, here he comes!"

It was a meadowlark. Big, bright, and bold as brass, the bird shouldered his way into the tray feeder and began scooping up millet.

Not an uncommon sight in the country-side, especially after snow. But to Betty, a meadowlark will always be something special.

Once your eyes are open to birds, you'll find yourself having a greater appreciation for everything else around you, too. Without even trying, you'll be noticing butterflies, ants, insects, wildflowers, and lots of other things that slipped right by before.

**Take a longer look at bunches of birds, and you may spot an oddball in their midst or find out the flock isn't what you'd thought. These are Eurasian tree sparrows, found only near St. Louis.**

Have your surroundings changed? Not a bit! You've simply learned to see.

## New Bird in Town

Spending the time to figure out the names of your backyard birds means that you'll be quicker to notice new birds.

Recognizing a certain bird quickly becomes automatic. You're training your eyes to discern the differences between species. And you're getting familiar with the posture and habits of each bird.

Once you've sorted out the details on a white-throated sparrow, for instance, you'll quickly notice when a white-crowned sparrow joins the flock.

Without even thinking about it, your eye will go right to the pine siskin mixed in with the goldfinches at the thistle feeder, or to the dark-eyed Oregon junco among the slate-colored juncos.

Pay attention to your first flash of "Hmm, doesn't look right." Often, that fleeting thought means your subconscious is doing a great job of alerting you to something different in the mix. Take a closer look!

## COLLECTING BIRDS

Keeping a collection seems to be an ingrained part of the human psyche. Even little kids like to line up their collections of rocks or Matchbox cars. That urge never seems to go away, although the collection may change. Jay Leno has accumulated dozens (Hundreds? Thousands? Can I have that red one?) of classic cars. A fellow I once met had so many pieces of sports memorabilia that he opened a restaurant so he could display it all.

## Table for 30?

How many different species of birds might show up in an average backyard over the course of a year? ("Average" meaning a medium-size yard of perhaps 8,000 to 10,000 square feet, with a bird feeder, some shrubs, and a flower bed or vegetable patch.)

Go ahead, take a guess. Five species? Ten? Maybe 15, if you're lucky?

How about 30 or more? That's about average for many backyards.

Add an older shade tree to that mix and the count will go up. Berry bushes or fruit trees? Expect other new friends.

If your yard is within easy flying distance of wild places, or if you live along a major migration route, look for your count to rise dramatically.

I recently moved to a small house on nearly an acre of land. In a few years it'll be bird heaven, but right now that acre is nothing but grass, plus one walnut tree and a couple of apple trees. But still I counted more than 50 different species in or over the yard in my first month! Most are just visiting from nearby wild areas, but they're here every day.

Venture outside your yard, and you might count 100 kinds of birds without too much trouble in any region of the country.

No wonder bird-watching can keep us busy for life!

It's hard to say what will set off that collecting urge. For some of us, it's decorated plates or frog figurines. Others go for first edition books or modern art. Maybe your collection leans toward designer shoes, postcards, or baseball cards. (Have you ever noticed how many mothers mistakenly sold that precious shoe box at a garage sale?)

I'm sure that our collecting urge is why birding has such strong appeal. Seeing a new bird is as much of a thrill as stumbling across a piece of Roseville pottery for your collection—the find is wonderful!

With this collection, you won't need a new set of shelves. Your mom can't sell it at a garage sale. And it doesn't have to cost a penny. All you need is a list.

Starting a list of the birds you've seen seems so innocent, but for many of us, it's the first step to a lifelong passion. Every new bird is an achievement, something to be proud of. There's nothing like constant ego gratification to keep us hooked!

Many birders keep more than one list: A master list of all the birds they've ever seen, plus smaller lists for nesting birds, winter birds, birds at the feeder, or any other category they like.

## Keeping a List

Keeping a list of the birds you see is a basic part of birding. Your list can be as casual or as complicated as you like. It may be a simple scribbled list of species on a sheet of paper; official checklists distributed by reputable organizations, such as those in the Peterson guides or used by the National Audubon Society for census-taking; or a computer database with details on sightings. The style of list is up to you and so is its content. You can keep your "Birds I've Seen" list as narrowly focused or as wide open as you like.

Here are some popular birding lists.

**The life list.** Keep this as your master list, in which you write down every bird you see, no matter where you see it.

**Does a kingfisher over your fish pond count as a backyard bird? It's up to you.**

**The backyard list.** Write down every bird you see in your backyard. I find this list just as much fun as the life list, because it's all about my own yard. I include birds that are flying over, too, even though it feels a bit like cheating.

**The feeder list.** Keep track of who's visited your seed, suet, nectar, and other feeders.

**Any other lists that you want to keep.** Note the birds that nest in your yard, birds of your state, birds you've seen on certain trips, birds that visit during spring migration, birds that stop by on the fall journey—whatever makes sense to you. It's your collection, so you get to organize it however you like!

## Listers

Mention your life list to other birders, and you're likely to get two very different reactions.

Phoebe Snetsinger is tops among listers. She was a birder who shifted into high gear after being diagnosed with melanoma. Instead of having treatment, Phoebe signed up for a birding tour to Alaska. Her cancer went into remission (though it later returned), and she spent the rest of her life "collecting" birds for her list. An heiress who could travel whenever and wherever she wanted, she added birds swiftly, most on guided tours. By 1995, she had hit the rarefied mark of 8,000 species.

Her autobiography, *Birding on Borrowed Time,* is quite a read. Traveling the world on an unlimited budget may sound pretty cushy, but some of Phoebe's experiences were horrifying. And she was a very busy person.

Besides traveling and writing a book, she kept incredibly detailed notes and records—and she managed to have a family. But what is evident throughout her life story is that she never lost the pleasure of watching birds.

On a November morning in 1999, Phoebe was looking for rare birds in Madagascar, off the coast of Africa. She'd added Bird #8,450 to her list that morning, the red-shouldered vanga, a species that had been discovered just 2 years earlier.

To a lister, though, the bird that really counts is the next one. A few hours later, Phoebe Snetsinger was killed in a bus accident while on her way to find #8,451, the Appert's greenbul.

At the time of her death, she had seen more birds than anyone else on earth.

**Phoebe Snetsinger: 8,450 birds on her list!**

One group will proudly announce the exact numbers of birds on their own life lists, or talk about a super trip when they added new species to their list.

The other group will have, at best, only a rough idea of the number of birds they've seen. Instead of comparing numbers, they'll talk about what the birds they saw were doing, or how beautiful they were.

For bird *listers,* the thrill of the hunt and the satisfaction of adding a new species to the count are the major reasons for birding.

Competition plays a big role. More birds on that list give you better bragging rights. Can you measure up? Or do you need another trip to the Rio Grande Valley to add more species to your list?

For bird-*watchers,* the list isn't as important as the pleasure of watching birds, any birds. Sure, it's a thrill to spot a new bird. But it can be just as satisfying to learn more about an old friend.

Naturally, there's plenty of overlap between the two. All of us are interested in birds, for starters. And while listers often look forward to competitive birding marathons such as the Big Day (see "Citizen Science" on page 32), most of them also enjoy watching bird behavior.

Roger Tory Peterson, America's most famous bird-watcher and a lifelong naturalist, was a dedicated lister. His goal was to see half of the birds on Earth in his lifetime. It took him until the mid-1980s, about 10 years before he died at age 88, but he made it.

Sometimes those who aren't listers are belittled as not being "serious birders." That's simply not true. Serious birders fall into both camps. And bird behavior is a science that's every bit as serious as tallying all the species in a given area.

### Going to Extremes

For some listers, birding veers into extreme territory. The collecting urge spins out of control. Adding birds to the list becomes an obsession. For some listers, getting to know the birds hardly matters: It's all about adding to the count.

Here's a sample of lister mania, from *To See Every Bird on Earth,* Dan Koeppel's book about his own father's quest: "He got in his car, drove ten hours to the dock where the bird had been seen, stepped out of his car, saw it, and then drove home. Bird Number 6559."

The listing craze is a fairly new phenomenon. It only really got going in the 1970s.

About 10,000 species of birds, give or take a few hundred, are on the Earth. About 800 species of birds can be found in the United States and Canada, not including Hawaii. (The exact number changes as the official list of species is fiddled with and birds are reclassified or new species discovered.)

Listers who've moved to the worldwide category are definitely the most obsessed. Some of them spend hundreds of thousands of dollars to reach remote areas with private guides so they can tick off one more bird.

By the mid-1970s, only 11 birders had tallied 2,500 on their worldwide lists. Thirty years later, 256 had hit that milestone. And among them were a few who had gone much, much further.

## Keeping a Bird Journal

I found out just how disorganized I am during a recent move. I was downsizing to a much smaller house, so I was weeding things out by sorting through boxes that had been stored away for many years.

That's when I came across my birding journals. There were maybe a dozen, the oldest dating back to 30 years ago. Some were spiral-bound, others black-and-white composition books, and a couple were beautifully bound journals. But all of them had something in common: Only the first few pages had anything written on them.

That's right. Despite my best intentions, I've never been able to make it a routine to write down daily happenings or musings, week after week.

Each notebook started out with a list. Usually it was an inventory of who was at the feeder, but a few lists were from outings to woods or lakes, and others were from birding trips to other states.

None of the journals continued for more than 3 days, I'm sorry to report. And most petered out after Day 1. I guess I was just too busy watching the birds, or too lazy to make any notes about them.

Still, I had a ball reading through the stack of barely touched notebooks. Wow, was it really 25 years ago that I saw my first blue-winged teal? I still vividly remember that day at Middle Creek Wildlife Refuge in Pennsylvania: Tree swallows and myrtle warblers were eating bayberries off the bushes by the visitors' center. Cedar waxwings were in every juniper tree. Huge swans flew overhead with a rush of wings. And the water was filled with ducks, my teal among them.

None of that was in my journal, though. All I had written was the name of a bird and a date, plus a quick sketch of the teal's head with its trademark crescent moon marking.

My record-keeping on paper may leave a lot to be desired, but at least my sightings are in order in my head.

## Learning More

It's way more gratifying to read about a brown thrasher once you know what a brown thrasher is. After you've identified a thrasher, you can read an account of the bird and say, "Yes, yes, I've seen him do that, too," or "Hmm, I'll have to watch for that," or "Now I know where to look for its nest."

Reading is a great way to learn more about our backyard birds. You'll find enough books and magazines about birds and bird-watching to keep you busy for years.

I generally find older books more engaging than most modern ones. The writing is usually more personal and more emotional (okay, florid!) than in today's books. Back then, nobody was worried about anthropomorphism, or assigning human emotions or motivations to birds and other animals. Today, many scientists scorn instances of anthropomorphism: "Cheerful chickadee," for instance, would be verboten.

Just try to match this enthusiasm:

> The song of the Goldfinch is, in part, very similar to that of the Canary. It is replete with the lively humor of the bird. One cannot listen to the full song of a characteristic singer without laughing involuntarily at the unmistakable glee with which it is executed. Only the Bobolink can excel the Goldfinch in spontaneity of feeling, and not even he can cram so much pure *fun* into one short musical sentence!

—F. Schuyler Mathews, *Field Book of Wild Birds and Their Music* (1904)

When your eyes get bleary from reading, let the birds themselves be your teacher. I love to read about birds, but I've learned way more just by watching them.

## SHARING EXPERIENCES

Birding is a one-size-fits-all hobby. You can tailor it to suit just about any personality.

- If you're feeling like a hermit at heart, you can watch birds all by yourself.

- If you prefer one-on-one or small groups, you can share your pleasure with your family or a small circle of friends.

- If you're a people person, you can connect with all kinds of groups, in person and online.

## Sharing with Other Birders

Other collectors usually play it close to the vest when it comes to sharing their finds. They're happy to show you—after the particular item is in their collection. And they're reluctant to disclose a good source. Bird collectors are different. Since no one is actually capturing the bird for his or her collection, most birders don't mind sharing their finds.

When it comes to a rare bird, there is cachet in being the first to find it. But a rare bird is still a thrill for the 100th or 10,000th birder to come along.

That's why group activities are common in birding. You'll find plenty of appealing possibilities.

## Birding Groups

The venerable National Audubon Society has chapters in every part of the country. Monthly meetings are usually announced in the newspaper. Members share sightings with each other and learn about conservation.

To find an Audubon chapter near you, check your phone book or Google "Audubon [YOUR STATE]." Or call the news desk of your local newspaper, or a local nature preserve. If all else fails, try the U.S.D.A. extension agent for your county, listed in the blue pages of the phone book.

Audubon is the oldest and best known birders' group. But other groups may also exist in your area. If you live in Kentucky, for instance, you also can check out the Eastern Kentucky Bird Club or the Kentucky Ornithological Society.

You'll find an excellent collection of bird clubs at www.birdingguide.com/clubs/. Just click on your state. As usual, Google is

your friend, too: Search for "bird clubs [YOUR STATE]." You can also keep an eye on information in your newspaper about local meetings.

## Citizen Science

Bird-watchers like you and me have contributed our observations to science for hundreds of years. Some of those stories have been found to be a little shaky (swallows burrowing into swamp mud for hibernation? I don't think so!), but anecdotal evidence still forms the basis for our understanding of birds.

The well-respected reference, *The Audubon Society Encyclopedia of North American Birds*, by John K. Terres, for instance, pulls much of its info from a 1900 to 1930 series of books edited by A. C. Bent, which was a collection of hundreds of stories from backyard birders as well as scientists.

Behavioral anecdotes may be my personal favorite, but science also needs cold, hard facts. That's where we come in, yet again! Birders like us have been researching bird populations and distribution patterns for decades. How? Through Audubon's Christmas Bird Count and other regular efforts.

On our end, we're busy marking down what type, how many, where seen, and so on for every bird we spot. That's important data to scientists, who tabulate, collate, and play with those numbers to come up with a yearly picture of American bird life and how it's changing.

Signing up to be part of a bird count is a regular ritual for many bird-watchers. Local counts are part of a national effort. Held on or about the same day, the counts collect valuable data about the distribution and population of birds. Here are the best known.

**Audubon Christmas Bird Count.** It takes place around Christmastime, which may sound crazy—aren't we all super busy then? Of course. That's why the count provides such a welcome change of pace. Instead of fighting traffic to buy gifts, give yourself (and your family) a gift by spending a day outside looking for birds. It's a great cure for holiday stress. Go to www.audubon.org/bird/cbc/ to find out the details.

**Project FeederWatch.** Organized by the Cornell Lab of Ornithology, this national count collects data from people with feeders. You won't even have to step outside, except to fill the trays! Go to www.birds.cornell.edu/PFW/.

**Breeding bird surveys.** These counts will take you outside to look for evidence of nesting birds in an assigned area. Don't worry, you won't have to find the nests! A singing male bird is enough evidence. Ask your local bird club or Google "breeding bird survey [YOUR STATE]."

**Great Backyard Bird Count.** This one functions as a mid-winter snapshot of bird life in the United States during a particular 4-day period. Birders of any level count birds over the period, then report their highest count for each species at an online site. Collected data is later available for viewing. Check it out at www.birdsource.org/gbbc/.

**eBird.** This project was developed by the Cornell Lab of Ornithology and the National Audubon Society to track bird populations and distribution, plus other data. You register online and send checklists to eBird's Web site; you can later review your own data or other records. Go to www.ebird.org/.

**Big Day.** An offshoot of the World Series of Birding (www.njaudubon.org/wsb/), which is held only in New Jersey,

"Big Day" bird counts can raise funds for good causes, with pledges collected for each species on the list.

this count is for anyone who loves listing. Be prepared to be exhausted: You'll be tromping around from before dawn to well after dusk. (Some die-hard participants start with owls at one minute after midnight, and never let up until 24 hours later.) In 2006, a team from East Brunswick, New Jersey, found 88 species in 11½ hours; it was only their second attempt and they expect to do better next year. If you're looking for a good cause to support, consider Earlham College, in Richmond, Indiana, which has produced more ornithologists than any other college in the country. Earlham uses the Big Day as a fundraiser, with money pledged for every species seen. So far, the counts have raised nearly a half-million dollars for the school. Find out more at www.earlham.edu/.

You can find details on all of these counts online. Or you can ask your local chapter of the Audubon Society or other bird club. More watchers are always welcome!

The brown sign that marks a National Wildlife Refuge promises good birding. This one, in arid eastern Washington, has water that draws swans, ducks, geese, and sandhill cranes in spring and fall.

## Planning a Vacation?

I'm a big fan of traveling by car because I can explore any place that catches my eye along the way. One of the roadside attractions I always stop for is heralded by a brown sign, often with a silhouette of a flying goose. That's the signature logo for a national wildlife refuge (NWR), public lands that I've learned are always teeming with great birds.

NWRs aren't nearly as crowded as national parks (which are also great for birds) and they're usually traversed by a well-kept dirt road as well as by hiking trails. You'll probably want to get out to stretch your legs for part of your visit. But birding by car is the best way to go: The car works like a blind, so you can approach much closer to birds than you could on foot.

The only drawback about NWRs is that parts of them may be open for hunting in season. Many of these areas serve as a stopping place for waterfowl or other game birds, which are great to look at. But I avoid the refuges during hunting season; personally, I'd rather bird-watch without the background blast of shotguns.

If you'd rather plan ahead, Google "NWR [STATE]" to find out if there are any near your destination. You can also find NWRs listed in AAA tour books, and they're marked on most maps, if your eyes are still up to scanning tiny type. Meanwhile, I keep looking for a bumper sticker that says "I Brake for Brown Signs," but so far, I haven't had any luck.

State and national parks are great places to see birds, too. Ask for suggestions about good spots to bird-watch in the park when you pay the entry fee.

If you prefer more guidance, you can reserve your spot on a birding tour. All kinds of mouth-watering destinations are available. Check the ads in the back of a birding magazine for ideas, or search online. A travel agent can be useful, too. Bird club members are usually brimming with suggestions as well.

Birding hot spots, such as hummingbird-heaven Ramsey Canyon in southern Arizona, offer comfortable inns to relax at while you go birding in the area. You'll meet plenty of like-minded folks to have a friendly conversation with, or to join for an outing at sunrise. Or if you'd rather, you can just kick back on the porch and watch the feeders.

# Chapter Three

# How to Get Started

I was so entranced by the first field guide I ever saw that it led to a 20-year friendship with the fellow who showed it to me.

We met because of a mutual love of music, but it was the field guide that cemented the deal. We were sitting at his comfortably cluttered kitchen table, having a cup of tea, when a flash of wings outside the window caught my eye. Leaning forward for a better look, I saw that a whole batch of birds were coming and going at a simple wood tray filled with seed.

My mom had fed birds for years, by tossing stale bread out the door in winter. But I'd never seen an actual feeder before. This setup drew the birds like magic and, better yet, put them right out in easy view.

"Oh, look, there's a chickadee! And a whole bunch of sparrows! And here comes a blue jay!" I was hogging the view out the little window, nose pressed to the glass.

"Is the nuthatch there?" my new pal asked.

"Nuthatch?"

He reached for a book on the table and flipped it open. "This one," he said, pointing at a drawing of a pointy-beaked gray and white bird with stubby legs.

"Oh, I know that guy, that's that upside-down bird! The one that goes headfirst down tree trunks? Says *ank-ank*? What'd you say he was called?"

"Nuthatch. White-breasted nuthatch."

"I always wondered what his name was," I said. "Hey, what is that book?" (And how

**The intriguing white-breasted nuthatch**

did I get to my twenties without ever knowing it existed?)

"Peterson's," he said, handing it over. "It's a field guide."

Trying not to act too grabby, I took the book and dove right in.

Look at all those birds!

I was in heaven. There were owls and gulls, pages of unbelievable hummingbirds, and whole flocks of sparrows. Even an albatross, like the one the Ancient Mariner had to lug around, which made me want to go back and read Coleridge's poem again, now that I knew the bird hanging around his neck had a 7-foot wingspan!

## FIELD GUIDE FRUSTRATIONS

Then I tried to actually find the handful of birds I already knew among the hundreds in the book.

Where was the cardinal? I flipped through, then flipped again. And again.

"Check the index," my friend suggested.

Oh, duh. Simple enough.

But what about the birds whose names I didn't know yet? It was overwhelming to sort through hundreds of birds, trying to find one particular kind.

"Where's that blue one," I asked him, "you know, the one you see singing from the very tip of the cornstalks in the fields? Or else he's on the wire along the road? Sings even in the afternoon when it's hot, when none of the other birds are singing?"

"Oh, I know who you mean," he said. "That's exactly what it says in the field guide: 'Conspicuous at midday.' Indigo bunting. Look in the index, under 'bunting.'"

"This is like a dictionary," I complained. "Don't know how to spell a word, can't look it up. Don't know what a bird's name is, can't look it up."

"Yeah, it takes a while," he agreed. "But you'll get faster at it. Like, all the sparrows are in one place, so you only have to look through those pages to find a sparrow."

As I learned how the birds were grouped, eventually I did get faster at it. And once I found the right section, I appreciated the detailed pictures that helped me pinpoint which bird I was looking at.

Still, I was often stumped.

"There's gotta be a better way to do this," I often thought when I was paging, paging, paging through the field guide yet again.

**The indigo bunting sings even at high noon.**

## That Lived-On Look ——

Paging through a field guide over and over is why most guides look like they've been through the war. Even with extra-sturdy bindings and covers, the books take on that well-thumbed look. Frequent consultation is also why many birders are on a first-name basis with their field guides: You'll hear folks talk about "the Peterson" or "the Sibley" like they're personal friends. And they are.

Experts apparently had had the same idea, which is what led to other field guides that were organized by color of bird rather than family, or by shape of body, or by habitat (water birds, land birds).

I soon had acquired enough field guides to fill a shelf—and none of them were simple enough. I still had to use the same method: Looking through page by page until I spotted a picture that made me say, "That's it!"

Why couldn't they just put in the birds I was probably going to see? Why did I need all those extra ones? Some of them didn't even live in my part of the country.

### A Focused Field Guide

What I wished I'd had, back at the beginning and every time I visited a new part of the country, was a field guide that showed me the birds I was *most likely* to encounter in that region.

Field guides to the East and the West narrowed down the possibilities a bit, but they still included way too many birds to easily find just one.

Those comprehensive guides are great, and you'll definitely want one on your shelf.

But the birds that visit your backyard will be a much smaller bunch than the hundreds of species in that full-scale field guide.

You're likely to see, at most, about 50 different species of birds in your yard—unless your backyard includes an ocean, a pond, a swamp, a desert, a grassy field, a deep woods, *and* a stream, plus every other niche that birds live in. Or unless you live close enough to those places that birds can fly by to check out your yard.

### START HERE

Even before you learn the basics of identifying birds, I have a simple trick that will cut your frustration to a minimum.

Simply focus on the species that you're most likely to see.

In Chapter 6, "Start Here," you'll find the 38 most common and most widespread birds. All of them range across nearly the entire country. All of them spend a lot of time in backyards and at feeders.

Page through that chapter and look at the pictures until you're pretty familiar with each bird. Don't worry, it's a lot easier flipping through pages of 38 species than it is paging through an entire field guide.

If you do this homework ahead of time, you'll have a giant head start. You'll be able to identify several species with little trouble, because you'll already be familiar with them.

After you have a nodding acquaintance with the "Start Here" birds, you may want to get acquainted with the birds that are likely to show up in your region of the country. You'll find them also profiled in Part 2.

Back in the Dark Ages before TV and computers, people spent a lot more time outside than most of us do today. There were lots more farmers and country folk, who plowed or tended to animals or grew big gardens to feed their families. Even in towns, life was way different than it is today: People grew vegetables, and raised chickens, chopped wood, hung laundry on the wash line.

Kids grew up running the woods and fields.

**Kids still love to be outside. Take a break from all those organized activities and go out and explore together?**

"Go outside and play," said moms everywhere, and we did. At supper time, neighborhoods would ring with parents' voices calling kids home to eat. I remember my sisters trying out possible names for their children-to-be by calling out the names in that special loud, drawn-out style in which kids were called into the house: "TRAAAAA-cey! TAMMMMMM-my!" (The last syllable was always called on a lower pitch—unless you were in trouble. Then it was "Sal-LY!")

We learned to identify birds without even thinking about it, because the names were passed along from one person to another, or from parent to child. "See the redbird?" "Listen to that catbird." "Chase those blackbirds out of the corn!" We didn't think twice about them.

Lots of that common knowledge got lost when we started spending most of our time indoors. No one showed kids what a robin's egg looked like, or how to whistle on a blade of grass.

Maybe whistling on a blade of grass has become a lost art among the cell phone/iPod generation. But a bird feeder outside the window will still catch the interest of even the most worldly teenager, especially if we give a gentle nudge.

No need to make a big deal out of it ("Oh, puh-*leeze!*"). A casual, "Oh, look at that chickadee," is enough to plant the seed for the next generation of nature lovers.

## Year-Round Feeder Birds with Wide Ranges

These widespread birds may drop in at your feeder on any day of the year, though fall and winter will be the busiest feeder seasons. Phone your friends a thousand miles away, and these birds may be at their feeder, too.

Mourning dove

Downy woodpecker

Blue jay

Black-capped chickadee

White-breasted nuthatch

Northern cardinal

American goldfinch

House finch

Song sparrow

Rufous-sided towhee

## Winter Feeder Birds with Wide Ranges

Look for these feeder friends to join the cast of year-round characters at your feeder (see "Year-Round Feeder Birds with Wide Ranges" above). They'll quickly become new friends when they arrive in fall. In most areas, they'll cheer up your winter days, then say goodbye in spring. But you can bet they'll be back next year.

Red-breasted nuthatch

Evening grosbeak

Pine siskin

Slate-colored juncos

Song sparrow

White-throated sparrow

White-crowned sparrow

## Nonfeeder Birds with Wide Ranges

These birds are not your usual feeder customers. They may drop in on occasion, or even become regulars at some folks' feeders, but in general they're more likely to find their own food, thank you very much. And where will they find that food? In your backyard!

Depending on the kind of plants your yard offers for food and cover, you might see:

Brown creeper

House wren

Golden-crowned kinglet

American robin

Hermit thrush

Northern mockingbird

Brown thrasher

Gray catbird

Cedar waxwing

Common yellowthroat

Yellow-rumped warbler

Northern oriole (Baltimore or Bullock's)

## Most Likely to Succeed

I have to admit that narrowing the focus of this book to the birds you're most likely to see isn't an original idea. I borrowed it from the visual aids I used to learn to identify birds some 25 years ago—not the field guide, but the posters that we hung flanking the door.

Each poster featured maybe a dozen beautifully drawn birds of a certain kind of habitat—the birds you would be most likely to see in that habitat. "Birds of the Forest," one was called, and I believe another may have been "Birds of the Garden."

We'd bought the posters in the 1970s for a very reasonable price at a national wildlife refuge in Pennsylvania; they were printed by Windsor Nature Discovery, I believe. They looked like posters meant for schoolteachers

**Hang a poster of common birds on a wall where you'll see it often, and you'll effortlessly learn to recognize many of the birds in your backyard.**

to hang on the wall, but I thought they were perfect art for our first home.

They worked incredibly well as a beginner course in bird identification. Just a few seconds of looking at the posters as I went in and out, and the pictures of birds and their names made enough of an impression on me that I could recall them when I actually saw the birds for the first time.

## FIRST THINGS FIRST

When my kids were little, one of our favorite games to play on long car rides was 20 Questions. One player thinks of an object; the rest ask questions to figure out what it is.

Bird identification works a lot like 20 Questions. You start by asking the big, general questions. Then you follow up with others that narrow down the possibilities even more.

Since you're usually playing this game by yourself, you'll want to get in the habit of looking for the clues in order of their importance.

## WHAT TO LOOK FOR

I can't tell you what to look for first when you see a bird, because each bird is different. Appearance and habits work together to create a first impression. And that's one of the keys to identifying birds. In a cardinal, that knockout color will grab your eye. Chickadee? Small size and lack of fear are likely to make the first impression. Goldfinch? Yellow color and that up-and-down flight that looks like it's riding a roller coaster.

That first impression may be fleeting. But it's packed with clues to bird ID. The more you watch birds, the more you'll trust your instincts.

## First Impressions

People often ask me "What bird is this?" questions. Most of them go something like this: "I have this bird in my yard, it's brown. Maybe there's a little white. Or is there? I forget. Anyhow, it's not all that big. What is it?"

Oh boy! It's just like playing 20 Questions. Before I can announce, "It's a white-throated sparrow," or "It's a rufous-sided towhee," or "It's a pine siskin," I have to narrow down the possibilities by asking questions.

What color brown? Pale? Dark? Gray-brown? Reddish brown?

How big is "not that big"? Smaller than a robin? Smaller than a sparrow?

Anything odd about its shape? Long tail? Pointy head? Really long legs?

Where was the bird? What was it doing?

Have you seen it before?

Some IDs take five questions to figure out. For others, I use up the entire 20 questions and still don't have a clue. The longer you get to look at a bird, the easier an identification is likely to be. But even a split-second glimpse of a bird may be all you need. If the bird has flown the coop, that fleeting glimpse may be all you have to go on. So take a minute to let it sink in, and try to consciously recall as many of the details as you can.

The first impression is a combination of appearance, habits, habitat, and possibly voice—all of the traits that make that particular bird what it is.

If the bird is still around, or shows up

**A speckled breast is the first clue to identifying a gray-cheeked thrush.**

again later, you can note the details step by step. Here's how.

### Appearance

Appearance alone is enough to ID many birds. What a bird looks like is one of the first things we notice. Sometimes it's knockout color, like that of a cardinal or bluebird. Sometimes it's an odd shape that veers from the typical "songbird style" to that of, say, a woodpecker's.

But often, appearance characteristics are subtle, with nothing that immediately grabs you. Whatever your first impression, try to note as many appearance details as you can.

A quick sketch—crude is fine!—will help you remember details later.

1. Notice the main color of the bird.

2. What color is the belly?

3. Any other colors?

4. Do the wings or the tail have any bars or bands across them?

5. Does the head have a splash of color on its crown or elsewhere?

6. Pay attention to the bird's shape. Does it look like a "regular bird"—basic songbird style? Or does it have unusually long legs, an odd beak, or an extra-long or extra-short tail?

7. Is there a pointy crest on its head?

8. Try to get an idea of its size—which isn't so easy unless there's a bird you already know nearby.

### Habits

Identifying birds is like juggling: You have to keep several points in mind at the same time, because any one of them could be the key to pinning down your bird's ID.

You may have already noticed some of the bird's habits as you checked its appearance. Often a bird's habits will linger in your mind after the bird is gone. Ask yourself these questions.

**You'll often see a flicker on the ground.**

1. Was the bird alone, or was there a group?

2. Where did you see it? On the ground? On a low branch? At eye level? Overhead in a tree? On a wire? In the sky?

3. If the bird was at your feeder, what was it eating?

4. Did you notice it do anything peculiar, almost like a nervous tic? Repeatedly flick its wings, perhaps, or raise and lower its tail?

### Habitat

Habitat is a big clue when you're looking at birds in the wild. It's less important in your backyard, where abundant food can cause birds to show up outside of their normal haunts. Still, backyard habitat can help steer you to an ID.

1. Was the bird on the lawn?

2. Did the bird spend most of its time in your shrubs? On the ground under your shrubs?

3. Which trees did the bird spend time in?

4. Did the bird visit your flower garden or veggie patch?

**A nervous tail helps ID a hermit thrush.**

## Voice

And finally, we get to the last characteristic you'll need to juggle in with the others: voice. You may not have heard the bird, or you may not have noticed its call. But if you did, you've got a bonus clue.

Matching a bird's song to the spelled-out translation in a book is tricky enough when the bird is right in front of you. Trying to remember a bird's call or song until you can listen to a recording later is way harder than it seems it should be. You can listen to bird recordings on the Internet, once you have a hunch what the bird is. I like www.mbr-pwrc.usgs.gov/id/songlist.html, the bird recordings Web site of the US Department of the Interior's Patuxent Wildlife Research Center. Or try www.birdsahoy.org/birdsong/, a Web site about birdsong that includes links to many sites with song recordings. For starters, though, stick to these basic questions.

1. Did the bird have a pretty, musical song? Or did the bird have more of a monotone trill or a harsh cackle?

2. Did the song last a long time?

3. Was the song repeated?

4. Did you notice any other sounds, perhaps a short, sharp chip!, a buzz, or a rattle?

## THE NEXT STEP

Now that you have the basics of birding under your belt, why not go out and find some birds to identify? The more practice you get, the easier it becomes to decide who's who.

If you get frustrated—and you probably will, as it happens to most of us!—try not to get too discouraged. Instead, come back and read the next chapter, "Quick Tips for Skill Building." There you'll find a frank discussion of the pitfalls of bird identification. But more important, you'll find lots of quick tricks for getting to know the birds and matching them up with their names. See you there!

**A nasal meow is a clue to the gray catbird.**

# Chapter Four

# Quick Tips for Skill Building

**M**y daughter, Gretel, can tell you every tiny detail that makes a Chanel a Chanel or a Prada a Prada. The style, the stitching, the material, the zippers or rivets, the lettering on the label, she knows it all. She can recognize a designer item from across the street or in a tiny photo. She can even tell the difference between the real thing and a clever copy.

Some years ago, she tried to educate me. We were in a consignment shop, and I'd found what I thought was a real buy, a classic Coach handbag for only $20.

"It's a fake," proclaimed my daughter. "Look how thin the leather on the name tag is. And the dye stops at the seams, so you know the purse was dipped after it was made, not dyed beforehand. This won't hold up like a real Coach."

She went on to point out half a dozen other details, none of which I'd noticed.

Now, if it had been a bird . . .

Learning the fine points of identifying *anything* comes with practice and study. Sound like a final exam? Not to worry. When you're "studying" something you love, the learning isn't just painless—it's fun.

## WHY IDING CAN BE A CHALLENGE

Most bird-watchers begin with a traditional field guide. All you need to do is match up what you're looking at with the pictures in the book, right? So how hard can this be?

Answer: much trickier than you'd think.

Identifying a bird can be straightforward and simple: yellow body, black wings and cap—American goldfinch, check.

But it can also be complicated enough to make you want to pull your hair out. Lots of birds look similar to other species. Often birds don't exactly match the picture. And no

**Head markings help differentiate sparrows. This one is the well-named white-crowned.**

**Sparrows with less flashy markings, like this golden-crowned, require a closer look.**

matter what your bird looks like, simply finding its picture in a field guide can be a tough task in itself.

## Sheer Size

Traditional field guides are necessarily large. With roughly 800 species of birds in the United States and Canada, it takes a lot of pages and a lot of pictures to fit them all in.

Ready for some major good news? You'll only be using the back half of that book for your backyard birds.

Field guides are arranged by bird order and bird families, and it's the back half that includes the passerines, the order of perching birds that includes the huge majority of our backyard friends.

The first half of the book will hold waterfowl, seabirds, marsh birds, and others that aren't likely to show up in your backyard. Save that part for later, when you look for birds outside your yard.

## Finding Your Bird

Practice, practice, practice. It's the only way to become faster at finding a bird in a field guide. That word "practice" still makes some of us shudder with recollections of being dragged by the ear to the piano bench as a kid. I never got any further than beginner pieces ("Für Elise," anyone? How about a "Chopsticks" duet?). I didn't like playing piano—I just wanted to be outside.

On the other hand, I've never minded looking at pictures of birds. And that's what "practicing" bird identification is all about.

Look through the 38 "Start Here" birds in Chapter 6, and the birds for your own region. Then look at them again. If you like, you can do the same with a more comprehensive field guide. I keep one in my car and one in my bathroom: Every few minutes of looking through them helps.

There's no need to consciously memorize the details of each bird. Instead, trust your wonderful brain to store those fine points while you simply look at the drawing or photo and read the name attached to it. You'll be surprised how much you remember when the actual bird is right in front of you. "Oh, I know that one," is likely to be your first reaction. (If you're like me, the next thought probably goes like this: "It's … it's … uh, I know I saw it, now what was it called? Streaky yellow, right, that's a, oh, I got it, it's a yellow warbler!")

## Look-Alikes

Remember that designer-savvy daughter of mine, with her handbag advice? As a kid, her favorite segment on *Sesame Street* was the one with the catchy ditty that went, "One of these things is not like the other … " No wonder she's so good at recognizing tiny differences.

The same kind of challenge—of sorting out the details—comes into play when you're trying to tell the difference between birds that look too darn much alike.

You'll quickly discover that one sparrow looks very much like another. Many species of warblers and vireos can look a lot alike. So can kinglets. Ditto woodpeckers. Hummingbirds? Unless their throat is lit like neon, lotsa luck. Farther afield, shorebirds are legendary for giving birders fits.

With look-alike birds, the only way to be sure of an ID is to pay attention to the details. Once you have the basics of appearance, habits, and habitat clues nailed down, then you'll need to look for the fine points.

That's why Roger Tory Peterson's system of "field marks" was such a stroke of genius. Look for those pointers on your bird, and it'll be much easier to single out from the crowd. You'll find information on field marks in "ID Aids You Can Count On," on page 50. Field marks for individual birds can be found in their profiles in Chapter 6. When I spot a bird that I know has look-alike friends, I make a conscious effort to cement those field mark details into my brain. A scribbled sketch works great, but if

This summer tanager looks a lot like a hepatic tanager. Checking details is vital.

Dramatic red and black make it a cinch to separate the scarlet tanager from its kin.

# Brown, Green, Gray

I'll never forget how I looked and looked to match up a little brown bird with my field guide. Diligently, I went through every sparrow pictured, while the cooperative bird stayed right in view. None of them matched.

Finally, months later, I found my bird in the book, purely by accident. It wasn't a sparrow at all, but a female indigo bunting.

Not many birds are as easy to recognize as a male oriole or cardinal. Most are colored to blend in with their surroundings, in shades of brown, green, or gray.

It's the little brown birds that are truly devilish. Little green birds aren't exactly a picnic, either. Little gray birds can look a lot alike, too, but they're much easier to sort out.

## "Little brown birds"

- Sparrows of all sorts
- House sparrow (which technically isn't a sparrow at all but a weaver finch from Africa)
- Female finches
- Some warblers
- Waterthrushes
- Ovenbird
- Female buntings
- Wrens
- Brown creeper
- Horned lark
- Water pipit

A female indigo bunting is a challenge to ID.

- Maybe female rufous-sided towhees and both sexes of other towhee species, also thrushes
- Female red-winged blackbird

## "Little green birds"

- Many warblers
- Most vireos
- Female goldfinches
- Female painted bunting
- Female towhees, tanagers, grosbeaks, or crossbills (larger birds)

## "Little gray birds"

"Little gray birds" are easier to separate because many of them have very different habits or habitat. They might be:

- Chickadees
- Titmice
- Nuthatches
- Kinglets
- Some warblers
- Some vireos
- Juncos
- Gnatcatchers
- Verdin
- Bushtits
- Wrentit

Tricolor plumage, without streaks, peg a female rufous-sided towhee. Other, plainer towhees are trickier.

I don't have paper, I find it helps to say the field marks out loud: "White wing bars. White corners on tail." Anything that makes you pay conscious attention will help remind you later, when you're sifting through look-alikes.

## VARIATIONS ON A THEME

Ornithologists like to write up fussy bird descriptions that try to mention every single characteristic in excruciating detail. Field guides follow Confucius's advice, and let a photo or drawing stand in for those 1,000 words. Too bad birds don't read the books.

Often, your bird will match the picture exactly. Hallelujah! But you'll quickly discover that there's a lot of variation in the appearance of birds of the same species. And that can be frustrating. Here are some tips for finding a match for a bird that just doesn't look like the one in the book.

### Individual Variations

Like the fugues you may have learned in those long-ago piano lessons, each individual bird echoes the main theme of the species, with its own slight twist. It's still instantly recognizable as the species. It's just a little different.

Sometimes it's better not to try to make every detail match the picture. Do check and double-check the field marks, though, such as color of bill or legs, or other details that peg your bird as a certain species. As long as the field marks line up, you can be sure of your ID.

I learned that lesson the hard way—by public humiliation.

### A Really Rare Sparrow

When I first began identifying birds with a field guide, I quickly became pretty cocky. I ran through the feeder birds, my ego expanding with every species I notched in the book. Goldfinch, chickadee, white-throated sparrow, song sparrow, fox sparrow, junco, even the red-breasted nuthatch—why, this was a cinch!

Then I came across a bird that stopped me dead.

It looked like some kind of a sparrow, I thought. But no matter how carefully I compared it to the pictures in the sparrow section of my Peterson's, I couldn't make it match up. The closest I could come was Harris's sparrow, a bird that would be totally out of place in Pennsylvania, which was where I was.

I looked again: Yes, the black bib was

**Harris's sparrow is a wanderer that sometimes strays from its Midwest home.**

right, and the gray cheeks, and the brownish back and wings. Harris's belly looked whiter than my bird's grayish tan, and the top of its head was black while my bird's was brown. But it had to be Harris's sparrow. Nothing else came close. I had a rare bird!

Excitedly I phoned a nearby bird sanctuary, where the staff had been terrifically encouraging about my fledgling efforts.

"I've got a Harris's sparrow at my feeder," I proudly announced. "Just showed up this morning."

Two birders from the sanctuary came right over. They quickly scanned the scene with their binoculars—once, twice, three times.

Why weren't they seeing it? "Right there," I pointed out.

"That one? The one with the black bib?"

I was ready to go down in the record books. "That's him!"

They seemed to be distinctly unexcited. Were Harris's sparrows more common than I'd thought?

"Got your field guide?" one of the fellows finally asked. I handed it over.

He quickly flipped past all those pages of sparrows I'd pored over. I saw goldfinches go by, and cardinals. Finally he stopped and handed the book back.

"What about this one?" he asked.

Oh. Instant deflation. House sparrow. Not exactly a sighting to trumpet.

The birders were kind. "They do look somewhat alike," they acknowledged. "If the book had had the house sparrow with the other sparrows, you would've seen the difference right away. But he's actually a weaver finch, not a sparrow, so they put him in a different section."

"Any way I might have known that?" I asked, hoping to learn a tip that would help me avoid future shame.

"Practice," they said. "Just keep looking at the pictures and looking up birds. You'll get there."

### Focus on Field Marks

I had one more question for the birders from the sanctuary. "How come this house sparrow's bib doesn't look like the picture? It's all spotty, like the bib on a Harris's."

They looked at each other and laughed, as if they'd been down the same path. "There's a lot of variation," they said. "You just learn what to look for. And make sure the field marks match. See that arrow? Harris's has a pink beak. Your bird doesn't."

By the way, this story does have a happy ending. I became an expert in recognizing house sparrows, for one thing. And for another, I did soon sight my rare bird: a tiny

**House sparrow plumage can vary, causing a newbie birder to think, "Rare bird!"**

heron called a least bittern that showed up at a pond down the road a few weeks later.

Much to their credit, my bird sanctuary pals once again hurried right over. This time, they confirmed it. Only the fifth sighting in the county, they told me.

Smug? Do I seem smug? Heck, 25 years later, I'm still bragging! Oh, and if you want some tips on house sparrow plumage, hey, just let me know.

## ID AIDS YOU CAN COUNT ON

Roger Tory Peterson was a genius. But he also was a birder, and he knew how tricky identification could be. So he invented a can't-miss system that was brilliant in its simplicity: field marks.

Field marks are those details of a bird that, taken together, confirm the species without a doubt. Just as important, they're details that you can spot at a glance—once you know to look for them. Every Peterson guide includes arrows pointing to field marks of that species.

Starting in Chapter 6, you'll find an entry called "Details, Details" for each bird, spelling out a few details you can quickly check.

## Finding Field Marks Quickly

Field marks are such a simple system; it takes just a few minutes to learn how to look for them. Mostly, it's a matter of where to look and what to watch for.

It'd be great if every bird sat still long enough for us to systematically run through its field marks. But that's not usually the case. So birders train themselves to look fast, since they may only get one glimpse.

### Head

Head color and shape are the watchwords. Look for:

◆ Color and shape of beak

◆ A pointy crest, as that of a cardinal or Steller's jay

◆ Raised feathers, a subtler effect than a crest, as often seen on purple finches

## Elvis Impersonator?

Field marks are taken so seriously by birders that they've led to some interesting arguments. One of the most notable recently has been the dispute over the identity of "Elvis," the possibly rediscovered ivory-billed woodpecker in an Arkansas swamp.

When the Cornell Lab of Ornithology announced the rediscovery of the ivory-billed in 2005, skeptics immediately surfaced. Code-named "Elvis," the ivory-billed had

been videotaped. Still, it was almost immediately branded an impersonator.

Elvis was actually an abnormal pileated, goes the hypothesis. Supporting evidence? Four of the five ivory-billed field marks, which you can count yourself in Peterson's, weren't seen in the Elvis video. Without those field marks, argue the skeptics, the ID isn't certain.

- A colored cap, like that of a chickadee or tree sparrow

- A colored bib, like that of the house sparrow or Harris's sparrow

- Eye ring, a narrow circle around the eye, often white

- Stripes above, below, or at the eyes

- Pattern on the face

- Eye color

## Wings

Wing decoration and sometimes wing shape in flight are clues to look for. Check for these details.

- Wing bars: a horizontal bar or bars of different colors, usually white or yellow, across the wing; take note of how many

- A dab of white, sometimes yellow, on the wing; often called a "pocket handkerchief"

## QUICK TIPS

While that bird is in your binoculars, check its field marks in this order: head, wings, tail—and if you still have time—legs. Give the bird a quick once-over, then go back and take a longer look if it hasn't flown away.

- White wing patches seen in flight

- White wing edges seen in flight

- Noticeably pointed wings, usually seen in flight

- Unusually long wings, noted when bird is perched or flying

## Tail

Tail details are usually noticed best when the bird takes off or lands. Scan for these possibilities.

- Noticeably long tail

- Noticeably short tail

**Wingbars and head stripes are clues that help set a golden-crowned kinglet apart from similar wood warblers.**

**A female American redstart sports a yellow "pocket handkerchief" and tail spots.**

## Make a Note

I'm always taken aback by how quickly I forget or mix up the details when trying to ID a batch of birds.

Warblers and sparrows are the worst because they often hang around in flocks of mixed species. It's not unusual to find six or eight kinds of warblers together, or four or five kinds of sparrows, especially during migration time.

When birds are coming through fast and furious, it's all too easy to lose track of the details you do note.

Was the one with the eye ring the same one that had the wing bars? And who had the white tail feathers—the one with the reddish cap or the one with the striped head?

Anytime you're checking details on more than one bird, it makes sense to jot down a few notes on field marks—as you notice them!

♦ Unusually shaped tail, such as the wide keel shape of a grackle

♦ Forked tail, such as a barn swallow or goldfinch

♦ Rounded or square corners of tail

♦ White feathers along edges of tail

♦ White or colored patch on tail

♦ White or colored corners of tail

### Legs

Details of legs and feet can help separate very similar birds, or can be an instant clue to ID. Look for:

♦ Noticeably long legs, such as a waterthrush

♦ Noticeably short legs, such as a nuthatch

♦ Color of legs

To ID juncos, look for white tail edges, back and head color, and eye and beak color. This is the red-backed race.

Long legs, bright pinkish in spring, are a big clue to identifying the Louisiana waterthrush.

- Color of feet

- Arrangement of toes, such as the two toes front and two toes back of woodpeckers, or the three-and-one of songbirds

## SIZING IT UP

I was so disappointed when I ripped open the package that held my newly ordered field guide to sub-alpine wildflowers. It was so small! It had looked like a normal book online. But in my hand, it was only the size of a small spiral-bound notebook.

That's the same reaction I have to a "bird in the hand." Whenever I see a dead bird, or happen to have the chance to look at a captive, I always exclaim, "It's so small!"

A bird in hand looks surprisingly smaller than the same bird at the feeder or in the yard. Or to put it another way, birds look bigger than they really are. Why? Because there's nothing familiar to compare them to.

### The Theory of Relativity

Maybe you've ordered a plant from a catalog that showed a gorgeous close-up of its flowers. Without any background to compare them to, you'd have no way of knowing that the plant was only 3 inches tall.

Same deal with my undersized alpine field guide. If the online photo of the book had included a person's hand, or even a penny, I would've had something familiar against which to judge its size.

Even movie stars can be startlingly short in real life, or so I hear. On the screen, they look 6 feet tall. In person, when we have

familiar benchmarks nearby, they suddenly shrink to 5-feet, 6-inches.

It works the same way with birds. Without a familiar reference point in the scene, most of us assume birds are bigger than they actually are.

I remember being stunned when I finally realized how small the shorebirds called "peeps" actually are. I knew that one of the peeps, the least sandpiper, is the smallest shorebird in the world. I'd read the description often enough to be able to rattle off its size: 6 inches.

Yet I still had an entirely inaccurate idea of the size of these birds. On the bare beaches and mudflats where I usually saw them, they didn't look like mini birds at all. I would've sworn they were at least as big as a starling—until a starling happened to land near a small flock of them on a mudflat one day. Either that starling was a relative of King Kong, or peeps are only the size of a sparrow.

**Least sandpipers seem much bigger than the sparrow-size birds they are.**

## A "Handy" Experiment

A few years ago, I was walking down the aisle of Halloween supplies in a local store when an eerie electronic laugh rang out. Apparently I'd set off some sort of motion detector, which had triggered a life-size fake hand to reach out of its plastic coffin. It wasn't exactly my kind of décor, but the thing had possibilities for a science experiment I'd been pondering.

I waited for the after-Halloween clearance sale, then snatched up the hand at a bargain price. A few minutes of brute-force disassembly, and I was the proud possessor of a disembodied pinkish hand and wrist, almost exactly the same size as my own.

Relying on duct tape and florist wire, I managed to secure the appendage to one of my thistle feeders, palm up. With a sprinkling of niger seed, the experiment was ready to begin. For a few minutes, the goldfinches and siskins were leery of this weird new feeder add-on. Not for long. As birds outnumbered perches, a couple of them soon made themselves at home on the hand's fingers.

Oh my gosh! You should see how small a goldfinch is! With the hand as a gauge, I suddenly realized just how big—I mean little—a 5-inch bird really is.

For a week or so, I varied the placement and the treats that the hand held out. It was enlightening to see the actual size of jays, starlings, chickadees, and other friends.

As soon as I removed the "handy" gauge of relativity, though, my unconscious view of the birds came back. I had to try hard to remember how small the chickadee had looked on "my" thumb. Maybe you can find your own plastic Halloween hand for experimenting. Just remember that the eye-opening effect only lasts as long as the visual aid does.

That's why I depend on another system for gauging the size of birds. It's not as exact, but it's a whole lot simpler.

## How Big?

Whenever I'm playing the birder version of 20 Questions with someone who's asked me to identify a bird she's seen, I start with one of the most general characteristics: How big was it?

No one I've ever met answers like this: "Uh, I'd figure 10¼ inches head to tail, with a 3-inch beak."

So instead of asking "How big was it?," I ask, "Do you know what a robin looks like?"

Almost everyone says yes.

"Was it bigger than a robin?"

It's funny, but this trick works great.

Try it yourself. You'll find that just having

**Gauge the size of an unfamiliar bird by comparing it to your mental image of a robin.**

the idea of a robin to compare to the mental image of another bird seems to be enough to give you a pretty good handle on size.

If the bird in question was smaller than a robin, I ask, "Was it about the size of a sparrow?" Seems like a lot more people have a mental image of a robin than they do of a sparrow. Often I hear, "I don't really know how big a sparrow is." If that's the case, I'll switch to a chickadee. Often that will do the trick.

### Imaginary Friends

A trio of imaginary birds is a terrific aid to bird-watching.

I've found that a quick and easy way to gauge the size of a new bird is to compare it to one of these three commoners:

- A 5¼-inch black-capped chickadee

- A 6- to 7-inch song or white-throated sparrow

- A 10-inch robin

Become familiar with these birds, and you'll have three excellent benchmarks to draw upon when you're looking at a new bird. Make it a point to watch these three as they move about your yard. Look at each bird

**The common grackle is one of a handful of backyard birds that are bigger than a robin.**

on the ground, at the feeder, in the shrubs or trees, and in flight. Learn to recognize each of the three from a distance. Meanwhile, your subconscious will be registering how big each of your benchmark birds looks against these different backgrounds.

When a new bird comes along, just picture one of the three nearby. With practice, the best-fitting of your comparison birds will pop up without any prompting. "Hmm, about the size of a robin," you'll think. Or maybe, "Wow, even smaller than a chickadee."

## HOW TO AVOID COLOR CONFUSION

The birds in your backyard won't always look like the pictures in this book. Many of these photos show birds at breeding time, when feathers are at their most vivid. And all of them show the birds in ideal light, not in dim shade or bright sun. They've been selected to best show the characteristics of each bird.

**QUICK TIP**

Fully or mostly albino birds can be most unsettling. When I saw a white bird on the lawn, acting just like a robin, it threw me for a loop. I was accustomed to robins that looked like robins, yet the silhouette and habits were unmistakable. Albinotic birds, which have only some white feathers, can be trickier to figure out. Pay attention to habits, and you'll get it.

How do backyard birds compare in size? Just use the three benchmark birds at the bottom of this page to create a mental image.

| OTHER BACKYARD BIRDS | RELATIVE SIZE (size relative to benchmark birds) | ACTUAL SIZE, BEAK TO TAIL |
|---|---|---|
| American goldfinch | Smaller than a chickadee | 5" |
| Blue jay | Bigger than a robin | 11" |
| Bushtit | Smaller than a chickadee | 4½" |
| Cardinal | Smaller than a robin | 8¾" |
| Carolina wren | Smaller than a sparrow; bigger than a chickadee | 5½" |
| Common grackle | Bigger than a robin | 12½" |
| Evening grosbeak | Smaller than a robin; bigger than a sparrow | 8" |
| House wren | Smaller than a chickadee | 4¾" |
| Hummingbird | Smaller than a chickadee | 3¾"–4¼", depending on species |
| Mourning dove | Bigger than a robin | 12" |
| Red-breasted nuthatch | Smaller than a chickadee | 4½" |
| Slate-colored junco | About the same as a sparrow | 6¼" |
| White-breasted nuthatch | Bigger than a chickadee; a little smaller than a sparrow | 5¾" |

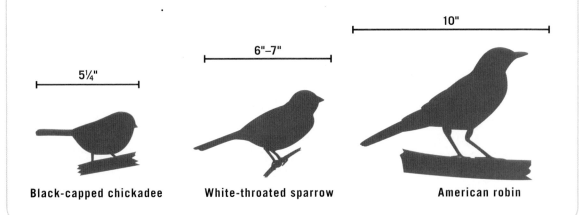

5¼"
Black-capped chickadee

6"–7"
White-throated sparrow

10"
American robin

**The red-breasted nuthatch, 4 inches long including beak and tail, is one of our tiniest birds.**

What you'll be looking at in your backyard is a lot less perfect.

Gender, age, season, geography, and individual idiosyncrasies can cause enough variations in color to make you doubt your birds' ID.

## Gender Differences

Plumage may or may not be different between the genders of a species. In many species, male and female birds look so much alike you'd have to get downright rude to find out for sure. Nearly all sparrow species are perfectly matched pairs. So are jays, chickadees, flycatchers, thrushes, thrashers, catbirds, wrens, and various others.

QUICK TIP

When you see two birds that are obviously interacting but are very differently colored, you're probably watching a male and female or a parent and young. Female or young birds, depending on species, may be greenish, brownish, or streaked.

In other species, you'll notice a slight difference between the sexes. Generally, the female is a slightly less vivid version of the male. You can pick the males out of a flock of robins, for instance, by looking for those birds with the deeper orange chests. Some female wood warblers, too, including the northern parula, look like a faded version of the brighter male.

That leaves the bird species whose genders are markedly different. I hate to generalize because I'm sure I'll overlook somebody, but typically these seem to be the birds with the brightest colors: the cardinal, orioles, tanagers, grosbeaks, crossbills, and on the smaller side, the finches, buntings, wood warblers, and hummingbirds. Males are

**A female slate-colored junco is slightly paler and a bit browner than this male.**

**Young birds look more like their mother than their father. In blue jays, the sexes look alike, so ID of this baby jay is easy.**

**QUICK TIP**

Baby birds often leave the nest before they've become accomplished fliers. They hide in shrubbery or plants for a few days, while the parent bird keeps an eye on them from a distance. If you come across a fledgling in your yard without its parent nearby, you may have a hard time figuring out who this kid belongs to. Listen for an adult bird scolding you: That'll be Mom or Dad. To ID the youngster, back off and look for its parent.

## Sorting Out Young Birds

Freshly hatched baby songbirds may be the homeliest creatures on earth. They're naked and blind, and bottom-heavy so that they stay right side up in the nest. They'll soon sprout fluffy down and then their first set of feathers.

When young birds are old enough to leave the nest, they usually display a family resemblance. Baby jays have a few stubby blue wing feathers. Baby goldfinches look something like their mom. In fact in many cases, an immature bird looks more like its mother than its father.

You'll find detailed descriptions of immature birds in comprehensive field guides. Or you can just keep watching, to see which adults your young bird joins up with.

vibrant, with feathers in strong shades of red, orange, yellow, magenta, or blue. Females lean toward the greenish or sometimes brownish side. If you didn't have a field guide, it'd be easy to mistake them for two different species. Rufous-sided towhees and many blackbirds—particularly red-winged and yellow-headed, plus the less showy Brewer's blackbirds—also have so much difference between genders that you may mistake them for other birds altogether.

**QUICK TIP**

Bird families usually stick together even after the youngsters are flying. Keep watching an immature bird, and you may see it futilely pestering its parents for food, or joining the group when they leave the area.

## Molting

Most birds change their feathers, or molt, at least partially in fall, after nesting. Some finish the molt in late winter through spring, before breeding.

The process takes place gradually, just a few feathers at a time, over a period of weeks.

Birds that are molting may look funny.

**In their first fall, male rose-breasted grosbeaks look like a warmer-colored version of their streaky brown mama.**

QUICK TIP

Pay attention to behavior. When you see a large, young gray bird begging from a smaller adult bird, it's likely that you're watching a young, parasitic cowbird with its unwitting stepparent. Cowbird parents sneak their eggs into the nests of other birds for them to raise.

Their plumage may be splotchy or blotchy, and their wings or tail may have a few gaps.

A chickadee looks like a chickadee year-round. But a few birds, notably goldfinches, look drastically different after the molt, resembling females. Some of the trickiest birds to ID are young male birds—hatched that year—of species in which adult males are brightly colored: tanagers, orioles, grosbeaks, and buntings. "First-year males," the young birds that stop in our yards on their way south in fall and on their way back in spring, look more like their mamas than their daddies. After next year's nesting season, they'll molt again, into adult dress.

## Regional Variations

I'll always cherish my Peterson field guide, but *The Sibley Guide to Birds* has supplanted it as my favorite. Not exactly a pocket guide, this 544-pager includes pictures of regional variations in color.

Often these variations in birds are slight. But they can be enough to trip you up on identity. When I first moved to Washington State, I thought I was seeing fox sparrows throughout the white-ash woods along the Columbia River. In spring, they began to sing—like song sparrows!

*Sibley* confirmed my hunch: Song sparrows in my part of the country are a few shades darker than the same species in my former backyards in the East and Midwest. Instead of a whitish breast streaked with reddish brown, song sparrows in the Pacific Northwest have a gray background for those stripes.

The red-tailed hawk, a common bird that may turn up in your backyard, is famed for color variations. Birds may be light, dark, or somewhere in the middle. The dark form looks like an entirely different species, until you spot that telltale chestnut tail.

QUICK TIP

You can see migration in action by watching the plumage of the birds in your yard. Adult males depart first, followed in a couple of weeks or so by females and juveniles. Keep an eye on plants with fall berries, and you'll see vivid adult male tanagers, orioles, grosbeaks, and others pause first. Later, if your dogwood is suddenly swarming with nondescript birds, look for clues that they're tanagers or grosbeaks in disguise.

In bright sunshine, the neck of a male rock dove, or pigeon, flashes iridescent purple.

Color isn't the only trait that can vary by region. Vocalizations may also be different. The white-breasted nuthatch in the Pacific Northwest looks very similar to birds of other regions. But instead of saying *ank-ank,* he makes a complaining *mew.*

That's why deciding on an ID means taking into account a bird's looks, habits, and voice. If one of them fools you, the others will help you figure it out!

## Tricks of the Light

I'm a poor photographer, because I always forget to think about the light. When the exposure is off, the color of the bird is all wrong. It's either much too dark, or way too washed out. And if I happened to snap the shutter when the bird hopped into shade, I

might not see any iridescent color at all in my subject. But nowadays, with the instant-replay feature of digital cameras, I can retake the photo if I messed up, and if the bird is still there (big if).

Light affects your eyes the same way it does a camera lens. A bird in shade looks darker, and details are obscured. A bird in blasting sun is paler. If light isn't hitting the iridescent feathers of a bird, it'll look dull and dark instead of like a shimmering jewel.

As always, the cure for tricks of the light is to keep watching. With a little luck, the bird will move into a better position, where you can see what it really looks like.

## ID Challenges

Some birds are just plain difficult to tell apart, even if you have a lot of experience behind those binoculars. Here's what I look for to pin down those too-close-to-call characters.

## Brown Thrushes

Is it a veery or a wood thrush? Or any of the other confusingly close species? Check these traits while the bird is in front of you, then double-check with your comprehensive field guide.

- Color of back—Is it reddish (wood thrush, veery, possibly young Swainson's), brown (hermit, young Bicknell's), or grayish brown (Swainson's, gray-cheeked, Bicknell's, hermit)?

- Breast spots—Are they big and bold and separated by white (wood thrush), do they look muted (veery, young Swainson's), or are they so dense they're almost blurred (interior West race of Swainson's, gray-cheeked, Bicknell's, hermit)? Are they concentrated on the throat and upper breast area, then fade out (veery, Swainson's, gray-cheeked, Bicknell's, hermit), or do bold spots extend down along the wings (wood thrush)?

- Color of tail—Is it distinctly reddish (wood thrush, veery, Bicknell's, hermit)?

- Tail movement—Does the bird raise and lower its tail (hermit)?

- Eye markings—Does the bird have a distinct eye ring (wood thrush, hermit) or "spectacles" (Swainson's)?

## Thrashers

The brown thrasher is a cinch to identify—until you see a long-billed thrasher, which is similar enough to make you wonder. The grayer thrashers of the Southwest are even trickier, despite those distinguished beaks. Check these details.

- Color of eye—Is it noticeably light (brown, long-billed, Bendire's, curve-billed, Crissal, LeConte's, sage) or dark (California)?

- Under-tail feathers—What color are the *under-tail coverts,* the feathers in that triangular patch at the base of the bird's tail, behind its legs? If they're white, it's a brown or long-billed thrasher; if they're orangish tan, it's a Bendire's, curve-billed, California, LeConte's, or sage thrasher; if they're dark rusty, it's a Crissal.

- Facial markings—Does the bird have a bold line at its eye, or is that line hard to make out or nonexistent? If it has a dark line, it's a California thrasher; if it has a pale line, it's a sage thrasher. All other species don't have eye lines.

- Breast spots or streaks—Does the breast show any marks, such as round, muted dapples (Bendire's, curve-billed) or streaks (brown, long-billed, sage)?

## Warblers

With dozens of species, sorting out wood warblers can be a lifetime hobby. Quickly check these field marks to make it easier. Then consult a comprehensive field guide to see which of the more than 50 North American warbler species you may have.

- Wing bars—How many does it have? How wide are they?

- Tail spots—What color are they? Where are they located?

- Eye markings—Is there an eye ring? An eye stripe?

- Head markings—Are there any other noticeable head markings, such as a cap? A cheek patch?

- Throat color—What color is the throat?

## Buntings

There are only a few species of buntings, and still they can be a challenge. Double-check these details and you'll have them mastered—or at least you'll get the males. The uniformly brown females are best identified by certain circumstantial evidence: Which male bunting are they hanging around with?

- Color of breast—Is it the same (indigo) or different (lazuli, varied, painted) than the color of the bird's head and back?

- Wing bars—Can you see any white wing bars on the closed wing? If you do, it's a lazuli bunting.

## Bluebirds

All three bluebird species—eastern, mountain, and western—may show up in the same region. Enjoy the treat—and look for these fine points to sort them out.

- Overall color—Is it entirely blue (mountain), with no orange or chestnut? If not, it's an eastern or western.

- Color of breast—Is it orange (eastern or western) or blue (mountain)?

- Color of throat—Is it orange (eastern) or blue (western or mountain)?

- Color of belly—Is it blue (western or mountain) or white (eastern)?

- Color of sides of neck—Are they orange (eastern) or blue (western, mountain)?

- Color of back and above wings—Is any chestnut showing? If yes, it's a western bluebird; if no, it's an eastern or mountain.

## Sparrows

Yes, this is the group of birds that causes even seasoned birders to pretend they didn't see its many members. But all it takes is patience—lots of patience—and a comprehensive field guide to sort them out. Try to get a look at these marks while you're looking at the bird, or better yet, snap a few digital pictures that you can pore over later. Consult a comprehensive field guide to pinpoint which of the nearly 50 species of North American sparrows you're looking at.

- Head markings—Is there a cap? Head stripes? Cheek patch? Eye stripes?

- Eye markings—Is there an eye ring? What color?

- Beak color—What color is it? Are both upper and lower halves of the beak the same color?

- Throat color—What color is it?

- Wing bars—Are there any? How many? What color?

- Breast markings—Are there stripes? Streaks? A darker "stickpin" in the center?

- Tail color—Is there any noticeable flash of white tail feathers when the bird flies?

# Chapter Five

# The Regional Approach

Somehow, despite my best intentions, I still haven't quite managed to make it to Central America to see the resplendent quetzal, a fantastic green, blue, and red bird of the rain forest. The bird of paradise of New Guinea is still waiting for me, too, quivering those extravagant plumes without my binoculars watching.

Those endearing penguins at the South Pole? Maybe someday. As for the "robin redbreast" of England, a small, chubby songbird that shares nothing with our own robin besides a taste for worms, I only recognize it because I met it in *Winnie-the-Pooh* books.

They're great birds, every one. But I haven't felt deprived in the least. (Okay, maybe when I see on TV a bowerbird adding blue—and only blue—objects to its nest, I do have to stop myself from jumping onto a plane to Australia right then and there.)

Our own great big country holds so many wonderful birds that there's been way more than enough to keep me busy for my whole life. Our continent is wildly diverse. We have rolling hills and snow-capped peaks. Flat farmlands and prairies, and at least three distinct kinds of desert. Every kind of water feature you can imagine—from oceans and big rivers on a grand scale, to tiny ponds and brooks.

When I get the itch to travel, all I have to do is visit a different part of the country. I know I'll see different plants, different terrain—and lots of different birds!

## WHY REGIONS?

Those exotic places you see on the nature shows are often surprisingly small compared to the United States. You could fit all of Great Britain, including its robin redbreasts, into the state of Oregon. Costa Rica would slip right into West Virginia with room to spare, even with all those quetzal tails. Even New Guinea, with all its marvels, is only twice the size of California.

Check any bird supplies store, and you'll find individual field guides for each of those places. Yet only a handful of states in our own country can lay claim to a field guide focused on that region.

Many birds are generalists, and adapt easily to different conditions, climates, and food. Our friend the American robin is one of them—you'll find it just about everywhere.

On my first trip to the Southwest, where it seemed that every bird I looked at was a new species to me, I was fooled good by a regular old robin. I was sure the brownish gray and rusty red bird I saw hopping about in the desert had to be something special. Straining my eyes, I tried hard to find some detail that would make it something else—a clay-colored robin, perhaps? Nope. It was simply a regular old robin, as at home among the cactus as it was on my lush green lawn back home.

In the "Start Here" chapter, beginning on page 75, you'll find many species that range across most or all of our country. All of the "Start Here" birds are widespread. They're also abundant. And they frequently visit backyards. All of that means you have a good chance of meeting them in your own yard.

Getting familiar with these birds is the basis of becoming a backyard bird-watcher. You probably already know quite a few of them—including that widespread robin.

These birds may not show up in your yard at the same time they visit other parts of the country. Many are seen year-round, but some may stay in your region only to raise a family, or to spend the winter, or to use your yard as a rest stop when they pass through on migration.

That's why I've taken the regional approach in this book. Using a regional approach makes it simpler for you to identify the birds in your own area. And it makes it easy to check out the bird life of other regions so you can dream about that next vacation.

You won't see the same birds in Boston as you do in Minneapolis, or in Seattle, or in Houston, or at Disney World. Sure, there's some overlap—we all get song sparrows, for instance—but there are also dozens of species that tend to stick to certain regions.

## Climate and Conditions

Visit New England in January, and you can bet you'll be wearing your warmest winter coat and snuggest hat. Now imagine that you're a ruby-throated hummingbird, and the only down jacket you own is right there on your back. You're not going to be celebrating Christmas in Boston anytime soon; instead, you'll have hightailed it for the sunny South months before.

Climate and weather conditions play a big role in determining which region sees which birds. Here are a few major ways in which the climate in your region may affect birds.

◆ If you live where winters are cold, you're not going to see birds that depend on insects after frost settles in—not unless the birds can ferret out overwintering insects or add other foods to their menu come the cold season. So you'll say goodbye to flycatchers in fall, but you'll still see more adaptable chickadees all winter.

- If your region gets a lot of deep snow, your winter birds are likely to be mostly those species that can find food in the trees, not on the ground. Ground-scratching sparrows—fox, white-throated, white-crowned, and others—will move to areas where seeds are easier to access. But the sparrows will be replaced by juncos, which can switch to finding insects, spiders, or seeds in shrubs, on fallen logs, or in trees, and also are adept at finding small areas where the snow has melted, such as at the base of trees.

- Sheer cold is enough to kill many species of birds. Bluebirds are notoriously susceptible to cold, so they'll winter in warmer regions.

Birds are always surprising the scientists, though, so don't depend on birds to follow the rules. Our feeders and other human changes to the natural landscape may create conditions that are easier for birds to live in.

And bird habits don't always follow rhyme or reason, either. Why do some birds migrate only as far as the South, while other species travel on for hundreds or thousands more miles? No one knows. But we do know that regional differences make an impact on the range and habits of birds.

## Habitat and Food

The seasonal divisions you'll find under the "Mark Your Calendar" heading in the individual bird profiles in the regional chapters are based on the species' life cycle. "Winter only" means that you may see the bird on fall migration, during winter, and on spring migration. "Spring to fall" means that you live within its nesting territory; you're likely to see the bird

**Cardinals find plenty to eat in snowy regions.**

when it arrives on spring migration, then during its nesting season, and finally, after nesting until it leaves on fall migration. "Migration only" means that the bird passes through your area and doesn't linger for long. "Year-round" means just that: You have a chance of seeing the bird at any time of the year.

The climate and geography of your region determine which plants grow there, too. Those plants create the different habitats of the wild land around you—the forests, brush, grasslands, deserts, swamps, and other niches that appeal to various species of birds.

Not only do the plants of a region make a home for birds; they also supply the food that sustains birds in every season. Their food includes seeds, from pinecones to grasses; wild fruits and berries; and the most important by a mile, the teeming thousands of insects that live on those plants.

Page through the regional introductions in this book, and you'll find pictures that show a sampling of the typical landscape of each region. There's such diversity, our regions may as well be separate countries! Swamps draped with Spanish moss; balsam forests gleaming with white birches; stately saguaros: We have enough variety to fill years of pretty picture calendars. And that's just scratching the surface.

Those dramatic differences are easy to see. It's simple to grasp why a bird of the Arizona desert, say, might feel a little out of its league up around the Great Lakes. But less spectacular signs can be equally important in determining the traditional range of a bird.

Many birds are specialists in their food habits, eating only certain kinds of seeds or insects or fruits. And who can say when one of those is the key to hosting a bird species while it's nesting, or simply waving to it when it flies through on April migration? Maybe it's an abundance of grasshoppers that does the trick—and the grasshoppers depend on a grass that only thrives when rainfall is within a certain range. Or maybe the bird needs a plethora of spiderwebs—so a region with drenching downpours that destroy the webs wouldn't work. It's fun to conjecture about why certain species are limited to certain areas. But the truth is that, in many cases, science simply doesn't know what causes a particular species to say, "Here, right here. This is home."

Those skills developed in birds so long ago that we don't even know how it happened. All we can see is the result: Each bird species is perfectly suited to living in its natural habitat.

### Going to Extremes

To make a living in places that go to extremes requires specialized behavior and habits—the innate knowledge of how to nest in a cactus, for example, or how to find food when it's 30 degrees below zero.

If you live in a region of extreme climate or conditions, you're likely to see a good number of species that's at home only in your particular region. If you could "transplant" a scissor-tailed flycatcher from the wide-open spaces of its home in Texas to the close quarters of a deciduous woods a few states over, say in Tennessee, that bird would soon be hitching a ride back home. Its body is built for swooping over grasslands to forage, not for finagling its way through forests. Besides, grasshoppers—its mainstay meal—would be few and far between in those Tennessee trees.

You can play the same game with all kinds of specialized birds, from the northern parula of southern swamps to the roadrunner of the Southwest to the crossbills that roam among northern conifers. Although there's some give and take to their habits, many birds from more extreme habitats need a certain kind of niche to be able to put their innate skills to use.

## Natural Barriers

You'd think having wings would mean you could travel anywhere you want, but no such luck. Birds are limited in their range by some pretty daunting natural barriers.

One of the biggest was the Great Plains. Those vast prairies of tall grass and short grass acted as a natural stop sign to birds that depended on trees for their food and homes.

As towns and cities sprouted across the Plains, bringing windbreaks and backyard trees, the situation changed—a little. There's still enough open space out there to stop many birds in their tracks.

It works in reverse, too: Many of the birds that developed skills to shine in a grassland setting can't transfer them to a forest. So they stay put, like the dickcissel, or they seek out a downsized version of the Great Plains, like a meadowlark moving into a hay field or pasture across one of those blurred regional boundaries.

**Birdlife in these foothill alders is different than birdlife high in the mountains.**

Mountains are natural barriers, too, because bird species would have to gradually expand their range up and over. Life at the top is very different from life in the foothills, so most birds stick to a certain level on one side and never make it to the other side.

Blue jays, for instance, are found only east of the Rocky Mountains, except for a scattering of intrepid souls that has made the trip to the far side of the Rockies. The Steller's jay of the West, by the way, has returned the favor. It's been spotted from South Dakota to Florida.

You'll notice that many comprehensive field guides are divided into Eastern and Western versions. That continuous spine of the Rockies is why. Many of the birds in the East are not the same as birds in the West. The barrier of the mountains keeps them separated.

### Extended Fingers

Mountains can also function to funnel birds into a region where they wouldn't otherwise occur. Bird life at high elevations often includes species that would never be seen in the lowlands, or that only occur in lowlands during a specific season. Many species nest in the mountains but spend only the winter at lower elevations.

That high-altitude habitat, and the conditions and food that go along with it, is very similar throughout a mountain chain. The slate-colored junco, for example, is only a winter bird from Pennsylvania to Georgia—unless you live in the Appalachians. For that entire stretch of mountains, a long finger extending deeply southward, the slate-colored junco is a year-round species. Instead of moving northward into New England, the species also nests in those cool woodlands

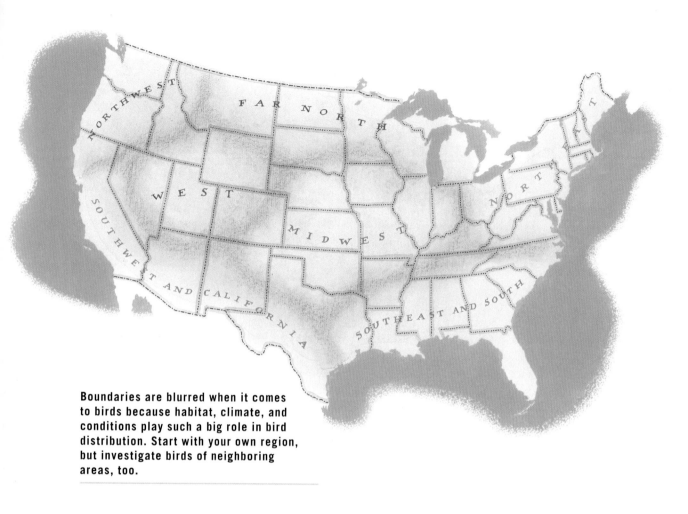

Boundaries are blurred when it comes to birds because habitat, climate, and conditions play such a big role in bird distribution. Start with your own region, but investigate birds of neighboring areas, too.

high up in the mountains. Another mountain inhabitant is the white-headed woodpecker, a bird of the West—the western mountains, that is. It rarely ventures into the lowlands, though it lives year-round in conifer forests in the Sierras and Cascades.

You can clearly see those fingers of mountain habitat extending into other regions in any comprehensive field guide. Once you start paying attention, you'll be quick to spot the differences in range created by the Appalachians, the Rockies, the Sierras, and even the mountains that extend upward from Mexico into the Southwest. More opportunities to see great birds!

## THE SEVEN REGIONS

The bird profiles in Part 2 are divided into eight chapters. First comes "Start Here," the common backyard birds shared by most of us across the country. After that, you'll find the seven geographic regions.

I've divided the country into these regions according to attributes that make each unique. Those natural attributes are what make each of the regions home to a wonderful array of interesting birds. As we've talked about, not all species will be unique to just one region; many will overlap into other areas.

In general, the more extreme the climate

and conditions of your region, the more specialized birds you'll see—which means more species that are unique to your region. The Northeast shares many birds with the Midwest and the Southeast. But the Southwest's collection of species includes many unusual, much more restricted birds.

You'll find a detailed description of the characteristics of each region in the regional chapters in Part 2. Here's a quick preview of the regions' most notable features and what kinds of birds you might find there.

## The Northeast

The most familiar backyard birds are icons in this region. Here's where you'll enjoy the company of cardinals, black-capped chicka-

**Northeast birds are "leaf peepers," too, but it's seeds and insects they seek.**

dees, and just about every other bird that shows up on sweatshirts or on those "singing" clocks decorated with birds.

A gentle landscape and relatively moderate climate bring an abundance of nesting birds and many year-round species. A wide variety of habitat, from forest to pasture to seacoast, also boosts the species count. Northern parts of this region, such as Maine, share some species with the Far North.

## The Far North

Lucky you—you can enjoy many species that the rest of the country rarely even sees. Those boreal chickadees and fantastic crossbills are simply specialists. They're birds that developed skills to thrive in the challenging conditions of this region.

One of the most extreme regions, this area features deep snow and penetrating cold. That creates specialists among birds, which have learned to exploit any food source they can find. Conifer forests and some deciduous woods sweep across the land. Birds that can extract the seeds of cones have a ready source of food, and so do those species that forage over tree bark and foliage.

## The Southeast and South

Hot and steamy in summer, your region is an ideal wintering ground for eastern bluebirds, catbirds, and many other species that are only a seasonal treat elsewhere. The deeper south you go in this region, the more unique birds you'll see. Blue grosbeaks, brown-headed nuthatches, and other winged wonders roam the lush vegetation.

Food is abundant. Insects are often annoyingly plentiful, and berries and small fruits tailor-made for birds grow with wild abandon. In the mountains, more-northern species raise their families in the cooler habitat.

## The Midwest

You may not have the endless prairie outside the door of your sod house anymore, but those amber waves of grain aren't a bad substitute. Here's where you'll find vesper sparrows and other interesting grassland birds, species that developed a successful way of life that didn't depend on trees.

Flat and open is the classic picture of the Midwest landscape, but there are also pockets of trees, especially around cities and towns and along rivers and lakes. Those trees shelter some fabulous birds, such as the beautiful orchard oriole, the summer tanager, and a selection of dramatic woodpeckers.

This region is a big one, and its climate changes considerably from the upper to the lower part. That means changes in bird life, too. Species that nest in the northern parts may be year-round or winter friends in the southern area.

**Steller's jay is at home in higher elevations.**

## The West

"Rocky Mountain High" is the theme song for this region, and don't you love it! Those spectacular peaks and endless jagged ridges are the defining feature here. Here's where you'll find many birds that can't scratch out a living on the Midwest Plains, as well as northern birds that live at high elevations.

Like the birds of the Far North, this area includes species that specialize in finding food on conifers, or that shrug off extreme cold. You also can enjoy many birds of lower elevations, such as the black-headed grosbeak and lazuli bunting.

## The Southwest and California

California sunshine is too good to resist, unless you live in Tucson or other parts of the Southwest where you have your own sunshiny days. With rain limited to a very small amount each year, the habitat here is comprised of plants that make the best use of a limited resource—and birds that do the same.

As the climate becomes drier, the birds become more specialized, so that each species can exploit some unusual niche in this unusual landscape. You get the lion's share of unique species in this region. How about thrashers with outrageous curved beaks? Wrens that live on spiders they find among the rocks? And hummingbirds that shine like gems in that Southwest sun?

## The Northwest

Did somebody say "rain"? Yes indeed. That notorious rain is what makes this region so green and lush and makes the trees grow so tall. After the rainy season, though, the next

6 months are extremely dry. Creeks and waterfalls slow to a trickle or dry up altogether, until the rains come again in fall.

It's a lopsided arrangement, and one that many birds have learned to thrive in. The dim forests are filled with thrushes, band-tailed pigeons, and other birds that like life on the shady side.

The closer to the Pacific Coast, the more rain that falls. Heading east, the land gradually becomes drier, until the dramatic shift from one side of the Cascade Mountains to the other: Because the mountains block the rain, the eastern part of this region is so dry it qualifies as desert. Still, those western forest birds can be found here, thanks to the mountain ranges that pick up again in the eastern part of this region.

## BLURRY BORDERS

My son used to have a whole collection of pictures of himself standing proudly beside the "Welcome to … " signs that mark the boundaries between our nation's states. He liked seeing the license plates change, too—a sure sign that he'd entered new territory.

But birds can't read, and state lines hold no significance to them. The only thing they pay attention to is the natural world: the habitat, food sources, climate, and natural features of the land.

When one region fades into another gradually, many bird species are likely to blend, too. That's why the lines on these maps aren't sharp: There's a lot of overlap between the regions.

If you live in the Northeast, for instance, you might see birds from three other regions: the Far North, Southeast and South, and Midwest. All share a blurry boundary with the Northeast.

Remember, too, that changes in elevation can affect which birds you see and when. In early summer, when I haven't seen a junco at my lowland Northwest feeder in months, I like to take a drive way up into the Cascades—until I see that flash of white tail feathers in the trees. Juncos live year-round in the mountains here, but they're a winter-only treat for me.

As I explained earlier, in this book I've divided the country into seven regions, based on their natural features that help determine bird life there. But the blurry edges indicate that birds from neighboring regions may visit, too.

Wherever you see a blurry edge on the map, it's a sign that birds from a neighboring region may also visit in your region. Keep in mind that the likelihood of seeing species from other regions also depends on how close to that blurred boundary you live. If you're clear on the other side of the region, your chances are much slimmer than if you live a hop, skip, and a flap over the line.

No matter how carefully birds are arranged in a bird book, in real life they're not so easy to categorize. The best advice, when it comes to bird-watching, is to *be ready for anything*. You never know who will show up in your backyard!

# MEET THE BIRDS

Ready to start matching names to faces? And to speckled breasts, crested heads, flicking tails, characteristic songs, and interesting behaviors? In Part Two, you'll meet more than 140 birds and learn the tricks that will help you identify each one— *at a glance.* Then you can confirm your good guess by checking details of looks, voice, and behavior.

Start with Chapter 6 where you'll make the acquaintance of the most abundant, most widespread backyard species. Regional chapters follow, chockful of birds that are also likely to visit backyards in your particular part of the country. Peruse the profiles for neighboring regions, as well as your own. And if you really want to see how diverse our American birdlife is, let your mouth water by looking at the birds of faraway regions, too. Seasoned birders know that any bird can show up anywhere—even far from its usual haunts.

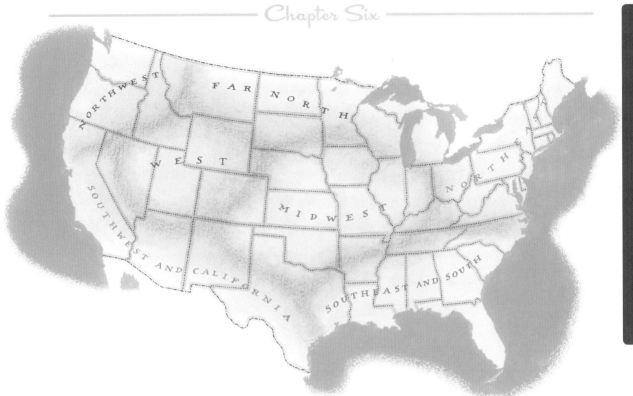

# Chapter Six

# Start Here

Getting an invitation to a party at a new friend's house is a lot of fun. But walking into a lively room full of people who already know each other can be intimidating. They're chattering away in little groups, smiling and laughing, comparing notes on other folks they know or experiences they've shared. Once I relax and look around, though, I realize I do know some of the guests—there's the fellow I met at the library, the woman I often exchange smiles with at the coffee shop, and the couple who sat next to me at the fund-raiser. Why, they're not all strangers—it's just a room full of friends I haven't yet met.

The birds in this chapter are like the guests at that party. You may expect to find no one but strangers, but I guarantee you'll discover a few familiar faces. If you've been feeding birds or watching your backyard birds for a while, you'll be able to greet many others that you already know. Maybe you haven't learned their names yet. But you soon will, just as I finally was able to put names to the friendly faces I already knew from the library, the coffee shop, and the fund-raiser.

That's why I call this chapter "Start Here." These birds are confidence builders.

Talk to your friends in Massachusetts and

Nebraska, and you can all compare notes on these birds. They're the most widespread of backyard birds. I think of them as our national cast of characters. They range across the entire country or a major part of it, nesting or wintering over huge areas.

You'll see a *lot* of these birds, too. They're abundant, which means you won't wait years for a glimpse at one. Most are well-adapted to life in our backyards, and they're not shy at all about visiting or moving in. They're the birds we're most likely to encounter.

Ready to get the party started?

## MEET THE "START HERE" BIRDS

These are the birds you're most likely to see in your yard, no matter where you live. Get a handle on them, and you'll have the basis for a lifetime of bird-watching. Once you have a nodding acquaintance with the "Start Here" birds, you'll find it much easier to notice when a stranger shows up in your yard.

**Downy woodpeckers eat suet everywhere.**

**Everyone knows the American robin.**

You'll soon find yourself saying, "Hmm, that gray bird looks just like my juncos, except for that dark head. Wonder if he's some new kind of junco?"

Congratulations! You're a bird-watcher.

### Consult a Map

Because these species are so widespread, I haven't included a detailed map of range for each one. You don't actually need a map to get to know these guys. You'll find range descriptions in each species entry.

If you do prefer to see a map, pick up any traditional comprehensive field guide, such as Peterson's or Sibley's. Then you can use it in conjunction with this chapter, to discover exactly who you can expect to see outside your window.

## Who's Who

You'll find profiles of 38 species in this section. Of these birds, 22 species are seen in every region of the country. Nearly all of the others are seen in most regions.

Some of these bird species include regional subspecies—birds that share many traits with the species but have some differences in color, song, or habits. You may find such subspecies mentioned in these entries, or you may find full-fledged entries for them in their appropriate regions.

The regions are abbreviated in this chapter and elsewhere. They are:

NE: Northeast

N: Far North

SE: Southeast and South

MW: Midwest

W: West

SW: Southwest and California

NW: Northwest

## HOW TO USE THIS CHAPTER

Here's how to use this chapter: Turn to the first page. Read. Look at the picture. Turn to the next page. Repeat.

That's all there is to it. The more often you page through this chapter, the more likely a bird name will spring to mind when that bird shows up in your yard.

You'll see that the birds in this section aren't all to be expected year-round. While some are full-time friends, others stay with us only in certain seasons. If the entry says "year-round,"

**Cedar waxwings wander widely to find food.**

**A song sparrow is likely in most backyards.**

it means you can expect to see birds of this species in your yard at any time of year. If the entry says "winter," it means the species is a seasonal visitor that will be around in winter, which in bird land runs from after fall migration until spring migration. So although I may call it "winter," that period may actually be from early fall to early spring.

If the entry says "spring through fall," that means the bird will nest in your region. It goes elsewhere to spend winter, but your backyard may be the place it calls home during spring and summer, until it's time to depart in fall.

No matter what seasons these birds show up in your yard, they're bound to be your most reliable friends. If all you ever saw were the "Start Here" birds, you'd still have a hard time tearing yourself away from your feeder window.

One other note: For each bird you'll find descriptions of wild foods it likes ("Wild

Blue spruce (*Picea pungens*) attracts birds.

Goldfinches seek out pretty cosmos (*Cosmos bipinnatus*) as soon as the first seeds mature. In winter, sparrows glean what the goldfinches dropped.

Menu") and plants you can consider adding to your landscape to attract it ("Plant Picks"). There are also recommendations for stocking your bird feeders ("Feeder Pleasers"), and for other special amenities you might want to offer ("Tricks and Treats").

That's just the beginning, of course. In subsequent chapters, you'll discover even more great birds who call your particular region home.

But that's for later. For now, just "Start Here."

## "Start Here" Birds

Here's a list of the birds you'll find in this chapter. The birds are organized by family, according to the checklist of the American Ornithological Union (AOU). You'll find this order also coincides with the arrangement of birds in many more comprehensive field guides, such as Peterson's.

# Mourning Dove

## First Impression
**Big, plump, short-legged, grayish tan bird**

### Mark Your Calendar
Year-round; but in northern parts of states, spring through fall

### Details, Details
- Bigger than a robin; 12 inches
- Small head and long tail
- Black spots on wings

### Listen Up!
- Easy to imitate, heartbreakingly sad, *ooAH! cooo cooo coo*

### Telltale Traits
- Rockets away on loudly flapping wings when startled
- Often in pairs or small group

### Look Here
- On ground

### Or Here
- In tray feeder
- Perched in trees at dusk to roost at night
- Perched on utility wires

**On the Home Front** Doves mate for life. But old age for a dove, what with hunting and predators, is only about 2 to 3 years old. The record holder in the wild lived to age 10. • Builds one of the flimsiest nests, a casual collection of sticks that you can see right through • A spruce or pine in the yard is a favorite homesite, but nests in deciduous trees, too • Early nester • Raises more than one family a year

*"Like the strokes of a distant bell"*

—**Ralph Hoffmann,** *A Guide to the Birds of New England and Eastern New York* (1904)

**The voice of the dove is easy to recognize. It's a plaintive cooing that travels far through the mild spring morning air.**

**Wild Menu:** Weed and grass seeds; other seeds, including grain; some insects

**Plant Picks:** Grow a mixed patch of buckwheat, millet, wheat, and broomcorn for a winter's worth of seeds on the stalk.

**Feeder Pleasers**
- Millet, milo, cracked corn

**Tricks and Treats**
- Doves need grit to help digest their food. Buy an inexpensive box of birdcage grit in the pet supply aisle, and pour some on bare ground.

## Public Displays of Affection

Doves aren't shy at all about courting in public. They look so romantic as they flirt and cuddle that they've become a symbol of enduring love.

Enduring lust is more like it. It only takes a month from nest to empty nest—and then doves are ready to start the next batch. No wonder they always seem to be kissing and cooing.

# Northern Flicker

## First Impression
**Big, brown woodpecker**

### Mark Your Calendar
Year-round; but in northern parts of states in this region, spring through fall; winter only in some areas of SW

### Details, Details
- Bigger than a robin; 12½ inches
- Shows a big white patch above tail in flight
- Dramatic black swash across breast
- Female lacks "mustache"

### Listen Up!
- A fun bird to imitate: a rapid, repeated *wick-a! wick-a! wick-a!*

### Telltale Traits
- Often on ground, but does cling to trees like a typical woodpecker
- Strong, fast, undulating flight, except on migration—then flies straight, without bouncy dips
- Colorful, golden or reddish undersides of wings and tail

### Look Here
- At feeder

### Or Here
- On lawn, eating ants or probing for grubs
- Hammering on a resonant tree, metal rain gutter, or other "drum"

**On the Home Front** Drills a good-size hole in a dead tree, often snitched by a pair of waiting starlings • Nests in wooden utility poles where trees are scarce • Quickly adopts a nest box

*"Few birds combine such charming colors and pleasing contrasts"*

—A. C. Bent, *Life Histories of North American Woodpeckers* (1939)

Flickers don't follow the crowd when it comes to color. Unlike most other woodpeckers, they're brown. Bright accents in their wings and on their head, plus a white rump and a bold black breast stripe, add plenty of flash.

**Wild Menu:** Ants; other insects; fruit

**Plant Picks:** Elderberries (*Sambucus* spp.), dogwood berries (*Cornus* spp.), Virginia creeper (*Parthenocissus quinquefolia*), other small fruits and berries

### Feeder Pleasers
- Suet, peanut butter, and other fat-based foods; mealworms and other insect foods

### Tricks and Treats
- Flickers enjoy a good splash in a birdbath. Make sure the edge isn't slippery, so they can get a good grip with their feet when they fly in. Old-fashioned concrete, or a nonslip resin, is a good choice.
- A nest box may also attract starlings; mount it in a woodsy area if you have one.

## Isn't That Just Ducky

Whenever I spot a fist-size hole in a dead tree in spring, I keep an eye on it to see who it belongs to. If the tree is in woods, it's usually a flicker residence (starlings tend to take over the holes closer to open space).

But a few times, I've had the thrill of seeing a wood duck emerging from the hole. Some ducks, including the beautiful "woodies" and flashy black-and-white buffleheads, nest high in trees, not near water like you'd expect. They move into an old woodpecker hole to raise their batch of duckies.

# Downny Woodpecker

## *First Impression*

Ubiquitous small, black-and-white woodpecker

START HERE

### Mark Your Calendar

Year-round; absent from parts of SW

### Details, Details

- As big as a large sparrow; 6¾ inches
- Female lacks red patch on back of head
- W and NW birds have less zebralike striping

### Listen Up!

- Keeps in touch with frequent *peek!* contact call
- Staccato *ki-ki-ki-ki-ki-ki,* usually descending in pitch; sounds something like a tiny horse whinnying
- Drums on resonant dead wood

### Telltale Traits

- Typical clinging woodpecker posture
- Often hitches around to other side of tree when observed
- Pals around with chickadees, nuthatches, titmice in fall and winter

### Look Here

- At suet or seed feeders

### Or Here

- On tree trunks or branches
- May visit nectar feeder

*On the Home Front* Digs out a nest cavity in dead wood • Often nests surprisingly low to ground, about 5 to 6 feet, but can nest to 50 feet • Gratifyingly quick to accept a birdhouse

*"When the woodpecker pecks low on the trees, expect warm weather."*

—**Old folk saying**

I never remember to note the temperature when I see my downy pecking away, which is probably why I've never noticed any connection between the two. But it's conceivable that movements of insects under tree bark may be susceptible to temperature.

**Wild Menu:** Insects; fruit; sap

**Plant Picks:** Common mullein (*Verbascum thapsus*), Virginia creeper (*Parthenocissus quinquefolia*), elderberries (*Sambucus* spp.), mulberries (*Morus* spp.)

### Feeder Pleasers

- Suet; mealworms and other insect foods; sunflower seeds; nuts and nut spreads, such as peanut butter or almond butter (mix with cornmeal to make this pricey treat go farther)

### Tricks and Treats

- Mount a nest box tailored to these small woodpeckers' size. It will also serve as shelter on cold or snowy winter nights.

## Polka-Dotted Zebra

Downies are daily visitors in our backyards, which means that at some point you may happen to find one of their feathers. Late summer to early fall is prime molting season; that's when I often come across a downy woodpecker feather under fruit trees or feeders.

Figuring out who dropped a feather can be tricky. Your downies may have zebra-striped backs, but the feather is likely to look more polka-dotted. Arranged in rows, those dots create the look of stripes.

# Blue Jay

*First Impression*

**Big, screaming, blue bird**

### Mark Your Calendar

Year-round, from the Rockies eastward; westward, the Steller's jay takes over

### Details, Details

• Bigger than a robin; 11 inches
• Female looks like male

### Listen Up!

• Loud and raucous, jays are screamers. You'll soon recognize their harsh, unmusical calls.
• You may occasionally hear a lovely, completely different, very musical phrase that sounds like *too-lee-lee-lee*.

### Telltale Traits

• Swoops in to feeding station with loud cries, scattering smaller birds like leaves
• Scoops up several seeds or nuts at once, then goes off to bury them
• Holds nuts or acorns in feet and whacks with bill
• Alerts other birds to danger by screaming and harassing predators in area

### Look Here

• At feeder

### Or Here

• Silently collecting acorns, walnuts, pecans, or other nuts from backyard trees
• Flying to and from your yard
• At birdbath

*On the Home Front* Blue jay nests in trees, shrubs, or vines, usually about 15 to 20 feet high • Sings sweet, quiet song to its mate

**Steller's Jay**

*"Several jays spent the entire day harvesting acorns"*

—**William Brewster, "The Birds of the Lake Umbagog Region of Maine" (1937)**

**Blue jays and other jays play a big role in keeping trees growing. They plant acorns, pecans, and other nuts by burying them, assuring plenty of trees for the future.**

**Wild Menu:** Nuts, including acorns; fruit; insects; plus frogs, salamanders, snakes, mice, and—sadly—eggs and nestlings of other birds

**Plant Picks:** Single-headed annual sunflowers (*Helianthus annuus*), corn, oak trees for acorns

### Feeder Pleasers

• Nuts, especially peanuts in the shell; sunflower seeds; corn

### Tricks and Treats

• You can train jays to come for nuts when you call. Just put nuts out at a certain time every day, call "Here, jays!" and stand nearby until the jays arrive. They'll soon learn when to expect feeding time.
• A simple pedestal birdbath will get attention, but a naturalistic ground-level bath with a dripper will attract more fans.

## Gardeners with Smarts

I've noticed that jays are much quicker to snatch up nuts still in the shell from my feeder than they are to grab chopped or hulled nuts. Peanuts, filberts, pecans, English walnuts—whatever I put out, it's the whole nuts still in their shells that jays home in on first.

Do they somehow know that those are the ones that will sprout after they poke them into the soil, ensuring a crop of trees for future generations of jays? Or is it because those nuts keep longest, so the jays know there'll be food during lean times?

# Black-Capped Chickadee

*First Impression*

**Active little gray bird with contrasting black head markings**

## Mark Your Calendar

Year-round

## Details, Details

- Chickadee size! 5¼ inches
- Female looks like male

## Listen Up!

- Seven different species of chickadees roam the country, and most say some version of the classic *chick-a-dee-dee-dee* of the black-capped.
- Chickadees are talkative, uttering high-pitched, buzzy notes, similar to titmice.

## Telltale Traits

- Always in action, moving on, over, and around branches and leaves, in a never-ending quest for food
- Usually in groups
- Often hangs upside down

## Look Here

- At feeder

## Or Here

- Moving through trees or large shrubs

*On the Home Front* Often nests in backyards, but is often overlooked • Happily accepts a nest box • Also nests in natural cavities, either abandoned by woodpeckers or dug out by chickadee pair, in decayed branches or stubs • Nests very low, which is why you might miss it—from 1 to about 10 feet tops • The nest is an invitingly cozy collection, thick with moss, feathers, hair, soft plant fibers, and silk cocoons.

*"Two days later he would perch on my finger"*

—John Woodcock, "A Friendly Chickadee" (1913)

**If you have the patience for standing quietly, chickadees are one of the easiest wild birds to hand tame. Nuts are an ideal bribe to bring them to your hand, but you can also try ordinary sunflower seeds.**

**Wild Menu:** Insects; seeds; nuts

**Plant Picks:** Annual sunflowers (*Helianthus annuus*) and just about any kind of tree or shrub for insects, including oaks (*Quercus* spp.), firs (*Abies* spp. ) or other conifers, and redbuds (*Cercis* spp.)

## Feeder Pleasers

- Sunflower seeds; chopped nuts; suet, peanut butter, and other nut butters; mealworms and other insect foods

## Tricks and Treats

- In late winter, make a collection of soft fibers to offer as nesting material. Short lengths of string, thread, moss, soft feathers, and cotton balls will catch their eye.
- Birdbaths are a hit with this tribe.

## Variations on a Theme

The black-capped is the most widespread species, ranging across much of the NE, MW, W, and NW. In the SE, S, and lower MW, it's the look-alike Carolina who entertains you. In the W and SW, look for the mountain chickadee. Coastal W and NW? You get the easy-to-recognize chestnut-backed. Some species overlap, so you might see more than one type in your yard.

Whichever chick-a-dee-dee-dee you host, you'll soon get to be best friends. Just watching these bright-eyed little guys brightens up a winter morning.

# White-Breasted Nuthatch

*First Impression*

**Odd "tuxedo-clad" gray bird, often clinging in upside-down posture**

### Mark Your Calendar

Year-round; but in some MW regions, winter only

### Details, Details

- About sparrow size; 5¾ inches
- Female similar but has paler head
- Stubby tail and long, pointy beak

### Listen Up!

- Song is a nasal *whi-whi-whi-whi-whi-whi-whi*—you get the idea.
- Call has regional variations, depending on the subspecies: east of the Rockies, a distinctive *yank-yank*; in the W, a nasal *yidi-yidi-yidi*; Pacific West, a mewling *eeern*
- Talkative like chickadees, with frequent soft, high-pitched notes

### Telltale Traits

- Clings to tree trunks with stubby legs, like a woodpecker—but travels upside-down!
- Grab-and-go eating habits at the feeder (except for suet or peanut butter, at which it lingers)
- Flies in undulating swoops

### Look Here

- At feeder

### Or Here

- Climbing rapidly down tree trunks or main branches, peering intently at bark
- Hammering nuts or seeds into crevices of wood posts, trees, or other hiding places
- With foraging bands of chickadees or kinglets in winter

*"Like mirthless laughter"*

—Frank Chapman, early American ornithologist, on the song of the white-breasted nuthatch

The "love song" of nuthatches is a monotone trill that gets lost among the music of spring songbirds. But once you start listening for it, you'll hear it often.

*On the Home Front* Nuthatches are cavity nesters, so they're likely to try a birdhouse. • Put the box up early, in late winter. • Keep your suet feeder filled in summer—parents may bring their young when they leave the nest.

**Wild Menu:** Insects; nuts; seeds

**Plant Picks:** Annual sunflowers (*Helianthus annuus*) and nut trees, such as oaks (*Quercus* spp.), hemlocks (*Tsuga* spp.), firs (*Abies* spp.), or other conifers

### Feeder Pleasers

- Suet, peanut butter; nuts (chopped last longer); sunflower seeds; mealworms and other insect foods

### Tricks and Treats

- Supply a birdhouse.
- Offer soft materials for lining the nest: feathers, moss, cotton balls, and dog hair.

## You Talkin' to Me?

He may look like a gentleman in those dapper evening clothes, but the white-breasted nuthatch can show a temper like a barroom brawler. Watch for bullying behavior at the feeder: If another bird gets too close to the food that a nuthatch has its eye on, the nuthatch will instantly flash its wings and spread its tail, while threatening with that wicked-looking beak. Guess who usually gets the goodies?

# Red-Breasted Nuthatch

START HERE

*First Impression*

**Tiny, unafraid gray-and-reddish bird that creeps as if it has Velcro feet**

### Mark Your Calendar

Year-round or winter only

### Details, Details

- Smaller than a chickadee; 4½ inches
- Stubby tail and pointy beak
- Female similar to male but paler

### Listen Up!

- Used to be described as sounding like a child's tin horn, but since most of us haven't heard that sound for, oh, half a century, just listen for an incessant bleating: a series of repeated *eeen, eeen, eeen* or weak, nasal *yank*s.

### Telltale Traits

- Unafraid of people; easy to approach
- Crawls around on trees and branches, often head-down
- Undulating flight

### Look Here

- At feeder

### Or Here

- Creeping on trunks or branches of trees, often upside down
- On small branches or at cones of firs, hemlocks, other conifers
- With foraging bands of chickadees, or kinglets in winter

*On the Home Front* Not usually a backyard nester, unless your yard looks like a coniferous forest • Reluctant to use a nest box; offer food instead

*"They exhibited no fear"*

—**Richard Miller, "The red-bellied nuthatch feeding among weeds" (1914)**

Tiny red-breasted nuthatches are completely unafraid of us. So it's easy to slowly and quietly walk right up when you see one, and watch whatever it's doing.

**Wild Menu:** Insects; seeds of conifers

**Plant Picks:** Annual sunflowers (*Helianthus annuus*), perennial sunflowers (*H. angustifolia, H. maximilianii,* and other spp.), any conifers

**Feeder Pleasers**
- Suet; insect-enriched suet and other insect foods; sunflower seeds

**Tricks and Treats**
- Adding a few pines, firs, spruces, or other conifers to your yard will make it inviting.

## *Thighmaster*

Nuthatches move about on tree trunks as easily as woodpeckers, but their style of motion is very different. Woodpeckers have super-stiff tail feathers that they can use to prop themselves up, so they can hitch along, both feet at a time. Nuthatches have to depend on the strength of their legs and feet to cling and get around.

Next time you have both birds in your yard, take a close look and see if you can spot which one is the thighmaster.

# Brown Creeper

*First Impression*

> Tiny, brown, mouselike bird spiraling up
> tree trunk

**Mark Your Calendar**

Year-round or winter only

**Details, Details**

- Chickadee size; 5¼ inches
- Mottled back feathers are perfect camou-
flage against tree bark.

**Listen Up!**

- You'll have to listen hard to catch the thin,
high, lispy notes, which sound very much
like the soft calls of the titmice, kinglets,
and chickadees it often travels with.

**Telltale Traits**

- Distinctive habit of creeping up tree
trunks
- One or two creepers often join mixed
groups of foraging chickadees, titmice,
and nuthatches in winter.

**Look Here**

- On tree trunks

**Or Here**

- Rarely at feeder

*On the Home Front* If you think the creeper
is well-camouflaged, just try finding its nest:
It's hidden behind a piece of bark. • Uses
cocoons and silken spider-egg cases to attach a
crescent of twigs to back of bark

*"Like a fragment of
detached bark that is
defying the laws of
gravitation"*

—Winsor Tyler, "Notes on nest
life of the brown creeper" (1914)

**The brown creeper is hard to see
but unforgettable. Once you spot
one of these odd birds spiraling up
a tree, you'll have it nailed. The
trick is seeing it in the first place!**

**Wild Menu:** Insects; occasionally seeds

**Plant Picks:** Mature trees

**Feeder Pleasers**

- Sunflower seeds; may pick at suet or insect
foods

**Tricks and Treats**

- The trick is yours: To spot one of these
interesting birds, try to get in the habit of
watching for what looks like that moving "piece
of bark" on the trunks of trees. Or look for a
creeper when it flies from one tree to the base
of another, to repeat its upward search for food.

## Foraging Friends

In winter, little bands of little birds may include your backyard as part of their foraging
territory. Look out bugs, because these birds are all adept at ferreting out insects.
Chickadees are the mainstay of the group, with a sprinkling of kinglets, titmice, and
nuthatches, and generally a downy woodpecker along for the tour.

Often there's a brown creeper in the mix, too, which is why I get excited when I hear
those tiny, soft calls that announce the band of birds is heading my way. It's fun to compare
their different foraging styles as they move through.

# Carolina Wren

*First Impression*

**Energetic, warm-brown bird with a white eye stripe**

### Mark Your Calendar

Year-round; not in upper part of country (except NW and NE)

### Details, Details

- Small sparrow size; about 5½ inches
- Carolina has warm buff-colored belly; similar Bewick's of western states has grayish white belly
- Male and female look alike

### Listen Up!

- Long and varied musical songs
- Harsh, scolding rattle
- Sharp *chip!* when alarmed

### Telltale Traits

- Stays hidden in vegetation
- Seems to be always in motion, nervous and quick
- Often cocks tail upward at an angle

### Look Here

- In shrubbery, vines, or garden beds

### Or Here

- May visit feeder

*On the Home Front* Bulky nest made of a conglomeration of materials, but well-hidden • May be in cavity or in dense tangle of vines or branches • Usually fairly low, within about 6 feet of ground • May build nests and then not use them for nesting

**Bewick's wren**

*"He comes of his own accord and installs himself . . . wherever it suits his taste."*

—**Robert Ridgway**, *Ornithology of Illinois* (1889)

These delightful birds aren't a sure thing, even in the most bird-friendly backyard. So you can feel honored if a wren chooses your backyard as its home.

**Wild Menu:** Insects; fruit

**Plant Picks:** Elderberries (*Sambucus* spp.), Virginia creeper (*Parthenocissus quinquefolia*), and other small fruits and berries; hedges, vigorous perennial vines, and shrub groups for cover

### Feeder Pleasers

- Mealworms and other insect foods; suet; crumbles of peanut-butter dough (mix peanut butter with flour or cornmeal); doughnuts

### Tricks and Treats

- For fast vegetative growth that may attract a wren, it's hard to beat sweet autumn clematis (*Clematis paniculata*) for quick cover in a single season. Grow it on a trellis against your house, garage, or shed for maximum cover.

## *Ad-Lib Artist*

Unlike most songbirds, these wrens don't reliably sing the same song. They mix up the phrases or the notes, like Ella Fitzgerald scat-singing up and down the scale. Plus they make a lot of strange noises—rattles and chatters and trills, often mixed with high, clear notes.

Whenever I find myself straining to figure out who's making those weird noises, I wait for the giveaway: Eventually comes the chirr that announces a wren.

# House Wren

## First Impression
**Small, hyperactive "Jenny wren"**

### Mark Your Calendar
Spring through fall; winter, too, in southern areas

### Details, Details
- Chickadee size or smaller; 4¾ inches
- Male and female look alike: little brown birds, not at all flashy

### Listen Up!
- Famed for its long, gurgling, burbling, beautiful song, the avian equivalent of water running over rocks

### Telltale Traits
- Busy, busy, busy; always in motion except when singing
- Cocks tail upward frequently
- Male regularly sings from a series of perches, in full view

### Look Here
- Constantly hopping about in low, dense cover

### Or Here
- Amidst vegetable or flower gardens
- In shrubbery or vines
- If you're lucky, at the feeder

**On the Home Front** Readily adopts a nest box, although in W, often chooses open woods or woods' edges instead of backyards • It's famed for its selection of oddball homesites. Any object outside with a place to stuff full of twigs and leaves may become a nest site: a boot, a shirt pocket, a scarecrow, an open mailbox.

## The Not-So-Nice Side

House wrens are notoriously aggressive toward other nearby nesting birds, destroying eggs and young with their long, lethal beaks. Back in the 1920s, a spirited campaign was waged to discourage people from putting up wren houses, with magazine articles such as "Down with the House Wren Boxes" (Althea Sherman in the *Wilson Bulletin*, 1925).

By 1948, the little brown birds were being compared to the world scourge of the times: "This Nazi trait has brought them into disfavor ... " tsk-tsked A. C. Bent (*Life Histories of North American Nuthatches, Wrens, Thrashers, and Their Allies*, 1948).

*"There were 637 pieces of food brought"*

—Lynds Jones, about house wrens in "Some records of the feeding of nestlings" (1913)

House wrens are one of the best friends a gardener could ever ask for. As Jones noted: "161 geometrid larvae, 141 leafhoppers, 112 young grasshoppers," and hundreds more yummy bugs.

**Wild Menu:** Insects; fruit

**Plant Picks:** Elderberries (*Sambucus* spp.), raspberries, blueberries, mulberries (*Morus* spp.), and other small fruits

### Feeder Pleasers
- May visit a feeder for mealworms and other insect foods or suet

### Tricks and Treats
- Wrens love an afternoon at the spa—or should we say, 10 minutes in a birdbath, especially if it has a spray or mister.
- Feathers offered are a hit at nesting time.

# Golden-Crowned Kinglet

Tiny, gray-green bird fluttering at branch tips

### Mark Your Calendar

Winter, most areas; year-round in W and NE; migration only in N

### Details, Details

- Smaller than a chickadee; about 4 inches
- Female has paler yellow on crown and doesn't raise head feathers like male

### Listen Up!

- Faint, very high-pitched, lisping notes, plus a chickadee-like *chi-chi-chi* chatter

### Telltale Traits

- Constantly flicks its wings while moving through branches
- Often hovers at branch tips while feeding
- Joins mixed flocks of chickadees, titmice, nuthatches, and other foragers in winter

### Look Here

- Fluttering among and at branches of conifers

### Or Here

- Fluttering at foliage of deciduous trees and shrubs
- At apples, crab apples, and other flowering trees, picking off insects at blossoms
- At nectar feeder

*On the Home Front* Rarely nests in backyards, unless yours is thick with spruces or other conifers • Nests high in a conifer

*"A tiny feathered gem"*

—A. C. Bent, the *Life Histories of North American Birds* series (late 1800s to mid 1900s)

You have to look hard to see where the "gem" part of the kinglet comes in. The golden crown is best seen at close range or through binoculars. The male bird's gold deepens to orange at the very top of his head, and he can raise those gem-colored feathers to form a rounded crest.

**Wild Menu:** Insects; some small fruits

**Plant Picks:** Short-needled conifers, such as spruce, hemlock, fir; elderberries (*Sambucus* spp.); and flowering crabs (*Malus* cvs.) for insects at flowers

### Feeder Pleasers

- May visit nectar or suet feeders; may eat mealworms and other insect foods

### Tricks and Treats

- A ground-level birdbath, such as a naturalistic resin style with more than one shallow basin, is ideal; draw them to it with a dripper.

## *Seasonal Treat*

Kinglets retreat to forested places during breeding season, so unless you live near their natural haunts, you may not see them for months at a time.

It's always a fun little surprise to see them again and to renew my acquaintance when they show up in my yard in fall. The birdbath is often a favorite stop—and even there, they can't seem to stop that nervous tic of flicking their wings.

# American Robin

## First Impression

Alert, gray-brown bird with reddish breast, on lawn

### Mark Your Calendar

Year-round; but in northern parts of states, spring through fall

### Details, Details

- Robin size! 10 inches
- Female looks like a faded version of male

### Listen Up!

- Beautiful long, whistled song
- Sharp alarm notes, and concerned— almost clucking—sounds

### Telltale Traits

- Pulling worms from ground
- Flipping through leaves to find worms and insects

### Look Here

- On lawn

### Or Here

- On ground beneath shrubs or trees
- In trees or shrubs
- In birdbath

On the Home Front Maybe the most frequent backyard nester • Builds sturdy cup with mud foundation • Nests at mid-level, in shrubs, roses, on limb or in crotch of trees, or in basket or wreath hanging on house

*"The harbinger of spring"*
—Old folk saying, still well known

In many regions, robins are present year-round, but many seek cover in wild areas over winter and act more wary. Then in spring, our backyard robins return to their "regular" habits, hopping about on the grass and raising our spirits.

**Wild Menu:** Worms; insects; fruit and berries

**Plant Picks:** Fruits of any kind; loves elderberries (*Sambucus* spp.), mulberries (*Morus* spp.), grapes (*Vitis* spp.), and lots of others; also fond of berries of holly (*Ilex* spp.), dogwood (*Cornus* spp.), and others

### Feeder Pleasers

- Rarely visits feeders but may eat mealworms and other insect foods, bread and other baked goods, and chopped and accessible suet

### Tricks and Treats

- Give them a bath! Robins will visit your birdbath daily. They also absolutely revel in sprays and misters.

## Head-Cock, Bill-Pounce

Have you ever watched a robin's hunting technique? First comes the "head-cock," which scientists have defined as "one eye points to the ground, 3 to 5 cm in front of the bird, along the longitudinal axis of the body. . ." (F. Heppner, 1965) There's more, but it boils down to this: Then the robin spies its prey with both eyes—and nails it with its coup de grace, the "bill-pounce," which is exactly what it sounds like. Down the hatch!

91

# Hermit Thrush

## First Impression

Brown bird with speckled breast, nervously flicking tail and wings

START HERE

### Mark Your Calendar

Winter in SE and S; spring through fall in W, NE, and parts of N; migration in MW and parts of N

### Details, Details

- Robinlike but smaller, only as long as a large sparrow; 6¾ inches
- Female and male look alike

### Listen Up!

- A fabled singer, with a haunting, flutelike song

### Telltale Traits

- Quickly flicks tail up, then slowly lowers it
- Flicks wings frequently
- Sings at dusk (as well as other times)

### Look Here

- In shrubs, especially berry bushes

### Or Here

- On the ground, usually near or under vegetation
- Eating berries in fall

*On the Home Front* Doesn't usually nest in backyards but has been known to nest on golf courses or in cemeteries—areas with big stretches of open land • East of the Rockies, usually nests on ground; west of the Rockies, usually in small trees • Only the female builds the big, bulky nest. • Eggs are beautiful pale blue to turquoise.

*"It is the sweetest, ripest hour of the day"*

—John Burroughs, on a hermit thrush at dusk, *Wake-Robin* (1887)

**The thrushes hold a special place in many bird lovers' hearts. As shadows begin to gather among the trees of the forest, the hermit thrush sings his pure, sweet song.**

**Wild Menu:** Insects; fruit

**Plant Picks:** Fall-bearing fruits and berries, such as dogwoods (*Cornus* spp.), possumhaw and other native viburnums (*Viburnum* spp.), and spicebush (*Lindera benzoin*)

### Feeder Pleasers

- Uncommon feeder visitor; try mealworms or other insect foods and suet

### Tricks and Treats

- Plenty of cover: Plant groups of shrubs, and let leaves accumulate beneath them in fall instead of raking them, to provide foraging opportunities.

## Far-Flung Hermits

On my first trip to the Southwest, when my neck was aching from looking right, left, up and down at all the new-to-me birds, I spotted a brown bird perched on a rock. It was near a patch of poison oak, in the middle of parched California grasslands.

Hmm, it sure looked a lot like the hermit thrushes I knew from the shady woods back East. It even had the same habit of raising and lowering its tail and flicking its wings.

I opened my field guide to pin down this rare California thrush—and discovered a hermit thrush can turn up anywhere across America!

# Northern Mockingbird

*First Impression*

**Slim, large, long-tailed gray bird**

**Mark Your Calendar**

Year-round. Oddly enough, the "northern" mockingbird is absent from the northern tier of states as well as parts of the NW and W.

**Details, Details**

- Same size as a robin but appears longer; 10 inches
- Female and male look alike

**Listen Up!**

- Long, musical song; includes imitations of other birds and mechanical sounds

**Telltale Traits**

- Chases away other birds from feeder
- Quick to harass a snake, cat, or other predator

**Look Here**

- Singing from a high, conspicuous perch— your chimney?

**Or Here**

- At feeders—eating or driving off other birds
- At apples, crab apples, and other flowering trees, picking off insects at blossoms
- Eating fruit or berries

*On the Home Front* Nests in shrubs or trees, usually less than 10 feet off the ground • Raises two or three families a year, and builds a new nest for each • Starts nesting very early, in late winter • Often includes trash—such as paper, foil, plastic—in its nest

*"A curious and most interesting performance"*

—Alice Bowers Harrington, "Observations on the mockingbird at Dallas, Texas" (1923)

*Dancing with the Stars*, pshaw. How about dancing with mockingbirds? In courtship, the male and female face each other to perform a series of flashy steps. And to scare off a snake, the male lifts and spreads his wings and tail in an impressive display.

**Wild Menu:** Insects; fruit

**Plant Picks:** Roses (*Rosa* spp.) with sprays of small hips, for nesting and winter food; raspberries and other brambles

**Feeder Pleasers**

- Suet and other fats; mealworms and other insect foods; millet

**Tricks and Treats**

- Delight your mockingbirds with a birdbath. They're big fans of water.

## Quiet! I Need to Sleep!

A mockingbird singing at night may sound romantic, but in reality it can be, shall we say, less than pleasant. Night after night the bird holds forth, usually tuning up well after midnight. Young, unmated males are believed to be the culprits for this behavior.

So how can you make them stop? You probably can't. Instead, try "white noise" to block out the singer: The whir of an electric fan or a soothing recording might save your sanity.

# Brown Thrasher

## First Impression

**Big, reddish brown bird with long tail**

### Mark Your Calendar

Spring through fall in MW, N, NE; year-round in SE and S; absent in W, NW, and SW, except for strays

### Details, Details

• Bigger than a robin; 11½ inches
• Female and male look alike

### Listen Up!

• Long, complicated, musical song of repeated phrases

### Telltale Traits

• No other bird looks like this!
• "Thrashes" through dead leaves on ground with its bill

### Look Here

• On ground, under shrubs

### Or Here

• In dense thickets: a hedge, a bramble patch, or a rampant perennial vine

**On the Home Front** Nests low in shrubs, sometimes on the ground • Young leave the nest only 9 days after hatching—an adaptation that improves survival chances for birds at low levels. • Often nests in backyard shrubs, including forsythia and privet

*"Seeks a bit of thick and tangled growth"*

—**Althea Sherman, "The brown thrashers east and west" (1912)**

For all their size and eye-catching color, thrashers can be tricky to find. They're skulkers who seek out the densest thicket. Listen for the song, then try to sneak up on the singer.

**Wild Menu:** Insects; fruit

**Plant Picks:** Small fruits, especially mulberries (*Morus* spp.) and grapes

### Feeder Pleasers

• Was occasional feeder visitor, but now appears more frequently; mealworms and other insect food; suet and other fats

### Tricks and Treats

• Provide a birdbath with a nonslip rim and bottom: Thrashers are energetic in the bath.

## Feathered Architects

Next time you visit a natural history museum, ask to see a brown thrasher nest. They're often constructed like a series of four nesting baskets: The outside basket is twigs. Inside that is a layer or cup mostly of leaves. Then comes a neat layer of very fine twigs and grass stems. Finally, the inner basket or lining: a cup of clean rootlets, probably from grasses.

All those layers are shaped in place by the female, who pats them down with sideways motions of her feet to help mesh them together.

# Gray Catbird

*First Impression*

A petulant, whining *meeurrr* from the bushes—and it's not Kitty.

START HERE

## Mark Your Calendar

Spring through fall; winter along extreme southern edge of the United States; year-round along the Atlantic Coast; absent from much of SW, W, and NW

## Details, Details

- A little smaller than a robin; 8½ inches
- Solid dark gray with black cap, and reddish brown beneath tail
- Female and male look alike

## Listen Up!

- That feline *meow* is unique among birds.
- Also a pretty, musical, whistled song of repeated phrases
- A grating chatter when alarmed
- May mimic other birds

## Telltale Traits

- Sings from within a dense bush
- Violently attacks snakes, which often prey upon its nest

## Look Here

- More often heard than seen, but may be spotted eating mulberries or other fruit

## Or Here

- In patches of raspberries and other brambles
- Foraging on the ground under shrubs

*On the Home Front* Builds a bulky nest low to the ground in dense, often thorny shrubs
- One of few birds that quickly recognizes and rejects eggs of parasitic brown-headed cowbird

*"Some of his improvisations are very sweet and musical"*

—Charles Townsend, "Mimicry of voice in birds" (1924)

Poor catbird. Famed for his meow, he's actually an accomplished singer with an ever-changing repertoire. Like the mockingbird, he can mimic other birds or sing his own rambling tune.

**Wild Menu:** Insects; fruit

**Plant Picks:** Mulberries (*Morus* spp.), cherries (*Prunus* spp.), blueberries, raspberries, blackberries, and other small fruits; native fruits and berries

## Feeder Pleasers

- An unusual but occasional feeder visitor; mealworms and other insect foods; accessible suet

## Tricks and Treats

- Occasionally a catbird will linger into winter in cold areas. Pump up its calories by offering chopped suet in a low, open tray feeder or on the ground. Lightly freeze a block of plain suet (or beef fat) to make it easier to chop.

## Bye-Bye, Bad Eggs

You'd think birds could easily recognize an egg of a different color laid in their nests. But that's not the case. Of the 220 bird species parasitized by the brown-headed cowbird, scientists say only a dozen have learned to spot the out-of-place eggs.

The gray catbird is one. Only six records are known of catbirds raising baby cowbirds. In experiments with fake cowbird eggs, the catbird gave the bad egg the boot in less than 24 hours.

# Cedar Waxwing

## First Impression

**Elegant, neat, smooth-feathered, grayish-tan bird perched with flock**

### Mark Your Calendar

Year-round in northern third of United States; winter, southern two-thirds. Larger, plumper Bohemian waxwing in northern tier in winter; sporadic visitor elsewhere

### Details, Details

- Smaller than a robin but looks much larger than a sparrow; 7¼ inches
- Pointy crest and dashing black mask across eyes
- Trademark dots of red wax on wings
- Female and male look alike

### Listen Up!

- Very high, one-note, hissy whistles

### Telltale Traits

- Always in a flock or with a partner
- The group flies around together, settling in trees or at food sources.

### Look Here

- At berries or other small fruits

### Or Here

- In treetops
- Flying, with distinctive high-pitched, single-note, whistling calls

**On the Home Front** One of the latest birds to nest; often not until July or August • Nests in fork or on branch of trees of many kinds, also in shrubs, high or low • Fashions a bulky cup of twigs, dead leaves, ferns, and other natural materials.

*"Few birds care to take life so easily"*

—Neltje Blanchan, *Bird Neighbors* (1897)

". . . not to say indolently," continues Blanchan. Placid waxwings are the opposite of peppy chickadees or frenetic warblers: They spend a lot of time just sitting around.

**Wild Menu:** Fruit; insects

**Plant Picks:** "People" fruits of any kind, particularly sweet or sour cherries (*Prunus* spp.) and mulberries (*Morus* spp.); berries of holly (*Ilex* spp.), dogwoods (*Cornus florida* and other spp.), mountain ash, and many others

**Feeder Pleasers**
- Not a feeder visitor

**Tricks and Treats**
- Waxwings may collect short pieces of string, narrow strips of white cotton cloth, or tufts of natural sheep's wool that you offer. Lay the materials over a branch of a shrub in your yard.

## "False Azure"

Cedar waxwings are frequent victims of head-on collisions into windows. Change your perspective when you look at a window from outside and you'll see why a pane of glass can be so deceptive. All you see is a reflection of sky and surroundings. Vladimir Nabokov (famed for *Lolita*) gave an indelible account in his poem, "The Waxwing Slain" (*Pale Fire*, 1962):

*I was the shadow of the waxwing slain / by the false azure of the windowpane;*
*I was the smudge of ashen fluff—and I / lived on, flew on, in the reflected sky.*

# Common Yellowthroat

## First Impression

Small, quick, secretive, olive-colored bird flashing into low vegetation

### Mark Your Calendar

Spring through fall; winter in parts of S, SE, and SW

### Details, Details

- Chickadee size; 5 inches
- Male sports a wide black mask
- Both male and female have a yellow throat.
- Female is paler

### Listen Up!

- More often heard than seen. Listen for a clear, loud *witchity-witchity-witchity*.
- Also has a short, buzzy *chip!* of alarm.

### Telltale Traits

- Hyperactive; darts here and there in bushes, gardens, or overgrown grass
- Stops momentarily to sing, while clutching a flower or grass stem

### Look Here

- Low to ground, usually at about 2 to 3 feet, in dense vegetation

### Or Here

- In overlooked, overgrown corners of the yard
- In flower gardens
- In vegetable gardens

**On the Home Front** Nests on or near the ground • Female builds the nest by herself • Very hard to spot the nest, since it's made from dead stems and leaves of surrounding vegetation, so it blends right in • Sometimes built with a roof, instead of as an open cup

*"A fine, clear voice"*
—**Amos Butler**, *Birds of Indiana* (1898)

*Witchity-witchity-witchity* **is an easy way to remember the distinctive song of the yellowthroat, but Butler correctly points out that it's actually closer to** *wit-ti-chee, wit-ti-chee, wit-ti-chee.* **Whichever way they enunciate, yellowthroats say it loudly and often.**

**Wild Menu:** Insects

**Plant Picks:** Go for habitat: Try growing ornamental grasses mixed with large, clumping, low-maintenance perennials, such as perennial sunflowers (*Helianthus angustifolia* and other spp.) in an undisturbed corner. The yellowthroat also likes meadows with occasional wild roses or other shrubs.

**Feeder Pleasers**

- Not usually a feeder visitor; you can try offering mealworms or other insect foods

**Tricks and Treats**

- May be tempted by a low-level naturalistic birdbath with a dripper

## Early Bird

The yellowthroat was one of the first New World birds described in science, and it was Swedish botanist Carolus Linnaeus, the father of genus/species scientific nomenclature, who did the honors.

That original specimen who gave up his life for science (I doubt anyone asked him to volunteer) was collected in 1766 in Maryland. The species was once commonly called the Maryland yellowthroat.

# Yellow-Rumped Warbler

## First Impression
Small, active, gray/black/yellow/white bird with bright yellow rump patch

### Mark Your Calendar
Winter in SE and S; spring through fall in much of W, NW, NE, and N; migration in parts of MW and N

### Details, Details
- Between chickadee and sparrow size; 5½ inches
- The myrtle race has a white throat; Audubon's race, a yellow throat.
- Spots of white on outer tail feathers
- Female is not so vivid, and young birds are brownish—but all have the signature yellow rump.

### Listen Up!
- High, soft warbling song
- Sharp *chip!* call note

### Telltale Traits
- Nervous-jervis! Warblers are constantly on the move, flitting to and fro.
- Sallies out to snatch insects in the air

### Look Here
- In trees or shrubs, often at mid-level

### Or Here
- Eating bayberries winter to spring

### On the Home Front
Does not nest in much of its American range • Nests in conifer forests, on a branch of a conifer; nests high or low • In the SW, nests in mixed forest, sometimes in maples or oaks • Female builds nest while male sings encouragement

*"Wherever bayberries are abundant"*

—**Ralph Hoffmann**, *A Guide to the Birds of New England and Eastern New York* (1904)

**Audubon's race**

Many folks know this bird as the "myrtle warbler," thanks to its love of bayberries, or myrtles (*Myrica* spp.). In winter, bayberry bushes are a magnet for these birds and a good place to approach quietly for a close-up look.

**Wild Menu:** Insects; berries

**Plant Picks:** This is one of the few warblers that can digest the wax of bayberries (*Myrica pensylvanica*) and wax myrtle (*M. cerifera*); plant male and female bushes to produce a crop of their fragrant berries. Also try other small berries, including Virginia creeper (*Parthenocissus quinquefolia*).

**Feeder Pleasers**
- It's becoming a more frequent feeder visitor from fall through late winter. You can try offering mealworms and other insect foods and suet.

**Tricks and Treats**
- Try a ground-level birdbath with moving water produced by a dripper, Water Wiggler, or mister.

## Beach Bums

After a winter storm, I was strolling along a New Jersey beach, just to see what I could see. Lots of pretty shells had washed in, and so had big piles of seaweed.

Those long windrows of kelp and eelgrass were buzzing with small brown flies and other insects—and with myrtle warblers! The birds had forsaken their usual haunts in the bayberry thickets, and like me, they were combing the beach.

# Northern Cardinal

*First Impression*
**Bright red bird with pointy crest**

**Mark Your Calendar**

Year-round; absent in W, NW, and parts of N and SW

**Details, Details**

- Smaller than a robin; 8¾ inches
- Heavy, conical, orange bill
- Female is reddish gray

**Listen Up!**

- A great song for beginners at birdsong to learn: *what cheeer! what cheeer!*

**Telltale Traits**

- Unmistakable appearance
- Often sings from exposed perch
- Pairs often stay together year-round.
- Stays at feeder for minutes at a time, cracking seeds

**Look Here**

- At feeder

**Or Here**

- In backyard trees or shrubs

*On the Home Front* Often uses dense backyard shrubs and roses as homesites • Puts in a good word for "invasive" honeysuckle: cardinals often build nest in tangle of honeysuckle vines (*Lonicera japonica*) • Cardinal nestlings look very much like brown-headed cowbird babies—and the cardinal is a frequent victim of that parasitic species.

*"Decidedly social, particularly in the winter"*

—**Maurice Brooks, "Notes on the Birds of Cranberry Glades, Pocahontas County, West Virginia" (1930)**

**Nothing warms up a winter day like a flock of cardinals. Whether they're perched in a pine tree or at your feeding station, those red birds are simply glorious—especially in snow.**

**Wild Menu:** Seeds; insects; fruit

**Plant Picks:** Large-headed, stout-stemmed sunflowers (*Helianthus annuus* 'Russian Giant')

**Feeder Pleasers**

- Sunflower seeds; corn; may eat safflower seeds

**Tricks and Treats**

- Cardinals often nest in grapevines—and sometimes in grapevine wreaths. Try hanging a wreath on a protected wall of your house, and see if you get any takers. Grapevine bark is used in nest construction, too.

## Winter Red

Cardinals in the snow are a popular theme on Christmas cards, and no wonder—it's a beautiful combination. These brilliant red birds gather in groups in winter, feeding and sheltering together. Stock up on sunflower seeds and shelled corn, and you can be their favorite friend all season.

# Evening Grosbeak

## *First Impression*
**Looks like a giant, darker goldfinch**

### Mark Your Calendar
Winter only in most areas; year-round in parts of W, NW, N, and SW

### Details, Details
- Smaller than a robin; 8 inches
- Male's big white wing patches flash as he flies
- Female is gray-green
- Massive, conical bill

### Listen Up!
- Distinctive, hard-to-describe calls make an almost constant chatter.

### Telltale Traits
- Usually visit in groups
- Eat sunflower seeds steadily for long periods of time
- Often an irregular visitor; plentiful one year, absent or scarce the next

### Look Here
- At feeder

### Or Here
- In flocks in treetops
- Flying in flocks from place to place

*On the Home Front* Nest is hard to see: a shallow saucer of loose twigs usually placed high in forest tree • So highly secretive about nesting, and nests so high in trees, that not much is known about it • Watch for birds in winter flocks to begin to pair off as spring approaches.

### "Grosspigs"
**—Nickname for evening grosbeaks**

Better stock up on sunflower seeds if evening grosbeaks descend on your feeders. These "pigs" go through seed like hogs at the trough, cracking one shell after another with their powerful bills.

**Wild Menu:** Seeds, especially tree seeds; insects; some fruit

**Plant Picks:** Just keep that sunflower tray stocked for success with grosbeaks. The birds may also eat maple, ash, box elder, and other seeds on your shade trees.

**Feeder Pleasers**
- Sunflower seeds, and plenty of them

**Tricks and Treats**
- Try a heater for your birdbath to give grosbeaks a welcome winter spa.

## *What's That Noise?!*

Many years ago, we had a kitchen fire with flames that moved faster than I would've believed possible. We smothered it quickly, but it scared the daylights out of us.

A couple of weeks afterward, I was sound asleep when the faint sound of crackling flames broke into my dreams. Heart pounding, I leaped out of bed and ran downstairs.

No fire, thank goodness. It was just a newly arrived crowd of grosbeaks going through the birdseed.

# Rufous-Sided Towhee

*First Impression*

**Big black, reddish, and white "sparrow" scratching on ground**

**Spotted towhee**

## Mark Your Calendar

Year-round in most areas; spring through fall in some areas; eastern towhee in eastern half of country; spotted towhee in West

## Details, Details

- A little smaller than a robin; 8½ inches
- Female is brown rather than black

## Listen Up!

- The call *che-WINK!* is shared by both eastern and western races.
- Calls are distinctive but variable. Once you recognize the timber of its voice, you won't have any trouble recognizing its notes.
- Eastern: also exhorts a buzzy, trilling *drink your teeee!*
- Western: rapid trill with that signature buzzy quality

## Telltale Traits

- Scratches vigorously on ground
- Usually shows up singly or as a pair

## Look Here

- On ground beneath shrubs

## Or Here

- In dead leaves
- Low in dense shrubs or hedges

*On the Home Front* Nests on ground under bush, or very low in vines or shrubs, to about 5 feet • Builds a cup of twigs, grasses, and rootlets, lined with hair and fine grass • If you get too close to the nest, you'll hear the parents calling *twee* apprehensively.

### *"Chewink"*

—Traditional common name for towhee

That name "towhee" sounds more like *toe-WHEE* when the bird says it himself. It's often preceded by a call that sounds almost exactly like *che-WINK!*

**Wild Menu:** Insects; fruit

**Plant Picks:** Plant a hedge or group of shrubs and let fallen leaves accumulate beneath.

**Feeder Pleasers**
- Millet

**Tricks and Treats**
- Towhees often visit a birdbath.

## Doin' the Hokey Pokey

Watch the legs and feet of a towhee next time you hear one rustling in the dead leaves under your bushes, or spot one going to town beneath the feeder. You'll see they only use a two-footed method for scratching: a quick hop forward, a quick drag back.

No fancy Fred Astaire dance steps here. It looks like they only learned one move from the Hokey Pokey: "You put your both feet in, you put your both feet out."

# American Goldfinch

*First Impression*
**Bright yellow and black little bird**

*"He stays with a happy company of friends."*

—J. H. Stickney, *Bird World: A Bird Book for Children* (1904)

### Mark Your Calendar

Year-round in a large swath; winter in southern states; spring through fall in northern

### Details, Details

- Chickadee size; 5 inches
- Female and male in winter are olive-green

### Listen Up!

- High, sweet, twittering, musical song
- Querying call note: *twee?*

### Telltale Traits

- Usually in flocks
- Flies in deep dips, often singing *potato CHIP!* (actually, more like *perchick-uh-wee*) along the way

### Look Here

- At feeder

### Or Here

- In flower garden, eating seeds
- On thistles, dandelions, or other weeds, eating seeds
- In treetops, with the flock

*On the Home Front* May nest in backyard, usually low in a hedge or shrub • May also nest in a maple or other deciduous tree, or in pines, to about 30 feet high • Watch for goldfinches collecting plant down for their nests about the time that thistles begin to go to seed. • The cup of a nest is so densely woven from plant fibers and so thickly lined with thistledown or other soft materials that it holds water; the parent bird shelters the nest with its wings during showers.

"Perhaps you know some boy or girl who is cheerful and lively all the day and all the year," writes Stickney, as the children's book author extols the goldfinch's supposed virtues. Wonder if that approach would fly with today's middle-schoolers?

**Wild Menu:** Weed seeds and other small seeds; insects

**Plant Picks:** Annual sunflowers (*Helianthus annuus*), Sensation cosmos (*Cosmos bipinnatus* 'Sensation'), garden lettuce you let go to seed, and a few choice weeds (dandelions, lamb's quarters, pigweed)

### Feeder Pleasers

- Niger seed; sunflower seed; canary seed and finch mix

### Tricks and Treats

- Water, water, everywhere—goldfinches can't seem to get enough of a birdbath. Expect to see several "wild canaries" splashing at once.
- Soft nesting materials are often welcomed. Try milkweed fluff, cotton balls, natural tufts of wool, or other soft or downy materials.

## Dandelion Appreciation

Goldfinches are just as sunny and yellow as America's most recognized weed, and they're a natural match. Dandelions' little parachute-topped seeds are a big hit with these birds.

I like the look of flowers in my grass, and I like watching goldfinches standing on tiptoe to pluck out their seeds. So I welcome every dandelion that moves in. Call them "goldfinch food," and maybe you, too, can learn to enjoy them.

# House Finch

## First Impression

Streaky, red-splashed "sparrow" at feeder

**Mark Your Calendar**

Year-round

**Details, Details**

- Sparrow size; 6 inches
- Female is streaky gray-brown

**Listen Up!**

- Sweet, long, warbled song
- *Qweet?* call

**Telltale Traits**

- Often in small to large groups
- Frequent presence at feeder

**Look Here**

- At the feeder

**Or Here**

- In backyard conifers
- In flocks, in trees, or on other perches

On the Home Front Often lives near people, but in W, also in desert and other open spaces; never nests in forests • Frequently nests in hanging baskets, in ivy on walls, or in backyard trees, usually spruce, pine, or palm • The fad for specimen conifers—think suburban brick rancher with blue spruce in front—helped give this once-western species the protected nesting places it needed to spread across the entire country.

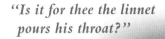

*"Is it for thee the linnet pours his throat?"*

—**Alexander Pope** (1688–1744), poet, *Essay on Man*

A sweet, pleasing song is always in the air when house finches—once called "linnets"—are around. Males sing year-round, slowing down some in winter but not stopping altogether like many other songbirds. Even the female sometimes sings.

**Wild Menu:** Buds; seeds; fruit; plus a few insects

**Plant Picks:** Annual sunflowers (*Helianthus annuus*) and almost any "people" fruit: cherries, peaches, plums, figs, blackberries, strawberries, and more

**Feeder Pleasers**

- Sunflowers; niger seed; finch mix

**Tricks and Treats**

- Provide a freshly filled birdbath every day.
- Salt is a hit; try a handful of rock salt in a clay saucer.

## Clothes Make the Man

Check out the male house finches at your feeder, and you'll see they show huge variation in the color that washes their head and breast.

Some males are as richly red as strawberry juice, others look faded, and some are even orange to pale yellow.

Females, science has found, go for the guys with the reddest feathers.

# Indigo Bunting

## First Impression
**A brilliant flash of metallic blue**

### Mark Your Calendar

Spring through fall; absent from W, NW, and part of N

### Details, Details

- Small sparrow size; 5½ inches
- Female is plain brown

### Listen Up!

- *Sweet-sweet-choo-choo-sweet-sweet*—or the more vivid interpretation *fire, fire, where, where, here, here!*
- During nesting season, the male gives a gushing, rippling, joyous song while in flight.
- Sharp *chip!* alarm note

### Telltale Traits

- One of the few birds to sing all day, even in heat
- Sings from an exposed perch

### Look Here

- At feeder

### Or Here

- Singing from a perch, often a utility wire or the tippy-top of a tree
- In brushy, overgrown areas, such as roadsides or old fields
- Eating weed seeds, especially dandelions

**On the Home Front** Not exactly a model of monogamy: A female may pair with more than one male, and a male may mate with more than one female. • Female raises nestlings by herself • Nests low to ground, usually at 3 feet or less, in shrubs, goldenrod, or other vegetation

*"Sang the livelong day"*

—**Thomas S. Roberts**, *The Birds of Minnesota* (1932)

**When there's an indigo bunting in your neighborhood, you'll know it. This is one of the "singing-est" birds in the country, holding forth even in the heat of a summer day, when other birds are silent.**

**Wild Menu:** Seeds; insects; some berries

**Plant Picks:** Dandelions! Let them go to seed to attract buntings passing through on spring migration.

**Feeder Pleasers**
- Millet

**Tricks and Treats**
- If you have a big yard, consider planting a meadow of grasses and rugged perennial wildflowers, such as goldenrods (*Solidago* spp.) and asters (*Aster* spp.), dotted with sumacs (*Rhus* spp.) or wild roses (*Rosa* spp.).

## Stay on the Sunny Side

The brilliant blue of a bunting's feathers is nothing more than a trick of the light. Just as the sun makes the sky look blue, hitting it at a certain angle, so does the sun light up a bunting like the rarest of sapphires. In shade, the bunting is just a little dark bird.

START HERE

# Pine Siskin

## First Impression
Streaky brown finch that looks a little different at the tube feeder

START HERE

*"Pine Siskins settled on the road to eat the salt"*

—Gordon Meade, "Calcium chloride—a death lure for crossbills" (1942)

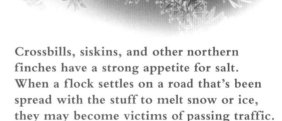

### Mark Your Calendar
Winter in eastern half of country; year-round in much of W and parts of N

### Details, Details
- Chickadee size; 5 inches
- Yellow bars on wings
- Noticeable notched tail
- Small, thin, sharp beak
- Female usually doesn't have as much yellow as male

### Listen Up!
- What a racket! Noted for its motormouth habit of rapid notes, plus a buzzy *zhreeeee*. Multiply by 50 when a flock descends.

### Telltale Traits
- Active little bird
- Generally visits feeder in groups, which explode into flight when disturbed
- Associates with goldfinches—and looks a lot like them at first glance

### Look Here
- At tube feeder, eating niger seed

### Or Here
- At other seed feeders
- Hanging out in a flock, in a tree near a feeder
- In conifers

### On the Home Front
Not a backyard nester
- Nests in conifer forests • The female builds a flattened nest of twigs, rootlets, and grass, lined with soft materials—which she may recycle from an old goldfinch nest.

Crossbills, siskins, and other northern finches have a strong appetite for salt. When a flock settles on a road that's been spread with the stuff to melt snow or ice, they may become victims of passing traffic.

**Wild Menu:** Seeds, including seeds from conifer cones; buds; insects

**Plant Picks:** Annual sunflowers (*Helianthus annuus*), weeds, weedy grasses

### Feeder Pleasers
- Niger seed; sunflower seed

### Tricks and Treats
- Siskins seem to do everything together—they even like group baths. Provide a shallow basin of fresh water.
- Salt is a big hit with flocks of siskins. Try a handful of ice-cream-maker rock salt in a tray feeder.

## Call Me Unpredictable

Feast or famine: That's often the way with pine siskins. They're famed for being irregular in their visits to backyards. Some years you'll host dozens, other years only a few—or none at all.

Most of the time they live in conifer forests, and some years, it seems, they just want a change of scenery—or maybe the cone crop failed. Then siskins "irrupt," traveling outside their usual haunts. If they told us they were coming, we could stock up on niger seed.

# Slate-Colored Junco

## *First Impression*

**Ubiquitous small gray birds with white bellies, on ground**

### Mark Your Calendar

Winter in most areas; year-round in some parts of W and NE

### Details, Details

- Sparrow size, 6¼ inches
- Flash white outer tail feathers when they fly
- Note the pinkish bill.
- Female is paler than male

### Listen Up!

- Fast chippering trill, usually a monotone
- Sharp *chip!* alarm note

### Telltale Traits

- Often in groups
- Scratches on ground to expose seeds
- Fairly unafraid of humans

### Look Here

- On ground beneath feeder

### Or Here

- In or at tray feeder
- Under shrubs or hedges
- Scratching for seeds in flower or vegetable gardens

*On the Home Front* Often nests on ground, in a cavity by a rock, at the foot of a tree, or along a log • May nest in higher places, such as vines on the side of a building or even a hanging basket • Female builds the nest, but male stays near during incubation and warns of intruders

Oregon junco

Pink-sided junco

## "Snowbird"

—Traditional common name, still in use

Is it because juncos portend the arrival of winter when they arrive in backyards that they got the name "snowbird"? Or is it because of their snowy underside and a back the color of a gray sky? I vote for the first. What do you think?

**Wild Menu:** Seeds; insects

**Plant Picks:** Sow a patch of finch mix or birdseed mix—right from the bag—for juncos to forage in all winter.

**Feeder Pleasers**
- Millet

**Tricks and Treats**
- Hold off on cutting back your flower garden until early spring, especially if you grow zinnias (*Zinnia* spp.), bachelor's buttons (*Centaurea cyanus*), and other annuals: Juncos will find cover among the dead stems as they scratch for seeds.

## *Regional Treats*

Not all slate-colored juncos look alike. The species includes several geographic variants, or races. All have dark eyes, a pink bill, and a general gray color. But details are different.

In the W and NW, the striking black hood and rusty brown trim of the Oregon junco add some spice. In the SW and W, you may spot the well-named pink-sided junco. Live in the SW? Watch for the gray-headed junco, which I think would have been better named the rusty-backed—it has a splash of bright rusty red on its upper back.

# Song Sparrow

## First Impression

**Little streaky brown bird scratching or hopping on ground**

### Mark Your Calendar

Year-round

### Details, Details

- Sparrow size; 6¼ inches
- Streaky white breast and distinctly striped head
- Some geographic races, including eastern and midwestern birds, have a distinct darker blotch on the chest, a thickening of their streaks. Juvenile birds, as well as western, northwestern, and southwestern races, may lack this mark.
- Slight color variations geographically: SW birds are ruddier, NW birds are grayer
- Female looks like male

### Listen Up!

- Varying gentle songs with musical trills
- Frequent *chip!* alarm note

### Telltale Traits

- Scratches on ground with both feet at once
- Usually stays somewhat hidden, in or beneath vegetation
- May remind you of a mouse, fast and secretive

### Look Here

- Under feeder, picking up small seeds on ground

### Or Here

- At tray feeder
- On ground under bushes
- At low levels, in flower garden, vegetable patch, or shrubbery

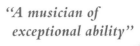

*"A musician of exceptional ability"*

—F. Schuyler Mathews, *Field Book of Wild Birds and Their Music* (1904)

START HERE

And we can enjoy this singer's concerts every day, right in the backyard. The little brown bird is an indefatigable performer, bursting into sweet songs many times a day.

**On the Home Front** Because song sparrows are so abundant, you have a good chance of enjoying a nesting pair in your own yard.
- Nests on ground or low in shrubs • The nest is surprisingly hard to spot; you may find it by accident when tending your garden.

**Wild Menu:** Seeds; insects; small fruits

**Plant Picks:** Strawberries, raspberries, blackberries, blueberries

**Feeder Pleasers**
- Millet

**Tricks and Treats**
- Keep that birdbath brimming; song sparrows like a daily splash. Place the bath near a shrub to make the bird feel more at home.

## Was That a Moo?

Parent birds work hard dawn to dusk to feed their nestlings. Now imagine trying to feed a baby that's a giant!

That's the predicament of many song sparrows. They're a favorite target of the brown-headed cowbird, which in some regions lays eggs in nearly 20 percent of song sparrows' nests.

You may spot the mismatched, hulking cowbird fledgling when its "parents" bring their family to your feeder. The cowbird will be gray and noisy (but it won't be saying *moo*).

# White-Throated Sparrow

**First Impression**
Streaky brown sparrow with white bib and eye stripe, scratching on ground

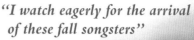

*"I watch eagerly for the arrival of these fall songsters"*

—Frank Chapman, *Handbook of Birds of Eastern North America* (1895)

### Mark Your Calendar

A winter friend in most areas; year-round in northern NE; migrant only in much of MW; absent from much of W

### Details, Details

- A large sparrow; 6¾ inches
- Male and female look alike
- Head stripe may be bright white or drab tan
- Yellow spots at bill are worth a close-up view through binoculars

### Listen Up!

- This sparrow sings one of the best beloved songs: a quavering, melancholy whistle to the cadence of "*old Sam Peabiddy Peabiddy Peabiddy.*" It's easy to imitate; give it a try.
- Clinking note, as of a chisel striking rock

### Telltale Traits

- Usually in groups of a few to several
- May join a group of mixed sparrows and juncos
- Scratches vigorously on ground with both feet simultaneously

### Look Here

- Beneath feeder with other sparrows

### Or Here

- At tray feeder
- In or under shrubs or hedges
- In flower garden or vegetable patch, scratching for seeds on ground

**Listen for the plaintive song of this sparrow when fall migrants arrive in your backyard. You might also hear what Chapman calls their "quarrier chorus," a collection of soft *chinks* as the birds settle down together for the night.**

**On the Home Front** Nests only in the very northern states, from Minnesota eastward
- Not usually a backyard nester • Builds nest on ground, often under wild blueberry bush
- Caterpillars are a big part of the nestlings' food.

**Wild Menu:** Seeds; a smattering of insects; some small fruits

**Plant Picks:** Scatter a few handfuls of birdseed in late spring to early summer, to grow a self-serve garden for these winter pals.

**Feeder Pleasers**
- Millet

**Tricks and Treats**
- White-throats appreciate a sip of water, even in winter. Set out a clay saucer of warm water, or try a birdbath heater. A Water Wiggler device may also keep water from freezing so quickly.

## Who's Snoozin'?

Got a dense conifer in your backyard? It may become the Do Drop Inn for white-throated sparrows, juncos, and other winter visitors. These birds gather in communal roosts at dusk, often in a spruce, fir, or juniper. The extra bodies share warmth as they sleep safely among the branches.

# White-Crowned Sparrow

*First Impression*

An elegant, large sparrow with plain gray front and boldly striped head

### Mark Your Calendar

Winter, most areas; year-round in parts of W, or spring through fall in other parts of W and NW; migration only, upper MW and NE

### Details, Details

- Large sparrow; 7 inches
- Some variation geographically
- Female and male look alike
- Young birds in their first winter have heads striped with brown instead of black, with tan instead of white between stripes.

### Listen Up!

- Starts out similar to that of white-throated sparrow, then goes into pretty trills
- Call note: sharp *pink!*

### Telltale Traits

- Watch for the bird to raise its head feathers into the crown that gives it its name.
- Scratches with both feet simultaneously
- Usually in small groups or with other sparrows and juncos

### Look Here

- On ground or in feeder

### Or Here

- In brushy areas, like a casual flower or vegetable garden
- In weedy corners

*On the Home Front* Mostly nests far to N, except in areas of W • May nest in parking lot shrubbery in W and NW • Often nests near water • A bird of grasslands and brush

*"One of the aristocrats of the family"*

—Frank Chapman, *Handbook of Birds of Eastern North America* (1895)

**It's the crown that does it, plus a habit of perfect posture. White-crowned sparrows have a proud look, especially when they erect their boldly striped head feathers.**

**Wild Menu:** Seeds; some insects; and small fruit

**Plant Picks:** Weeds! Dandelions are a big favorite. Don't have any weeds or any tolerance for them? Sow a "sparrow garden" of any inexpensive wildflower mix along with a few handfuls of birdseed, and let the plants stand through fall and winter.

**Feeder Pleasers**
- Millet

**Tricks and Treats**
- Water, water everywhere: Provide a birdbath, a dripper tube, a water-filled plant saucer on a rock, or a naturalistic "creek."
- Pour birdcage grit on bare ground at your feeding station or in a tray feeder.

## Parking Lot Pals

When I moved to Washington State, I was stunned to find these special sparrows nesting in ordinary bushes in the supermarket parking lot. And the library parking lot. And the coffee shop parking lot. And, it seemed, every other parking lot with a few shrubs or trees.

I'm still not quite used to seeing them there. But I am enchanted by hearing their songs as I load my groceries and push my cart into the corral.

# Chipping Sparrow

## *First Impression*

**Tiny, unafraid, streaky brown bird with reddish cap, hopping on ground**

### Mark Your Calendar

Spring through fall in most regions; year-round or winter in SE, S, and parts of SW

### Details, Details

- The size of a small sparrow (which it is!); 5½ inches
- Look for that reddish cap and an eye stripe.
- Plain gray breast, unlike similar tree sparrow (larger, with dark spot)
- Female looks like male

### Listen Up!

- Long, monotone trill from the trees
- Sharp *chip!* alarm call

### Telltale Traits

- Listen for that trill—you'll hear it a lot.
- Not a low-level skulker like most sparrows; often in trees, though it does also forage on the ground

### Look Here

- Singing from small backyard trees

### Or Here

- At feeder or on ground beneath it
- Foraging for seeds on ground in winter flower garden or vegetable patch
- Singing from a perch, usually moderately high in a tree

**On the Home Front** Frequent backyard nester • Mostly nests in conifers • Builds in trees or shrubs • Often picks a yew near the house as a nest site

*"Who does not know this humblest . . . little neighbor that comes hopping to our very doors?"*

—**Neltje Blanchan,** *Bird Neighbors* **(1897)**

Chipping sparrows still come hopping to our doors, so why not get to know these little neighbors? They're common summer residents in town and country, in just about any yard that has at least a small tree and garden.

**Wild Menu:** Small seeds, especially grass and weed seeds; a few insects

**Plant Picks:** Weedy grasses, including foxtail grass and crabgrass, are a big hit. Or plant millet or finch mix for a self-serve banquet.

### Feeder Pleasers

- Millet

### Tricks and Treats

- Chippies eagerly accept horsehair for their nests. Ask at a stable for tail or mane combings.
- Pour a handful of birdcage grit on bare ground below the feeder, or in an open tray feeder.

## *Finding the Nest*

I always like to know where the birds in my yard are nesting. Most are so secretive, it's usually winter before I find out where they raised their family during summer.

But I've had good luck finding chippy nests, because these birds seem to lack any fear of me. Just keep an eye open for a chippy coming and going to the same place day after day. Binoculars will help you see what's happening without taking the chance of disturbing its family.

# House Sparrow

## First Impression

Big, brown, stocky sparrow with black bib, usually with a bunch of loudly chirping friends

### Mark Your Calendar

Year-round

### Details, Details

- Large sparrow size; 6¼ inches
- Gray crown and white cheeks
- Female is much drabber and lacks the bib

### Listen Up!

- Frequent chirps
- The flock produces a constant chorus of chirping.

### Telltale Traits

- Always in a flock
- Frequently squabbles with companions
- Dust baths are a popular activity; look for a few to several birds "splashing" in a dusty spot in your yard.

### Look Here

- At the feeder

### Or Here

- In a bush near the feeder
- On the ground

**On the Home Front** Unloved by bluebird fans, due to habit of commandeering nest boxes • Nests in cavity, birdhouse, dense vine, or sometimes in a tree—in spaces that can be completely filled up with leaves and other nesting materials • Often leaves nest materials trailing from entrance of birdhouse

*"Too pestiferous to mention"*
—**H. E. Parkhurst**, *The Birds' Calendar* (1894)

**A bulletin issued in about 1900 by the Department of Agriculture warned that the progeny of a single pair of house sparrows could amount to precisely 275,716,983,698 in only 10 years! Introduced as "English sparrows," though they actually hailed from Africa, the birds are still abundant but not pestilential. They're common city birds, but not nearly as plentiful as they once were.**

**Wild Menu:** Seeds; insects

**Plant Picks:** You won't need to do anything special to attract house sparrows. But they'll enjoy a birdseed garden for fall and winter foraging.

### Feeder Pleasers

- Millet; any other seed they can crack

### Tricks and Treats

- House sparrows relish a good, splashing bath, and they're fun to watch.

## Let Me Introduce You

The introduction of new species of birds to America rapidly lost its charm after the population explosion of the house sparrow and the starling. But not all intros met with such "success."

If you're visiting near St. Louis, watch for a bird that looks a lot like a house sparrow, but has a bright reddish brown crown and not much of a bib. That's the Eurasian tree sparrow, introduced in 1870 to "enhance the North American avifauna." Unlike the pushy house sparrow, this one stayed in a relatively confined area and behaved itself.

START HERE

111

# Common Grackle

## *First Impression*

Big, shiny, long-tailed black bird stalking proudly on ground

### Mark Your Calendar

Year-round in many areas; spring through fall in parts of W, N, MW, and NE; absent in parts of W, NW, and SW

### Details, Details

- Bigger than a robin; 12½ inches
- Pale yellow eye
- Beautiful blue/purple iridescence on head; bronze iridescence on body and wings
- Wedge-shape tail is distinctive in flight
- Male is more iridescent than female

### Listen Up!

- Creaking, grating *kuh-reeez* or other harsh noises

### Telltale Traits

- Stalks around, doesn't hop
- Drops wings and bows while *screek*-ing
- Eats eggs and young from other birds' nests so often is pursued by other birds
- May arrive in large flocks during migration

### Look Here

- On lawn

### Or Here

- At feeder
- Singing from top of conifer
- Scything through leaves for insects

*On the Home Front* Begins nesting early in season • Usually builds nest in conifer, such as spruce or juniper • Makes a large nest, often with strips of paper, string, and bits of wire

*"Squeaking and whistling like creaking sign-boards"*

—Ralph Hoffmann, *A Guide to the Birds of New England and Eastern New York* (1904)

Grackles have quite a repertoire of wheezy, mechanical songs—like the repeated creaking of a swinging signboard that needs a drop of oil.

**Wild Menu:** Seeds; grain; insects; plus other birds' eggs and nestlings, mice, salamanders, fish, and fast-food leftovers

**Plant Picks:** Your lawn and feeder will be enough of an attraction to lure all the grackles you could possibly want. If you let fall leaves nestle into place below trees and shrubs instead of raking them, you also may be visited by migrating flocks.

**Feeder Pleasers**
- Millet; cracked corn; sunflower seeds

**Tricks and Treats**
- Grackles enjoy a birdbath.

## *Wearing Out Their Welcome*

Some backyard bird lovers aren't fond of grackles, because the birds arrive in groups that can clean out a feeder in no time.

Imagine if you were tending a hundred-acre "feeder." In South Dakota, where huge farm fields are planted with sunflowers whose seeds are targeted for our backyard bird feeders, grackles have become huge fans of the stuff. The birds' traditional mixed diet has given way to one that's almost entirely sunflower seeds, eaten from the field. That can put quite a dent in the harvest.

# Red-Winged Blackbird

## First Impression
**Black bird with vivid red shoulders**

### Mark Your Calendar
Year-round in most areas; spring through fall in parts of NE and N

### Details, Details
- A little smaller than a robin; 8¾ inches
- Look closely for the yellowish border below the red epaulets
- Female is streaky brown with yellow tinge on face and throat

### Listen Up!
- A screaking *oh-kuh-REE!*
- A sharp *chack!* call note
- Harsh rattle

### Telltale Traits
- Often walks about on ground, hopping when necessary to catch up with flock
- Male is usually on visible perch; female generally stays hidden
- Often in groups or flocks
- Males often battle fiercely over females.

### Look Here
- At or below feeder

### Or Here
- On lawn

**On the Home Front** May nest in cattails in water; at edges of bodies of water; in dense, grassy, or weedy fields; or in brush • Usually nests in colonies • Nest is large, woven from coarse grasses or cattails and finished with a finer lining • Raises two broods a season

*"Most effective when seen from in front"*

—**Charles Townsend**, *The Birds of Essex County* **(1920)**

The red patches of the male redwing are nearly covered up when he is feeding. But as Townsend says, "when his love passions are excited," the redwing puffs out his gorgeous scarlet epauletes.

**Wild Menu:** Seeds; insects; some fruit and berries

**Plant Picks:** Try growing a patch of broom-corn or milo to supply fall and winter food for this species.

**Feeder Pleasers**
- Millet; cracked corn; birdseed mix; chick scratch; stale bread, corn muffins, and other grain-based products

**Tricks and Treats**
- You won't need anything but a steady supply of feeder food to keep these birds coming around.

## A Cloud of Smoke

When I used to drive home in southern Indiana, I'd often notice what looked like a cloud of smoke on the horizon, far out across the endless flat fields of corn or soybean stubble. The smudge would darken, then dissipate until it was hard to make out, then just as suddenly draw together into a black puff again. Sometimes the "smoke" would veer suddenly in one direction or another, even when there was no wind.

What I was watching wasn't smoke at all, but the cloud made by 30,000 or so far-off red-winged blackbirds. All winter long, they'd range here and there over the farm fields, settling down to feed after a while, then swirling up and regrouping to try another spot.

# European Starling

*First Impression*

**Dumpy, waddling, voracious, *screal*-ing, blackish bird**

### Mark Your Calendar

Year-round

### Details, Details

- A little smaller than a robin; 8½ inches
- Female and male look alike
- From fall through winter, the birds acquire a spattering of little "stars" on their bodies—actually the pale tips of their new coat of feathers—and a darker beak.
- From late winter through summer, the birds wear breeding plumage, gleaming with a pretty greenish purple iridescence and lacking their spots. Their beaks also turn yellow.
- It's easy to mistake young starlings for young cowbirds: They're plain, soft gray-brown.
- Often wrongly called grackles, the starling has a much squatter appearance and shorter tail than those svelte, long-tailed birds.

### Listen Up!

- A wild array of squeals, squeaks, and hissing chatter
- Also a lovely, liquid, musical song
- Often mimics other birds or mechanical sounds that it hears frequently: Does your garden gate need a drop of oil?
- One of the first birds to begin singing, often in late winter

### Telltale Traits

- Usually in flocks, which descend en masse on a likely food source
- Notorious for taking advantage of the hard work of flickers and other woodpeckers, starlings often wait until the other birds have excavated a nest hole, then intimidate them into leaving it. Sometimes all it takes is a lurking pair of starlings to "encourage" the homebuilders to seek another site.

*"Even then they do not mean to be a bother"*

—**Wilfrid Bronson**, *Starlings* (1948)

If starlings were rare birds, we'd probably find them fascinating. But familiarity, in this case, definitely breeds contempt. It's hard to find a starling appreciator, which is why I adore Bronson's little book. The birds do have their good points, if you can look beyond their pest potential. These common birds are tops at destroying many of the six-legged pests that plague our backyards—particularly Japanese beetles.

### Telltale Traits—*Continued*
- Often walks about on ground, stabbing into the soil
- In winter, starlings join together in flocks that can number in the tens of thousands.

### Look Here
- Scarfing down your feeder foods, especially suet and other soft (and expensive) treats

### Or Here
- On the lawn
- In a fruit tree or bush, eating the fruit
- At the birdbath

*On the Home Front* One of the reasons for starling unappreciation is the birds' habit of commandeering other species' nest holes. Woodpeckers are frequent victims. • Another reason most folks aren't fans of starlings: They often cram their huge, bulky conglomeration of a nest into an opening they create or discover around your house. Under an eave, in a porch ceiling, or in a chimney are prime locations. • The nest itself is a messy affair, spilling over with twigs, straw, grasses, plastic wrap, paper trash, and other flotsam. (At least they recycle.) • Typically several broods a year are raised, so once the first set of fledglings flies the coop, remove the nest and plug up its place.

**Wild Menu:** Ah! This is where the praise comes in. Starlings eat countless numbers of destructive insects and their larvae, including Japanese beetles and European crane flies. If you're an alfalfa farmer, you may appreciate their position as No. 1 destroyer of the clover weevil. They also eat a lot of fruit, plus weed seeds, grain, and leftovers gleaned from the trash.

**Plant Picks:** You probably won't want to encourage starlings, but they do love holly berries (*Ilex opaca* and other spp.).

### Feeder Pleasers
- Suet, soup bones, meat scraps; any kind of bread products; halved apples, which will provide you plenty of entertainment as the birds pick them completely clean, leaving nothing but the thin peel; softened dog food; millet, birdseed mix, and just about anything else they can get down the hatch. Sunflower seeds are not attractive, although they may be eaten if nothing better is around.

### Tricks and Treats
- To keep starlings from swamping your feeders, give them their own diner, away from other offerings. Stock it with the foods they enjoy, and they may stay there instead.
- Starlings are fun to watch splash in a birdbath. A heated birdbath is a huge hit in winter.

## Shakespeare, Mozart—and Starlings

The first starlings were released in New York's Central Park by Eugene Schiffelin, a well-meaning and eccentric New Yorker who wanted to import every bird ever mentioned in Shakespeare's plays. Starlings only get one mention in all of the bard's works, in a scheme intended to disturb King Henry IV by repeating the name of a distrusted earl:

> The King forbade my tongue to speak of Mortimer. But I will find him when he is asleep, and in his ear I'll holler 'Mortimer!' Nay I'll have a starling shall be taught to speak nothing but Mortimer, and give it to him to keep his anger still in motion. (*Henry IV*, Part 1, Act 1, Scene 3)

Mozart kept a starling for a pet and was so attached to it that he gave it a funeral when it died, complete with veiled mourners and a procession to its grave.

Whatever your feelings toward starlings, you're likely to see less of them. The species is declining both here and in Europe, for reasons no one yet knows.

# Brown-Headed Cowbird

## First Impression

A unique color combo: black body with brown head

### Mark Your Calendar

Year-round in many regions; spring through fall in most of W

### Details, Details

- Smaller than a robin, bigger than a sparrow; 7½ inches
- Black feathers are iridescent green in sun
- Female is dull grayish brown all over

### Listen Up!

- Quiet, gurgling notes interspersed or followed by high, thin whistle
- Rattling *kkkkk* when alarmed

### Telltale Traits

- Usually seen in pairs or flocks
- Males engage in weird poses: drooping wings, puffed chest, stretched neck.
- Female is extremely sneaky when approaching other birds' nests

### Look Here

- At or below feeder

### Or Here

- Walking on lawn
- Got a horse or other livestock? Look for cowbirds in your barnyard.

**On the Home Front** Cowbirds are parasitic: The female lays her eggs in other birds' nests for them to raise. • Usually only one cowbird egg is laid in a host's nest. • The eggs are white, speckled with brown. • Many birds don't recognize the eggs as not their own, even if they lay eggs of a completely different size or color.

*"Then he would bow or bend his head"*

—Herbert Friedmann, *The Cowbirds: A Study in Biology of Social Parasitism* (1929)

Blackbirds, including the cowbird, are famed for odd postures during courtship. Charles Townsend wrote to Friedmann: "A male would look up, puff up feathers, spread wings and tail, and fall on head." *Fall* is right: The bird simply keels over, with head and breast hitting the ground.

**Wild Menu:** Seeds; insects; small fruits

**Plant Picks:** Don't encourage these birds if you can help it. You probably can't, since cowbirds eat many of the same foods that songbirds do.

**Feeder Pleasers**

- Cowbirds will eat just about any seeds or grain you put out for other birds.

## Buffalo Bird

Way back when shaggy bison roamed the country in huge numbers, and cattle were much fewer, the cowbird was known as the buffalo bird. Flocks hung out wherever buffalo congregated. The reason for the attraction? Food, just as it is with cattle today.

As they lumber along, grazing beasts stir up millions of insects from the grass. Nimble cowbirds scoot among those heavy hooves to scoop up the insects. You may also spot cowbirds perched on the animals' heads or backs, searching for ticks or other tasty insects.

# Northern Oriole

*First Impression*
**A shocking flash of orange**

## Mark Your Calendar

Spring through fall

## Details, Details

- A little smaller than a robin; 8¾ inches
- Baltimore race, the bird in the eastern two-thirds of the country, has a black hood; Bullock's race, the western counterpart, has an orange head with black cap and nape and black throat.
- Bullock's also shows flashy white wing patches, even with wings folded
- Females of both are paler yellow-orange, with drab brown-gray back and wings.

## Listen Up!

- Loud, whistled song sounds like short, emphatic sentences
- Rattling *churr* when alarmed

## Telltale Traits

- Usually seen in pairs or alone, except at good food sources during migration, particularly in fall
- Males can be pugnacious

## Look Here

- Usually in tops of deciduous trees

## Or Here

- At flowering trees, picking off insects
- Pulling fibers for nest from plants in flower garden, or collecting string or fibers you supply
- At nectar or fruit feeder
- At birdbath

*On the Home Front* In winter, when orioles are long gone, the old nests are easy to spot in bare trees

**Bullock's oriole**

START HERE

*"The herald of spring"*

**—Alexander Wilson,** *American Ornithology* **(1832)**

**Orioles return in spring with a fanfare of robust, whistled songs. Their voices are so distinctive that they can wake you up and pull you to the window to see who's singing.**

**Wild Menu:** Insects; fruit

**Plant Picks:** Fruits of any kind, particularly sweet or sour cherries, mulberries (*Morus* spp.), and grapes

## Feeder Pleasers

- Nectar feeder; halved oranges, pushed onto a spike; grape jelly and other preserves

## Tricks and Treats

- Baltimore orioles immediately get busy courting after returning in spring.
- An old white sheet will give you a lifetime supply of thin strips of cloth to offer nesting birds. Keep strips about 6 to 10 inches long.
- Supply a source of fresh water; an old-fashioned birdbath is often popular.

## Overdose of Ardor

Male Baltimore orioles are often at war over females. Frequently a third male will attempt to cozy up to a female while her mate is distracted by an interloper. Male orioles are fearless fighters, but they're, um, birdbrained. In my own yard, an ardor-crazed oriole attacked my dog's toy—a stuffed orange and black tiger. Made me laugh, but the hero was proud of himself.

# Ruby-Throated Hummingbird

## First Impression

**Unmistakable tiny buzzing bird with dazzling ruby throat**

START HERE

### Mark Your Calendar

Spring through fall in eastern half of country; year-round at tip of Florida; black-chinned, the western counterpart, is also spring through fall in most areas

### Details, Details

- Tiny! Smaller than a chickadee; 3¾ inches
- Ruby-throated has a green back that shines golden; male, a ruby-colored iridescent throat patch
- Black-chinned, a similar western species, has a purple throat and a significant black chin
- The colorful throat feathers, or "gorgets," look black when not in sunlight.
- Females of both species are green with a whitish belly.

### Listen Up!

- Soft, chippering or warbling calls, like whistling through teeth
- A hum from the whirring wings; black-chinned's wings may produce a whistle in flight

### Telltale Traits

- Flies like no other bird: backward, forward, and hovering in place.
- Black-chinned often pumps its tail while hovering, as if for balance.
- Both species engage in fly-catching behavior, zooming out from a perch to nab a passing insect, then returning to perch until the next one comes along.
- Ruby-throat can be aggressive, driving away much larger birds from anywhere near a favored food source.
- May also bathe during rain showers by perching with fluffed out feathers.
- Collects small insects from spiderwebs, as well as silken spider egg cocoons and web strands to use in nest-building.

**Black-chinned hummingbird**

*"The old lilac bush by the well was 'swarming' with Hummingbirds"*

—Jane Hine, "Observations on the Ruby-Throated Hummingbird" (1894)

During spring migration, hummers often gather in numbers at a flowering shrub or tree. Listen for the hum around lilacs (*Syringa vulgaris*), azaleas (*Rhododendron calendulaceum* and other spp.), weigela (*Weigela florida*), red buckeye and other buckeyes (*Aesculus pavia, A. parviflora,* and other spp.), red horse chestnut (*A. × carnea*), and tulip tree (*Liriodendron tulipifera*). Hummingbirds also visit early flowers during spring migration. Look for them nectaring at columbines (*Aquilegia* spp.), especially wild red columbine (*Aquilegia canadensis*), fire pink (*Silene virginica*), sweet William (*Dianthus barbatus*), and the popular groundcover, ajuga (*Ajuga reptans*).

### Telltale Traits—*Continued*

- Hummingbirds rarely wallow in a birdbath, but they will eagerly "bathe" in the spray from a garden hose, fountain, or mister. Look for them zipping back and forth through the falling water, or sitting on a perch to catch the spray, then reteating to a dry place to fluff and preen their feathers.
- Frequently visits nectar feeders, but traffic will slow dramatically during nesting season, when hummingbirds become homebodies.

### Look Here

- At nectar feeder

### Or Here

- Drinking nectar at flowers, especially at red or orange-red blossoms and at tubular blossoms
- Drinking nectar at paloverde tree (black-chinned)
- Drinking nectar at mimosa tree (ruby-throated)
- Hummingbirds spend a lot of time resting their wings. Get in the habit of scanning for the silhouette of the tiny, long-beaked bird perched atop a metal shepherd's crook or the tippy-top of a shrub or trellis. You may also spot one on a slender branch of a young tree, usually in a relatively bare spot where foliage and twigs won't impede takeoffs and landings.

**On the Home Front** May nest in backyards, but incredibly hard to find—or even to notice • Looks like a knot on a tree limb • Builds a tiny cup about the size of a walnut, of plant down and spider silk; ruby-throat adds lichens to the construction • Black-chinned nests low, from 4 to 8 feet aboveground, often on branch over water or dry creek bed • Ruby-throat also often chooses a site on a branch over water, but builds higher, about 5 to 20 feet up

**Wild Menu:** Nectar; small insects; small spiders; tree sap

**Plant Picks:** Salvias (*Salvia* spp.) of any kind, beebalm (*Monarda* spp.) and other mints, trumpet vine (*Campsis radicans*), penstemons of any kind (*Penstemon* spp.), and a host of others

### Feeder Pleasers

- Nectar feeder. Be sure your feeder is equipped with a water-filled "ant moat," to prevent a stream of six-legged nectar seekers from draining the feeder (and drowning inside), and with small grids called "bee guards" over the holes, to help deter stinging insects that may harass hummingbirds.

### Tricks and Treats

- A misting device, attached to a birdbath or spraying into open air, provides a highly appealing, gentle bath for these birds.

## Courtship Capers

In general, male birds of most species impress females by showing they can do it better—whatever "it" happens to be. Those with flashy feathers usually find some way to show off their colors. Others sing their hearts out, or find homesites that a potential mate might like.

With hummingbirds, it's superior flying skills that males use to say "Pick me!"

So how does a bird that can already perform miracles in flight stand out from the crowd? With aerial acrobatics, that's how. Each hummingbird species performs its own "air show," tracing loops, figure eights, and other gymnastics above a female they hope to impress.

The black-chinned and ruby-throated use a similar style of courtship flight: They trace deep U-shapes above the perched female to win her favor, climbing to a height of 15 feet or more, then swinging like a pendulum to and fro. It's jaw-dropping to watch. Focus on the birds in your yard, and you may see it for yourself.

# Chapter Seven

# Birds of the Northeast

The Northeast is home to an abundance of backyard friends. The number of species found here, and the numbers of individuals, show that this long-settled region is prime bird territory.

Yet a megalopolis and birds just don't seem to go together. From New York to Boston, it sometimes seems like one big gridlocked expressway, dense with subdivisions and people, people, people. It's a major hub of commerce, and it's home to the people who make that commerce run.

Wild things? Good luck to them would seem to be the rule.

Crazy as it seems, though, this intensively settled part of the country is actually heaven for backyard birds.

Cities and towns dating back to the 1700s did change the landscape long ago. But that means that their street trees, city trees, and backyard trees have had plenty of time to grow into grand old specimens. Their leafy boughs create an oasis of green around, over, and among the buildings and roadways.

Next time you fly over the area, take a peek down below. You'll see lots of green—and that's what keeps the Northeast so inviting to birds.

## A REAL MIX

The Northeast is densely settled in most parts, although some areas (Hello, Maine! How's it going, upstate Pennsylvania? Good afternoon, northern New Jersey) are still surprisingly wild. They haven't totally paved paradise—yet.

The sprawl from New York City often gets the blame—or credit, depending on how you look at it—for creating the eastern megalopolis. But even today, you can drive out of the city for 45 minutes and end up in a rural, or at least rural-feeling, area.

A big part of the reason for that country feel is the trees.

In the cities, plentiful public parks, old cemeteries, and other open spaces are filled with trees and shrubbery that make birds feel at home.

**Chipping sparrows may roost in lilac bushes.**

Backyards here are often comparatively large in these days of more typical postage-stamp-size lots. The big yards also are filled with big forsythia bushes, lilacs, and other mature plantings. Those hedges and shrubs

**Evening grosbeaks eat maple seeds.**

**Forsythias may hold a cardinal nest.**

are home to cardinals, brown thrashers, and many other backyard birds.

This region is Roger Tory Peterson's old stomping ground. It's also the birthplace of the Audubon Society and the American Ornithological Union (A.O.U.), the organization that keeps the official names and records of American birds nicely straightened out.

## THE LAY OF THE LAND

Residential areas new and old share the region with small farms and pastures. Fertile river valleys and lakes created by spring-fed creeks and clear-running streams supply plenty of water year-round, making the region prime bird territory.

Well-weathered mountain ranges, their sharp spines worn to gently rounded slopes, provide totally different habitat for other bird species. Along with good skiing, you'll find nesting juncos, white-throated sparrows, warblers, and other northern birds in the Green Mountains of Vermont, the Poconos of Pennsylvania, the Catskills of New York, and other mountains of this region.

## FOOD AND SHELTER

Native trees in the Northeast are a mix of oaks, maples, beeches, and other deciduous types along with some conifers, including the patrician eastern white pine and the eastern hemlock, under siege by woolly adelgids in

There are still plenty of wild places in the well-settled East, and even the cities are green with trees. From the air, it's easy to see the connected corridors of trees along the Connecticut River Valley that provide a safe route for many birds as they move from town to country.

**Asters and goldenrod paint fields in fall.**

## CLIMATE

Four seasons, and what beauties they are! The Northeast is famous for its trilliums, bloodroot, and other spring wildflowers, and for its summer field flowers of asters and goldenrod. In fall, the red maples, sugar maples, and other trees are so spectacular that national bus tours run sight-seeing trips. Winter brings a snowy frosting and scarf-snuggling cold, well below freezing.

Rain is pretty evenly distributed over the seasons, including winter's snow. Summers are humid, often with gusty thunderstorms that can knock a robin's nest right off its branch.

Northerly parts of the region have more intense and longer-lasting cold. But extreme summer heat usually lasts only a few days at a time. Droughts and floods may occur.

some areas. All offer plenty of seeds, cones, and insects for birds. Wild cherries (*Prunus* spp.), beach plums (*Prunus maritima*), and other fruit-bearing trees and bushes give birds some variety in their diet. Street-side plantings and backyard trees broaden the menu mix even more. And all of the plants supply nesting places and cover.

Smaller seed-eating birds, including goldfinches and native sparrows such as tree sparrows and field sparrows, find abundant food in the meadows, along roadsides and woods' edges, and in backyards, where dandelions and other weed seeds are often abundant. Farm fields and pastures give ground-dwelling birds, such as grasshopper sparrows, Henslow's sparrows, and meadowlarks, a perfect homesite. And wooden fence posts and old orchards supply the habitat that's most desired by the bird that's most desired—the eastern bluebird.

**Keep a reserve supply of seed in case of ice storms. Your cardinals will thank you.**

## BIRD LIFE
## IN THE NORTHEAST

Birds are abundant in this region, thanks to ample cover and water throughout the area. Most of them spread out to cover other territories besides the Northeast; only a handful is limited to this region.

Many backyard birds, including feeder friends such as blue jays, song sparrows, and downy woodpeckers, are year-round residents in the Northeast. Catbirds, house wrens, and other species stop in just for summer, retreating to warmer regions for winter.

### Start Here

Because the Northeast is home to so many widespread species, you'll want to turn back to Chapter 6, "Start Here," to find your most familiar backyard friends.

These are the birds you share with other parts of the country—chickadees, white-breasted nuthatches, tufted titmice, goldfinches, juncos, cedar waxwings, and many others.

Every single one of the "Start Here" birds is happily at home in the Northeast region.

### Regional Specialties

You'll find other favorite friends spotlighted in this regional section. Some of these birds also occur in other regions. But every single one of them may turn up in your northeastern backyard.

Be sure to page through the birds of the Far North, too. Many of them pay a brief visit to northeastern backyards as they pass through on migration to and from more northern areas or mountainous parts.

## Birds of the Northeast

Here's a list of the birds you'll find in this chapter. Remember to consult the "Start Here" birds, starting on page 79, for the most common birds to be found in the Northeast.

# Yellow-Bellied Sapsucker

*First Impression*

**Nondescript woodpecker playing peekaboo around a tree trunk**

## Mark Your Calendar

Spring through fall

## Details, Details

- Slightly smaller than a robin; 8½ inches
- Female has white, not red, throat

## Listen Up!

- Mewling or squealing, repeated *clee-ah*
- Sound is peculiar, like a complaining cat

## Telltale Traits

- Look for black throat and yellow belly in flight
- Quiet and inconspicuous on migration, but real loudmouths once they get to where they're going
- Drills neat rows of small holes in tree bark and returns frequently to same tree

## Look Here

- Usually clinging to trunk or major limb of a living deciduous tree

## Or Here

- Males noisily chase each other in mating season in spring, making quite a racket.
- Can be a hog at nectar feeders, drinking sugar water for an hour or longer

*On the Home Front* Nests in a hole high in a tree • The male bird does most of the excavating of the nest hole and shares incubating duty and those incessant feeding chores.

*"Each pair have a 'sugar orchard' of maple or birch, to which they resort constantly to drink the sap"*

—**Ralph Hoffmann,** *A Guide to the Birds of New England and Eastern New York* (1904)

**Sapsuckers drill neat rows of holes in tree trunks and keep them in good working order. They return daily to maintain the holes and to sip the sap and nibble the insects that have accumulated there.**

**Wild Menu:** Sap; insects at sap

**Plant Picks:** Sapsuckers drill at more than a thousand kinds of trees: Apple, maple, birch, and pine are perennially popular.

**Feeder Pleasers**

- Nectar feeder; shelled pecans; suet feeder nailed to vertical board or tree

**Tricks and Treats**

- May use a birdbath

## Tapping the Sap

Before you snicker at a sapsucker, consider this: Even our best scientists haven't figured out yet how these birds get tree sap to keep flowing.

Phloem sap is a tree's lifeblood, so the tree quickly stanches the flow. But not so at sapsucker holes, where the sap stays liquid. The latest theory is that sapsucker spit may contain some kind of anti-coagulant that enables the phloem sap to fill the holes that sapsuckers drill.

If it weren't for sapsuckers, ruby-throated hummingbirds couldn't survive so far north, where flowers are few. Their spring arrival is timed to the period of peak sapsucker activity. Bats, flying squirrels, porcupines, warblers, and nuthatches share the sap, too.

# Hairy Woodpecker

*First Impression*

**A big "downy woodpecker" with a long, heavy bill**

### Mark Your Calendar

Year-round

### Details, Details

- Almost as big as a robin; 9¼ inches
- Female lacks red patch on head

### Listen Up!

- Sharp, loud *peek!*
- Long bursts of very fast drumming with beak on hollow tree or other resonant object

### Telltale Traits

- Much rarer than the common downy woodpecker
- Never found on mullein or other weed stalks, unlike downy
- Often flakes off pieces of bark, a giveaway to its location overhead
- Sticks close to mature forests in summer; wanders about in fall and winter and may show up in backyards

### Look Here

- On tree trunk or large branch, often of dead wood

### Or Here

- At suet feeder

*On the Home Front* Drills out a hole in dead wood for its nest

*"The young when first hatched are repulsive-looking creatures with enormously large heads . . . "*

—Charles Bendire, *Life Histories of North American Birds* (1895)

Good thing the hairy woodpecker's nest is in a cavity in a tree, hidden from bird-watchers with delicate sensibilities! The big-headed babies soon grow feathers and look like punk rockers when they leave the nest 3 weeks later.

**Wild Menu:** Insects drilled from wood; acorns and nuts; a small amount of fruit

**Plant Picks:** Blackberries or raspberries

### Feeder Pleasers

- Suet; insect foods; nuts and peanut-butter-based concoctions

### Tricks and Treats

- It may take a while before a hairy investigates, but once it does, it'll be a firm fan of mealworms at your feeder.
- Rig up a harness of string or wire and hang a big, meaty bone with marrow intact. A ham bone is perfect for winter woodpecker feeding, if not exactly picturesque.

## When in Doubt

I'm always trying to make downy woodpeckers into hairies. Listen—isn't that call a little louder? And the bird a little bigger? And doesn't that beak look thicker than a downy's?

Sorry, but no. What I've learned over the years is a simple guideline: When in doubt, call it a downy. When you see a hairy, you'll know. A hairy woodpecker is so much bigger than a downy (practically robin size!) and its beak is so much stouter, that there's no mistaking it.

It's always a good idea to take a second look at any woodpecker. But when you can't tell immediately whether you're looking at an ultra-common downy or a rarely seen hairy—sorry, but it's probably a downy.

# Red-Bellied Woodpecker

*First Impression*

**Big, calm, red-headed woodpecker at feeder**

### Mark Your Calendar

Year-round

### Details, Details

- Almost as big as a robin; 9¼ inches
- Female has red only on back of neck, not top of head

### Listen Up!

- Loud, harsh, querulous *quirrrr?,* as if asking, "Where's my food?"
- Steady, medium-speed drumming

### Telltale Traits

- Back and wings look grayish from a distance; up close, appear finely black–and-white zebra striped
- Undulating flight, with deep dips
- Often very tame; slow to fly away when you approach

### Look Here

- At the feeder eating sunflower seeds or squirrel corn

### Or Here

- Clinging to tree trunks or large branches
- Foraging on the ground
- At suet or nectar feeder

*On the Home Front* Happily accepts a nest box • Also drills out its own home in a dead tree or limb, or in a wooden utility pole or fence post • Often returns to same nest box or cavity the next year • Both parents incubate the eggs and care for the young.

*"The drumming and tapping of the busy feathered workmen on a resonant limb is a solace, giving a sense of life and cheerful activity which is invigorating."*

—**Neltje Blanchan,** *Bird Neighbors* (1897)

**Unless that resonant woodpecker drumming happens to be on your house, that is. Try a big squirt gun or a spray from a hose to prevent that Swiss cheese look in your siding.**

**Wild Menu:** Insects; seeds; nuts; fruit

**Plant Picks:** Pecans, oaks, hazels, for nuts; corn or Indian corn; tall, large-headed sunflowers (*Helianthus annuus*); mulberries (*Morus* spp.), elderberries (*Sambucus* spp.), blackberries, raspberries, grapes, and apples

**Feeder Pleasers**

- Whole ears of dried corn on cob; sunflower seeds; suet and suet-based foods

**Tricks and Treats**

- Squirrel feeders that hold a fixed ear of corn work great for this big guy to peck at, too.
- Fasten a wire suet cage firmly to a vertical board or tree to give this bird a place to prop its tail to help support its big body.
- May become a nectar drinker

## Belly Up!

I'd love to know who first decided this bird's name, because I have a feeling it's someone who didn't like to admit a mistake. The splashy red-decorated head is the first thing you'll notice about this bird. But since there's already a "red-headed woodpecker," this poor bird was named after its red belly—which is really hard to see. As the woodpecker contorts itself at your feeders, you may catch a glimpse of the tiny red-tinged feathers centered low on its belly. If you get a glimpse, then you, too, can say, "Red-*bellied* woodpecker? Ya gotta be kidding me!"

# Eastern Phoebe

*First Impression*

**Erect, perched, plain bird with nervously dipping tail**

**Mark Your Calendar**

Very early spring through early fall

**Details, Details**

- Smaller than a robin and just a little bigger than a sparrow; 7 inches
- Female and male look alike

**Listen Up!**

- This one's easy: The bird says its own name, except it sounds more like *FEE-we*. The hoarse, whistled song goes like this: *fee-wee-we, FEE-we*. It's repeated over and over and over.
- Also makes a clear, high *chip*

**Telltale Traits**

- Long, loose tail that's in constant motion: Dip down, raise; dip down, raise—as if tracing and retracing the letter U.
- Sits quietly perched for long stretches, then sallies out after an insect

**Look Here**

- On a low, conspicuous perch, such as a fence post

**Or Here**

- Making a nest above a door frame or on a rafter in a shed

*On the Home Front* The sweet mossy nest, lined with feathers, is saddled to a support, such as a rafter or door frame. The birds often recycle materials from an old nest; they may also reuse an old nest after some remodeling.

*"It is not only fine feathers that make fine birds."*

—**Aesop**

**The quietly colored phoebe may not be a glamour queen, but its early spring arrival and its habit of building its nest on the garden shed make it a special friend in the backyard.**

**Wild Menu:** Insects, especially flying insects

**Plant Picks:** No particular plants attract phoebes. Avoid pesticides: Tent caterpillar moths are a big favorite of phoebes.

**Feeder Pleasers**

- Doesn't visit feeders

**Tricks and Treats**

- Buy sphagnum moss at a florist or craft shop. Soak a generous handful in water for several hours, then gently squeeze and shake out some of the excess water. Keep moist and it will begin to green up in a few days. Offer to phoebes and other nest-builders by draping it on a twig.
- A birdbath is welcomed, especially one with a spray or dripper.

*Many Happy Returns* _____

Phoebes nested behind John James Audubon's house along the Perkiomen Creek, west of Philadelphia. In 1803, curious if the same birds returned year after year, the famed ornithologist wrote about an experiment he'd tried:

"When they were about to leave the nest, I fixed a light silver thread to the leg of each, loose enough not to hurt the part, but so fastened that no exertions of theirs could remove it. At the next year's season when the Phoebe returned to Pennsylvania, I ... caught several of these birds on the nest, and I had the pleasure of finding two of them had the little ring on the leg."

129

# Great Crested Flycatcher

*First Impression*

**Sudden swooping dash by big grayish and chestnut bird with long tail and loud voice, saying *wheeEEEEP!***

### Mark Your Calendar

Spring through early fall

### Details, Details

- A little smaller than a robin but seems larger due to its habits; 8¾ inches
- Female and male look the same

### Listen Up!

- Raucous voice; a distinctive, loud *wheep* or *kweep* call with a rising tone
- Combination of *kweeps* and *kwips* in an excited chatter

### Telltale Traits

- Feisty and irascible—fights with other males, sometimes battling in midair
- Flashes rusty tail and wing feathers in flight
- Raises and lowers head feathers when perched or agitated

### Look Here

- Perches alertly on conspicuous treetop branch or other perch, near or in woods or big shade trees

### Or Here

- Flying from one perch to another, near or in woods or shady yards
- Eating small fruit in trees

*On the Home Front* Adopts old woodpecker cavities as nest holes • Called the "snakeskin bird" for habit of tucking a shed snakeskin into its nest

*"The wheep bird"*

—Old traditional country name

That's a perfect name for this large flycatcher of woodsy places and shaded yards. The birds announce their spring arrival with ringing, musical *wheep* calls. Males seem to be always in a bad mood, yelling loudly while picking fights and threatening others of their kind.

**Wild Menu:** Insects, especially beetles; fruit

**Plant Picks:** Wild cherries, mulberries, grapes, blackberries, and raspberries

### Feeder Pleasers

- Doesn't usually visit feeders; may be tempted by mealworms or other insect foods

### Tricks and Treats

- Great cresteds are quick to make a home in your nest box, if you live near woods or in a neighborhood with plenty of old shade trees. Mount the box about 8 to 12 feet high on a tree, facing an open area. Better to use a too-big box than a too-small one; the birds will stuff it with leaves, grasses, and other filler to set their nest at the right level from the opening.
- May use a birdbath

## Too Busy to Wheep

One year, a crop of mulberries on a tree down the road drew all kinds of fruit-eating birds, including fabulous orioles, tanagers, and bluebirds. It was easy to admire them among the greenery. I spent long stretches with my neck craned back, watching the feasting.

I didn't realize great crested flycatchers were there, too, until I caught a familiar flash of long, rusty tail. Sure enough, there were my big noisy friends, eagerly choffing down mulberries without a hoot or holler. I guess their beaks were too full of berries to make a fuss.

# Tufted Titmouse

## First Impression

**Hyperactive little gray bird with pointy head**

## Mark Your Calendar

Year-round

## Details, Details

- Sparrow size; 6½ inches
- Female looks like male

## Listen Up!

- Clear, loud, whistled *Pete-o, Pete-o, Pete-o*
- High, thin, lisping notes when foraging in trees

## Telltale Traits

- Never sits still for long
- Grasps sunflower seed or nut in feet and pecks with beak

## Look Here

- Flying to or from feeder

## Or Here

- In trees or sometimes in shrubs, picking off insects
- On ground below trees or feeder, briefly, snatching up bits of nuts or dropped seeds

## On the Home Front

Often nests near houses • Builds nest in a natural cavity such as an old woodpecker hole, or in a birdhouse • Lines nest with soft hair • Brings young to feeder soon after they leave the nest

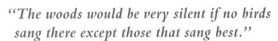

*"The woods would be very silent if no birds sang there except those that sang best."*

—Henry Van Dyke, American poet, author, and clergyman (1852–1933)

**The tufted titmouse is a loud and enthusiastic singer, with a limited two-syllable repertoire. Yet his song is always a treat: It signals the end of winter long before the groundhog checks out his shadow.**

**Wild Menu:** Seeds; nuts, including acorns; insects, especially caterpillars; small fruits

**Plant Picks:** Oaks, pecans, beeches, and other nut trees; mulberries, serviceberries (*Amelanchier* spp.), elderberries (*Sambucus* spp.)

## Feeder Pleasers

- Sunflower seeds and chips; chopped nuts; suet, peanut butter, and other fat-based foods

## Tricks and Treats

- Stuff a wire suet cage with soft materials for nesting: feathers, dog fur, hairbrush combings, and cotton balls.
- Birdbaths, from simple to elaborate
- Nest boxes mounted about 6 to 20 feet high

## Helping Hand

Titmice are loyal feeder friends. And friendly they are—they often fly in to grab a bite while you're standing right there filling the feeder, especially if it's a cold or snowy winter morning.

Like chickadees, titmice are easy to hand tame. Just hold out a handful of whatever they like best at your feeder (nut pieces are usually a good bet), and stand quietly. You may get a taker right away, or it may take several mornings of patience before your new "feeder" is accepted.

# Veery

*First Impression*

**Cinnamon brown, robinlike bird with white belly**

### Mark Your Calendar

Spring through fall

### Details, Details

- About the size of a large sparrow but looks like a downsized robin; 7 inches
- Female looks like male

### Listen Up!

- The veery says its own name, with some poetic license, of course, in three or four phrases, gently spiraling downward. Most sound like some version of *vreee-uu*, as played on a wooden flute—or a melodious kazoo.

### Telltale Traits

- Sings at dusk
- Male often sings from same perch in tree

### Look Here

- On ground in shady gardens or woods, especially near streams

### Or Here

- At naturalistic water features or birdbath
- At fruit trees and berry bushes in summer
- Flying overhead at night, on migration

*On the Home Front* Not usually a backyard nester • Nests on ground in its favorite haunts near a stream or in a wet, young woods • Visits backyards near its nesting grounds, or visits during migration

*"If you would enjoy it you must bring an ear to hear."*

—**Bradford Torrey, on the delights of the veery's song,** *Birds in the Bush* (1885)

**Fans of the thrush family, which includes the veery, like to debate which of these birds is the best singer. Is it the fabled wood thrush, with its fluting melody? The ethereal hermit thrush? Many vote for the veery, with its haunting, delicate song.**

**Wild Menu:** Insects, including gypsy moth caterpillars; small fruits

**Plant Picks:** Strawberries, Juneberries (*Amelanchier* spp.), blackberries, dogwood (*Cornus* spp.) berries eaten on fall migration

### Feeder Pleasers

- May sample mealworms from a low feeder, but not usually a feeder visitor

### Tricks and Treats

- The sound of water may lure the veery during migration. Try a ground-level naturalistic birdbath or constructed stream, with very shallow, nonslip pools for drinking and bathing.

## The Woods at Dusk

The dawn chorus of songbirds is justly famous. But if you're rushing around getting kids off to school or yourself off to work in the morning, then you can reserve a seat for the evening performance instead.

Just make yourself comfortable near or in a woods, and listen quietly. Before long, you'll hear the sweet, unearthly voices of thrushes start up all around you. It's an experience you won't forget.

# Wood Thrush

*First Impression*

**Rusty robinlike bird with boldly spotted breast**

### Mark Your Calendar

Spring through fall

### Details, Details

- Smaller than a robin; 7¾ inches
- Female looks like male

### Listen Up!

- The flutist of the woods: languid, liquid, *ee-oh-lay, ee-oh-lay*
- Like other thrushes, a short, terse call note when alarmed

### Telltale Traits

- Sings in late afternoon and at dusk
- Often sings when rain is on the way

### Look Here

- On ground in woodsy areas or shade garden near woods

### Or Here

- Eating small fruits or berries, especially in summer or on fall migration
- At naturalistic low-level water feature or birdbath

*On the Home Front* Unless your yard adjoins a woods, you're unlikely to host nesting wood thrushes. • Well-hidden nest is similar to robin's, usually saddled on a branch or tucked in a crotch at eye level or above • Keep cats indoors if you live in thrush territory; their depredations contribute to the declining numbers of these storied singers.

*"If I keep a green bough in my heart, the singing bird will come."*

**—Chinese proverb**

And maybe, just maybe, it will be a wood thrush. All thrushes have beautiful voices. But in my memory, the melancholy evensong of the wood thrush will always have a special place.

**Wild Menu:** Insects; small fruits and berries

**Plant Picks:** Mulberries (*Morus* spp.), serviceberry (*Amelanchier* spp.), elderberry (*Sambucus* spp.), dogwood (*Cornus* spp.), spicebush (*Lindera benzoin*)

### Feeder Pleasers

- May eat mealworms and other insect foods from low feeder

### Tricks and Treats

- If you live near a thrush woods, tear a few strips of white cotton cloth about ½ inch wide and 6 inches long, and lay them on the ground in a shady garden. The birds may collect them to weave into their nests.
- Coax them into your yard with a birdbath equipped with a dripper or moving water.

## Cowbird Competition

The woodsy ravine beside our Indiana house was thick with sugar maples, silver beeches, wildflowers—and wood thrushes. Often the birds visited our yard, feeding beneath the shrubs and splashing in the birdbath. In summer, nearly every pair brought its young.

Only problem was, each pair of thrushes was busily tending a big, noisy, cowbird baby instead of a young thrush. Wood thrushes are a prime target of parasitic cowbirds. Unless the thrush nest is deep within a large woods, the cowbird will lay an egg in it and then abandon it.

# Eastern Bluebird

*First Impression*

**Unbelievable blue that takes your breath away**

### Mark Your Calendar

Spring through fall, and year-round in parts of Pennsylvania, New Jersey, and New York

### Details, Details

- Smaller than a robin, as big as a large sparrow; 7 inches
- Female is duller, looks faded

### Listen Up!

- Sweet, gurgling, whistled, *tru-a-ly, tru-a-ly!*
- Brief, husky call note that seems to keep birds in touch: *chew*

### Telltale Traits

- Travels in short, slow, fluttering swoops from one perch to another
- Often glides from low perch to ground with wings spread, to catch insects

### Look Here

- Perched near or in open areas, often near the edge of a woods or an orchard

### Or Here

- In golf courses, cemeteries, large parks, pastures, and along roadsides
- At apples, crab apples, and other flowering trees, picking off insects at blossoms
- At feeders or birdbaths

*On the Home Front* Eagerly accepts a birdhouse but will face stiff competition from house sparrows • Very early nester, so mount boxes in late winter • Nesting may fail if late snow, ice, or freeze arrives; the birds will try again.

*"The bluebird carries the sky on his back"*

—**Henry David Thoreau, American naturalist (1827–1862)**

People have wondered at the magnificent blue of the bluebird for centuries. The signature color is best admired in sunlight. It's a prismatic layer, suggested the scientist V. Fatio, writing in French in 1866. He was on the right track. Thoreau, too, was closer than he knew: The same refraction that makes the sky look blue also makes bluebirds look blue.

**Wild Menu:** Insects; fruit; berries

**Plant Picks:** Flowering trees; small fruits, including mulberries (*Morus* spp.), serviceberries (*Amelanchier* spp.), winterberry and evergreen hollies (*Ilex* spp.), and Virginia creeper (*Parthenocissus quinquefolia*); dogwood (*Cornus* spp.)

**Feeder Pleasers**

- Mealworms and other insect foods; accessible suet, peanut butter dough (peanut butter mixed with cornmeal), and fat-based foods

**Tricks and Treats**

- The sound of trickling water is a big draw.
- Put up a roost box so bluebirds can stay cozy at night.

## Target Your Feeding

If bluebirds are in your area, you can catch their attention with food that's clearly visible in an open feeder. But since many other birds will eagerly scarf up those treats, it pays to invest in a bluebirds-only feeder once they're regular customers.

These feeders play on bluebirds' attraction to an entrance hole; in this case, the hole leads into a feeding area, not a nest box. The birds won't have to compete with more aggressive feeder visitors, and those expensive treats will last longer.

# Blue-Winged Warbler

*First Impression*

**Tiny, bright yellow bird with gray-blue wings**

**Mark Your Calendar**

Spring through fall

**Details, Details**

- Smaller than a chickadee; 4¾ inches
- Female is similar to male but with olive, not yellow, forehead

**Listen Up!**

- Song sounds like a loud insect: *beeeee-buzzz*
- Call note a short, sharp *chik!*

**Telltale Traits**

- Male often stays perched and singing for long stretches of time
- Forages slowly and deliberately, like a chickadee rather than a typically frenetic warbler

**Look Here**

- Singing from top of tree, small tree, or bush

**Or Here**

- Foraging in trees or shrubs, from near ground to tallest treetops
- Often in conifers

*On the Home Front* Nests have been found from 8 inches above the ground to 80 feet up in a tree. • Usually not a backyard nester

*"Rather deliberate in movements for a Warbler"*

—Frank Chapman, *The Warblers of North America* (1907)

**Not as hyperactive as most warblers, the blue-winged often acts more like a chickadee or vireo. Instead of constant fluttering, it often investigates possible food while hanging upside down or sneaking through the foliage.**

**Wild Menu:** Insects; poison ivy berries

**Plant Picks:** Native conifers of your area for insect foraging, such as eastern red cedar (*Juniperus virginiana*), larches (*Larix* spp.), pines (*Pinus* spp.), hemlocks

**Feeder Pleasers**

- Has been spotted visiting nectar feeder

**Tricks and Treats**

- A ground-level naturalistic birdbath with trickling water, or a created stream with very shallow areas, may attract them.

*Thanks, People!*

Habitat destruction usually means bird loss, but in the case of this warbler, the impact of civilization was a boon. The pastures, fields, and second-growth woods that this bird prefers flourished when European settlers cut the dense forests, so it rapidly expanded its range from Tennessee far northward.

Unfortunately, the pendulum is now swinging the other way, as forests regrow and as old fields sprout into subdivisions. Catch this warbler while you can!

# Cape May Warbler

*First Impression*

**Tiny, hyperactive, streaky greenish bird with yellow face**

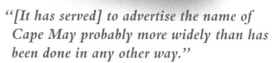

### Mark Your Calendar

Spring and fall migration only, except in northern areas

### Details, Details

- Smaller than a chickadee; 5 inches
- Chestnut ear patch
- The female is dull greenish, streaky below. Female warblers are very tricky to identify with certainty, and so are juvenile birds. Just pegging them as warblers is already an accomplishment.

### Listen Up!

- And listen hard; warbler voices are tiny. This one buzzes a fast *seet seet seet seet*.
- Call note is a sharp, short *tee!*

### Telltale Traits

- Shows white patches in tail feathers and yellow rump in flight
- Constantly on the go

### Look Here

- Examining branch tips and flitting through foliage as part of a wave of migrating warblers

### Or Here

- At conifers, looking for insects
- At birdbaths with trickling water
- At Cape May, New Jersey, on migration, which peaks in mid-September

*On the Home Front* Nests only in boreal forest areas far in the North • Builds a round cup on the branch of a spruce or fir • Usually nests near the top of the tree, from 30 to 60 feet aboveground

*"[It has served] to advertise the name of Cape May probably more widely than has been done in any other way."*

—**Dr. Witmer Stone,** *Bird Studies at Old Cape May* (1937)

**Cape May warblers are only fleeting visitors to Cape May. Blame the name on Alexander Wilson, who described the bird from a dead specimen taken in Cape May County, New Jersey, in 1811. He never saw it alive (neither did Audubon). Wilson never knew his "Cape May" bird was in the middle of a marathon journey, possibly from Costa Rica to Maine.**

**Wild Menu:** Insects

**Plant Picks:** Conifers native to your area, and spruces

### Feeder Pleasers

- Usually uninterested in feeders, but it may like mealworms; has been seen at nectar feeders

### Tricks and Treats

- Attract thirsty travelers with a naturalistic, low-level birdbath or homebuilt stream. Make sure there are shallow, nonslip areas for sipping and dipping.

## Budworm Boom

These teeny-tiny birds are Nature's defense against spruce budworm, a caterpillar that can be devastating to northern conifers.

Budworm populations increase and decrease in cycles. When they become plentiful, Cape May warblers lay more eggs. More beaks to eat budworms!

# Nashville Warbler

*First Impression*

**Tiny, fast, plain gray and yellow bird with a wide-eyed look**

### Mark Your Calendar

Spring through fall

### Details, Details

- Smaller than a chickadee; 4¾ inches
- Female is similar, not quite identical, but lacks the small dab of red crown feathers that the male wears

### Listen Up!

- And hear them you will: When Nashvilles come in, their trilling *seta-seta-seta-seeta-plee-plee-plee* seems to be everywhere.

### Telltale Traits

- Distinct white ring around eye
- Has a stubby look due to shorter tail
- Typical active warbler

### Look Here

- At catkins of oaks, birches, or other trees, picking off insects

### Or Here

- At spring-flowering trees, collecting insects at flowers
- In any tree or shrub, from low levels to very high branches; females forage lower than males

*On the Home Front* Builds its well-hidden nest directly on the ground under a bush, beside a log, or otherwise disguised • Doesn't usually nest in backyards; prefers undisturbed places

*"Nature does nothing uselessly."*

**—Aristotle, Greek philosopher (384–324 B.C.)**

Wood warblers, including the Nashville, are always in motion, because they have a lot of work to do. They're a dead-serious defense for guarding the health of trees. These tiny birds are made for moving quickly through branches and leaves. The sharp beak of a single warbler can nip up hundreds of potential tree eaters every day.

**Wild Menu:** Insects, including tent and gypsy moth caterpillars

**Plant Picks:** Birches, firs, oaks, poplars, pussy willows, and many other trees; trees with dangling catkins are a likely choice

### Feeder Pleasers

- Doesn't usually visit feeders but may like mealworms

### Tricks and Treats

- Offer sphagnum moss in spring; it's a popular nesting material and the birds may accept your handout.

## Changing Times

Nashville warblers are fairly common as warblers go, which means you have a good chance of spotting one in your yard. Scientists surmise that's because they can nest in a variety of habitats, from spruce bogs to second-growth woods to overgrown fields. This bird isn't a fan of deep, dark forests. As early settlers cleared the massive eastern hardwood forests, Nashvilles responded with boom years. Even today, soon after areas are logged, Nashvilles are likely to investigate the new territory.

# Northern Waterthrush

*First Impression*

**A bobbing, swaying, tail-wagging brown bird walking on the ground with a springy step**

### Mark Your Calendar

Spring through fall

### Details, Details

- Sparrow size but looks like a small thrush; 6 inches
- Streaked white belly and white eye stripe
- Female looks like male

### Listen Up!

- Musical, vigorous song, *sweet-sweet-sweet-see-swee,* falling off into a jumble of *chirps* and *chews*
- Call note an emphatic *whik!*

### Telltale Traits

- Constantly bobs tail up and down, weaves and dips body
- Seems to have springs in its legs as it walks along; hops over obstacles
- Perches often

### Look Here

- In your yard on lawn or under bushes

### Or Here

- Near lakes or rivers, often on banks
- In swamps, bogs, or other standing water

*On the Home Front* Doesn't nest in backyards • Nests in the Far North, from Alaska to Labrador, on the ground, usually in sphagnum bogs or along lakeshores • Nest is hidden amid roots or in stumps • Green moss, twigs, pine needles, and animal hairs are used in construction.

*"The world is mud-luscious and puddle-wonderful."*

—E. E. Cummings, American poet (1894–1962)

**The northern waterthrush agrees wholeheartedly with Cummings. These birds adore muddy banks, swampy pools, and puddle bogs. Give them a log with one end in the water, and it'll become a favorite promenade to stroll along.**

**Wild Menu:** Insects; spiders; snails

**Plant Picks:** It's not particular during backyard visits; it may show up near shrubs and hedges, or on lawn. Rake additional leaves under your bushes in fall to attract beetles and snails and mimic wild habitat where the bird forages.

**Feeder Pleasers**

- Uninterested in feeders

**Tricks and Treats**

- If you're lucky enough to have a small pond or boggy area, place a dead tree limb or log with one end in the water, as an inviting perch.

## The Thrush That Isn't

Waterthrushes look a lot like other thrushes at first glance. That brown back, streaky white breast, and habit of walking on the ground all say "thrush." And like thrushes, they're likely to show up in your backyard during migration. But the waterthrushes get their own genus in the wood warbler family, because they're not really thrushes at all.

The ovenbird looks a lot like the waterthrush, but it doesn't have the bobbing and swaying habit.

# Scarlet Tanager

## *First Impression*

**Brilliant red with black wings**

### Mark Your Calendar

Spring through fall

### Details, Details

- Smaller than a robin; 7 inches
- Male's color can vary from bright red to orange-red
- Female is greenish yellow

### Listen Up!

- It has a long, hoarse, slurry song. A good way to find a tanager is to listen for a song from the treetops, then try to locate the singer.

### Telltale Traits

- Vivid color and beauty are the best ways to ID a tanager.
- Slinks through tree foliage

### Look Here

- High in trees, usually deciduous and especially oaks

### Or Here

- At apples, crab apples, and other flowering trees, picking off insects at blossoms
- At your feeder in spring

### On the Home Front Usually nests in woods

- Loose, shallow nest attached to tree limb, well out from trunk • Often high up, but may be at eye level

## *"Seldom conspicuous"*

—A. C. Bent, *Life Histories of North American Blackbirds, Orioles, Tanagers, and Their Allies* (1958)

**Despite its brilliant color, the scarlet tanager rarely catches our eye. It stays in the treetops, for one thing, and it moves quietly and smoothly through the branches, without flashing wings or squawking cries.**

**Wild Menu:** Insects; fruit

**Plant Picks:** Fruits of any kind, particularly sweet or sour cherries and mulberries (*Morus* spp.); early spring flowering trees (crab apples, redbuds); dogwoods (*Cornus* spp.)

### Feeder Pleasers

- Millet and other birdseed; chopped suet; mealworms and other insect foods

### Tricks and Treats

- A simple saucer of fresh water is welcomed by tanagers on migration. A naturalistic birdbath with trickling water is even more effective.

## Watch the Birdie

So much is going on in springtime, when tanagers arrive, that I often forget to watch for them. Besides, they're darn hard to see among all those newly leafed-out branches. Often I find one when I'm casually scanning the trees and spot a dark bird shape against the bright spring sky. A look through binoculars often reveals enough color to say, "Hey, that's a tanager!" Then all I have to do is wait until it moves from a backlighted spot to a place where the sun hits its feathers and turns them fire-engine red. Beautiful!

# Rose-Breasted Grosbeak

## First Impression

**Flashy black and snow-white bird with rosy chest**

*"The potato-bug bird"*

—Neltje Blanchan,
*Bird Neighbors*
(1897)

### Mark Your Calendar

Spring through fall

### Details, Details

- A little smaller than a robin; 8 inches
- Female is streaky brown

### Listen Up!

- Warbling song, similar to robin's
- Squeaky call note; Sibley describes it as "sneakers on a gym floor"

### Telltale Traits

- Flashes big white wing patches in flight
- Female looks like an overgrown female purple finch

### Look Here

- In shade trees or small trees

### Or Here

- At apples, crab apples, and other flowering trees, picking off insects at blossoms
- At feeder

*On the Home Front* Nests usually fairly low to ground, eye level to about 15 feet • Birches and other small trees are popular nest sites. • Has adapted to nesting in backyards and city parks

Rose-breasted grosbeaks were once famed for their appetite for potato bugs; they still indulge in our gardens today. Blanchan commended Pennsylvania farmers for recognizing the bird's effort—noting it was "more useful to their crop than all the insecticides known"—and protecting the bird from being shot.

**Wild Menu:** Insects, including gypsy moth caterpillars and Colorado potato beetle; tree buds; some fruit and seeds

**Plant Picks:** Mulberries (*Morus* spp.), Virginia creeper (*Parthenocissus quinquefolia*), grapes, maples native to your area for winter seeds

**Feeder Pleasers**
- Sunflower seeds

**Tricks and Treats**
- Becoming a regular feeder visitor, so experiment with mealworms and other insect foods
- Birdbaths are popular with migrants.

## You Go, Girl!

I'm always leery when I spot two male birds giving each other "the eye" in spring. Battles over a female can be ferocious, and twice I've seen birds (not grosbeaks) actually kill an opponent.

But in the case of the rose-breasted grosbeaks that nested in my front yard, it was the female who took up the attack. When an unattached female arrived and started throwing coy glances toward the already-taken male, the original female didn't take any chances. Instantly she launched into action and fiercely drove the interloper far out of the yard. Then she returned to tenderly reunite with her mate.

# Pine Grosbeak

*First Impression*

**Very tame, rosy red bird**

**Mark Your Calendar**

Winter; year-round in northern Maine

**Details, Details**

- A little smaller than a robin; 9 inches
- Blackish wings with white bars
- Female is greenish and gray

**Listen Up!**

- Soft, whistled song
- Quiet call notes keep a flock in touch

**Telltale Traits**

- Hangs around in small groups
- Very calm and easily approached

**Look Here**

- Eating berries in winter

**Or Here**

- Quietly perching
- At feeder
- In spruce, pine, or other conifers

*On the Home Front* Does not nest in NE except in northern Maine • Builds its bulky nest on a limb of a spruce, fir, or possibly a shrub • The open cup is loosely constructed of twigs and roots, with a wonderfully soft inner lining of rabbit fur and grasses—which also provide insulation on those chilly northern nights.

*"It seems stupidly tame."*

—A. C. Bent, *Life Histories of North American Cardinals, Grosbeaks, Buntings, Towhees, Finches, Sparrows, and Allies* (1968)

**Maybe it's the lack of people in their Far North homeland, but pine grosbeaks and other northern birds are exceedingly tame when they periodically pay a visit to other regions. If you move quietly, you can refill the sunflower seeds while they sit at the feeder.**

**Wild Menu:** Tree seeds, seeds from conifer cones, weed seeds; tree buds; also fruit and insects

**Plant Picks:** Junipers (*Juniperus* spp., with berries), barberries (*Berberis* spp.), American bittersweet (*Celastrus scandens*), mountain ashes (*Sorbus* spp.), many others

**Feeder Pleasers**

- Sunflower seeds

**Tricks and Treats**

- Pine grosbeaks are a great reason to have a reserve bag of sunflower seeds on hand: Winter flocks may number 100 or more birds!

*Just Moping Around*

In Newfoundland, home to that breed of big, black, seafaring dogs and hordes of pine grosbeaks, these sedate birds go by the name of "mopes." That means someone who just sits around, and sitting motionless is something pine grosbeaks do a lot.

But when they're eating, pine grosbeaks are great fun to watch, because they feed for much longer stretches than most birds do. That's because they're equipped with an extra-large *gular pouch,* which they can stuff full when they find a good food source—a nifty survival trick in a harsh climate.

# Red Crossbill

*First Impression*

**Very tame, rosy red birds that twist and turn upside down like parrots—and get a load of that beak!**

> " . . . *everything in nature is lyrical in its ideal essence, tragic in its fate, and comic in its existence.*"
>
> —George Santayana, philosopher, essayist, poet (1863–1952)

### Mark Your Calendar

Winter; year-round in Maine

### Details, Details

- The size of a big sparrow; 6¼ inches
- The similar white-winged crossbill has two flashy white bars on black wings.
- Female is grayish green

### Listen Up!

- Mechanical trilling song, often sung in chorus by flock
- Thin, weak call notes

### Telltale Traits

- Travels in groups
- Uses beak and feet like parrot to crawl on branches
- Very approachable

### Look Here

- Extracting seeds from conifer cones with that remarkable bill

### Or Here

- At feeder
- In trees

*On the Home Front* Crossbills nest only in the northern parts of this region. • The nest is built in a pine, cedar, spruce, or other conifer, and cozily lined with moss, feathers, and fur. • Parents feed nestlings for weeks after they fledge, until their beaks cross into the shape that allows them to efficiently extract seeds from cones.

**Did someone say comical? Take a gander at the beak on the red crossbill, and you may think you're looking at Nature's sense of humor. Not so. It may look funny to us, but it's actually a serious tool for slipping between the scales of a pinecone and extracting the nutritious seeds.**

**Wild Menu:** Seeds of conifer cones; also other tree seeds and buds; insects

**Plant Picks:** Any conifer native to your area; pines (*Pinus* spp.) are fast-growing

### Feeder Pleasers

- Sunflower seeds; suet and other fat-based foods

### Tricks and Treats

- Even in the dead of winter, birds enjoy fresh water. Invest in a heater for your birdbath, or set out a shallow container of warm water for a short-term solution.
- If you live in nesting territory, offer soft materials such as feathers or a scrap from an old fur coat.
- Crossbills, like other northern finches, are huge fans of salt. Try some rock salt in an open tray feeder.

## Here Today, Gone Tomorrow

If somebody invites you to come over and see the flock of crossbills in her backyard, drop everything and get going! These birds are sporadic wanderers; there's no guarantee they'll be at the same place tomorrow. And when one leaves, the whole flock picks up and goes. A chance to admire these oddballs is worth putting other responsibilities off 'til tomorrow. Errands will wait, but the crossbills might not. Oh, and don't forget your camera.

# American Tree Sparrow

## First Impression

**Small brown bird with reddish cap and dark spot on breast**

### Mark Your Calendar

Winter

### Details, Details

- Sparrow size, of course; 6¼ inches
- Female looks like male
- Reddish stripe at eye (an "eye line")

### Listen Up!

- Talks with others in a musical twitter, *teedle-eet, teedle-eet*
- High, sweet, warbling song not usually heard in winter

### Telltale Traits

- Often in small flocks
- Bounding, zigzagging flight when crossing open space—hard for predators to follow

### Look Here

- In feeder or on ground beneath it

### Or Here

- Hanging on stems, eating weed seeds and grass seeds in garden beds
- Scratching for dropped seeds on the ground in flower beds or brushy places

### On the Home Front
A winter visitor only
• Nests way up North, near Santa Claus's homeland • Despite the name of "tree sparrow," the birds build their nests on the ground in the tundra.

*"I once had a sparrow alight upon my shoulder for a moment, while I was hoeing in a village garden … "*

—**Henry David Thoreau (1817–1862)**

**He continues: " … and I felt that I was more distinguished by that circumstance than I should have been by any epaulet I could have worn." Maybe this winter a tree sparrow will sit on *your* shoulder?**

**Wild Menu:** Seeds of weeds, grasses, and sedge; some insects

**Plant Picks:** Plant a few handfuls of finch mix or white proso millet to make these little guys happy all winter long. They'll clean off the seeds of any weeds you may've missed, too.

### Feeder Pleasers

- Millet, by a mile
- Finch mix

### Tricks and Treats

- A heated birdbath is the ultimate tree sparrow spa. An electric birdbath heater will pay you back with entertainment all winter long.

## The Winter Chippy

You'll soon learn to glance at the breast of your sparrow visitors to verify the dark spot or "stickpin" that marks the plain breast of the tree sparrow. Without that dot, this little bird looks almost the same as its summertime cousin, the chipping sparrow, a favorite friend in the backyard.

But chipping sparrows ("chippies" for short) leave town when winter rolls in. That leaves the feast of seeds in your yard to the tree sparrow, or "winter chippy."

# Field Sparrow

*First Impression*

**Small brown bird with blank, wide-eyed look**

### Mark Your Calendar

Spring through fall; year-round in southerly part of region

### Details, Details

- Small sparrow size, what else? 5¾ inches
- Pink bill
- Reddish cap and white eye ring; no dark spot on breast
- Female looks like male

### Listen Up!

- Plaintive *see-a, see-a, see-a, see-a, wee, wee, wee, wee*
- Sharp, short *chip!* of alarm

### Telltale Traits

- Vigorous scratcher on ground
- Often in flocks of mixed sparrow species

### Look Here

- On ground beneath feeder, or in tray feeder

### Or Here

- Scratching elsewhere in your yard for seeds, in flower beds or vegetable garden
- Hanging on weed or grass stems to reach seeds

*On the Home Front* Nests in thicket or thorny bush, usually in field but possibly in backyard • Well-made cup of dead grasses is placed on or near ground • Once called "huckleberry bird" for habit of nesting in those bushes

*"There is not a sprig of grass that shoots uninteresting to me."*

—Thomas Jefferson, American naturalist, gardener, and US president from 1801 to 1809

**What's so special about a sparrow? Everything! Once you begin looking at birds, you'll find out that every species, even the commonest sparrow, can keep you fascinated for hours. There's not a single boring creature under the sun.**

**Wild Menu:** Insects; weed and grass seeds

**Plant Picks:** A scattering of millet seed in your vegetable garden or flower bed will give you hours of fun, watching field sparrows and other sparrows at the stalks. No need to buy special seed; just plant some of your birdseed.

**Feeder Pleasers**
- Millet; canary seed and other small seeds

**Tricks and Treats**
- Like other winter sparrows, the field sparrow appreciates a warm bath on a cold day. Check out a heater for your birdbath.
- Nests are often lined with horsehair from the animal's mane or tail. Ask at a nearby stable for the currycomb leavings if you don't have your own trusty steed.

## Bird Barometer

The number of sparrows at your feeder is a quick clue to the weather. Field sparrows and others will arrive in force at your feeder just before a snow or ice storm sweeps in. Apparently they can feel the change in air pressure, or perhaps some other clue alerts them to stock up in case food might soon be in short supply.

After a snow, field sparrows won't wait for you to clear off the feeders. They'll scratch deep holes to reach buried seed in a tray or on the ground. I once watched a field sparrow taking turns with a larger fox sparrow in the little clearing they'd managed to make after a snow—it only had room for one bird at a time.

# Purple Finch

*First Impression*

**Small raspberry-red bird with alert look**

### Mark Your Calendar

Year-round

### Details, Details

- The size of a sparrow; 6 inches
- More intense all-over color and stouter than a house finch
- Female is streaky brown with distinctive light eye stripe

### Listen Up!

- Fast, rising and falling, warbled song
- Call note is a sharp metallic *tick!*

### Telltale Traits

- Can raise head feathers for an almost crested effect
- An erratic wanderer; some years may bring many, other years only a few

### Look Here

- At tray or tube feeder

### Or Here

- In trees

*On the Home Front* Nests in spruces and other conifers, often high aboveground • Often adds bits of shed snakeskin to nest • Nest lined with hair, wool, or other fine fibers

*"Eats many of the seeds of the most destructive weeds"*

—Edward Forbush, *Useful Birds and Their Protection* (1913)

Snifflers of America, rejoice! Ragweed seeds are a favorite of the purple finch. Small finches (and their cousins, the sparrows) do a gargantuan job of destroying future weeds. As with everything in nature, it's always a matter of balance.

**Wild Menu:** Seeds of trees and weeds; tree buds; some berries

**Plant Picks:** Red maple (*Acer rubrum*), birch (*Betula* spp.), conifers, sunflowers (*Helianthus annuus*), raspberries or blackberries

### Feeder Pleasers

- Sunflower seeds; finch mix

### Tricks and Treats

- Northern finches, of which this is one, are fond of salt—and also of the mortar used in brickwork. Put a small handful of rock salt into an open tray feeder, or set up a salt block.
- Purple finches usually retreat to the woods to raise their families. But if your yard is nearby, or has large conifers that might be considered for nest sites, try offering soft materials, such as tufts of natural wool, for lining.
- Birdbaths are popular year-round with purple finches.

*Lover's Dance*

A tango looks tame compared to the male purple finch's courtship dance routine.

When ardor grabs hold, the male flutters his wings vigorously while hopping and contorting. He thrusts out his breast, cocks his tail up, raises his crest feathers, and sings a love song, often while holding out a bit of nesting material to his beloved—just to help her get the hint, I suppose. Eventually, he's so overcome that he flies up, comes back down, and poses with drooping wings, tail propped, and head tilted to the sky.

Who could resist?

# Chapter Eight

# Birds of the Far North

So you live in the land of cold, snowy winters? Lucky you! Your region is home to many fabulous birds, including redpolls and tundra species that move in when they need a respite from homelands even farther north.

You get to see a whole other world of birds that other people only dream about. Meanwhile, birds such as crossbills, which folks in milder climes can only hope to host during an irregular irruption year, are yours to enjoy as nesters and summer residents.

## WATER, WATER EVERYWHERE

This region is swimming in water. There are the Great Lakes, for starters, then countless smaller and shallower lakes formed by gla-

ciers. Freshwater marshes called "prairie potholes" dot the landscape in some areas, too. And you can't go far without finding a river, stream, or creek.

## Add Heat and Wait

Summers are warm here. Add that heat to all that water, and you have the perfect breeding ground for one of the North's most famous "assets"—insects.

Millions of insects live in the water when immature, spending months creeping around on the bottoms of ponds and lakes. When warm weather comes, they emerge from the water, hatching into airborne hordes of black flies, mosquitoes, and the notorious no-see-ums.

Those insects make us slap and swear,

especially when we forget the repellent. But birds have another reaction: Yum!

## A Bounty of Birds

Those tiny bugs bring hordes of birds into this region. Tiny wood warblers, svelte waxwings, and many other species flock to the feast of winged insects. Toss in the caterpillars and other bugs among the branches of the region's many trees, and you have ideal habitat for insect-eating birds and their nesting families.

## Room to Stretch

The northern tier of states is sparsely populated compared to many other regions of the United States. Cities are few and generally far

**Snow can be frequent, deep, and drifting.**

**Canada or gray jays may visit your yard.**

between. Homesteads are generously sized, with acres of elbow room. Small towns dot the landscape, and cows graze on the lush grass of dairy farms. Countless clear blue lakes and ponds, from "pothole"-size to acres-wide, are dotted across the land, many of them fringed by wild rice and rushes.

Why are there so few people in such an idyllic place?

Winter, in a word.

## COLD CALLS THE TUNE

You'll need your mittens and your warmest coat when you live in the North. Winter is the defining quality of this region, where snow comes early and stays late. You're probably used to a thermometer that reads below zero, and so are your birds.

A challenging climate calls for specialized birds. In the North, you'll enjoy species that can make the most of conditions that would leave less well-adapted birds begging for mercy.

Here's where cold-hardy birds, including boreal chickadees and Canada jays, are thoroughly at home. Their diet and their dense feathers make them able to withstand the worst Mother Nature can dish out.

Although you'll find many of the familiar friends of the "Start Here" chapter in this region, you'll also see other wonderful birds that you can call your own.

## THE LAY OF THE LAND

Fragrant balsam firs and other conifers thrive in this region, filling forests big and small, and springing up fast on any open patch of ground. Elegant white birches gleam against the dark-needled evergreen boughs.

Tree seeds—including a bounty of conifer cones—provide many a meal for nuthatches, crossbills, and other northern birds. Their big advantage is that these seeds stay above the snow, unlike weed and grass seeds.

In fall, the woods come alive with the foliage of golden birches, flaming maples, and other deciduous trees. In spring, if you're

**Lakes and ponds provide abundant insects for birds of the North. So do the forests.**

lucky, you may come across a knee-high patch of drop-dead-gorgeous pink lady's slippers (*Cyprideum acaule*).

Forests are one big feature of the North. But water is just as important.

Parts of the Far North are promoted as vacation hot spots: The turbulent water of the Wisconsin River at the Dells, the canoeing areas of Boundary Waters in Minnesota, and other places draw visitors from many miles away.

Even avian vacationers get into the act. To birds of the extreme North, up near the Arctic Circle, the Far North must feel like Hawaii. In some winters, those extreme northern species, such as Bohemian waxwings, pine grosbeaks, and redpolls, show up here in huge numbers.

**Showy ladyslipper orchids glow in the woods.**

## INSECT HEAVEN

All those lakes and creeks for canoeing make the North a haven for water lovers. Don't forget to count insects among those fans. Many bugs spend part of their lives underwater, emerging into the air as hungry adults.

The North is famous for its swarms of pesky insects, including mosquitoes. In Roseville, Minnesota, you can take in the "Bluegrass Buzz," a festival that celebrates music *and* mosquitoes.

In other, more heavily populated regions, and in places with big agriculture, pesticide use is common. But in the wide-open North, pesticide use is relatively restrained. That's another reason why the region is a haven for insects—and the birds that eat them.

Many migrant birds, especially tiny wood warblers, are thick in the North. The insects they depend upon are wildly abundant here—*slap! slap!*

## BIRD LIFE IN THE NORTH

Birds are abundant in this region.

Some backyard birds, including feeder regulars such as blue jays and downy woodpeckers, are year-round friends here.

Others, including the song sparrow and American goldfinch, are only warm-weather friends in the *brrrr!* North. In other regions, these birds are at home year-round.

Bird populations may shift from year to year in this region, because so many species depend on tree seeds—one of the few bird foods that remains accessible above deep snow. When the cone crop is slim, many birds depart southward. That's when bird lovers in other regions look out their window and exclaim, "Oh, look! Pine grosbeaks!"

**Include evergreens for shelter in your yard.**

Familiarize yourself with those common and abundant "Start Here" birds to get to know your most basic backyard friends. These are the birds you share with other parts of the country—chickadees, white-breasted nuthatches, tufted titmice, goldfinches, juncos, cedar waxwings, and many others. Then dive into the regional specialties here.

## Regional Specialties

You'll find other favorite friends spotlighted in this regional section. Some of these birds also occur in other regions. But every single one of them may turn up in your northern backyard.

Be sure to page through the birds of the Northeast, Midwest, and West, too. Many of them pay a brief visit to northern backyards as they pass through on migration to and from more southern areas.

### Start Here

The North shares many of the birds in Chapter 6, "Start Here," with other regions.

## Birds of the Far North

Here are the birds you'll find in this chapter. Remember to consult the "Start Here" birds, starting on page 79, for the most common birds to be found in the Far North.

# Black-Backed Woodpecker

*First Impression*
### Medium-size black woodpecker

**FAR NORTH**

**Mark Your Calendar**

Year-round

**Details, Details**

- Robin size; 9½ inches
- Glossy black has blue sheen in right light.
- Male has bright yellow patch on crown
- Only has three toes; the bird lacks the second back toe.
- Resembles the three-toed woodpecker, but back is solid black instead of barred

**Listen Up!**

- Loud, sharp, *peek!* call
- Has a "scream-rattle-snarl" warning call. Easy to imagine!
- Long bouts of drumming with beak, starting slow but accelerating

**Telltale Traits**

- Flakes off bark as well as digs into wood
- Tame and easy to approach
- Awkward climber; may hop on ground
- Flies with typical woodpecker style: a wing flap followed by a bound

**Look Here**

- In irruption years, may show up in backyard or visit feeder

**Or Here**

- On conifers
- Foraging on logs
- On burned trees; listen for their calls.

*On the Home Front* Nests relatively high, in live or dead trees, especially conifers

*"One bird will annually destroy 13,675 of these grubs"*

—**Foster Beal, "Food of the Woodpeckers of the United States" (1911)**

**Black-backed woodpeckers are eating machines when it comes to the larvae of wood-boring beetles. They help keep forests from being overwhelmed by wood eaters.**

**Wild Menu:** Mostly larvae of wood-boring and other beetles, and a few other insects; acorns; small fruits

**Plant Picks:** During irruption, may visit a backyard conifer

**Feeder Pleasers**
- Try mealworms or suet

**Tricks and Treats**
- Plant a conifer native to your area.

*Safety Glasses?*

This woodpecker is one of the hardest-pecking birds around. Most woodpeckers keep their tails propped against the tree while pecking, but this guy gives such a strong whack that its tail actually lifts up for even more leverage.

Got a headache already? Not the woodpecker, which has special head bones that absorb the shock. The black-backed woodpecker does take one precaution: It closes its eyes when whacking wood, which helps protect them from flying splinters.

# Hairy Woodpecker

*First Impression*

**A big "downy woodpecker" with a long, heavy bill**

### Mark Your Calendar

Year-round

### Details, Details

- Almost as big as a robin; 9¼ inches
- Female lacks red patch on head

### Listen Up!

- Sharp, loud, *peek!*
- Long bursts of very fast drumming with beak

### Telltale Traits

- Less often seen than the common downy woodpecker
- Never on mullein or other weed stalks, unlike downy woodpecker
- Often flakes off pieces of bark, a giveaway to its location overhead
- Sticks close to mature forests in summer; wanders about in fall and winter and may show up in backyards

### Look Here

- On tree trunk or large branch, often of dead wood

### Or Here

- At suet feeder

*On the Home Front* Drills a cavity high or low; excavation takes 1 to 3 weeks • The cavity is used for roosting, too: In Minnesota, the winter temperature inside averaged a whopping 37.4°F to 42.8°F warmer than the temperature of the tree surface outside.

> *"They utter a soft 'puirr, puirr'"*
>
> —Charles Bendire,
> *Life Histories of North American Birds* (1895)

Baby woodpecker voices are the best clue to locating a nest hole. When you hear their unusual noises, try to track them down. But don't disturb them, or you'll miss out on the fun of watching the family grow up and leave home.

**Wild Menu:** Insects drilled from wood; acorns and nuts; a small amount of fruit

**Plant Picks:** Blackberries or raspberries

**Feeder Pleasers**

- Suet; mealworms and other insect foods; nuts and peanut-butter-based concoctions

**Tricks and Treats**

- It may take a while before a hairy investigates, but once it does, it'll be a firm fan of mealworms at your feeder.
- Rig up a harness of string or wire and hang a big, meaty bone with marrow intact. A ham bone is perfect for winter woodpecker feeding, if not exactly picturesque.

## Telltale Tapping

Sometimes I don't know which I depend on more—my eyes or my ears. Listening has led me to many a woodpecker I never would've noticed just by looking. Even the big hairy is surprisingly well camouflaged against bark.

Listen for repeated tapping—much softer than drumming—and you may find a hairy, downy, or even a chickadee working away. Listen for the patter of something falling to the ground, and you're likely to track down a hairy at work, flaking off pieces of bark.

# Gray Jay

## First Impression

Tame, curious, large gray bird, like a giant chickadee

### Mark Your Calendar

Year-round

### Details, Details

- Bigger than a robin; 11½ inches
- Male and female look alike
- Plumage varies in different areas; head may be dark or whitish

### Listen Up!

- Soft, whistled notes, not at all like a typical jay's screeches and squawks
- When alarmed or squabbling, the "jay-ness" comes out in a harsh rattle.

### Telltale Traits

- Delightfully tame
- Hangs out in small groups
- Curious; investigates anything out of the ordinary, probably in hopes of food

### Look Here

- At feeder—or on your hand

### Or Here

- Nearby! They flock to people to see what's going on, and often follow us through the woods.

## On the Home Front

Nests very early, when it's still cold and snowy • Nests on branch of conifer, near trunk, at low to high levels • Breaks off dead twigs from branches for nest material; doesn't pick them up from ground

*"The boldest of all our birds"*

—Manly Hardy (now, there's a name!), *Life Histories of North American Birds* (1895)

**Gray jays will be your best friends forever—if you give them a bite to eat now and then. They'll eat out of your hand with very little coaxing. Or off of your hat, or from your picnic plate, or out of your lunch bag, or anywhere they can find accessible edibles.**

**Wild Menu:** Carrion and small rodents; caterpillars and other insects; wild fruit; and just about anything else they can get down their gullets

**Plant Picks:** Conifers native to your area for cover, and oaks (*Quercus* spp.) or Virginia creeper (*Parthenocissus quinquefolia*) for food

### Feeder Pleasers

- Suet; meaty soup bones; bread and other scraps; dog food

### Tricks and Treats

- Offer facial tissues and cotton puffs for nest materials; the birds may take them right from your hands if they happen to be building nearby.

## King-Size Comforter

*Brrr!* There's nothing like a downy quilt on a cold winter night! Within minutes, the air from your body is trapped between the feathers, and you feel as if you're floating in a cozy cloud.

The same principle keeps gray jay babies from freezing—in fact, it keeps them snug and warm. Mama jay stuffs silken moth cocoons into the chinks between the twigs that form the foundation of her nest. Then she builds a deep, insulating cup of feathers or fur inside it. One nest that was dissected and inventoried contained 437 feathers, mostly those of ruffed grouse—a fine substitute for an expensive eiderdown quilt!

# Boreal Chickadee

## First Impression

**A gray and brown (not black), super-friendly chickadee**

### Mark Your Calendar

Year-round

### Details, Details

- Chickadee-dee-dee size; 5½ inches
- Female and male look alike

### Listen Up!

- Wheezy, distinctive call, not the classic; says *yesterdaaay* or *fee-lay-dee* in a chickadee voice
- Also a clear trill and a single, sharp, *dee!* note

### Telltale Traits

- Like the typical chickadee: swinging from branch tips, flitting through foliage
- Always on the move
- But usually in a small group of like members; doesn't often pal around with other species like the black-capped chickadee does

### Look Here

- At feeder

### Or Here

- Branch tips and among foliage of conifers
- At conifer cones, often high up in balsam firs or other trees

**On the Home Front** Uses both conifers and deciduous trees • Usually nests low, less than 10 feet aboveground • One week after leaving the nest, fledglings are already adept at hanging from branch tips like their parents.

*"Chick-chick"*

—Old common name in parts of Canada

Tamest of all the chickadees, this friendly little mite is a favorite with northerners. Old timers (and some folks today) call it the chick-chick or fillady. The names reflect the calls the little bird frequently makes.

**Wild Menu:** Insects; conifer cone seeds; other seeds

**Plant Picks:** Any native conifer; annual sunflowers (*Helianthus annuus*)

### Feeder Pleasers

- Suet; sunflower seeds; mealworms and other insect foods; peanut butter and other fats

### Tricks and Treats

- Offer nesting materials, such as sphagnum moss, deer fur, rabbit fur, or any other soft materials, in a clean wire suet cage.

## Saving for a Snowy Day

Winters are long in the North Woods, but this little bird has adopted a way to get through most of the lean times: It hides food in nooks and crannies, to retrieve later.

Even insects it has caught and killed are put aside for a snowy day. Most are the caterpillars of moths and butterflies, but researchers have even found the birds setting up a stash of aphids.

Like other birds of this region, boreal chickadees are an irruption species: Sometimes they move south, especially when the conifer crop is scanty and the pantry is bare.

# Ruby-Crowned Kinglet

## First Impression

**Tiny, hyperactive, grayish bird with wide-eyed look, fluttering at branches**

### Mark Your Calendar

Spring through fall in some areas; migration only in others

### Details, Details

- Smaller than a chickadee; 4¼ inches
- Distinct whitish eye ring
- Female lacks the male's ruby crown

### Listen Up!

- Song is a lively melody of high, clear, whistled notes, falling in pitch near the end
- Call note is a husky *jit,* easy to recognize

### Telltale Traits

- Always in motion; even more nervous in habit than golden-crowned kinglet
- Tame and easily approached
- Constantly flicks wings
- Often forages as part of a mixed flock of chickadees and others
- Jerky, undulating flight

### Look Here

- Fluttering at branch tips of conifers

### Or Here

- Among foliage of any trees or shrubs, often at eye level or low to ground
- May visit nectar feeder

**On the Home Front** Nests mid-level to high in conifers, especially spruce • Builds a deep, narrow, hanging nest; only the tail tip of the female is visible when she's in it

*"One of our most brilliant songsters"*

—A. C. Bent, *Life Histories of North American Thrushes, Kinglets, and Their Allies* **(1939)**

This is one of our tiniest birds, but with one of the loudest voices. Bradford Torrey described it in 1885 as "a prolonged and varied warble, introduced and often broken into, with delightful effect, by a wrennish chatter."

**Wild Menu:** Insects

**Plant Picks:** Any native short-needled conifer, or any native small tree, evergreen or deciduous, will host the insects these birds seek.

### Feeder Pleasers

- A rare visitor, but try mealworms or other insect foods; may visit nectar feeders

### Tricks and Treats

- Avoiding pesticides is the best thing you can do for tiny kinglets. No extra inducement is needed when your yard has insects to offer.

## Migration Music

Fabulous birds are everywhere during spring migration, and I'm constantly swinging my binoculars and craning my neck to see who's singing now. With so many birds to look at— rose-breasted grosbeaks! scarlet tanagers! orioles!—it's easy to let kinglets slip by.

Except for their voice. When I hear that remarkable song, I automatically think it must come from a bigger bird, and I start scanning for the singer in the treetops. After way too long, I remember, "Oh, right, it's a *kinglet!*" And there he'll be, right under my gaze, pouring out his heart as beautifully as any "famous" songbird.

# Swainson's Thrush

## *First Impression*

Quiet olive-brown robinlike bird with speckled breast, on ground

### Mark Your Calendar

Spring through fall in some areas; migration only in others

### Details, Details

- Smaller than a robin; 7 inches
- Look for pale eye ring to distinguish from similar thrushes
- Female and male look alike

### Listen Up!

- A long song of repeated phrases, in typical fluting thrush style. One transcriber suggests *whip-poor-will-a-will-e-zee-zee-zee,* rising at the end, and adds helpfully, "sometimes with an extra *a-will.*"
- Piping call note sounds like a spring peeper.

### Telltale Traits

- Often on ground, but also in shrubs and treetops
- Moves around on ground in long, bouncy hops
- May sing at night

### Look Here

- On ground

### Or Here

- At berry bushes

*On the Home Front* Usually nests in shrubs or in young spruce or other conifers, beneath taller trees • Seeks out delicate, lacy, skeletonized leaves to use in the lining of its mossy, grassy cup • Female is very wary when approaching the nest, giving nervous *whit* calls.

*"These birds easily escape observation"*

—**Frank Chapman,** *A Handbook of the Birds of Eastern North America* (1924)

**Plant its favorite berry bushes and you may get to be friends with this quiet-colored thrush. By the way, Chapman, one of America's premier ornithologists, dedicated his handbook in this way: "to my mother, who has ever encouraged her son in his natural history studies."**

**Wild Menu:** Berries; insects; snails

**Plant Picks:** Blackberries and raspberries; for migrants, shrubs and trees with fall-ripening berries, including spicebush (*Lindera benzoin*), flowering dogwood (*Cornus florida*), shrubby native dogwoods (*Cornus* spp.), and many others

### Feeder Pleasers

- Doesn't usually visit feeders, but it may like mealworms and other insect foods

### Tricks and Treats

- Offer moss for nest building.
- May visit a birdbath, particularly one near the ground

## *Love at First Song*

Seems like every bird lover has a favorite thrush. For me, it's the Swainson's, which I often think of by an earlier name, the olive-backed thrush.

It was twilight on a soft spring day when a sweet, plaintive, spiraling song rose from the ravine I was following. Soon I heard a faint, fluting echo, equally sweet and mellow, then another and another. Swainson's thrushes were all around, making magic in the gathering dusk. That was it—I was in love.

# Eastern Bluebird

*First Impression*

**Unbelievable blue that takes your breath away**

### Mark Your Calendar

Spring through fall

### Details, Details

- Smaller than a robin, as big as a large sparrow; 7 inches
- Female is duller, looks faded

### Listen Up!

- Sweet, gurgling, whistled *tru-a-ly, tru-a-ly!*
- Brief, husky, *chew* call note that seems to keep birds in touch

### Telltale Traits

- Travels in short, slow, fluttering swoops from one perch to another
- Often glides from low perch to ground with wings spread, to catch insects

### Look Here

- Perched near or in open areas, often near the edge of a woods or orchard

### Or Here

- In golf courses, cemeteries, large parks, or pastures, or on roadsides
- At apples, crab apples, and other flowering trees, picking off insects at blossoms
- At feeders or birdbaths

*On the Home Front* Nests in natural cavity or nest box • The female alone builds the nest. You may see a male carrying nesting material, but this "nest demonstration display" actually hinders the female's progress. • Nest is often made entirely of grasses or pine needles

*"Somewhere there's a bluebird of happiness"*

—From the song "Bluebird of Happiness," recorded by Art Mooney & His Orchestra (1948)

Happiness, indeed. Introduced at Radio City Music Hall, the song produced a best-selling record for Mooney and friends. Bluebirds seem to be irresistible, no matter what they're selling.

**Wild Menu:** Insects; fruit and berries

**Plant Picks:** Flowering trees; small fruits, including mulberries, serviceberries (*Amelanchier* spp.), winterberry and evergreen hollies (*Ilex* spp.), Virginia creeper (*Parthenocissus quinquefolia*), flowering dogwood (*Cornus florida*)

**Feeder Pleasers**

- Mealworms and other insect foods; accessible suet, peanut butter mixed with cornmeal, and other fat-based foods

**Tricks and Treats**

- The sound of trickling water is a big draw.
- Put up a roost box for bluebirds to stay at night.

## Enemy No. 1: Jack Frost

Cold weather is the culprit in many bluebird deaths. Thousands of these pretty birds have died due to extreme cold, which may swoop in after the birds come back in spring.

Just as bad are spring snowstorms and ice storms, which prevent the birds from eating. You can help in tough times by keeping your feeder stocked with high-fat foods, such as peanut butter and finely chopped suet, so bluebirds don't waste precious calories to forage.

# Bohemian Waxwing

## *First Impression*

**Plump, sleek, taupe bird, very tame, one of a flock**

### Mark Your Calendar

Winter, all areas except W near Canadian border, where it's year-round

### Details, Details

- Smaller than a robin; 8¼ inches
- Get out your binocs! Like the cedar waxwing, this bird is beautiful in every detail. Look for the white wing patches and rusty patch under the tail that set it apart from the similar cedar waxwing.
- Female looks like male

### Listen Up!

- Trilled *screee* calls similar to cedar waxwing

### Telltale Traits

- Almost always in flocks, small or large
- Very tame
- May be mixed with a flock of cedar waxwings; check for a bigger bird in their midst
- Wanders sporadically in winter
- Expert at fly-catching: flying from a perch to nab an insect, then returning to perch

### Look Here

- At berry bushes, eating berries

### Or Here

- At feeder
- Perched with a flock in a tree
- Fly-catching from a perch

*On the Home Front* Nests far to the N, from Canada to Alaska • Usually nests near lake or stream, in swampy areas, or near beaver ponds

*"The very incarnation of peace and harmony"*

—Neltje Blanchan,
*Bird Neighbors* (1904)

Unexpected and unpredictable, Bohemian waxwings may descend upon your city or backyard in winter, in flocks great or small. Windows are a danger to these gentle Northland birds, which aren't accustomed to the deceptive reflections of the glass.

**Wild Menu:** Fruits; buds; insects, including many mosquitoes

**Plant Picks:** Fruits and berries that linger into winter, including hollies (*Ilex* spp.), junipers (*Juniperus* spp.), hawthorns (*Crataegus* spp.), mountain ashes (*Sorbus* spp.), crab apples (*Malus* cvs.)

### Feeder Pleasers

- Dried fruit, raisins, possibly apples cut in half

### Tricks and Treats

- Plant a mixed hedge to pack lots of fruits and berries into your yard.

## *Friendly One in the Family*

If you approach cedar waxwings slowly and quietly, they may let you walk right up to the bush where they're feeding. But their Bohemian cousins make cedar waxwings look like snobs. Like many birds of the Far North, Bohemians are unbelievably tame.

   The very first one I saw, mixed in a flock of cedar waxwings scarfing down mountain ash berries, came right to my hand when I held out a branch of berries. The next one landed on my head when I was filling the feeders!

# Bay-Breasted Warbler

*First Impression*

**Quick, pretty little bird boldly marked with rusty brown**

### Mark Your Calendar

Migration in most of region; spring through fall along northern tier near Canadian border

### Details, Details

- Chickadee size; 5½ inches
- Two noticeable white wing bars and white corners of tail, visible in flight
- Female is greenish with a flush of rusty red along sides

### Listen Up!

- Short, high, thin, monotone trill: *tee-te, tee-te, tee-te, tee tee tee*
- Typical warbler call note: a sharp *chip!*

### Telltale Traits

- Active, darting movements amid foliage
- Rarely see more than one at a time, usually among other warbler species
- Tame and unsuspicious; will allow you to approach—but most likely will have moved on before you can do so

### Look Here

- Usually in treetops of deciduous trees, moving quickly through foliage

### Or Here

- With a "wave" of other warblers, often in a group that includes blackpoll warblers

*On the Home Front* Nests in very northern edge of region, then northward into Canada
- Builds fragile nest on limb of spruce, balsam fir, or other dense conifer

*"Little Chocolate-Breasted Titmouse"*

—Name bestowed upon the bay-breasted warbler by Alexander Wilson in *American Ornithology* (1832)

No matter what you call it, this pretty little bird is always a treat to see. In *The Warblers of North America* (1907), Frank Chapman described this species as "among the rarer Warblers the mere sight of which is stimulating."

**Wild Menu:** Insects; it's a major eater of spruce budworms

**Plant Picks:** Spruces and other conifers host its natural insect foods, but it may visit any tree in your yard during migration.

**Feeder Pleasers**
- Not a feeder visitor

**Tricks and Treats**
- Trees, to provide a safe corridor for travel and plenty of snacking on the go, are all you need to boost your chances with this little guy.

## Happy Family

If you could watch a family of bay-breasted warblers at home, you'd see some heartwarming behavior. The pair of birds is devoted to their nest and to each other. While the female sits on her eggs, the male serenades her from a nearby treetop—and sometimes she sings back to him. During heavy rain and on hot days, the female stands in the nest, shielding her babies with outstretched wings.

# Blackburnian Warbler

*First Impression*

A tiny, active bird with a vivid orange head and throat, quickly moving through foliage

## Mark Your Calendar

Spring through fall in many areas; migration only in others

## Details, Details

- Chickadee size; 5 inches
- Body is streaky black and white, with white lower belly
- Female is yellower instead of deep orange

## Listen Up!

- Super-high wheezy notes that sound as if they should be on a secret "dogs only" whistle—*tsi-tsi-tsi* and so on
- Typical warbler *chip* call note

## Telltale Traits

- Striking color is the best clue.
- Like most warblers, constantly in motion, gleaning insects as it moves through trees

## Look Here

- Often in hemlocks

## Or Here

- Hopping through foliage of conifers or deciduous trees
- Foraging with a mixed group of chickadees, kinglets, and other small birds

*On the Home Front* Builds nest in conifers, especially hemlocks or occasionally spruces
- Dense cup of twigs, rootlets, fibrous lichens, and soft materials

## "The hemlock warbler"

—John James Audubon, on the female Blackburnian, in *Birds of the Connecticut Valley in Massachusetts* (1937)

Warblers were tough for early ornithologists to get a handle on—the birds traveled so far, the sexes looked so different, and their plumage and habits changed from one season to another. Audubon thought the female was a different species and called it the hemlock warbler. "Blackburnian" is for a Mrs. Blackburn, a patron of ornithology who collected stuffed birds.

**Wild Menu:** Insects

**Plant Picks:** Hemlocks, other conifers any deciduous trees

## Feeder Pleasers

- Not a feeder visitor

## Tricks and Treats

- Many warblers appreciate a birdbath during their travels in spring and fall. A mister, drip tube, or other device that creates the sound of moving water may help draw them in.

## Sit Tight!

Years ago, I was lucky enough to find a nest of Blackburnian warblers in a gracious old hemlock tree, within easy reaching distance. The female seemed unperturbed by my presence and stayed sitting on her nest. After several days of observing her, I couldn't resist and reached out a finger to gently stroke her back. She didn't even flinch.

"Never before have I seen a bird harder to flush or more loath to leave the nest," noted R. C. Harlow, cited in *Ecology* (October 1958). Harlow took a slightly different approach than I did: He reported hitting the female several times with small twigs before she flew off. But even after that, he noted, she returned immediately to her eggs.

# Black-Throated Green Warbler

### First Impression

Tiny, active bird with striking black throat and snowy belly, combing the trees with similar greenish yellow birds

### Mark Your Calendar

Spring through fall in many areas; migration only in others

### Details, Details

- Smaller than a chickadee; 5 inches
- Bright yellow face
- Large white corners of tail
- Female is paler and has black only on sides of throat, not in center

### Listen Up!

- Short, high buzzes, sounding like "trees, trees, murmuring trees"
- Sharp *chip!* call note

### Telltale Traits

- Male is tireless singer; when these guys are in your area, you'll know it
- Behaves like most other warblers: fast and active, moving quickly amid foliage
- Males and females are strongly territorial and may attack other trespassing warblers during nesting season.

### Look Here

- Usually hopping quickly through foliage

### Or Here

- Flying from one tree to another
- Hopping on ground
- Perched and singing

*"Trees, trees, murmuring trees"*

—Traditional transliteration of the species' song

Despite their name, warblers are no great shakes as singers. Most have high, wheezy little voices without much melody. Birders use handy phrases to try to sort them out.

On the Home Front Gets down to business soon after arriving in spring • Female chooses a site, usually in a conifer, close to trunk and low to ground • The well-built cup is a pretty thing, with white birch bark woven among twigs held together by spider silk. • Nestlings are so loud you can hear them from hundreds of feet away.

**Wild Menu:** Insects, including many caterpillars

**Plant Picks:** Conifers and deciduous trees, especially insect-rich trees such as spruces and other conifers, birches, willows, oaks

### Feeder Pleasers

- Not a feeder visitor

### Tricks and Treats

- May visit a naturalistic ground-level birdbath basin with a pump or trickling tube

## Tiny Target

Black-throated green warblers are tiny birds, only 5 inches from beak tip to tail tip. Yet, like many warbler species, they're a frequent target of the parasitic brown-headed cowbird.

At 7½ inches long, the cowbird is much larger than an adult warbler—and its babies are bigger, too. Yet the cowbird often deposits an egg into a warbler nest.

And the pint-size adoptive parents obligingly raise the giant without ever seeming to wonder, "Hey, why is Junior so big?"

# Canada Warbler

## *First Impression*

Striking black necklace on bright yellow breast of a small gray bird moving quickly through low foliage

## Mark Your Calendar

Spring through fall in many areas; migration only in others

## Details, Details

- About chickadee size; 5¼ inches
- Yellow spectacle-effect eye ring
- Female has only a faint necklace and lacks black "whiskers" of male

## Listen Up!

- One of the better singers among warblers: a long, loud, clear song of varied notes
- Sharp *chip!* call note

## Telltale Traits

- Cocks tail and flicks wings constantly when foraging
- Feeds mostly in flight, instead of scouring foliage like many other warblers

## Look Here

- Foraging through branches of rhododendron and other understory shrubs, low to ground

## Or Here

- Fly-catching for insects

## *On the Home Front* Not a backyard nester

- Nests in dense cover, including mossy, ferny places, thickets, or rhododendrons • Builds bulky cup of leaves, grass, and bark on or near ground • Like many warblers, reluctant to flush from nest when disturbed • Parasitized by brown-headed cowbird

### *"Listen to that beak snap!"*

—Mary Roth, my mother, watching Canada warblers fly-catch for insects in her yard

Most warblers pick insects off branches, but Canada warblers take to the air, chasing down zigzagging mosquitoes and other fast fliers. Listen hard, and you can hear the wind rushing through their wings as they dash and dart after prey—and the snap of their beak when they snatch it.

**Wild Menu:** Insects, including many mosquitoes

**Plant Picks:** Native shrubs, great for harboring yummy insects, are always a likely pick.

### Feeder Pleasers

- Not a feeder visitor

### Tricks and Treats

- You won't need anything but bountiful bugs to bring this warbler in.

## Sphagnum Specialist

Whenever I find myself stepping on springy, spongy sphagnum moss in a moist northern forest (wet sneakers, anyone?), I start looking for Canada warbler nests. Haven't had any luck so far, no doubt because they're well hidden, often between the roots of a tree that keeled over, or tucked into a mossy lump that looks just like every other mossy lump.

Sphagnum wetlands and bogs are a likely locale for nesting pairs, so keep your eyes open for these little birds where the skunk cabbage grows.

# Mourning Warbler

## First Impression

**Tiny gray bird with gray hood and yellow belly**

### Mark Your Calendar

Spring through fall in many areas; migration only in others

### Details, Details

- About chickadee size; 5¼ inches
- Dark face
- Female has a paler gray hood and face

### Listen Up!

- Short, churring song that sounds something like, *"Kiss me Charlie, Charlie, Charlie"*
- *Chip!* call note

### Telltale Traits

- Creeps around in brush like a wren, giving you only teasing glimpses
- Males often sing from a conspicuous perch

### Look Here

- Near or on ground

### Or Here

- Low in shrubs or brush
- Singing from top of bush or small tree

### On the Home Front Not a backyard nester

- Nests on or near the ground • Well-concealed in dense vegetation, such as horsetail (*Equisetum* spp.), blackberries, or ferns • Like other warblers, parasitized by brown-headed cowbird • Family groups remain together for weeks after young birds leave the nest.

*"Its song is a paean of joy"*

—Edward Forbush, *Birds of Massachusetts and Other New England States* (1929)

**As active as any other warbler, this species gets its name from its coloring, which suggests the once traditional wearing of black crepe by the grief-stricken. But as Forbush wrote, "It seems as happy and active as most birds."**

**Wild Menu:** Insects

**Plant Picks:** Shrubs and shade gardens

### Feeder Pleasers

- Not a feeder visitor

### Tricks and Treats

- A ground-level birdbath with moving water of some sort may attract all kinds of interesting warblers on migration.

## Sneaky Skulker

It's hard to remember to look down when there's so much going on in the trees above during migration. But when you see flocks of mixed warblers moving through your trees in spring, take a look lower down, too. Watch for a quick glimpse of this shy skulker, who sometimes seems like he's playing hide-and-seek with us, hopping in and out of view.

# Scarlet Tanager

*First Impression*
**Brilliant red with black wings**

**Mark Your Calendar**
Spring through fall

**Details, Details**
• Smaller than a robin; 7 inches
• Female is greenish yellow

**Listen Up!**
• Long, hoarse, slurring song

**Telltale Traits**
• Vivid color and beauty are the best ways to ID a tanager.
• Slinks through tree foliage

**Look Here**
• High in trees, usually deciduous and especially oaks

**Or Here**
• At apples, crab apples, and other flowering trees, picking off insects at blossoms
• At your feeder in spring

*On the Home Front* Usually nests in woods
• Loose, shallow nest attached to tree limb, well out from trunk • Often high up, but may be at eye level

*"The appointed guardian of the oaks"*

—Edward Forbush,
*Useful Birds and Their Protection* (1907)

Scarlet tanagers and oak trees go together like red and green for Christmas. Oak trees harbor plentiful insects, including many resting moths, a favorite of tanagers. The birds often use oaks as nest sites, too.

**Wild Menu:** Insects; fruit
**Plant Picks:** Fruits of any kind, particularly sweet or sour cherries and mulberries (*Morus* spp.); early-spring-flowering trees (crab apples, redbuds); flowering dogwood (*Cornus florida*)

**Feeder Pleasers**
• Millet and other birdseed; chopped suet; mealworms and other insect foods

**Tricks and Treats**
• A simple saucer of fresh water is welcomed by tanagers on migration. A naturalistic birdbath with trickling water is even more effective.

*Branching Out* _____

Spectacular scarlet tanagers seem to have a split personality when it comes to filling their bellies. In the wild, they eat almost entirely insects and fruit. In all my years of exploring and observing, I've never once seen one of these birds nibbling at seeds in their natural haunts. But in the backyard, these beautiful birds broaden their menu to include birdseed! Sure, they love mealworms and suet, too, just as you'd expect. But, at least during spring migration, they gobble down millet and seed mix with gusto.

# Red Crossbill

*First Impression*

**Strawberry red, very tame bird—and get a load of that beak!**

### Mark Your Calendar

Year-round; in some areas, winter only

### Details, Details

- The size of a sparrow; 6¼ inches
- Dark wings—but that bill is the only detail you'll need
- Female is grayish green
- The similar white-winged crossbill, also an erratic wanderer, has two white bands across its wings.

### Listen Up!

- Mechanical clicking or trilling song, often sung in chorus by flock
- Thin, weak call notes

### Telltale Traits

- Travels in groups
- Uses beak and feet like a parrot to crawl on branches
- Very approachable

### Look Here

- At conifer cones

### Or Here

- At your feeder
- In trees

*On the Home Front* Depending on when the conifer crop ripens, the birds nest anytime from December to September! • Well-concealed nest is placed in a spruce, pine, or other conifer • Makes good use of nearby materials, including conifer twigs, lichens, and conifer needles.

*"Capricious little visitors"*

—Neltje Blanchan, *Bird Neighbors* (1897)

**Crossbills can't be taken for granted. Their movements are unpredictable, so they may show up in your backyard every day in winter—or not! Enjoy them when you can.**

**Wild Menu:** Seeds of conifer cones; also other tree seeds and buds; insects

**Plant Picks:** Pines, spruces, larches, firs, and other conifers

**Feeder Pleasers**
- Sunflower seeds

**Tricks and Treats**
- Crossbills are greatly fond of salt. Offer a handful of rock salt in your feeding tray when crossbills arrive.

## The Legend of the Crossbill

Crossbills and Christianity? According to an old German legend that American poet Longfellow turned into verse, the bird tried its hardest, but without success, to pull the nails from the Crucifixion cross. Because of its efforts, the crossbill became stained with blood.

*"In the groves of pines it singeth / Songs, like legends, strange to hear"*

—"The Legend of the Crossbill," by Henry Wadsworth Longfellow, in *Longfellow's Poetical Works* (1893)

# Pine Grosbeak

*First Impression*
**Very tame, rosy red bird**

**Mark Your Calendar**
> Winter

**Details, Details**
- A little smaller than a robin; 9 inches
- Blackish wings with white bars
- Female is greenish and gray

**Listen Up!**
- Soft, whistled song
- Quiet call notes keep a flock in touch.

**Telltale Traits**
- Hangs around in small groups
- Very calm and easily approached

**Look Here**
- Eating berries in winter

**Or Here**
- Perched quietly for long periods of time
- At feeder
- In spruce, pine, or other conifers

*On the Home Front* Not a backyard nester
- Nest is well-hidden in dense branches of conifers, usually about eye level or lower
- Like many other northland birds, this one builds its nest out of whatever's close at hand: conifer twigs, rootlets, and grasses, lined with needles, lichen, and a few feathers. • Parents feed young birds a yummy regurgitated paste of vegetable matter and insects.

*"They persistently gourmandize"*

—Neltje Blanchan, *Bird Neighbors* (1897)

Slow-moving pine grosbeaks feature a special adaptation of a throat pouch, which allows them to eat way more at one time than other birds can. Then they sit around digesting. See if you agree with Blanchan, who wrote, "[I]f the truth must be confessed, they appear to be rather stupid and uninteresting."

**Wild Menu:** Tree seeds, seeds from conifer cones, weed seeds; tree buds; fruit; insects

**Plant Picks:** Junipers (*Juniperus* spp.) with berries, barberry (*Berberis* spp.), American bittersweet (*Celastrus scandens*), mountain ash (*Sorbus* spp.), many others

**Feeder Pleasers**
- Sunflower seeds

**Tricks and Treats**
- Pine grosbeaks are a great reason to have a reserve bag of sunflower seeds on hand: Winter flocks may number 100 or more birds!

## Boring? Maybe

But brightening up a winter day, definitely. Even Neltje Blanchan, who seems to have had a low opinion of the birds because of their gluttonous ways and lack of activity, gave them credit for making the winter scene a lot cheerier: "They visit us at a time when we are most inclined to rapture over our bird visitors." Got those sunflower seeds ready?

# Common Redpoll

## First Impression

**Little, plump, streaky bird splashed with red on throat and head**

### Mark Your Calendar

Winter

### Details, Details

- Chickadee size; 5¼ inches
- A small black bib
- Female lacks wash of pinkish red on breast; has only red patch on forehead

### Listen Up!

- Constantly "talking" in trilling, tinkling notes
- Listen for the distinctive *churrrrr* when the flock flies from place to place

### Telltale Traits

- Acrobatic and active
- Exuberant birds, with lilting, bounding flight
- A redpoll or two may mingle among your other finches; or you may be visited by a small or large flock of only redpolls.

### Look Here

- At the feeder

### Or Here

- Gleaning seeds from weeds and grasses
- Deep in a hole in the snow, dug to reach buried seeds
- Hanging acrobatically at branch tips in birches or other trees

### On the Home Front

Not a backyard nester
- Well-built nest is made from fine twigs woven with rootlets and grasses, and lined with a thick layer of feathers or other soft material.

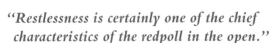

*"Restlessness is certainly one of the chief characteristics of the redpoll in the open."*

—**A. C. Bent**, *Life Histories of North American Cardinals, Grosbeaks, Buntings, Towhees, Finches, Sparrows, and Allies* (1968)

**Watch redpolls in your garden and you'll see that the flock is almost constantly moving. At the feeder, though, redpolls feed calmly for many minutes at a time.**

**Wild Menu:** Seeds; buds; some insects

**Plant Picks:** Birches (*Betulus* spp.); any plants with seeds remaining in your garden, such as seed-rich annual bachelor's buttons (*Centaurea cyanus*), cosmos (*Cosmos bipinnatus*), and zinnias (*Zinnia* spp.); also weeds and grasses

### Feeder Pleasers

- Niger and finch mix; black oil sunflower seeds

### Tricks and Treats

- Like other northern finches, redpolls appreciate an offering of salt.
- Fresh water is always welcome; try providing a heated birdbath.

## Take a Closer Look

Even after years of feeding birds, I'm surprised by how often redpolls slip in without my noticing right away. A few redpolls can easily blend right in among goldfinches, house finches, and pine siskins at my feeders.

The big difference? These birds don't fly away when I come outside to restock feeders. They're so tame—especially when there's snow on the ground—that I sometimes have to shoo them away so I can refill the seed tube.

# American Tree Sparrow

## First Impression

Small, streaky brown bird with reddish cap and dark spot on breast, scratching on ground

### Mark Your Calendar

Winter

### Details, Details

- Sparrow size, of course! 6¼ inches
- Female looks like male
- Reddish stripe at eye ("eye line")

### Listen Up!

- Talks with others in a musical twitter, *teedle-eet, teedle-eet*
- High, sweet, warbling song not usually heard in winter

### Telltale Traits

- Often in small flocks
- Bounding, zigzagging flight when crossing open space—hard for predators to follow

### Look Here

- In feeder or on ground beneath it

### Or Here

- Hanging on stems, eating weed seeds and grass seeds in garden beds
- Scratching for dropped seeds on the ground in flower beds or brushy places

### On the Home Front

Not a backyard nester
- Usually nests on ground in tundra, often in clump of grass near small tree or shrub
- Female gathers nesting material from the general vicinity of the nest and builds nest alone • Nest is kept cozy with an inner ring of fine grass almost half an inch thick, lined with a layer of feathers—usually ptarmigan
- Both parents feed young.

*"Winter chippy"*
—An old name

Tree sparrows look a lot like chipping sparrows, another common backyard bird. But there's one big difference—that dark dot in the middle of their breast. It's often called a "stickpin," and it's the key to telling the species apart. Of course, by the time tree sparrows move into your yard for the winter, chipping sparrows are long gone.

**Wild Menu:** Seeds of weeds, grasses, and sedges; some insects

**Plant Picks:** Plant a few handfuls of finch mix or white proso millet to make these little guys happy all winter long. They'll clean off the seeds of any weeds you may've missed, too.

### Feeder Pleasers

- Millet, by a mile; finch mix

### Tricks and Treats

- A heated birdbath is the ultimate tree sparrow spa. An electric birdbath heater will pay you back with entertainment all winter long.
- Got any lemming fur? How about a snowshoe hare pelt? Put them, or any other fur, out for nesting material possibilities.

## Waste Not, Want Not

Tree sparrows are adept at ferreting out stray seeds. And that's another great reason not to hurry to clean up your garden.

These loyal winter friends appreciate the cover of those dead standing stems, whether they're annuals, perennials, or those weeds that sneaked their way in. Let them stand, and all winter long, you'll see tree sparrows searching for seeds on and below them.

# Fox Sparrow

## First Impression

**Big, plump, rusty sparrow with heavily streaked or speckled breast**

### Mark Your Calendar

Migration only, but still a treat!

### Details, Details

- A big sparrow; 7 inches
- Much geographic variation in color and song; some are redder, grayer, or thicker-billed
- Female looks like male

### Listen Up!

- With 18 subspecies divided into at least four distinct groups, fox sparrows show a lot of variation in song. The group of this region is the red or Taiga fox sparrow, which sings a rich, melodious, whistled song.

### Telltale Traits

- Scratches vigorously on ground; can dig a hole through several inches of snow to reach seeds
- Secretive when not at feeder; stays concealed in brushy areas
- Usually arrives singly at feeder

### Look Here

- On ground beneath feeder

### Or Here

- In or at feeder
- Scavenging seeds from a winter garden or weeds

## On the Home Front Not a backyard nester
- Nests on ground, in low bushes, or in small trees

*"In their search for food they make the snow fly"*

—A. C. Bent, *Life Histories of North American Cardinals, Grosbeaks, Buntings, Towhees, Finches, Sparrows, and Allies* (1968)

**The big fox sparrow is a powerful and determined digger who scratches vigorously to uncover seeds buried in the snow. Often the bird will scratch for buried seeds instead of eating at leisure in the feeder.**

**Wild Menu:** Seeds; insects; fruits

**Plant Picks:** Fall-ripening berries may catch the eye of migrants. Try elderberries (*Sambucus* spp.), burning bush and other euonymus (*Euonymus* spp.), eastern red cedar (*Juniperus virginiana*), pokeweed (*Phytolacca americana*).

**Feeder Pleasers**
- Millet

**Tricks and Treats**
- A birdbath is often welcomed.

## Snow Removal Service

Fox sparrows are great at digging through snow to reach the seeds below. They use their feet like little snow scoops, clawing the snow out of the way. In minutes, they can excavate a surprisingly deep hole.

One morning, after a 6-inch snow, I looked out and saw some smart white-throated sparrows taking advantage of an energetic fox sparrow's efforts. While Foxy dug away, the white-throats gathered behind him, where the excavated snow was piling up, and methodically picked out every bit of millet the fox sparrow was unearthing.

# Clay-Colored Sparrow

*First Impression*

**Small sparrow with plain breast and striped head**

## Mark Your Calendar

Spring through fall

## Details, Details

- A small sparrow; 5½ inches
- Strongly striped head; markings become less distinct once breeding season is over
- Similar to tree sparrow, but without the eye ring that gives that bird its typical wide-eyed look
- Also looks a lot like chipping sparrow; look for the reddish cap of the chippy
- Female looks like male

## Listen Up!

- Rasping, monotone buzzy notes: *zhee zhee zhee*
- Sharp *chip!* alarm note

## Telltale Traits

- Hops on ground
- Hangs out in flocks unless nesting
- Often in large flocks, sometimes with other species, such as Brewer's sparrows in the western part of this region

## Look Here

- At feeder

## Or Here

- In shrubs, hedges, and brushy places
- In garden, eating seeds

*On the Home Front* Nests are usually built low, in snowberry shrubs (*Symphoricarpos albus*). • The nest is made of grass, fine twigs, rootlets, and lots of hair. • More than a third of nests may be parasitized by brown-headed cowbirds.

*"Shrub cover may be a more important factor"*

—J. A. Dechant, "Effects of management practices on grassland birds: clay-colored sparrow" (2004)

**Although this species is often considered a grassland bird, researchers have shown that it prefers areas with shrubs among the grass. Western snowberry and silverberry are its favorites in the wild and in the backyard.**

**Wild Menu:** Seeds; insects

**Plant Picks:** Flowers with many small seeds, including sweet alyssum (*Lobularia maritima*), cockscomb (*Celosia* spp.), amaranth (*Amaranthus* spp.), and others; also weeds and weedy grasses, such as foxtail (*Setaria* spp.)

**Feeder Pleasers**

- Sunflower seeds; cracked corn; millet

**Tricks and Treats**

- Plant shrubs to provide cover to make this sparrow feel at home. Native western snowberry (*Symphoricarpos occidentalis*) and American silverberry (*Elaeagnus commutata*) are perfect candidates.

## The Hand of Man

This sparrow has greatly benefited from human activities—or in this case, the cessation of certain human activities. In olden days, the northern prairie frequently was burned, either by natural or man-made fires. Regular blazes prevented shrubs and trees from gaining a foothold.

Then setting fires was stopped. The grassy prairie grew up into shrubs, creating ideal habitat for the clay-colored sparrow, which expanded its range to take advantage of it.

171

# Purple Finch

## *First Impression*
### Small raspberry-red bird with alert look

*"One of the most delicious songsters"*

—Neltje Blanchan,
*Bird Neighbors* (1897)

### Mark Your Calendar

Year-round, spring through fall, winter only, or migration only, depending on location

### Details, Details

- The size of a sparrow; 6 inches
- More intense all-over color and stouter than a house finch
- Look for the raised feathers on the head, which give the bird an alert look that's different from a house finch.
- Female is streaky brown with distinctive light eye stripe

### Listen Up!

- Fast, rising and falling, warbled song
- Call note is a sharp, metallic *tick!*

### Telltale Traits

- Can raise head feathers for an almost crested effect
- An erratic wanderer; some years may bring many, other years only a few

### Look Here

- At tray or tube feeder

### Or Here

- In trees
- At fruit trees, eating buds or blossoms

*On the Home Front* Nests in spruces and other conifers • Often adds bits of shed snakeskin to nest • Nest lined with hair, wool, or other fine fibers

Called a purple linnet in olden times, this pretty species is quite the vocalist. Often I only get to enjoy the purple finch as a winter visitor, so I miss out on his long, warbling song. If you live where he nests, you may be fortunate enough to hear his full, rich melody.

**Wild Menu:** Seeds of trees and weeds; occasionally tree buds or flowers; some berries

**Plant Picks:** Red maple (*Acer rubrum*), birches (*Betula* spp.), conifers; sunflowers (*Helianthus annuus*); raspberries or blackberries

### Feeder Pleasers

- Sunflower seeds; finch mix

### Tricks and Treats

- Northern finches, of which this is one, are fond of salt—and also of the mortar used in brickwork. Put a small handful of rock salt into an open tray feeder, or set up a salt block.
- Purple finches usually retreat to the woods to raise their families. But if your yard is nearby, or has large conifers that might be considered for nest sites, try offering soft materials, such as tufts of natural wool, for lining.
- Birdbaths are popular year-round with purple finches.

## *Christmas Present*

Growing Christmas trees for sale is big business in the North. Truckloads are cut and shipped to points hundreds of miles away, or mail-ordered across the country.

One year, the Christmas tree we bought held a bird nest like I'd never seen before. After some research, I figured out that the cup of twigs and sticks, lined with animal hair and fur, probably had belonged to a purple finch—who had raised its family in Minnesota or points north. We felt especially honored.

# Yellow-Headed Blackbird

*First Impression*

**Unmistakable! Big black bird with striking yellow hood**

**Mark Your Calendar**

Spring through fall

**Details, Details**

- Smaller than a robin; 9½ inches
- Male flashes white wing patches in flight
- Female is much less dramatic but still has yellow tinge

**Listen Up!**

- Or maybe you should cover your ears—a menagerie of squawks, squeeps, rattles, shrieks, and clacks, plus a noise like a chainsaw

**Telltale Traits**

- Sight alone is enough to positively ID this dramatic bird
- Usually in flocks
- Nervous tail flicks

**Look Here**

- At feeder

**Or Here**

- In marshes with cattails or other reeds
- In winter, turns to grain fields for food. Huge flocks "roll over" fields, the birds in back moving to front as the field is scoured of waste grain.

*On the Home Front* Not a backyard nester, unless you have a large, reed-fringed pond • Nests in colonies, in a marsh • Nests are built within a clump of reeds, and woven from reeds.

*"Xanthocephalus xanthocephalus"*

—Scientific name of yellow-headed blackbird

*Xantho* means yellow; *cephalus* means head. Why repeat the word as both genus and species epithet? No doubt because once just isn't enough to emphasize what an astounding bird this is!

**Wild Menu:** Weed seeds; grain; aquatic insects

**Plant Picks:** Your feeder will keep these birds content.

**Feeder Pleasers**

- Sunflower seeds; cracked corn

**Tricks and Treats**

- A birdbath or water feature may attract a yellow-headed splasher.

## What's That Noise?

We were watching our local colony of nesting yellow-heads when all of a sudden, they simultaneously began making a peculiar harsh rattle. All the usual cacophony halted instantly. No birds were then visible, but the cattail marsh buzzed with this unsettling call.

What could it be, we wondered. Then we sighted a Cooper's hawk—a bird eater—flying through. One of the blackbirds had spotted it when it was still far off and raised the alarm. Scientists call that the "hawk alarm call," and note that it's given only by males.

# Birds of the Southeast and South

# Chapter Nine

The Southeast and South share many bird species with the Northeast and the Midwest. But you also get some species that are mainly at home in the mild climate of your region, such as the charming little brown-headed nuthatch. And you get to enjoy the company of hummingbirds, bluebirds, and many other beloved birds in winter, long after they've retreated from less hospitable regions.

Everyone from chickadees to flamingos is at home here. Gracious old cities, brand-spankin'-new suburbs, small and large farms, and plenty of woods—plus lots of water—supply habitat for a hugely varied population of birds.

Plants grow like mad in this kind of climate, which is great news for gardeners and birds. Insects flourish spectacularly well, too, which is another boon to birds.

## THE LAY OF THE LAND

Long, steamy summers, mild winters, and abundant rain make this region a nearly tropical paradise in some places. The farther south, the more extreme the steam heat, until

175

it becomes subtropical. Coastal marshes and Spanish-moss-draped sloughs are part of the scenery, too, as the highlands relax into plains as they near the sea. The sandy beaches of the Atlantic and the Gulf of Mexico add another element to the region.

Yet, in other parts of this area, you might think you were in New England. The southern Appalachian Mountains pass through several states in this region, providing homes for forest birds. Piney woods and stands of magnificent deciduous trees, such as tulip poplar, sycamore, and sweet gum, plus a plethora of oaks, dominate other parts of the landscape.

**Woodsy streams thread through the Appalachians.**

**Pine cones provide seeds for nuthatches.**

## FOOD AND SHELTER

That immense diversity of habitat means an equal variety of plant life—and that means food choices galore for birds. Wood warblers can thrive on the myriad of insects in the trees, while gnatcatchers flit after gnats in the swamps, and sparrows feast in the fields. Nuthatches and woodpeckers can patrol tree bark for bugs, while tanagers take care of those insects found in treetop foliage. For every niche in this varied landscape, there's a bird ready to take advantage of it.

Trees are rich in insects and insect larvae, a real draw for woodpeckers. Bayberries (*Myrica pensylvanica*) and wax myrtles (*M. cerifera*) supply fall and winter food for tree swallows, waxwings, and yellow-rumped warblers. Swamps offer even more choices, with swarms of mosquitoes and gnats ready for feasting upon.

Rampant growth means plenty of shelter, too. Evergreens are abundant here, and not only conifers: This region is home to spectacular live oaks, magnolias, laurels, and other broad-leaved evergreens, too—all of them adding to the possibilities of year-round cover for backyard birds.

Dense undergrowth of various heights supplies cover that appeals to thrushes, blue grosbeaks, vireos, and sparrows. Vines are another big part of the southern landscape, and birds make good use of them, too. Curtains of ghostly Spanish moss (*Tillandsia usneoides*) supply protection, when birds are moving from place to place or looking for a nesting site.

## CLIMATE

Hot, humid summers seem a small price to pay for winters that often are so mild that you can get by with just a sweater against the nighttime chill. More northerly areas in this region and mountainous locations are much colder, of course, with occasional opportunities for sledding or making a snowman.

In some parts of the region, flowers bloom year-round—and so hummingbirds stay, too. Strong summer storms and drenching rains are common, which can spell trouble for robins' nests and others that may topple from their supporting branches. Occasional ice storms can swoop in, wreaking havoc on trees still carrying a burden of leaves.

This area is winter vacationland for many northerners—including those with feathers. The brown thrasher, eastern bluebird, gray catbird, and oriole leave their summer homes in the more northern states to winter here.

## BIRD LIFE IN THE SOUTHEAST AND SOUTH

Birds are abundant in this region. Most of them spread out to cover other territories besides this one. While this region gets bragging rights for its many fabulous wading birds, such as wood storks and flamingos,

that's not true for birds that visit backyards. Only a handful of backyard bird species are limited to this region.

Nearly all migrants swarm through this region on their way to points north in spring, or when they're retracing their flight in fall. Other species stick around much longer. Many backyard birds, including feeder friends such as cardinals, song sparrows, and downy woodpeckers, are year-round residents in the Southeast. White-crowned sparrows, white-throated sparrows, fox sparrows, and vesper sparrows are here all winter, while chipping sparrows remain all year.

**Bayberries (*Myrica* spp.) are bird favorites.**

## Start Here

Because the Southeast and South are home to so many widespread bird species, you'll want to turn to Chapter 6, "Start Here," to find your most familiar backyard friends.

These are the birds you share with other parts of the country—chickadees, white-breasted nuthatches, tufted titmice, goldfinches, juncos, cedar waxwings, and many others.

Every single one of the "Start Here" birds is happily at home in the Southeast and South.

## Regional Specialties

You'll find other favorite friends spotlighted in this regional section. Some of these birds also occur in other regions. But every single

**Blue grosbeaks may be in shrubs in this region.**

one of them may turn up in your southeastern backyard.

Be sure to page through the birds of the Northeast and Midwest regions, too. Many of them are also at home in your region. Flip through the birds of the Far North, too, because in order to reach those haunts, they'll have to pass through your area during migration.

## Birds of the Southeast and South

Here's a list of the birds you'll find in this chapter. Remember to consult the "Start Here" birds, starting on page 79, for the most common birds to be found in the Southeast and South.

# Red-Bellied Woodpecker

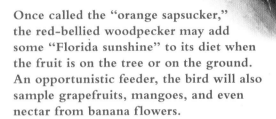

*First Impression*

> Big, calm, red-headed woodpecker at feeder

**Mark Your Calendar**

Year-round

**Details, Details**

- Almost as big as a robin; 9¼ inches
- Female has red only on back of neck, not top of head

**Listen Up!**

- Loud, harsh, querulous *quirrrr?* as if asking, "Where's my food?"
- Steady, medium-speed drumming with beak

**Telltale Traits**

- Back and wings look grayish from a distance; up close, finely black-and-white zebra striped
- Undulating flight, with deep dips
- Often very tame; slow to fly away when you approach

**Look Here**

- At the feeder eating sunflower seeds or squirrel corn

**Or Here**

- Clinging to tree trunks or large branches
- Foraging on the ground
- At suet or nectar feeder
- In citrus or other fruit trees

*On the Home Front* Excavates a cavity in a dead tree, dead limb, or wooden fence post for a nest site; may accept a nest box • In southern areas, often raises more than one brood

*"I frequently found oranges that had been riddled by this woodpecker"*

—Benjamin Mortimer, "Notes on habits of a few birds of Orange County, Florida" (1890)

Once called the "orange sapsucker," the red-bellied woodpecker may add some "Florida sunshine" to its diet when the fruit is on the tree or on the ground. An opportunistic feeder, the bird will also sample grapefruits, mangoes, and even nectar from banana flowers.

**Wild Menu:** Insects; seeds; nuts; fruit

**Plant Picks:** Pecans or oaks for nuts; mulberries (*Morus* spp.); citrus in mild-winter areas; field corn or Indian corn; tall, large-headed sunflowers (*Helianthus annuus*)

**Feeder Pleasers**

- Whole ears of dried corn on cob; sunflower seeds; suet and suet-based foods

**Tricks and Treats**

- Squirrel feeders that hold a fixed ear of corn work great for this big guy to peck at, too.
- May become a nectar drinker

## *Love Your Hat!*

When I was a kid, I spent many an afternoon poking into forgotten corners of my father's secondhand store. In one room, crammed to the ceiling with antique clothing, I came across stacks of hatboxes. I expected to find fantastic creations, but instead I found raw materials for making hats a hundred years ago. Birds, to be exact. I dropped the box in horror. Onto the floor tumbled glossy wings of purple martins, white egret plumes—and the striking black-and-white backs of red-bellied woodpeckers, which were once slaughtered wholesale for their feathers.

# Red-Headed Woodpecker

*First Impression*

**A breathtaking bird! Bold white and black patches with a vivid crimson head**

**Mark Your Calendar**

Year-round

**Details, Details**

- A little smaller than a robin; 9¼ inches
- Female looks like male
- Juvenile has brown head

**Listen Up!**

- Rattles, *chirr*s, and makes a loud, wheezy *queeer queeer queeer*
- Doesn't usually excavate into wood for insects; does drum weakly on occasion

**Telltale Traits**

- Fly-catches! The bird flies from a perch after an insect, then returns to eat it.
- Usually seen alone or in pairs; after nesting, may forage in family groups
- Not a rare bird in general, but "locally common" in some parts of its range
- Stores acorns, nuts, and sometimes grasshoppers to eat later

**Look Here**

- Fly-catching from a utility pole, fence post, or tree

**Or Here**

- Flying across an open area
- On ground beneath trees, eating nuts
- Eating fruit or berries in bushes or trees
- Scavenging corn in farm field

*On the Home Front* Nests in dead trees or utility poles, near the top • May reuse same cavity for several years or excavate a new one below it

*"Strongly contrasted blotches of black, white, and crimson flashing in the sunlight"*

—**Spencer Trotter,** *Life Histories of North American Woodpeckers* **(1939)**

**You'll never forget your first sighting of this fabulous bird, whether it's flying across a field, clinging to a tree, or contentedly eating corn at your feeder. It's perfectly gorgeous.**

**Wild Menu:** Insects; fruit and berries; corn; nuts and acorns

**Plant Picks:** Cherries, grapes, mulberries; corn; oak trees for acorns; pecan trees for nuts; crab apples and other flowering trees for insects

**Feeder Pleasers**

- Dried corn on the cob, pushed firmly onto a spike; nuts; suet

**Tricks and Treats**

- Got any weathered wooden posts around? Install them as inviting perches for fly-catching.

## The Shores of Gitche Gumee

Why does the red-headed woodpecker have a red head? In Longfellow's classic poem "Hiawatha," there is a climactic scene in which the hero slays a great and evil magician. Hiawatha receives advice from a woodpecker, who tells him that the only place the evil one can be mortally wounded is at the roots of his long hair. Hiawatha releases the arrows, and the magician falls. In gratitude, the hero daubs the woodpecker's head with blood.

# Pileated Woodpecker

*First Impression*
**Humongous "Woody Woodpecker"**

### Mark Your Calendar

Year-round

### Details, Details

- As big as a crow; 16½ inches
- The cartoon character Woody Woodpecker was drawn from the pileated woodpecker.
- Big, strong beak
- Watch for big white patches on the wings, and even bigger white patches underneath, when the bird flies.
- "Pileated" means "crested"—that pointy tuft of feathers on the head.
- Female is similar to male but lacks the red forehead and red mustache

### Listen Up!

- Hollers *awoik! awoik!* in a ringing voice
- Sounds very similar to the flicker, but louder and slower

### Telltale Traits

- Often pecks at logs as well as dead trees
- Pries off long strips of dead wood to reveal its favorite food, carpenter ants
- Flies like a crow, with deep wing beats
- Noisy; can be heard from far away
- Can raise and lower that red crest

### Look Here

- At your suet feeder

### Or Here

- Clinging to tree trunk
- Hammering at dead trees, logs, or stumps, looking for ants
- Flying across open space or swooping from tree to tree

*"Easily located by the half-bushel of big fresh chips scattered about on the ground"*

—George Simmons, *Birds of the Austin Region* (1925)

For all their size, pileated woodpeckers are often easy to overlook. Watch for wood chips: the remains of their excavating. Look up, and you may spot the big-beaked bird itself.

*On the Home Front* May nest in backyard or even accept a nest box • Usually excavates its nest hole high up in a dead decaying tree

**Wild Menu:** Insects, mostly carpenter ants and wood-boring beetle larvae; fruit and berries

**Plant Picks:** Hackberry (*Celtis occidentalis*), sassafras (*Sassafras albidum*), blackberries or raspberries, shining sumac (*Rhus copallina*), Virginia creeper (*Parthenocissus quinquefolia*), flowering dogwood (*Cornus florida*), persimmon (*Diospyros virginiana*), and other berried plants

**Feeder Pleasers**

- Suet, served in a stationary feeder that supplies a sturdy place to get a grip and prop a big tail

**Tricks and Treats**

- Keep that old stump in your yard to attract ants. This big woodpecker may be close behind.

## Pileated by Phone

Is there a bird you're yearning to see, but which, for some reason, you never quite catch? For one of my friends, that bird was the pileated woodpecker.

One day, as he was talking to his father on the phone, his dad broke in: "A giant woodpecker just landed on the tree right outside the window!" Yep, it was a pileated. My friend tried not to whimper while his dad described every detail with gusto.

# Brown-Headed Nuthatch

*First Impression*

**Acrobatic plain gray bird with brown cap, often poised upside down**

**Mark Your Calendar**

Year-round

**Details, Details**

- Smaller than a chickadee; 4½ inches
- Female looks like male

**Listen Up!**

- Says *cha-cha-cha* or *cah-cah-cah,* and sometimes a conversational twitter of *pit-pit.*

**Telltale Traits**

- Creeps up and down trees, looking for insects
- Often hangs head-down from a bunch of pine needles, alertly looking for insects
- Picks off flakes of bark, making a pattering sound below as the flakes fall

**Look Here**

- At your feeder

**Or Here**

- On tree trunks, fence posts, or even buildings
- Hanging like a tiny, drab parrot from a cluster of needles on a pine branch
- Flying from one tree to another
- Tilt your neck way back: These little birds often stay high in pines. Listen for their calls, then track them down with binocs.
- At a nest box or nest hole, fairly low to ground

*On the Home Front* Digs out a cavity or recycles a woodpecker hole • May use a nest box • Most nests are at lower than 10 feet aboveground

*"Its favorite haunts are in the pines"*

—A. C. Bent, *Life Histories of North American Nuthatches, Wrens, Thrashers, and Their Allies* (1948)

This nuthatch spends much of its time on or about loblollies, long-leaf, and other pine trees. It's often so high up it's hard to see—except at nesting time, when oddly enough, it makes its home close to eye level.

**Wild Menu:** Insects

**Plant Picks:** Pines native to your area, such as loblolly (*Pinus taeda*) or long-leaf (*Pinus palustris*)

**Feeder Pleasers**

- Suet feeder, including insect-enriched suet; sunflower seeds; peanuts and other nuts

**Tricks and Treats**

- Mount a birdhouse at about 4 to 8 feet high (ideally on a pine tree), and you may be able to see utterly adorable baby nuthatches being fed by their parents. Chickadees or titmice might become tenants instead, though.

*Tool Time*

The tiny brown-headed nuthatch has a remarkable habit that sets it apart from most other species: This bird often uses a tool when feeding.

This bird's daily grub consists of insects hiding on trees, often under the bark. To get at these tidbits, the nuthatch has been seen using a flake of bark to pry off another piece of bark. It makes for better leverage, I suppose, because the bark chip is wider than the bird's sharp little bill. Like they say, the right tool makes the job faster and easier.

# Blue-Gray Gnatcatcher

*First Impression*

**An active mini-mockingbird with up-tilted tail, in the branches overhead**

### Mark Your Calendar

Spring through fall in most areas; year-round along Gulf Coast and in Florida and Deep South

### Details, Details

- Smaller than a chickadee; 4½ inches
- Male is blue-gray during breeding season; pale gray otherwise; female is similar
- Whitish belly and noticeable white eye ring
- Watch for the distinctive white edges of the black tail; they show best in flight.

### Listen Up!

- A constant barrage of thin, very high, lisping or buzzy notes, generally *zee-u, zee-u, zil, zeet, zee-e*, sometimes with a mewing tone like a catbird. It's so distinctive you won't confuse it with any other sound.

### Telltale Traits

- Look for that nervous tail—rising, lowering, twitching from side to side.
- Often cocks tail up, like a wren
- Highly active, always in motion, constantly searching foliage or flitting about
- In winter, gnatcatchers hang out with all kinds of great birds, from kinglets to cardinals—enough to keep your binoculars busy for an hour or more.

### Look Here

- Fly-catching, by flying out from a branch to nab a gnat or other insect in mid-air

### Or Here

- Flitting among branches of trees

*"It tends to maintain an upright position"*

—A. C. Bent, *Life Histories of North American Thrushes, Kinglets, and Their Allies* **(1949)**

**Unlike chickadees and kinglets, which may contort themselves into acrobatic postures to reach a morsel among the leaves, this gnatcatcher species gleans its insects without ever hanging from twigs.**

*On the Home Front* Builds its pretty nest far out on a branch, near the tip; look just above halfway up the tree • Builds a strong cup of delicate materials

**Wild Menu:** Insects, including plenty of—can you guess?—gnats!

**Plant Picks:** Oaks (*Quercus* spp.), which apparently host a myriad of gnatcatcher-approved insects

**Feeder Pleasers**
- Not a feeder visitor

**Tricks and Treats**
- The best inducement for a gnatcatcher will be the insects in your yard. Avoid using insecticides to make sure your little pals have plenty to eat.

## *Roaming with Friends*

A friend and I headed south for the warm sunshine of the Gulf one winter. In Georgia, we pulled off the highway to stretch our legs. Naturally, I headed for the trees beside the gas station, to see what I could see. As I stepped close, I could hear the familiar high-pitched *zee-zee* calls of a band of little birds: chickadees, check; titmice, yep; kinglets, hello little guys. But, wait, what was that familiar voice? Cheerfully calling *zee-e-e-e*, blue-gray gnatcatchers were also part of the little band. Welcome to a winter haven!

# Eastern Bluebird

*First Impression*

**Unbelievable blue that takes your breath away**

## Mark Your Calendar

Year-round

## Details, Details

- Smaller than a robin, as big as a large sparrow; 7 inches
- Orange-red throat and breast; white belly
- Female is duller, looks faded

## Listen Up!

- Sweet, gurgling, whistled, *tru-a-ly, tru-a-ly!*
- Brief, husky call note that seems to keep birds in touch: *chew*

## Telltale Traits

- Travels in short, slow, fluttering swoops from one perch to another
- Often glides from low perch to ground with wings spread, to catch insects

## Look Here

- Perched near or in open areas, often near the edge of a woods or an orchard

## Or Here

- In golf courses, cemeteries, large parks, or pastures, or on roadsides
- At apples, crab apples, and other flowering trees, picking off insects at blossoms
- At feeders or birdbaths

*On the Home Front* Eagerly accepts a birdhouse, but will face stiff competition from house sparrows • Very early nester, so mount boxes in late winter • Nesting may fail if late snow, ice, or freeze arrives; birds will try again.

*"They are gathered sociably in companies of half a dozen or more"*

—Winsor Tyler, *Life Histories of North American Thrushes, Kinglets, and Their Allies* **(1949)**

**When you see one bluebird in your yard, you're probably soon going to see more. Bluebirds usually flock together in family groups. In winter, the families may join together to make much bigger flocks. Got that mealworm feeder ready?**

**Wild Menu:** Insects; fruit and berries

**Plant Picks:** Flowering trees; small fruits, including mulberries (*Morus* spp.), serviceberries (*Amelanchier* spp.), bayberry (*Myrica* spp.), sumac (*Rhus* spp.), winterberry and evergreen hollies (*Ilex* spp.), Virginia creeper (*Parthenocissus quinquefolia*); flowering dogwood (*Cornus florida*)

## Feeder Pleasers

- Mealworms and other insect foods; suet, peanut butter mixed with cornmeal, and other fat-based foods, in an accessible feeder

## Tricks and Treats

- The sound of trickling water is a big draw.
- Put up a roost box so bluebirds can stay cozy at night.

## Foraging Friends

Some birds band together into small flocks of mixed species in wintertime and forage together in their feeding territory. Each species in the group seeks food in a slightly different way and in a different place, so they don't compete with one another.

In winter, look for bluebirds roaming in open places, such as cornfields, cotton fields, or sugarcane fields, as well as your own backyard. Watch for warblers, too, when you notice bluebirds: Their winter foraging friends include palm warblers, myrtle warblers, and pine warblers. No one knows why they hang out together. Maybe they just like the company!

# Wood Thrush

*First Impression*

**Rusty robinlike bird with boldly spotted breast**

### Mark Your Calendar

Spring through fall; migration only on the Florida peninsula

### Details, Details

- Smaller than a robin; 7¾ inches
- Female looks like male

### Listen Up!

- The flutist of the woods: languid, liquid, *ee-oh-lay, ee-oh-lay*
- Like other thrushes, a short, terse call note when alarmed

### Telltale Traits

- Sings in late afternoon and at dusk
- Often sings when rain is on its way

### Look Here

- On ground in woodsy areas or shade garden near woods

### Or Here

- Eating small fruits or berries, especially in summer or on fall migration
- At naturalistic low-level water feature or birdbath

*On the Home Front* Unless your yard adjoins a woods, you're unlikely to host nesting wood thrushes. • Well-hidden nest is similar to robin's, usually saddled on a branch or tucked in a crotch at eye level or above • Keep cats indoors if you live in thrush territory; their depredations contribute to the declining numbers of these storied singers.

*"Beryl green"*
*"Pale sulphite green"*
*"Nile blue"*

—Descriptions of the color of wood thrush eggs

How about "robin's egg blue"? Whatever name you call them by, thrush eggs are pretty things. All thrushes, including the robin and bluebirds as well as the wood thrush, lay greenish blue or blue eggs.

**Wild Menu:** Insects; small fruits and berries

**Plant Picks:** Mulberries (*Morus* spp.), serviceberries (*Amelanchier* spp.), elderberries (*Sambucus* spp.), dogwoods (*Cornus* spp.), spicebush (*Lindera benzoin*)

### Feeder Pleasers

- May eat mealworms and other insect foods from low feeder

### Tricks and Treats

- If you live near a thrush woods, tear strips of white cloth about ½ inch wide and 6 inches long and lay them in a shady garden. The birds may weave them into their nests.
- Coax thrushes with a birdbath equipped with a dripper or moving water.

## The Better to See You With

Next time you're lucky enough to spot a wood thrush, take a close look with binoculars at its eyes. See how big they are? The bird's eyes are larger than most similar size birds, a trait emphasized by their white eye ring. Dr. Arthur A. Allen, a dean of American ornithology, theorized in 1934 that the wood thrush sticks to the shady side, staying in woodsy places, because its eyes are so large that too much sunlight makes the bird uncomfortable ("The Veery and Some of His Family," *Bird-Lore*).

# Palm Warbler

## First Impression

**Tiny greenish yellow bird with eye-catching reddish brown cap, flicking tail up and down**

### Mark Your Calendar

Winter, along Gulf and Atlantic Coasts and Florida; inland, migration only

### Details, Details

- Small sparrow size; 5½ inches
- This species comes in two different variations: brown or yellow forms or races.
- "Yellow" birds have a rich yellow breast heavily streaked with reddish brown in breeding season; when not in breeding season, they are dull yellowish brown with no cap or streaky breast.
- "Brown" birds are much duller, being brownish with a brownish white belly, but they still wear that noticeable reddish cap.
- Female and male look alike

### Listen Up!

- A weak, buzzy trill
- Sharp *chick!* call note

### Telltale Traits

- When you watch this bird constantly raising and lowering its tail, you'll see why it's such a great clue to identification.
- Often in small groups, especially during migration

### Look Here

- On the ground. Look hard: They're tricky to see against dead leaves.

### Or Here

- In flower or vegetable gardens
- In brush along fences
- Flitting through shrubbery
- In palmetto clumps

*"A prominent feature of winter bird life in Florida"*

—**Arthur Howell,** *Florida Bird Life* **(1932)**

This warbler often sticks to low levels or the ground, instead of taking to the tall treetops like many other warbler species. In winter, the birds are a regular sight in backyards and city parks, as well as along roadsides and on grassy or weedy open ground.

### On the Home Front

Nests far, far to the North • Nests in sphagnum peat bogs, generally at the foot of a short conifer • It's a mystery to science about which bird does the building, how long it takes, and other details.

**Wild Menu:** Insects; some small fruits

**Plant Picks:** Bayberries (*Myrica* spp.) and raspberries, for winter berries; groups of shrubs or hedges, palmettos (*Sabal* spp.), and willows (*Salix* spp.) for good foraging possibilities

### Feeder Pleasers

- Not usually a feeder visitor; try mealworms

### Tricks and Treats

- The usual insects in your yard are enough.

## Poinsettias and Palms

Flocks of 50 or more seemed to be everywhere in the old days, but palm warblers are still common in their winter range. On a trip to the Deep South one winter, I enjoyed watching a flock of these birds inspect the yellow centers of big red poinsettias for insects. Of course, to a northerner, the poinsettias themselves were jaw-dropping—blooming outside at Christmastime!

# Northern Parula

*First Impression*

**A plump, *cute*, blue, yellow, and white little bird flitting through foliage**

### Mark Your Calendar

Spring through fall; also winter in Florida peninsula

### Details, Details

- Smaller than a chickadee; 4½ inches
- Rusty and black band across upper breast
- White wing bars show up well in flight.
- Snow white belly
- Admire the fine points with binoculars—if you can focus on this active little guy.
- Female is paler version of male

### Listen Up!

- Unmusical buzz that rises in pitch, punctuated by a sharp note at very end
- Call note: a sharp *chip!*

### Telltale Traits

- Forages more like a chickadee and nuthatch than like the typical fluttering wood warbler: It often hangs head down to reach the underside of leaves; creeps along branches; or clings to trunk.
- Often with mixed flocks of other warblers

### Look Here

- In any backyard tree or shrub, gleaning insects

### Or Here

- In Spanish moss (*Tillandsia usneoides*), where its bright feathers blend in
- In deciduous trees

*"Small, dumpy, and short-necked"*

—**David Allen Sibley, in my favorite comprehensive field guide,** *The Sibley Guide to Birds* **(2000)**

Dumpy?! A stubby tail, compact shape, and plump breast make this an adorable little bird—it looks more like a baby bird instead of the usual sleek warbler.

*On the Home Front* Usually picks a homesite in swamps, where Spanish moss grows • The nest is a bowl hollowed out of the surrounding moss or lichen.

**Wild Menu:** Insects, including many spiders

**Plant Picks:** Spanish moss is a natural draw for this bird, if you live where it thrives. Otherwise, any backyard tree not sprayed with pesticides may catch its attention.

### Feeder Pleasers

- Not a feeder visitor

### Tricks and Treats

- You won't need anything other than trees and shrubs with insects.

## PAR-you-luh, Please

I've called this bird the *pa-ROO-luh* warbler my whole birding life. Wrong on two counts: pronunciation and that word "warbler." "Parula," properly accented on the first syllable, is a Latin word that means "little titmouse." Our friend the tufted titmouse belongs to the genus *Parus*; "parula" is the diminutive of that word, indicating smaller size. That's why the official common name of this bird doesn't include the word "warbler." If we said "northern parula warbler," we'd really be saying "northern little titmouse warbler."

# Prothonotary Warbler

## First Impression
**Small, vivid, golden yellow bird**

### Mark Your Calendar
Spring through fall

### Details, Details
- About chickadee size; 5½ inches
- Blue-gray wings and some snowy white under the tail add nice contrast.
- Female very similar to male

### Listen Up!
- Most warblers don't have a melodic song, but this one will catch your ear. It sings a series of rising notes: *tsweeet tsweeet tsweeet tsweeet*. The song fades into the background, though, because it never changes.
- A sharp *chip!* call note

### Telltale Traits
- Constantly on the move, examining crevices or hopping over logs to pick insects from hiding places
- Clings to tree trunks like a nuthatch to extract insects

### Look Here
- At a nest box in your yard

### Or Here
- In trees or shrubs in your yard with flocks of other warblers during migration
- In swamps

**On the Home Front** Nests in a cavity • Eagerly accepts a nest box • Often uses an old downy woodpecker hole in dead snag or branch of live tree • Cypress knees are a favorite homesite. • Fills hole with plenty of moss before adding other materials, including fishing line

*"What a name to saddle on the Golden Swamp-Bird!"*

—Aaron Bagg and Samuel Eliot, Jr.,
*Birds of the Connecticut Valley in Massachusetts* (1937)

"Wrongly compounded in the first place, wrongly spelled, wrongly pronounced!" the authors fumed. All because a certain papal official—"first notary" or *protonotary*—wears a yellow hood. Still, whatever you call this bird, or however you pronounce its name, it's still a beauty, gleaming like a yellow flame in the dim swamps.

**Wild Menu:** Insects

**Plant Picks:** Bald cypress trees (*Taxodium distichum*), sweet gum (*Liquidambar styraciflua*), or any other native tree of your area, for best insect possibilities

**Feeder Pleasers**
- Not usually a feeder visitor; you might try mealworms

**Tricks and Treats**
- Mount a small birdhouse—wren or chickadee size works well—in a shady spot to attract nesting pairs.

## The Voice of the Swamp

Early ornithologists had to do quite a bit of bushwhacking back in the old days. Often it was hard to tell when their next step would bring them blundering into a swamp.

William Brewster (1851–1919), a cofounder of the American Ornithological Union, didn't stay behind his desk for long. At the age of 27, he wrote about slogging through the Southeast. The prothonotary warbler was abundant, he wrote, and useful: The male's song was as good an indicator as frogs' croaking for where the explorers should watch out for water.

# Summer Tanager

*First Impression*

**Vivid, rosy red bird, without a crest— usually being chased by another**

## Mark Your Calendar

Spring through fall

## Details, Details

- Smaller than a robin; 7¾ inches
- Note absence of black wings. The scarlet tanager, which has black wings and tail, also appears in backyards in the S and SE.
- Female is greenish yellow, sometimes with tinges of red-orange

## Listen Up!

- A short, musical song of hurried phrases, repeated after a pause
- Call sounds like *chicky-chucky-chuck*

## Telltale Traits

- Your best chance of spotting one is in spring when the males return. They chase each other, sing constantly, and very actively establish territories.
- Forages alone in mid- to upper levels of trees, usually deciduous
- Skilled at fly-catching
- Moves through foliage very deliberately and slowly
- Despite its color, it's very inconspicuous.

## Look Here

- Usually in deciduous trees

## Or Here

- Chasing other males or a female
- Flying after wasps or other winged insects

*On the Home Front* Usually nests high in trees • Only the female gathers nest material and builds the nest.

*"Tanagers in uncountable abundance"*

—Francis Weston, *Life Histories of North American Blackbirds, Orioles, Tanagers, and Allies* (1958)

**Weston was describing the summer tanagers that piled up on the Gulf Coast when stormy weather in spring prevented the birds from continuing their migration flight inland. Look for a swarm of tanagers in city parks, street trees, or your own backyard in April, if heavy rain, fog, or north winds prevail.**

**Wild Menu:** Insects, especially bees and wasps; fruit and berries

**Plant Picks:** Fruits of any kind, particularly bite-size mulberries (*Morus* spp.) and blackberries. To attract tanagers, bluebirds, and other fabulous fruit eaters, you might try letting a plant of the common pokeweed (*Phytolacca americana*) grow in your yard.

## Feeder Pleasers

- Not usually a feeder visitor, but may eat bananas; you might try mealworms, too.

## Tricks and Treats

- Add a drip tube or mister to your birdbath and you may manage to see summer tanagers freshen their feathers.

## Bee Eaters

Not my kind of a meal, but summer tanagers eagerly eat bees and wasps, to such an extent that they've become pests around beehives. Next time you come across a paper wasp nest (*Polistes* spp.), make it a habit to look for tanagers. Not only have the birds been seen snatching flying wasps from the colony, they've even been noted pecking through a wasp nest to get at the plump larval grubs inside.

# Blue Grosbeak

*First Impression*

**A dark, nothing-special, sparrow size bird hopping about on the ground—until it moves into the sun and reveals its deep, rich, cobalt blue**

### Mark Your Calendar

Spring through fall; migration only in South Florida

### Details, Details

- The size of a big sparrow; 6¾ inches
- Big, heavy bill
- Cinnamon wing bars and a big bill set this species apart from the similar indigo bunting.
- Female is grayish brown
- Juvenile females are warm reddish brown; juvenile males are blotched with blue.

### Listen Up!

- Rarely sings at midday, unlike the similar-looking indigo bunting
- Long, warbling song with a quiet quality that doesn't grab attention
- Metallic *zink* call note

### Telltale Traits

- Flies low, from one shrub to another
- Often forages on ground

### Look Here

- Hopping on ground, often beneath shrubs, looking for food

### Or Here

- Singing from within a shrub
- Perched in the top of a bush or small tree
- Foraging in flocks on plowed fields

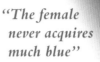

*"The female never acquires much blue"*

—Jonathan Dwight, Jr., "The Sequence of Plumages and Moults of the Passerine Birds of New York" (1900)

The male blue grosbeak is easy to confuse with the male indigo bunting. The female grosbeak also looks a lot like the female bunting. Both are brown, but the female blue grosbeak has tinges of blue on her wings.

*On the Home Front* Nests usually not more than 8 feet aboveground, in small trees, shrubs, brambles, or vines • May nest in backyard

**Wild Menu:** Insects; grain; weed seeds; fruit

**Plant Picks:** Plant shrubs in groups, or add a hedge or a patch of blackberries to supply the cover these birds crave.

### Feeder Pleasers

- Millet; birdseed mix

### Tricks and Treats

- Often incorporates shed snakeskins and other unusual, soft, or crinkly materials into its nest: cotton, rags, newspaper, string, cellophane, and plastic snack wrappers. Try an offering of these or similar materials at nesting time.

*Let's Get Together*

Blue grosbeaks aren't abundant birds. But they gather together after nesting, at first in small groups, but then in larger ones as other families join in. These flocks roam about, foraging in grain fields and sometimes backyards, until it's time to pack up and leave on fall migration. I used to mentally say "blackbirds" when I saw such a flock—until the day I lifted my binoculars because something just didn't seem quite right. I was stunned to see that every one of them was a blue grosbeak.

# Painted Bunting

## First Impression

**Unbelievable parrotlike colors—red and blue and lime green**

### Mark Your Calendar

MW, spring through fall; may stray to other areas

### Details, Details

- Small sparrow size; 5½ inches
- Female is yellowish green
- Not until fall of its second year does the male bird acquire its full, stunning plumage. Until then, males look like females.

### Listen Up!

- Sweet, high-pitched, tinkling, melodic song
- Low *chip!* alarm call

### Telltale Traits

- Acts like a sparrow, foraging in grassy or weedy places
- Male sings from exposed, elevated perch, to about 30 feet high
- A "scrapper": Male birds fight viciously with each other over females and territories, sometimes to the death.

### Look Here

- At feeder

### Or Here

- Eating seeds of foxtail grass or other weeds, while clinging to the stems
- Singing from top of bush

**On the Home Front** May nest in an appealing, shrubby backyard • Nests in low vegetation, usually less than 6 feet from ground

*"The* nonpareil*"*
—French for "without an equal"; traditional name for this bunting in the South

**You won't believe your eyes the first time you see a painted bunting. It looks just too outrageous to be true. Each blotch of color is clearly defined, so that the bird looks like Joseph's coat-of-many-colors.**

**Wild Menu:** Seeds, especially grass and weeds; grain; some insects

**Plant Picks:** Scatter a few handfuls of birdseed mix or finch mix in a sunny patch of soil, cover lightly, and keep your fingers crossed for buntings.

### Feeder Pleasers

- Millet; birdseed mix; sunflower seeds; cracked corn

### Tricks and Treats

- Don't be too fussy a weeder, and your payoff could be painted buntings—they seek out weedy grasses, especially foxtail grass, as well as dock, pigweed, and other common weeds.
- Add more birdbaths, fountains, or water features of any kind for drinking and bathing.

## Aggressive Beauty

I first met painted buntings one April, when the males had just returned to the Augusta, Georgia, area from their winter vacation. I felt lucky to spot three of the birds, each already singing lustily from its claimed territory. Their colors were simply amazing.

When the females arrived a few days later, those gorgeous birds began to fight like junkyard dogs. I shooed apart two birds joined in battle because males have been known to fight to the death. But as soon as I stepped away, they returned to the fray.

191

# Field Sparrow

*First Impression*

**Small brown bird with blank, wide-eyed look**

## Mark Your Calendar

Year-round; winter only in some parts of Deep South

## Details, Details

- Small sparrow size, what else? 5¾ inches
- Pink bill
- Reddish cap and white eye ring; no dark spot on breast
- Female looks like male

## Listen Up!

- Plaintive *see-a, see-a, see-a, see-a, wee, wee, wee, wee*
- Sharp, short *chip!* of alarm

## Telltale Traits

- Vigorous scratcher on ground
- Often in flocks of mixed sparrow species

## Look Here

- On ground beneath feeder, or in tray feeder

## Or Here

- Scratching elsewhere in your yard for seeds, in flower beds or vegetable garden
- Hanging on weeds or grass stems to reach seeds

*On the Home Front* Nests in thicket or thorny bush, usually in field but possibly in backyard • Well-made cup of dead grasses is placed on or near ground • Ground nests are usually close to a shrub or tree. • Raises several broods a season, making a new nest each time

*"Can be closely imitated by anyone willing to practice"*

—Arthur A. Allen, *The Book of Bird Life* (1930)

**Field sparrows have a simple song that's easy to mimic. Whistling back to a singing male bird often lures the bird in, to investigate the intruder—which will give you a better look at the bird.**

**Wild Menu:** Insects; weed seeds and grass seeds

**Plant Picks:** A scattering of millet seed in a corner of your vegetable garden or flower bed will give you hours of fun, as you watch field sparrows eating seeds from the stems. There's no need to buy special seed; just plant some of your birdseed.

**Feeder Pleasers**
- Millet; canary seed and other small seeds

**Tricks and Treats**
- Like other winter sparrows, the field sparrow appreciates a warm bath on a cold day. Check out a heater for your birdbath.
- Nests are often lined with horsehair from the animal's mane or tail. Ask at a nearby stable for the currycomb leavings if you don't have your own trusty steed.

## Slow in Summer

You've probably noticed that birds are abundant at your feeders in fall, winter, and early spring. But suddenly their traffic drops off. What's happened? Nothing but natural behavior.

As field sparrows and other feeder birds disperse to breeding territories, they tend to stick close to their nest area as they search for food. And that might not include your feeding station. They also switch to eating more insects in summer, and bugs are also what they usually feed their babies. Don't worry, though, the birds will be back come fall.

# Vesper Sparrow

*First Impression*

Nondescript streaky grayish brown sparrow, with white outer tail feathers

## Mark Your Calendar

Winter only in most parts of this region; spring through fall in upper tier of states in this region

## Details, Details

- Sparrow size; 6¼ inches
- Brown streaks may show against a tan or white background.
- White eye ring
- Male and female look alike

## Listen Up!

- Two long, low whistles give way to pretty, musical trills, something like the song of a song sparrow.
- Sharp *chip!* alarm note

## Telltale Traits

- Walks or runs on ground
- "Grass sparrow" and "grass finch" are old names reflecting its habit of hanging out in fields, meadows, and pastures.
- Male sings from highest available perches within nesting territory, not on ground

## Look Here

- At feeder

## Or Here

- In grassy areas
- Singing from fence post, tree, or other elevated perch

The vesper sparrow and song sparrow look a lot alike, but the vesper has white feathers on the outside edges of its tail. It's also a grayer bird than the song sparrow, which is a warmer brown color.

*On the Home Front* Not a backyard nester
- The female alone builds the nest, at the base of a plant or by a clump of crop residue. • The nest is a woven cup of grasses and other plants, camouflaged among the vegetation.

**Wild Menu:** Insects, especially grasshoppers; seeds; grain

**Plant Picks:** Try planting a prairie or meadow to entice a vesper sparrow to your yard.

**Feeder Pleasers**
- Millet; birdseed mix; might like mealworms

**Tricks and Treats**
- Provide a low-level birdbath.

## Tail Betrayal

I was exploring an old farm road in South Carolina without my binoculars when I noticed a bunch of sparrows on the ground ahead of me. As I drew closer, they ran ahead of me, then immediately returned to feeding on the ground. I took several more steps; the same thing happened.

Squinting to see better, I focused on one of the birds facing me. Song sparrows, I decided, going by the streaky breast with a "stickpin" spot. Even the sweet snatches of song sounded like those of song sparrows. Then my dog came bounding up from behind, and the birds instantly flushed. White tail feathers! It was my introduction to vesper sparrows.

# Fox Sparrow

*First Impression*

**Big, plump, rusty sparrow with heavily streaked or speckled breast**

### Mark Your Calendar

Winter only; only rarely spotted along the coast and on Florida peninsula

### Details, Details

- A big sparrow; 7 inches
- Much geographical variation in color and song; some are redder, grayer, or thicker-billed. The fox sparrow in this region is the red or Taiga race; it's a beautiful rusty-red bird.
- Female looks like male

### Listen Up!

- With 18 subspecies divided into at least four distinct groups, fox sparrows show a lot of variation in song. The group of this region is the red or Taiga fox sparrow, which sings a rich, melodious, whistled song.

### Telltale Traits

- Scratches vigorously on ground; can dig a hole through several inches of snow to reach seeds
- Secretive when not at feeder; stays concealed in brushy areas
- Usually arrives singly at feeder

### Look Here

- On ground beneath feeder

### Or Here

- In or at feeder
- Scavenging seeds from a winter garden or weeds

*"They scratch lustily for their food amongst fallen leaves"*

—A. C. Bent, *Life Histories of North American Cardinals, Grosbeaks, Buntings, Towhees, Finches, Sparrows, and Allies* (1968)

**Fox sparrows certainly do have a passion for scratching—you'll often hear one rustling in the leaves before you see it. The big sparrow forages with fervor among the fallen leaves beneath shrubs and hedges.**

*On the Home Front* Not a backyard nester in this region • Other subspecies nest in the United States, but the red fox sparrow group nests far to the north, from Canada to Alaska. • Nests on ground, in low bushes, or in small trees

**Wild Menu:** Seeds; insects; fruits

**Plant Picks:** Weeds are wildly popular in winter, especially smartweeds (*Polygonum* spp.), ragweed, lamb's quarters, and other plants we usually get rid of rather than encourage. If you have a discreet place for a weedy patch, the sparrows will flock there.

**Feeder Pleasers**
- Millet

**Tricks and Treats**
- A birdbath is often welcomed.

## Here Today, Gone Tomorrow

Migrant visitors are a delightful surprise in the backyard, but I'm especially fond of those temporary guests who come immediately to the feeder, where I'll spot them first thing in the morning.

I also like birds who stick out like a sore thumb, so you know you've got someone different. The fox sparrow fills the bill on all counts, plus he's a beauty to see against fall colors or an early snow.

# Boat-Tailed Grackle

*First Impression*

**Huge, beautifully iridescent blackbird with exaggeratedly long tail, stalking about on ground**

## Mark Your Calendar

Year-round along the Gulf and Atlantic Coasts and in Florida; absent in other areas

## Details, Details

- Way bigger than a robin: male, 16½ inches; female, 14½ inches
- Gulf Coast birds have dark eyes; Atlantic Coast birds, north of Florida, have light eyes.
- Female is brown, not iridescent black
- Boat-tailed grackle gleams with greenish blue iridescence; similar great-tailed grackle leans toward purple-blue

## Listen Up!

- Loud, piercing "wolf whistle" calls
- Also a variety of rattles, *churrs*, and other rasping, guttural noises

## Telltale Traits

- Unmistakable by sight alone—except in Louisiana, where this species overlaps with the similar great-tailed grackle, once considered a subspecies of the boat-tailed
- Watch for weird display postures, with up-tilted head, spread wings, and ruffled feathers.

## Look Here

- On lawn

## Or Here

- At feeder

## "Clarinero"

**—Name for male boat-tailed grackle in Mexico**

**This species of grackle ranges into Mexico and Central America. *Clarinero* means "trumpeter" in Spanish; it's an appropriate name for these powerful vocalists.**

*On the Home Front* Pairs begin nesting as early as February. • Nests in colonies, usually in a marsh, and often where alligators are present

**Wild Menu:** Just about anything it can get into its beak: fish, shrimp, crabs, frogs, snails, crayfish; small birds, nestlings of other marsh birds (including herons and red-winged blackbirds); insects; grain

**Plant Picks:** Just food in the feeder

**Feeder Pleasers**
- Millet; birdseed mix; cracked corn

**Tricks and Treats**
- A big, sturdy birdbath may be welcomed.

## Not Very Neighborly

Gators may seem like the creature to be wary of in the swamp, but many marsh birds are opportunistic when it comes to eating—and they have a taste for meat.

Although ibises are much bigger than boat-tailed grackles, ibis eggs and their newly hatched young are suitable for a grackle's gullet. Black vultures and fish crows also lick their lips—er, beaks—over the poor ibis's family. Even the fish that an ibis catches aren't safe—the boat-tailed grackle often grabs fish right out of the ibis's bill.

# Brewer's Blackbird

## First Impression

**Glossy blackbird with pale yellow eyes walking on ground**

### Mark Your Calendar

Winter only in some parts of this region; not at all or only as strays in other parts

### Details, Details

- A little smaller than a robin; 9 inches
- Part of this bird's Latin name means "blue head," referring to its iridescence: blue to purple on head and breast, green on body.
- Female is dull gray-brown with dark eye

### Listen Up!

- Squeaks, trills, and whistles
- Harsh *check!* call note

### Telltale Traits

- Walks on ground
- Head jerks forward with every step
- Holds back end of body and tail raised up when feeding on ground

### Look Here

- Walking about on ground beneath feeder

### Or Here

- Walking on lawn or other open areas
- In fall and winter, in large mixed flock with other blackbirds and starlings

## On the Home Front

Not a backyard nester • Nests in colonies • A colony often nests near water, in a variety of habitats, including willow thickets, wet meadows, and swamps. • Usually nests low to ground, at about 3 to 5 feet, but may also nest on ground or at higher level

*"Walking and feeding on pad-lily (Nymphaea) leaves, even one leaf serving to hold up a bird"*

—Frank Richardson, "Water surface feeding of blackbirds" (1947)

In sloughs and other quiet waters where water lilies grow, Brewer's blackbirds often walk about, perfectly at home, on the wide, flat leaves held at the water's surface. Watch closely and you may see them catching newly emerged damselflies and other aquatic insects.

**Wild Menu:** Insects; seeds and grain; occasionally fruit

**Plant Picks:** Try planting a patch of milo (sorghum) and let it stand in winter to attract visits from Brewer's blackbirds.

**Feeder Pleasers**

- Birdseed mix; millet

**Tricks and Treats**

- Blackbirds are fond of bathing. Provide a birdbath, and for an extra treat, a mister so they can loll in the spray.

## Pretty Posers

Blackbirds of all sorts are fascinating to watch, because some of their communication is done by dramatic physical posturing. The "ruff-out" display of the Brewer's blackbird is done mostly by males, as part of courtship. The bird fluffs out all the feathers of its head, neck, and breast, while partly fanning and drooping its wings and spreading its tail. When the ruffing is at its peak, the bird lets loose with a *squee* or other harsh noise. Then he immediately goes back to normal. The whole sequence only lasts for a couple of seconds, but it's a great show.

# Rufous Hummingbird

*First Impression*
**A flash of iridescent copper and orange**

*"The pugnacity of these birds is the most prominent characteristic"*

—William Kobbé, "The Rufous Hummingbirds of Cape Disappointment" (1900)

### Mark Your Calendar

An occasional stray in fall or winter, but seems to be expanding its range and becoming more frequently sighted

### Details, Details

- Tiny! 3¾ inches, and a good part is beak
- Female is iridescent green with a dab of orange-red on throat

### Listen Up!

- Buzzy sounds and variations of *zee-chew-chew-chew*
- Male dives from a great height, producing a stuttering *v-v-v-vroooom*

### Telltale Traits

- Unmistakable: He hovers! He buzzes! He goes backward, forward, sideways!
- Pugnacious personality

### Look Here

- At nectar feeder

### Or Here

- At flowers, especially red or red-orange blossoms or tubular-shape ones
- Perched on a slender twig or other raised spot, often at top of young tree or shrub

*On the Home Front* Nests in the Pacific Northwest, not in this region • The nest is well-camouflaged; it looks exactly like a knobby bit of a lichen-covered branch. • The tiny cup, about the size of a Ping-Pong ball cut in half, is made of plant down and bits of bark and moss, held together with spider webs and lichens.

Kobbé was writing about the hummingbirds he saw on the coast of Washington, a hundred years ago. Today, that same personality trait is evident even in birds who make the long trek across the country to the Southeast.

**Wild Menu:** Nectar; insects

**Plant Picks:** "Hummingbird flowers": tubular blossoms, especially in red or orange-red, which bloom in your area during fall or winter. Scarlet milkweed (*Asclepias curassavica*), Hong Kong orchid (*Bauhinia* × *blakeana*), and powderpuff (*Calliandra haematocephala*) are three possibilities for wintertime hummingbird flowers.

**Feeder Pleasers**
- Nectar feeder

**Tricks and Treats**
- A mister or garden sprinkler may attract bathing hummers.

## Chicken or Egg?

Or, in this case, hummingbird or hummingbird feeder? No one really knows why in recent years rufous hummingbirds have been spotted far outside their usual western range. Is it because people have put out more nectar feeders? Are there more nectar feeder watchers? Or is it a real shift in the migration pattern for the species?

I vote for "all of the above." I think that as we hummingbird fans hang more feeders, the birds find more to support them in the off-season. And maybe they say, "Hey, why should I fly all the way to Central America when I can just *laissez les bon temps roulez* in New Orleans?"

# Common Ground Dove

*First Impression*

**Small, ruddy dove on ground**

### Mark Your Calendar

Year-round

### Details, Details

- The length of a large sparrow, but much plumper; 6½ inches
- Stocky and short-necked, it looks as if its shoulders are hunched.
- Female is paler
- Also look for the larger (13-inch) Eurasian collared dove, with black collar at the back of its neck, and the white-winged dove (11½ inches), with a strip of white outlining the edge of its folded wing.

### Listen Up!

- A series of rising *woot, woot*s that gave it its nickname of "moaning dove"

### Telltale Traits

- Very tame; lets you approach very closely
- Won't fly until you almost step on it
- Spends most of its time on the ground
- Walks briskly with head nodding

### Look Here

- On the ground

### Or Here

- At the feeder
- Perched on fence or in tree
- In tobacco fields

*On the Home Front* Nests nearly year-round
- Builds its casual nest on the ground or in a low shrub, vine, fence, or stump

## Double the Doves

*"Oh that I had wings like a dove!"*

—**Psalms LV.6**

Doves have long, pointed wings built for fast flying. But this species seems to be reluctant to use them. The ground dove is almost always seen walking about on the ground, not flapping through the air.

**Wild Menu:** Seeds, especially weeds and grain; insects; small berries

**Plant Picks:** Plant a patch of birdseed by scattering handfuls of inexpensive seed mix. Let the plants stand to provide seed all fall and winter.

**Feeder Pleasers**
- Millet; birdseed mix; cracked corn

**Tricks and Treats**
- Doesn't need any extra enticement to visit

The South is home to several kinds of interesting doves, who will happily raise their families right in your backyard. Since doves feed their young "pigeon milk," which they produce from food they've eaten themselves, the time of nesting isn't dependent on, say, a boom crop of caterpillars. So doves tend to nest just about all year.

Look out also for the Eurasian collared dove, which may nest in cabbage palm (*Sabal palmetto*), magnolias (*Magnolia* spp.), ficus (*Ficus* spp.), black olive (*Bucida bucera*), eastern red cedar (*Juniperus virginiana*), live oak (*Quercus virginiana*), and other trees. White-winged doves, which often visit backyards, prefer to nest in colonies in woodlands.

# Northern Bobwhite

*First Impression*

**A flock of plump, streaky brown "footballs" scuttling through**

**Mark Your Calendar**

Year-round

**Details, Details**

- About the same length as a robin, but much plumper; 9¾ inches
- Stubby tail
- Female is streakier, with tan rather than white face markings
- The scaled quail, with quiet gray plumage, ranges through the lower western part of this region.

**Listen Up!**

- Clear as a whistle: *bob-WHITE!*
- The flock (called a covey) talks quietly with soft, low calls.

**Telltale Traits**

- A secretive bird; you'll hear bobwhites much more often than you'll see them
- Always in a covey, except when nesting
- Walks and runs over the ground
- Flies only when absolutely necessary; prefers to run away

**Look Here**

- On ground at feeder

**Or Here**

- In brushy fields or prairie plantings
- Foraging amid standing stems from last year's garden

*On the Home Front* The male and female build a ground nest together, weaving an arch of weeds and grasses overhead to conceal it.

*"They sometimes become very tame"*

—J. H. Stickney, *Bird World* (1898)

Bobwhites and other quail are creatures of habit. Once they discover that your feeding station holds a reliable feast, they're likely to become regulars. And, as Stickney writes, they may "come shyly into the barnyard or about the house for food."

**Wild Menu:** Seeds; grain; insects; berries; fruits

**Plant Picks:** A birdseed patch, mixed with corn and milo, supplies cover and food.

**Feeder Pleasers**

- Cracked corn; birdseed mix; millet

**Tricks and Treats**

- Provide a ground-level birdbath, such as a naturalistic molded resin type, with a drip tube

*Feed Store Finds* _____

I'm a big fan of "feed stores," those country places where you can pick up a 100-pound sack of grain, a fly swatter, or any other staples you might need. I often stumble across a product I never knew existed, but definitely want to try. One of my best finds was a poultry waterer—basically, an overturned jar in the center of a saucer that automatically refills when needed. Works great for bobwhites, if you can live with an object that definitely looks utilitarian. You can also buy one online at www.lehmans.com.

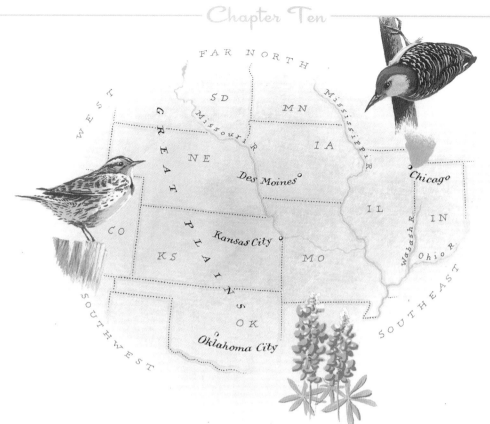

# Chapter Ten

# Birds of the Midwest

The region we call the Midwest was once home to such vast grasslands that early travelers could get lost for days. The grass was waist- or shoulder-high, and there were no landmarks to help you get your bearings. No mountain peaks cracked the horizon, and deep forests were mostly to the east and west.

Farm fields dominate the region now, with crops flourishing in the deep, fertile soil the prairies left behind. Those huge fields mean lots of open space—and birds that are adapted to that kind of habitat.

It's the plaintive whistled notes of the meadowlark and the sweet trills of ground-hugging sparrows that are the signature songs of many parts of this region, although you'll also find sweet-voiced thrushes and other forest birds in pockets of woods in the Midwest. In backyards with big shade trees, orioles and tanagers are often fixtures.

Many of the backyard birds of this region will look familiar to backyard bird-watchers in many parts of the country. That's because dozens of the most common and most widespread species are just as at home here as they are in other regions.

## WILD WEATHER

The Midwest has a geography all its own. Travel here from the East or West, and you'll notice that mountains and hills gradually give way to gentle slopes, then to land that's so flat you can see forever. From the air, you can easily spot the Midwest, too: It's a vast crazy quilt of green corn, golden wheat, blue-gray oats, and other crops, stitched together by roads and decorated with far-flung farmhouses and occasional towns. Skyscraper cities are here, too, but they quickly give way to wide open spaces on their outskirts.

Wind is a constant in this region. With few landforms to impede its movement, the wind—from soft, breezy caress to laundry-whipping gust—is a part of life here. Windbreaks of hedges and trees shield yards and gardens, especially in rural areas. Humidity is part of midwestern living, too. Summers can be mighty muggy.

**Productive fields cover what once was prairie.**

Storms are simply a fact of life in the Midwest. When warm air from the South hits that cold air sweeping down from the North, wild weather is the result. Crashing thunderstorms, towering lightning, and tornadoes blow through in spring and summer. Blizzards or icy cold can blast in with little warning in winter.

Those storms can sweep birds off course by a few miles or by hundreds of miles. Keep an eye out for oddballs, which can show up far outside their usual range or customary habitat. On a smaller scale, summer storms can also disrupt bird life by dislodging nests from trees, or by downing trees, nests and all. That's sad to see, but bird parents will usually quickly get busy on replacement nests.

You'll want to plant trees and shrubs and other plants in your yard to soften the blow of weather extremes for your bird friends. Food sources help, but cover is just as vital. Deciduous trees offer summer shade and nesting sites, while conifers and broad-leaved evergreens help keep birds cozy in winter. If your yard is exposed to open fields, you'll want a hedge or windbreak; include some evergreens in it for a four-season wind shield.

Include scattered groups of evergreens or

**Electrical storms are common in the Midwest and can disrupt bird activities.**

single specimen evergreens in your yard, too, for shelter in unpredictable weather. They'll offer extra safety when storms roll in.

## THE LAY OF THE LAND

Like other regions of the United States, the Midwest is a mix of cities, towns, and country land. But the rural areas are huge, with fields of soybeans, wheat, corn, and other crops as far as the eye can see. Most of our grain is raised here—and a lot of our birdseed!

Streams and rivers water the land, but drought cycles often occur every few years. Sparrows and other birds teem along every watercourse, from ponds to lakes to rivers, wherever they can find a bit of brush for cover. The grasslands and farm fields are also full of birds accustomed to that kind of a life. These are often ground nesters, such as meadowlarks, or birds that form gigantic flocks, such as blackbirds of various kinds.

The Midwest is well-known for being flat, but you'll find plenty of rolling hills, too, as well as sandstone bluffs, shale outcroppings, and other changes in elevation. Still, it's not exactly the nosebleed section of the US: The highest point in Indiana, where I lived for a decade, is only 1,257 feet above sea level. Stand there on Hoosier Hill—the exact highest point is tucked in a little thicket—and you'll feel the wind coming across miles of openness.

The Midwest grows acres of sunflowers for oil, snacks, and birdseed.

## FOOD AND SHELTER

Midwesterners are proud of their prairie heritage. Fabulous grasses, as high as your ears, whisper and sing as they rustle in the breeze. In summer and fall, the grasses are splashed with confetti colors from tall, bright wildflowers. Many of the prairie flowers belong to the composite or daisy family, which means they're chock-full of seeds for any birds nearby or passing through.

I learned a lot about the wonderful prairie plants when I lived in the Midwest. But what really took me by surprise were the glorious trees, and the huge colonies of spring wildflowers blooming beneath them.

Some parts of this region are dotted with gorgeous forests, nearly totally deciduous in nature. Guess what that means? Yep, fall colors that will take your breath away. Flaming sugar maples are as good as any in Vermont, and they're bolstered by scarlet oak, coppery beech, golden hickory, and purple ash leaves.

Oh, and don't forget one of the trademark trees of the Midwest: the sweet gum (*Liquidambar styraciflua*), whose leaves look burnished deep red from a distance, but are actually a spectacular mix of red, orange, honey gold, and maroon—often on the same leaf! They're so incredible, I used to wear them as jewelry, by simply pinning a leaf to my sweater.

Those deciduous trees produce tons of acorns and seeds for jays, titmice, nuthatches, and other birds; they also supply shelter and

**Maturing soybeans dominate the view, but hedgerows and field edges hold many birds. Little patches of woods hold wonderful spring wildflowers.**

**Purple spikes of *Liatris* punctuate a prairie.**

nest sites to scarlet and summer tanagers, thrushes, and many other shade-loving species. In winter, finches pry apart the seeds of tulip trees (*Liriodendron tulipifera*), box elders (*Acer negundo*), and other big trees, while titmice and chickadees work at the seedpods of smaller redbud trees (*Cercis canadensis*).

Shrubs and small trees are a hit with many birds in this region, whether they're the lilac in your backyard or the spicebush (*Lindera benzoin*) in the woods. They supply cover and places to move about safely, and they also serve as a handy diner. Insects on foliage, flowers, or bark, plus any fruits or berries or seeds, add variety to the birds' menu.

In fall, berried shrubs are a huge draw for birds. Look for migrating rose-breasted grosbeaks and tanagers to gather at dogwood trees (*Cornus* spp.); native dogwood shrubs, such as silky dogwood (*Cornus amomum*); and native viburnums, including arrowwood (*Viburnum dentatum)* and other species.

Thrushes and bluebirds seem to be partial to deciduous hollies, such as winterberry (*Ilex verticillata*) and spicebush (*Lindera benzoin*).

The deciduous woodlands are home to another well-kept secret of this region: the unbelievable spring wildflower show. Immense colonies of dense mayapple (*Podophyllum peltatum*), or vast sky-blue stretches of wild sweet William (*Phlox divaricata*) or knee-high Virginia bluebells (*Mertensia virginica*), are just a few of the dozens of species that make spring a delight.

Although the wildflowers don't supply much food for birds, they do make spring bird-watching a pleasure that's hard to beat anywhere in the country. Don't forget to keep an eye out for the delectable mushrooms called morels, too!

Every spring, I looked forward to spending a long day in the woods, welcoming back spring migrants and admiring wildflowers, then coming home with my sack of loot—a mess of morels to dip in cornmeal batter and fry up to hot, juicy perfection.

## CLIMATE

The Midwest gets four seasons, but they're not always evenly distributed. Intense cold and intense heat mark the seasonal extremes in winter and summer, but spring and fall can be glorious.

Winters are long, especially in the upper Midwest, where snow and cold may seem to last forever. Ice storms are more the order in the lower part of the region, though they can occur anywhere. Snow and ice may make it impossible for birds to find food, so your feeders can be a literal lifesaver in winter.

**A drought will bring birds to your birdbath.**

By the time summer rolls around, you may find yourself wishing for another taste of that winter weather! The air is hot and humid in summer, and 90°F days can set in even while the daffodils are still blooming. Seasonal dry stretches and even drought occur fairly often. A birdbath or water feature in your yard will be popular with birds during dry times, and may even pull birds from surrounding fields.

Spring is famous as tornado season, and most midwesterners are used to taking sensible precautions. A weather radio that broadcasts important alerts is a common fixture in midwestern homes.

One way you'll know when the threat of bad weather has passed is to listen to the birds. When the black clouds move on, you'll hear birds singing again as they come out of their storm shelters.

## BIRD LIFE IN THE MIDWEST

Birds are abundant in this region, thanks to plenty of wide open spaces, plus inviting backyards in farms, small towns, and cities. Roadsides and scattered patches of woods support thriving bird life, too.

Large expanses of open land encourage grassland birds, such as meadowlarks, dickcissels, scissor-tailed flycatchers, buntings, and kingbirds. Once, they were the natural inhabitants of the vast, grassy prairies that covered this area. Now, they live in or along farm fields and other open land. Not all grassland birds will come into backyards, but many, including sparrows, blackbirds, and quail, have expanded their horizons to include a welcoming backyard.

With its bounty of grasses, prairie wildflowers, and grain crops, seed-eating birds are in heaven here. You'll notice an abundance of seed-eating species such as black-

**Grasslands support all kinds of wildlife as well as seed-eating birds.**

**Summer tanagers are a seasonal treat.**

birds and native sparrows in this region. And you can easily tempt them to your yard by planting a garden of seed-rich sunflowers (*Helianthus annuus*), millet, and other bird-seed plants. Birds will find plenty to pick at in your flower or vegetable garden, too, over fall and winter.

Birds that usually stick to open fields often show up in backyards in fall or winter, wherever there's a welcoming handout of seeds on the stem or in the feeder. When I lived in the Midwest, I hosted meadowlarks every winter—at my in-town feeder.

Some backyard birds, including feeder friends such as blue jays, song sparrows, and downy woodpeckers, are year-round residents in the Midwest.

Other species are more of the fair-weather variety. They return reliably each spring to raise their families and spend the summer. But winter vacation? No thanks, they say, as they flock south. As soon as the days grow shorter, they're off for a more hospitable climate. Insect eaters such as summer tanagers, scissor-tailed flycatchers, and orioles, for instance, are only seasonal pleasures instead of year-round friends.

A few unusual species can really liven up a winter day in the Midwest. This is vacation land for some of the super-hardy birds of the Far North, including Lapland longspurs, red-breasted nuthatches, and tree sparrows.

## Upper and Lower Midwest

This region covers a wide area from north to south, which means that the seasonal aspects of bird-watching may be different for some species.

In the more southerly part of the region, say, Oklahoma, chipping sparrows may stick around all year. While you're enjoying those chippies at Christmas, your friends in Iowa are looking forward to the return of "their" birds next spring.

Other species, such as the vesper sparrow, may be present in summer in the northern parts of the region and in winter only in the southern sections. And some only pass through the lower Midwest on their way to nesting grounds in the upper part of this region.

You'll find general range and seasonal info for each species in this chapter. But you may also want to check a more comprehensive field guide, such as Peterson's or Sibley's, to pinpoint birds' ranges in your particular area.

## Start Here

Like other regions, the Midwest is home to many common and widespread species of backyard birds. That's why you'll want to begin your tour of midwestern bird life by turning to Chapter 6, "Start Here." That's where you'll find many familiar backyard friends that you may already know by name, such as the cardinal, chickadee, goldfinch, and robin.

These are the birds you share with other parts of the country. You'll also find white-breasted nuthatches, tufted titmice, juncos, cedar waxwings, and many others who are happy to pay a visit to your backyard.

Every single one of the "Start Here" birds is happily at home in the Midwest region. You'll see some of these species more often than others. But if you keep looking, eventually you may get to know them all.

## Regional Specialties

"Start Here" birds are just the beginning! In this chapter, which spotlights birds of the Midwest region, you'll meet other interesting friends. Some of these birds also occur in other regions. But every single one of them could turn up in your midwestern backyard.

Because of your location smack-dab in the middle of the country, you're likely to see birds whose ranges are to your east or west, too, as well as your regulars. Strong storms—and you know all about those!—may carry them astray into your region. Or they may just be wandering.

Paging through the other regional sections will help you get acquainted with possible travelers. Then, if they do turn up in your backyard, you'll find it's more like saying hello to a new friend for the first time than trying to identify a stranger.

Be sure to page through the birds of the Far North region, too (Chapter 8). Many of them pay a brief visit to midwestern backyards as they pass through on migration to and from more northern areas or mountainous places.

## Birds of the Midwest

Here are the birds profiled in this chapter. Remember to consult the "Start Here" birds, starting on page 79, for the most common birds to be found in the Midwest.

# Red-Headed Woodpecker

*First Impression*

**A breathtaking bird! Bold white and black patches with a vivid crimson head**

### Mark Your Calendar

Spring through fall in part of region; year-round in other areas

### Details, Details

- A little smaller than a robin; 9¼ inches
- Female looks like male
- Juvenile has brown head

### Listen Up!

- Rattles, *chirr*s, and a loud, wheezy *queeer queeer queeer*
- Doesn't usually excavate into wood for insects; does drum, weakly, on occasion

### Telltale Traits

- Fly-catches! The bird flies from a perch after an insect, then returns to eat it and wait for another one.
- Usually seen alone or in pairs; after nesting, may forage in family groups
- Not a rare bird in general, but locally common: in some parts of its range, it's easy to spot; in other areas, it's absent
- Stores acorns, nuts, and sometimes grasshoppers to eat later

### Look Here

- Fly-catching from a utility pole, fence post, or tree

### Or Here

- Flying across an open area
- On ground beneath trees, eating nuts
- Eating fruit or berries in bushes or trees
- Scavenging corn in farm field

*"A bird of the open country"*

—A. C. Bent, *Life Histories of North American Woodpeckers* (1939)

**Most woodpeckers stick close to the woods. Look for this drop-dead-gorgeous bird winging across fields or hollering from a utility pole out in the open.**

*On the Home Front* Nests in dead trees or in wooden utility poles, high up near top • May use a nest box • Male does most of excavation

**Wild Menu:** Insects; fruit and berries; corn; nuts and acorns

**Plant Picks:** Cherries, grapes, mulberries (*Morus* spp.), and other fruits; corn; oak trees for acorns; pecans for nuts; crab apples and other flowering trees for insects

### Feeder Pleasers

- Dried corn on the cob, pushed firmly onto a spike; nuts; suet

### Tricks and Treats

- Got any weathered wooden posts around? Install them as inviting perches for fly-catching in your yard. You can also try "planting" a new wood post; the taller, the better.

## Cavity Karma

Birds that nest in cavities can get pugnacious when it comes time to lay claim to a nest hole. The bird that dug it doesn't always get to enjoy its new home! Starlings are famed for snitching holes from woodpeckers. Great crested flycatchers may also usurp the holes for their own use.

Before you start feeling too sorry for red-headed woodpeckers, keep in mind that this species may use the same tactics to steal a nest hole from red-bellied woodpeckers.

# Red-Bellied Woodpecker

*First Impression*

**Big, calm, red-headed woodpecker at feeder**

## Mark Your Calendar

Year-round; absent from western part of this region

## Details, Details

- Almost as big as a robin; 9¼ inches
- Female has red only on back of neck, not top of head
- Tiny, hardly noticeable patch of red-tinged feathers on lower belly

## Listen Up!

- Loud, harsh, querulous *quirrrr?*
- Steady, medium-speed drumming

## Telltale Traits

- Back and wings look grayish from distance; up close, appear finely black-and-white zebra striped
- Undulating flight, with deep dips
- Often very tame; slow to fly away when you approach

## Look Here

- At feeder eating sunflower seeds or corn

## Or Here

- Clinging to tree trunks or large branches
- Foraging on ground
- At suet or nectar feeder

*On the Home Front* Excavates a cavity in a dead tree, usually deciduous, often in woods • May adopt a nest box • Breeding activity begins very early; in Illinois, breeding begins in late winter, with nesting as early as March.

*"Drinking the sweet sap from the troughs in sugar camps"*

—**Charles Bendire, describing the diet of this species,** *Life Histories of North American Birds* **(1895)**

**Red-bellieds have a definite sweet tooth. One of these big birds may appropriate a nectar feeder, clinging in an acrobatic position while it guzzles the feeder dry.**

**Wild Menu:** Insects; seeds; nuts; fruit

**Plant Picks:** Pecan or oak trees for nuts; field corn or Indian corn; tall, large-headed sunflowers (*Helianthus annuus*); mulberries (*Morus* spp.)

**Feeder Pleasers**

- Whole ears of dried corn on cob; sunflower seeds; suet and suet-based foods

**Tricks and Treats**

- Squirrel feeders that hold an ear of corn fixed in place work great for this big guy to peck at, too.
- Fasten a wire suet cage firmly to a tree or post to give this bird a place to prop its tail.
- May become a nectar drinker

## Easier Excavating

Get in the habit of looking for dead limbs and snags in your yard and neighborhood, and you may spot a woodpecker nest hole. Often you'll spot more than one, with the older ones at top and the freshest-looking one at bottom.

There's a reason for this: fungus. Wood-decaying fungi usually enter at the top of a stub, carried into the wood by rain. As the fungi break down the wood, they make digging easier for woodpeckers. As the fungi work their way down the dead snag, so do the woodpeckers, excavating the softening wood underneath last year's hole.

# Scissor-Tailed Flycatcher

*First Impression*

**Pale gray bird with outrageously long, skinny tail, usually perched**

## Mark Your Calendar

In upper MW, an occasional stray; in lower MW, spring through fall

## Details, Details

- From tip to tip, the flycatcher measures 10 inches—but that tail is 6 inches all by itself! Bird's body is about sparrow size.
- Female has a shorter tail than male, but it's still notably long
- Tail is deeply forked, easily visible in flight
- Look for salmon-colored undersides of wings and sides of body in flight.

## Listen Up!

- Series of rapid, twittering notes
- Calls *ko-peek*!

## Telltale Traits

- Opens and closes tail in flight, like a pair of scissors
- Perches for hours, sallying forth to snatch insects from the air or on the ground
- Swoops to ground from perch, or dashes out into air, returning to same perch
- Can hover in mid-air
- Sometimes hops on ground

## Look Here

- On perch near open space

## Or Here

- On ground, capturing grasshoppers or other insects
- In flight across open land
- Eating fruit or berries

*"Most fantastic of feathered sky-dances"*
—**Herbert Brandt,** *Texas Bird Adventures* **(1940)**

**Like an exotic bird-of-paradise, this all-American species uses his fantastic feathers to wow the female in a courtship extravaganza that lasts for weeks.**

*On the Home Front* May nest in backyard in small tree or shrub

**Wild Menu:** Insects, especially grasshoppers, crickets, wasps, and beetles; some fruit

**Plant Picks:** Try a meadow or prairie planting with posts for perching.

**Feeder Pleasers**
- Hulled sunflower chips; insect-enriched suet

**Tricks and Treats**
- Avoid pesticides to ensure grasshoppers.

## Sky Dancer

John Terres, in the *Audubon Society Encyclopedia of North American Birds* (1980), notes that the male scissor-tail makes a remarkable courtship flight. First the flycatcher flies to about 100 feet high, until he's just a dot against the blue sky. Then he plunges down partway and zigzags, while vocalizing in a cackle that sounds like rapid hand clapping.

Hold your applause, though, because the best is yet to come. Climbing straight up again, he then goes into a series of backward somersaults that show off his incredible tail. Watch for the show when you're in scissor-tail country in May or June.

# Eastern Bluebird

## First Impression

**Unbelievable blue that takes your breath away**

### Mark Your Calendar

In upper MW, spring through fall; in lower MW, year-round

### Details, Details

- Smaller than a robin, as big as a large sparrow: 7 inches
- Female is duller, looks faded

### Listen Up!

- Sweet, gurgling, whistled *tru-a-ly, tru-a-ly!*
- Brief, husky call note that seems to keep birds in touch: *chew*

### Telltale Traits

- Travels in short, slow, fluttering swoops from one perch to another
- Often glides from low perch to ground with wings spread, to catch insects

### Look Here

- Perched near or in open areas, often near the edge of a woods or an orchard

### Or Here

- In golf courses, cemeteries, large parks, or pastures, or along roadsides
- At apples, crab apples, and other flowering trees, picking off insects at blossoms
- At feeders or birdbaths

**On the Home Front** Early nester, even in upper Midwest • Cavity nester • Prefers a site in open area or at edge of woods, not in forest • Only the female incubates and broods young, but the male pitches in when it's mealtime.

*"Cows use the box to scratch their backs"*

—Thomas Musselman, on why he had to mount 200 nest boxes (near Quincy, Illinois) *outside* of fences, "Three Years of Eastern Bluebird Banding and Study" (1935)

Finding just the right spot for a bluebird box can be a matter of trial and error—or frustration, thanks to house sparrows claiming the box. Why not start a trail like Musselman's on a rural road where bluebirds can live in peace?

**Wild Menu:** Insects; fruit and berries

**Plant Picks:** Flowering trees; small fruits, including mulberries (*Morus* spp.), serviceberries (*Amelanchier* spp.), winterberry (*Ilex verticillata*) and evergreen hollies (*Ilex* spp.), Virginia creeper (*Parthenocissus quinquefolia*); dogwood (*Cornus* spp.)

**Feeder Pleasers**

- Mealworms and other insect foods; accessible suet, peanut butter mixed with cornmeal to form a crumbly dough, and fat-based foods

**Tricks and Treats**

- The sound of trickling water is a big draw.
- Put up a roost box so bluebirds can stay cozy.

## Shaking Out the Sheets

Female bluebirds are good housekeepers, according to evidence from video cameras placed inside nest boxes. They even shake out their nests, with a motion that scientists call "tremble-thrusting." The female pokes her beak deep into the nesting material and, with a rapid trembling motion, shakes her entire nest. According to the evidence on camera, this helps shake loose parasitic larvae from the bedding.

# Summer Tanager

*First Impression*

**Vivid rosy red bird, without a crest**

### Mark Your Calendar

Spring through fall in some parts of this region; only a stray in northern and western areas

### Details, Details

- Smaller than a robin; 7¾ inches
- Note its absence of black wings. The scarlet tanager, which has black wings and tail, also appears in backyards in the MW.
- Female is greenish yellow, sometimes with tinges of red-orange

### Listen Up!

- A short, musical song of hurried phrases, repeated after a pause
- Call sounds like *chicky-chucky-chuck*

### Telltale Traits

- Your best chance of spotting one is in spring when the males return. They chase each other, sing constantly, and actively establish territories.
- Forages alone in mid- to upper levels of trees, usually deciduous
- Skilled at fly-catching
- Moves through foliage slowly

### Look Here

- Usually in deciduous trees

### Or Here

- Chasing other males or a female
- Flying after wasps or other airborne insects

*On the Home Front* Usually nests high in trees
- Female gathers nest material and builds nest

## *"The summer redbird"*

**—Traditional name**

The cardinal is more often called "redbird," but the name certainly applies to this species, too. Unlike the cardinal that resides year-round, the "summer redbird" is gone before the autumn leaves change color.

**Wild Menu:** Insects, especially bees and wasps; fruit and berries

**Plant Picks:** Fruits of any kind, particularly mulberries (*Morus* spp.) and blackberries. To attract tanagers, bluebirds, and other fabulous fruit eaters, let a plant of the common poke-weed (*Phytolacca americana*) grow in your yard.

### Feeder Pleasers

- Not usually a feeder visitor, but has been reported to eat an offering of bananas; may like mealworms, too.

### Tricks and Treats

- Add a drip tube or mister to your birdbath and you may see summer tanagers freshen up.

## Taking Inventory

In the 1950s, researchers in the Midwest disassembled a summer tanager nest to take a detailed inventory of what it was made from. The materials weren't what you might expect. Instead of being gathered from treetops, they'd been collected from fields or roadsides. The base was constructed entirely of panicles of white vervain (*Verbena urticifolia*), a common, easily overlooked, weedy wildflower. The second layer was made of at least 46 pieces of a grass called *Bromus japonicus*. And the soft inner layer was woven from 215 fine stems of muhly grass (*Muhlenbergia schreberi*).

# Blue Grosbeak

*First Impression*

A dark, nothing-special, sparrow size bird hopping about on the ground—until it moves into the sun and shows its deep, rich, cobalt blue coloring

### Mark Your Calendar

Spring through fall

### Details, Details

- The size of a sparrow; 6¾ inches
- Cinnamon wing bars and a big bill set this species apart from the indigo bunting.
- Female is grayish brown
- Juvenile females are warm reddish brown; juvenile males are blotched with blue.
- Look close to see the big, heavy bill.

### Listen Up!

- Long, warbling song with a quiet quality that doesn't grab attention
- Metallic *zink* call note

### Telltale Traits

- Flies low, from one shrub to another
- Often forages on ground

### Look Here

- Hopping on ground, often beneath shrubs

### Or Here

- Singing from within a shrub
- Perched in the top of a bush or small tree
- Foraging in flocks in plowed fields

*On the Home Front* Nests usually not more than 8 feet up, in small trees, shrubs, brambles, or vines • May nest in backyard • The female provides most of the food for the young in the nest.

*"A very diligent singer in the early morning hours"*

—Henry Nehrling, *Our Native Birds of Song and Beauty* (1896)

But, continues Nehrling, "I have rarely heard its lively strain during noontide." That helps set this species apart from the very similar and much more abundant indigo bunting, who's famed for singing during the heat of the day.

**Wild Menu:** Insects; grain; weed seeds; fruit

**Plant Picks:** Plant shrubs in groups or add a hedge or a patch of blackberries to supply the cover these birds crave.

**Feeder Pleasers**
- Millet; birdseed mix

**Tricks and Treats**
- Often incorporates shed snakeskins and other unusual, soft, or crinkly materials into its nest: cotton, rags, newspaper, string, cellophane, and plastic snack wrappers. Try offering these or similar materials at nesting time.

## Bring on the Blue

Blue grosbeaks are easy to confuse with indigo buntings, but they have their own behavior that sets them apart. Indigo buntings don't hang out in flocks, although you may see several of them feeding in the same place during migration. Blue grosbeaks are more social.

After the young birds leave their parents, they form small flocks that forage together. When the parents are finished raising their second brood, that batch of birds joins the flock, too. Look for them in grainfields and grasslands. They'll look black—like a flock of cowbirds—until you take a closer look with binoculars.

# Rose-Breasted Grosbeak

## First Impression

Flashy black and snow-white bird with rosy chest

### Mark Your Calendar

Spring through fall in some areas of the region; migration only in others

### Details, Details

- A little smaller than a robin; 8 inches
- Female is streaky brown

### Listen Up!

- Warbling song, similar to robin's
- Squeaky call note; Sibley describes it as "sneakers on a gym floor"

### Telltale Traits

- Flashes big white wing patches in flight
- Female looks like an overgrown female purple finch

### Look Here

- In shade trees or small trees

### Or Here

- At apples, crab apples, and other flowering trees, picking off insects at blossoms
- At feeder

**On the Home Front** Nests in a wide variety of habitats, including deciduous, mixed, and coniferous woodlands, overgrown fields and pastures, roadsides, along railroads, city parks, and of course in backyards • Nests usually less than 20 feet from ground • Makes a loose, open cup, often so thinly constructed that eggs can be seen right through the bottom of it.

*"Within a stone's throw of brick buildings"*

—**A. C. Bent,** *Life Histories of North American Cardinals, Grosbeaks, and Allies (1968)*

Bent noted that in the 50 years since he was a boy, this bird that formerly nested far from human dwellings "learned to find sanctuary ... closer to the haunts of man in our towns, villages, and suburban grounds."

**Wild Menu:** Insects, including gypsy moth caterpillars and Colorado potato beetles; tree buds; some fruit and seeds

**Plant Picks:** Elderberries (*Sambucus* spp.), mulberries (*Morus* spp.); Virginia creeper (*Parthenocissus quinquefolia*); grapes; maples native to your area for winter seeds

**Feeder Pleasers**
- Sunflower seeds

**Tricks and Treats**
- It's becoming a regular feeder visitor, so offer mealworms and other insect foods.
- Birdbaths are popular with migrants.

## Ever-Lovin' Elderberries

I didn't know I had rose-breasted grosbeaks nesting in my Pennsylvania yard years ago until I spotted a male grosbeak flying to and from my patch of elderberry bushes. Through binoculars, I could see the bird's beak was splashed with purple juice from the berries. More exciting, he was carrying berries in that beak—and that meant there were nestlings nearby! Sure enough, the birds had a nest in a young red maple that I walked beneath several times a day. I'd never even been aware that a family was getting started there. Did they choose the nest site because of the berries nearby? Or just by a happy coincidence? They never told.

# Painted Bunting

*First Impression*

**Unbelievable parrotlike colors—red and blue and lime green**

### Mark Your Calendar

Lower MW, spring through fall; may stray to other areas

### Details, Details

- Small sparrow size; 5½ inches
- Female is yellowish green
- Not until fall of the second year does the male bird acquire its full stunning plumage. Until then, males look like females.

### Listen Up!

- Sweet, tinkling, melodic song
- Low *chip!* alarm call

### Telltale Traits

- Acts like a sparrow, foraging in grassy or weedy places
- Male sings from exposed, elevated perch
- A "scrapper": Male birds fight viciously with each other, sometimes to the death.

### Look Here

- At feeder

### Or Here

- Eating seeds of foxtail grass or other weeds, while clinging to the bending stems
- Singing from the top of a bush

*On the Home Front* Not usually a backyard nester • Nests in low vegetation, usually less than 6 feet aboveground • Makes a well-woven, deep cup of plant fibers and stems

*"The most common cage bird they have"*

—Edward Wilson, noting the common practice of keeping this species as a pet, *American Ornithology* (1832)

Wilson also noted that "Many of them have been transported to Europe." Audubon commented on the practice, too, describing how the birds were trapped when attracted by a live or stuffed bunting decoy, and remarking that "Few vessels leave the port … without taking some Painted Finches."

**Wild Menu:** Seeds, especially grass and weeds; grain; some insects

**Plant Picks:** Scatter a few handfuls of birdseed mix or finch mix in a sunny patch of soil.

### Feeder Pleasers

- Millet; birdseed mix; sunflower seeds; cracked corn; chick scratch (a crushed grain mixture available at farm feed stores)

### Tricks and Treats

- Don't be too fussy a weeder. Painted buntings seek out weedy grasses, as well as dock, pigweed, and other common weeds.
- Add more birdbaths, fountains, or water features of any kind for drinking and bathing.

## *Caging Nature*

When I was a little girl, my mom kept canaries. One day, the pet shop we visited had new birds for sale: beautiful creatures that the sign called "painted buntings." My mom couldn't resist those colors; even though the birds were extremely nervous, so she took one home to join the canaries. Within a few days, it had calmed down and learned the routine.

The bunting lived to a ripe old age of 12. Years later, I was looking through my first field guide when I stopped, stunned. There was my mom's painted bunting—a wild songbird of the lower Midwest and South. It must have been trapped in the wild, not raised in an aviary like her singing canaries. No wonder the poor thing had been so frantic.

# Dickcissel

*First Impression*
**A prettier, yellow-splashed house sparrow; or a miniature meadowlark!**

### Mark Your Calendar

Spring through fall

### Details, Details

- Same size as house sparrow: 6¼ inches
- From the front, the dickcissel bears a surprising first-glance resemblance to the meadowlark, thanks to a dramatic black V on its upper chest.
- Use binoculars to see its yellow facial markings.
- Female is paler and lacks black V at throat

### Listen Up!

- All together now: *dik-dik-dik-SISSEL! dik-dik-dik-SISSEL!*
- Actually, that *sissel* may sound more like *siss-siss-siss*, with sibilant emphasis.
- Call note, a quick *check*

### Telltale Traits

- Forages on or near ground
- Often turns up among house sparrows
- Sings incessantly in nesting season

### Look Here

- At the feeder or on ground beneath it

### Or Here

- On ground, in nearby open land, such as overgrown pastures or weedy fields
- Low to ground, on brushy roadsides or in shrubby areas of your yard

*On the Home Front* Usually nests in old fields or prairie, low but not on ground

*"What's with that name?"*

—**Bird-watchers who first hear about the dickcissel**

There's a simple explanation for the name of this bird: That's exactly what its song sounds like—the syllables *dick-sis-sel* repeated over and over and over, from dawn to dusk, throughout breeding season.

**Wild Menu:** Seeds; grain; insects, including many grasshoppers and cankerworms

**Plant Picks:** Bluestem (*Andropogon* spp.), switchgrass (*Panicum virgatum*), and other prairie grasses and wildflowers will make this species feel at home.

### Feeder Pleasers

- Millet; birdseed mix; cracked corn and chick scratch (a crushed grain mixture available at farm feed stores)

### Tricks and Treats

- Occasionally a dickcissel will linger long into fall, even winter. That's when it's likely to show up at your feeder.

## Hello, My Name Is ...

In my early days as a bird-watcher, I glanced at a letter posted on the wall of the visitor's center at Hawk Mountain in Pennsylvania. It remarked on a sighting of a dickcissel, in what seemed to be a joking tone. Years later, after I had moved from Pennsylvania (where dickcissels don't exist) to Indiana (where they are common), I was walking along a field when I heard what I thought was a new kind of grasshopper or other insect. From every side, I heard the same song: three quick *dik-dik-dik* syllables, ending with a sibilant burst of *sss-sss-sss*—dickcissels, holding forth on all sides. I never snickered at their name again.

217

# Harris's Sparrow

*First Impression*

**A very big, white- or gray-bellied sparrow with a black bib and head**

## Mark Your Calendar

Most areas, winter only; in northern part of this region and a few other areas, only seen on migration

## Details, Details

- Our biggest sparrow; 7½ inches
- Look for the dramatic black facial markings of adult birds.
- A lot of variation in plumage: belly, for instance, may be white or gray
- Note adult's pink bill.

## Listen Up!

- Single, plaintive, whistled note, repeated several times; similar to white-throated sparrow's whistle, but all on same pitch
- Sudden *week!* alarm call
- Winter flocks make a wide variety of calls.

## Telltale Traits

- Kicks and scratches on ground
- When alarmed by a person, flies up into trees instead of seeking low cover
- When alarmed by a hawk, takes shelter in low cover, instead of up in trees.
- May visit singly, in pairs, in flocks, or mixed in a flock of other sparrows

## Look Here

- At feeder or beneath it

## Or Here

- Scratching in flower or vegetable garden
- In hedges, shrub groups, overgrown corners, and other brushy places

*On the Home Front* Nests *waaaay* up near Arctic Circle • Nests on ground, in scraped-out depression under small shrub

*"The only North American songbird that breeds exclusively in Canada"*

—**The National Audubon Society Watchlist**

The Midwest is the winter home of this big, pretty sparrow, which nests in remote boreal forest edges and tundra. Because its Canadian summer home is so hard to reach, the nesting habits of this species were not discovered until 1931.

**Wild Menu:** Seeds; grain; insects; snails

**Plant Picks:** Scatter a few handfuls of birdseed mix to grow a patch for winter foraging. Let flower garden stalks stand, so sparrows can seek seeds on or under them.

**Feeder Pleasers**

- Millet; birdseed mix; cracked corn and chick scratch (a crushed grain mixture available at farm feed stores); accessible suet; leftover bread

**Tricks and Treats**

- For a high-calorie winter warm-up, toss crumbled, stale doughnuts and cornmeal with chopped suet.
- Puddles from melting snow are favorite spots for a bath. Try a low-level basin with a heater for backyard visitors.

*Sharing Lessons*

Harris's sparrows can create dissension at your bird feeder. Often they act aggressively, chasing other birds away. Cut down on the competition by supplying chicken scratch and millet in a low tray feeder or directly on the ground, away from other feeders.

# Lark Sparrow

*First Impression*

**Big, slender sparrow with white-cornered tail**

### Mark Your Calendar

Spring through fall

### Details, Details

- Sparrow size; 6½ inches
- Dramatic white corners of tail, like towhee
- Whitish or pale breast with black spot in center
- Striking head pattern in chestnut, gray, white, and black—like the patches of a Harlequin
- Female looks like male
- Immature birds show a distinct but less bold version of the head pattern.

### Listen Up!

- A pretty song, full of liquid trills, with the occasional rattling note—often sung in flight
- Alarm call, a sudden *chewp!*

### Telltale Traits

- Spends a lot of time on ground or lawn
- Forages on ground with much scratching
- Frequent singer from ground, fence post, trees, and wires, or in air
- The male struts like a turkey to court the female, with his tail spread to show off its white corners.

### Look Here

- On the ground, usually scratching for food

### Or Here

- Foraging in vegetable or flower garden
- Foraging on lawn
- Singing from a perch or in the air

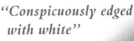

*"Conspicuously edged with white"*

—Ralph Hoffmann, on the tail of the lark sparrow, *Birds of the Pacific States* (1927)

**Sparrows can be tricky to tell apart, so any flashy markings are a big help. With this species, watch for the conspicuous white-edged bottom and sides of its tail in flight.**

*On the Home Front* Nests low to or on ground, often hidden by overhanging branch

**Wild Menu:** Seeds, especially of grasses; insects, particularly grasshoppers

**Plant Picks:** Tolerate a few weedy grasses, such as foxtail, in your garden, or sow millet. Your lawn is inviting to these birds.

### Feeder Pleasers

- Doesn't often come to feeders during breeding season, but may on migration. Offer millet, birdseed mix, or chick scratch (a crushed grain mixture available at farm feed stores).

### Tricks and Treats

- A birdbath, especially one low to the ground, may be welcomed during drought.

## Recycled Nests

No one knows why, but this species has a penchant for "recycling" the nests of other birds as its homesites. Nests of scissor-tailed flycatchers, western kingbirds, thrashers, and especially mockingbirds are often sought out—sometimes while the original owner is still in residence!

Those owners can get mighty aggressive defending their real estate. If you spot one chasing a sparrow, you may be seeing the home-front defense in action.

# Vesper Sparrow

## *First Impression*

**Nondescript, streaky brown sparrow—
with white outer tail feathers**

### Mark Your Calendar

Spring through fall in upper MW; migration only or winter in most of lower MW

### Details, Details

- Sparrow size; 6¼ inches
- Brown streaks may show against a tan or white background.
- White eye ring
- Male and female look alike

### Listen Up!

- Two long, low whistles give way to pretty, musical trills, something like the song of a song sparrow.
- Sharp *chip!* alarm note

### Telltale Traits

- Walks or runs over the ground
- "Grass sparrow" and "grass finch" are old names, reflecting its habit of hanging out in fields, meadows, and pastures.
- Male sings from highest available perches within nesting territory, not on ground

### Look Here

- At feeder

### Or Here

- In grassy areas
- Singing from an elevated perch

### *On the Home Front* Not a backyard nester

- The female alone builds the nest, placing it at the base of a plant or by a clump of crop residue.

*"Two or three long, silver notes of peace and rest, ending in some subdued trills and quavers"*

—**John Burroughs,** *Wake-Robin* **(1871)**

"Vesper" means "of or pertaining to the evening," and that's what gave these birds their name. Although vesper sparrows also sing at other times, it's after sunset, when most birds have ceased singing, that you can really appreciate their pretty song.

**Wild Menu:** Insects, especially grasshoppers; seeds; grain

**Plant Picks:** Try a prairie planting or meadow to entice a vesper sparrow to your yard.

**Feeder Pleasers**

- Millet; birdseed mix; chick scratch (a crushed grain mixture available at farm feed stores); maybe mealworms

**Tricks and Treats**

- Provide a low-level birdbath.

## *After-Dinner Treat*

Vesper sparrows range across almost the entire country, according to the maps in field guides. Yet many folks still miss out on the pleasures of vesper sparrows. They sing at what has become, in modern life, one of our busiest times of the day. We're eating dinner, or helping with homework, or watching kids or grandkids at school events.

If your calendar is jam-packed, why not pencil in "vesper sparrows, twilight" on a few dates in spring and summer? Once you catch this romantic concert, you'll never forget it.

# Field Sparrow

*First Impression*

**Small brown bird with blank, wide-eyed look**

*"Sometimes sings on moonlit nights"*

—John K. Terres,
*The Audubon Encyclopedia of North American Birds* (1980)

## Mark Your Calendar

Spring through fall in upper Midwest; year-round in lower; absent in extreme western part of this region

## Details, Details

- Small sparrow size, what else? 5¾ inches
- Pink bill
- Reddish cap and white eye ring; no dark spot on breast
- Female looks like male

## Listen Up!

- Plaintive *see-a, see-a, see-a, see-a, wee, wee, wee, wee*
- Sharp, short *chip!* of alarm

## Telltale Traits

- Scratches vigorously on ground
- Often in flocks of mixed sparrow species

## Look Here

- On ground beneath feeder, or in tray feeder

## Or Here

- Scratching elsewhere in your yard for seeds, in flower beds or vegetable garden
- Hanging on weeds or grass stems to reach seeds

*On the Home Front* Not usually a backyard nester; as its name says, prefers old fields with scattered shrubs—but keep looking! • Female builds early nests on or near ground, often in grass clumps or below shrubs

**Field sparrows may seem like ordinary little brown birds at the feeder, but they have an unusual and charming habit of breaking into song on bright nights in nesting season.**

**Wild Menu:** Insects; weed seeds and grass seeds

**Plant Picks:** A scattering of millet birdseed on a patch of your vegetable garden or flower bed will give you hours of fun, as you watch field sparrows and other sparrows eating seeds off the stems.

**Feeder Pleasers**

- Millet; canary seed and other small seeds

**Tricks and Treats**

- Like other winter sparrows, the field sparrow appreciates a warm bath on a cold day. Check out a heater for your birdbath.
- Nests are often lined with horsehair from the animal's mane or tail. Ask at a nearby stable for currycomb leavings if you don't have your own trusty steed.

## Cowbird Culture

Parasitic brown-headed cowbirds are common in the Midwest, and that's bad news for field sparrows, as they're frequent victims. The cowbird sneakily lays its own eggs in the sparrow's nest, passing off parenting chores to the poor field sparrow.

In one Iowa study, nearly 80 percent of nests were parasitized by cowbirds. That doesn't necessarily mean boom times for cowbirds, however: Once the field sparrow discovers the foreign eggs, it often deserts its nest—even if it has already laid its own eggs.

# Bobolink

## First Impression

**Flock of startling black-and-white birds flying across a field, singing tinkling, joyous songs**

### Mark Your Calendar

Upper MW, spring through fall; lower MW, migration only

### Details, Details

- The size of a large sparrow; 7 inches
- Sometimes called the "skunk blackbird," thanks to its black-with-white feathers
- Female looks like a sparrow, gray-brown with streaky back and wings
- After breeding season, the male loses his dramatic colors and turns to a warm tan version of the female

### Listen Up!

- A warbling, bubbling song that sounds like *"bob-o'-link, bob-o'-link, spink, spank, spink"*
- Also a low *chuck* call

### Telltale Traits

- Walks slowly over ground, grabbing bites of food as it goes
- Male sings while flying, constantly warbling; flies low, almost hovering
- When not nesting season, birds stick together in flocks

### Look Here

- In grassy fields

### Or Here

- In cultivated fields, especially hay fields for nesting and grainfields when foraging
- Possibly at your feeder; look closely at those "sparrows" in case they're bobolinks not in breeding plumage.

*"Robert of Lincoln is gayly drest"*

—American poet William Cullen Bryant (1794–1898), "Robert of Lincoln"

As for that gay dress, here are the details: "Wearing a bright black wedding-coat; White are his shoulders and white his crest." Bryant was a little off. Maybe he didn't use binoculars to see that the bobolink has no white crest, but a large straw-colored patch on the back of his head.

**On the Home Front** Usually nests in fields; many nests destroyed by farm machinery

**Wild Menu:** Insects; seeds; on southward migration and in winter, eats grain

**Plant Picks:** Acreage with hay and crops attract bobolinks, but your best bet is your feeder.

### Feeder Pleasers

- Millet or birdseed mix

### Tricks and Treats

- Go for a ride in the country in spring and look for bobolinks. They're a delight to watch.

## Made in the Shade

On a summer day in the Midwest, temperatures regularly climb into the nineties or above. Cattle and horses in a pasture gather under a tree, and farmers do the same when it's time to take a break. Parent birds keep their precious babies out of the strong heat of the sun also. They start by building their nest in a shady location, usually beneath an overarching plant. If the sun's rays still peek through, the parents shade their nestlings by crouching over the nest with wings spread like a parasol.

# Meadowlark

## First Impression

Dumpy, waddling, streaky brown bird with a glorious yellow chest marked by a broad black V

## Mark Your Calendar

Spring through fall in upper part of this region; year-round in lower part

## Details, Details

- A bit smaller than a robin; 9¼ inches
- Both the eastern and western meadowlarks are in this region. They look very much alike.
- Yellow breast is paler when not in breeding season
- White outside feathers on tail, in flight
- Female and male look alike
- Reminiscent of starling body shape and walking style

## Listen Up!

- Eastern: clear, slurred, simple whistle of a few syllables, with hint of melancholy
- Western: lives up to the name "lark," with its rich, clear, gurgling, whistled song; notes descend toward end

## Telltale Traits

- Busily walks about on ground
- Sings from clump of tilled soil, hillock of grass, fence post, or other perch
- Generally flies low, often in flock

## Look Here

- On ground in grassy places

## Or Here

- At feeder, especially in winter or during migration

*"The very spirit of the boundless prairie"*

—A. C. Bent, *Life Histories of North American Blackbirds, Orioles, Tanagers, and Allies* (1958)

The clear, piercing whistle of the meadowlark carries over a long distance. It's so distinctive that despite almost endless variation in its song, its voice is instantly recognizable as the soul of the prairie.

On the Home Front Nests in old fields, pastures, meadows • Its interesting roofed nest is almost impossible to find, as it's woven right into surrounding grasses.

**Wild Menu:** Mostly insects; some seeds and grain

**Plant Picks:** Plant native prairie grasses and wildflowers, such as Indian grass (*Sorghastrum nutans*) and bluestems (*Andropogon* and *Schizachyrium* spp.), with perennial sunflowers (*Helianthus* spp.), silphiums (*Silphium* spp.), or others, to create a bit of grassland for this bird to forage in.

**Feeder Pleasers**

- Birdseed mix; cracked corn; millet

**Tricks and Treats**

- In fall, set up a ground-level feeder to attract migrating or winter-territory meadowlarks.

## Meat on the Menu

Meadowlarks have a song that's ethereal, but their eating habits can be really down to earth. Like other members of the Blackbird family, they occasionally engage in a meal of meat. I've seen meadowlarks eating what they could from roadkill. Horned larks, abundant in open land, have an unfortunate habit of gathering along roads—and waiting until the very last second to take flight. Driving through Oklahoma after a snowstorm one year, I saw some pragmatic meadowlarks putting dead horned larks to good use.

# Brewer's Blackbird

## First Impression

**Glossy black bird with pale yellow eyes walking on ground**

### Mark Your Calendar

Likely visitor but it may be migration only, nesting, winter only, or year-round

### Details, Details

- A little smaller than a robin; 9 inches
- Part of this bird's Latin name means "blue head," referring to the iridescent blue to purple on its head and breast, and green on its body.
- Female is dull gray-brown, not shiny, with dark eye

### Listen Up!

- Squeaks, trills, and whistles
- Harsh *check!* call note

### Telltale Traits

- Walks on ground
- Head jerks forward with every step
- Holds back end of body and tail raised up when feeding on ground

### Look Here

- Walking about on ground beneath feeder

### Or Here

- Walking on lawn or in other open areas
- In fall and winter, in large mixed flock with other blackbirds and starlings

**On the Home Front** Nests in colonies, often near water, in a variety of habitats, from fields to swamps • Usually nests low to ground, about 3 to 5 feet up, but may also nest on ground or at higher level

*"Satin bird"*

—Old common name

**The name "Brewer's blackbird" tells us nothing about this bird; Audubon named it that in honor of his friend, Dr. Thomas Brewer of Boston, a fellow ornithologist. On the other hand, the old name of "satin bird" fits this species perfectly: The male's glossy feathers gleam like candlelight on a long satin cape.**

**Wild Menu:** Insects; seeds and grain; occasionally fruit

**Plant Picks:** Try planting a patch of milo (sorghum) to attract summer to winter visits from the Brewer's blackbird.

**Feeder Pleasers**

- Birdseed mix; millet

**Tricks and Treats**

- Blackbirds are fond of bathing. Provide a birdbath, and for an extra treat, a mister that they can loll under.

## Building Supply

I always enjoy trying to figure out what old bird nests I come across are made of. In southern Indiana, where soybean fields are a fixture, I happened across many Brewer's blackbird nests. Often the cup was constructed of familiar material: pieces of dried soybean stems, with empty seedpods dangling here and there like festive decorations.

# Yellow-Headed Blackbird

*First Impression*

**Unmistakable! Big black bird with striking yellow hood**

### Mark Your Calendar

Spring through fall in most parts of this region; migration only in some lower MW areas

### Details, Details

- Almost as big as a robin; 9½ inches
- Male flashes big white wing patches in flight
- Female is much less dramatic but still has yellow tinge

### Listen Up!

- A cacophony of squawks, *squeeps*, rattles, shrieks, and clacks, plus a noise like a chainsaw

### Telltale Traits

- Sight alone is enough for positive ID
- Usually in flocks
- Nervous tail flicks

### Look Here

- At feeder

### Or Here

- In marshes with cattails or other reeds
- Stalking about on lawn in flock
- In winter, in grainfields. Huge flocks "roll over" fields, birds in back moving to front as they scour field for wasted grain.

*On the Home Front* Not a backyard nester, unless you have a large, reed-fringed pond • Nests in colonies, in marsh • The male selects a breeding territory, then females in his harem build nests within it.

*"A wail of despairing agony"*

—**William Leon Dawson, on the love song of the male yellow-headed blackbird,** *The Birds of California* **(1923)**

**This species' courtship has been described as "more spectacular than beautiful," and weird sounds are certainly part of it.**

**Wild Menu:** Weed seeds; grain; aquatic insects

**Plant Picks:** Your feeder will keep these birds content.

**Feeder Pleasers**

- Sunflower seed; cracked corn

**Tricks and Treats**

- A birdbath or water feature may attract a yellow-headed splasher.

## Wails and Shrieks

Yellow-headed blackbirds nest in many places in this region, and it's well worth looking for a colony near your neighborhood, if only to get an earful of their incredible vocalizations. No other bird has so many weird sounds up its sleeve. And talk about loud!

William Leon Dawson wrote his description of the male's love song in the 1920s, but it's apt today. "When you have recovered from the first shock, you strain the eyes in astonishment that a mere bird, and a bird in love at that, should give rise to such a cataclysmic sound."

# Orchard Oriole

*First Impression*

**Reddish chestnut bird with black hood singing from shade tree as he hops from twig to twig**

### Mark Your Calendar

Spring through fall

### Details, Details

- A little larger than a sparrow; 7¼ inches
- No other male bird has this unusual coloring.
- Female is yellow-green with gray wings
- White wing bars

### Listen Up!

- A rich, musical, warbled song that sounds something like this: *look here, what cheer, what cheer, whip yo, what cheer, wee yo*
- Song is different from that of Baltimore or Bullock's orioles; sounds more like a robin

### Telltale Traits

- Constantly hops from twig to twig in foliage, even when singing
- Often obscured by leaves, but not shy

### Look Here

- In deciduous trees

### Or Here

- At apples, crab apples, and other flowering trees, picking off insects at blossoms
- In city parks, golf courses, or cemeteries with scattered trees, or along shaded streets
- Near streams, rivers, and other water

*On the Home Front* May nest in backyard
- Usually nests low, in small trees • The nest is an open pouch of grass suspended from a fork near the tip of a branch.

*"A gentle, friendly, and sociable bird"*

—**A. C. Bent,** *Life Histories of North American Blackbirds, Orioles, Tanagers, and Allies* **(1958)**

Nowadays, describing birds in terms of human characteristics is frowned upon by scientists. But Bent hit this bird's personality right on the mark, no matter what language he used. This species, he wrote, "lives in perfect harmony with many other birds ... and seems to enjoy human environments."

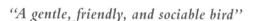

**Wild Menu:** Insects, mainly; plus a bit of fruit

**Plant Picks:** Shade trees for nest sites and insects; also mulberries (*Morus* spp.), cherries, strawberries, raspberries, and grapes

### Feeder Pleasers

- Not usually a feeder visitor; may visit a nectar feeder

### Tricks and Treats

- A birdbath may appeal, especially one with trickling water.
- Offer nesting materials in spring: cotton balls, tufts of natural wool, snippets of yarn, and other soft bits.

## Birding by Ear

The spring chorus of birdsong can sound like a confusing mess when you first begin trying to sort out the singers. But if you spend a little time each day listening and looking, you may soon find yourself admiring a lovely orchard oriole through your binoculars.

Listen for a musical song that seems to move slowly through the foliage, instead of coming from the same place. Then focus your glasses on the singer. It's not tricky, because sooner or later the bird will slip into view. All it takes is a bit of patience.

# Northern Bobwhite

*First Impression*

**A flock of plump, streaky brown "footballs" scuttling through**

### Mark Your Calendar

Year-round

### Details, Details

- About the same length as a robin, but much plumper; 9¾ inches
- Stubby tail
- Female is streakier, with tan rather than white face markings
- The scaled quail, another football-shape bird but with gray plumage, ranges through the lower western part of this region.

### Listen Up!

- Clear as a whistle: *bob-WHITE!*
- The flock (called a covey) talks quietly with soft, low calls.

### Telltale Traits

- Secretive birds; you'll hear bobwhites much more often than you see them
- Always in a covey, except when nesting
- Walks and runs over the ground
- Flies only when it needs to make a fast getaway; prefers to run

### Look Here

- On ground at feeder

### Or Here

- In brushy fields or prairie plantings
- Foraging amid standing stems from last year's garden

*On the Home Front* The male and female build their nest together, often weaving an arch of weeds and grasses overhead. • Nest on ground • May nest in backyard, in undisturbed corner

*"He seeks the home, garden, farm, and field"*

—Edward Forbush, *A History of the Game Birds, Wild-fowl, and Shore Birds of Massachusetts and Adjacent States* (1912)

Forbush had other praise to bestow on the bobwhite: "He is the friend and companion of mankind; a much needed helper on the farm; a destroyer of insect pests and weeds; … and, last as well as least, good food, a savory morsel, nutritious and digestible."

**Wild Menu:** Seeds; grain; insects; berries; fruits

**Plant Picks:** A birdseed patch, mixed with corn and milo, will supply all-important cover as well as months' worth of food.

**Feeder Pleasers**

- Cracked corn and chick scratch (a crushed grain mixture available at farm feed stores); birdseed mix; millet

**Tricks and Treats**

- Provide a ground-level birdbath, such as a naturalistic molded resin type, with a drip tube for extra coaxing power, and bobwhites may become regular visitors to your spa.

## Overdose of Ardor

In spring, that *bob-WHITE!* call can be a cry of battle. If another male dares to answer, the birds may advance on each other, calling as they go. Whenever I hear bobwhites trading insults, I try to sneak up on the scene. A few times, I've seen the actual clash, in which the "cute little birds" rush at each other with beating wings and claws and tearing beaks, like a couple of dueling roosters. In all cases, one of the birds gave up quickly and made his getaway.

# Chapter Eleven

# Birds of the West

The West has some of the most spectacular scenery in America, with high mountain ranges, flower-filled flatlands, and sunsets that set the sky on fire. This region is wildly diverse, with those staggering mountains yielding to sagebrush, and dense, well-watered forests giving way to arid scrub. Yet to birds, the scene all makes sense.

Many of the species in this area, from woodpeckers to hummingbirds, treat it as one world, but with seasonal homes. In spring, many birds move to cooler, higher elevations to raise their families. In fall, the "vertical migration" changes direction, and nesting birds of the mountains retreat downward to lower elevations, where the cold isn't quite as brutal and food can still be easily found.

## THE LAY OF THE LAND

This region is the most wildly diverse of all of the seven regions in this book. Aromatic sagebrush flatland, cut by canyons, leads to gentle foothills, then upward to the high mountains of the Rockies.

Blizzards are common in the long, harsh winters of this region. But summers are pure delight. They're relatively cool and short, although it can be hot at times. Spring brings fantastic spreads of wildflowers, and autumn gilds the scenery with glowing aspens.

Big cities and their suburbs are here, but there are still plenty of wide open spaces. Occasional towns and ranches, from mini-size to huge working spreads, add another twist to the habitat available for birds. Native plants are popular in backyards here; they're so well adapted to the rigorous conditions.

## FOOD AND SHELTER

Conifers, aspens, and other trees of this region harbor a host of insects on their foliage, and in and under their bark. That's a real draw for nuthatches, chickadees, and woodpeckers, among the most dedicated guardians of the trees.

In the sagebrush country, where trees are mostly absent except for junipers (*Juniperus* spp.) and other small trees, dryland birds such as quail, native sparrows, and thrashers find a home. These birds live on or near the ground, so they're well suited to the open sagebrush country. Wildflowers abound in this region, all of them well-adapted to the challenging climate. Explore the possibilities of growing penstemons (*Penstemon* spp.), native perennial flowers that are magnets for hummingbirds.

Also plant fruits and berries; their water content makes them a real treat for many birds of this area. Native shrubs are your best choice, because the birds already know and love them. Try buffaloberry (*Shepherdia argentea*), golden currant (*Ribes aureum*), wax currant (*R. cereum*), or any others that catch your eye. You'll find other suggestions in the following profiles of individual birds. If your locally owned nursery doesn't have a good

**Mmm, smell that sagebrush! Drier parts of the West, where trees give way to plants that can thrive with little water, also bring a change in birdlife. Quail and sparrows stay low among the cover.**

selection of natives, ask around. The West is full of passionate gardeners who have learned how to work with their climate instead of struggle against it.

## CLIMATE

*Brrr!* Winters are extreme in the western mountains. Even in the foothills, snows fall deep and often. The deserts in this area get their share of snow, too. And wind is a fact of life. Folks don hooded parkas and face masks to protect themselves from frigid air and blowing snow. All the more reason to add an extra metal trash can full of emergency supplies of birdseed. Running out feels awful when your birds are facing a blizzard. Weather can swing dramatically in this region, with temperatures dropping like a rock as fast-moving fronts roar through. It can be 70°F one day—and snowing the next!

Spring comes earlier to lower elevations, while mountains are still sleeping under snow. Eventually the warming air melts the white stuff, and waterfalls and rivulets course and drip off every slope.

Summer is fabulous in the mountains, with meadows of wildflowers, sometimes called mountain "parks," creating staggering sweeps of color. Lower down, summer brings the dry season, and the early wildflowers soon give way to brown and gray. This is a fairly dry climate, with most of the precipitation from fall through spring; summers are dry, and humidity is low. Cyclical droughts can be a problem, too. Those are good reasons to include several birdbaths in your backyard, with at least one of them at ground level.

Westerners take pride in their hardiness, and the birds are pretty tough, too. Birds in

**Black-headed grosbeaks are common.**

this region seem to follow two paths to thrive in this climate: Either they adapt to the conditions, like the rosy finches that call from rocky cliffs even in winter, or they move lower down in cold weather and range higher up in warm seasons, like the hummingbirds.

## BIRD LIFE IN THE WEST

Birds are abundant in this region, with some species seen only in the mountains, some in the deserts, and a good number adjusting to life both high and low. Most species are found in neighboring regions, too, because similar terrain and habitat are found elsewhere.

The elevation at which you live will affect the birds you see in your backyard—and when you see them. Steller's jays, broad-tailed hummingbirds, and other species move up the mountains in spring and down in late summer to fall. So depending on where your homestead is on their journey, you may enjoy them as nesting birds, winter residents, or only as passersby.

Because of all the variation in western terrain, you may want to invest in a comprehensive field guide with detailed range maps for each bird species. That way you can see at a glance whom you can expect, and when they'll be arriving.

## Start Here

Even though the West is home to many birds that would never be seen in the East, it also harbors a lot of familiar friends. Turn to Chapter 6, "Start Here," to find many of your loyal backyard friends, the birds you share with other parts of the country—chickadees, white-breasted nuthatches, tufted titmice, goldfinches, juncos, cedar waxwings, and many others.

## Regional Specialties

The West is where the bird life changes. Eastern species thrive also across the Midwest. But once you hit those mountains, it's time for a change. The birds here are very different from eastern birds.

Suddenly there's the vivid western tanager, flickering like a flame in the conifers. Striking black-headed grosbeaks take over from the rose-breasted ones found eastward. Grassy fields are full of lazuli buntings instead of the indigo species. Just about everywhere you look, you'll find unique birds that never cross the Great Plains.

Be sure to page through the birds of the Far North, Northwest, and Southwest and California regions, too. Those regions are your neighbors, and many of their birds also range into your territory.

## Birds of the West

Here are the birds you'll find in this chapter. Remember to consult the "Start Here" birds, starting on page 79, for many other common birds in the West.

WEST

# Lewis's Woodpecker

## First Impression

A large black woodpecker with a pale collar, gliding across an open area between trees

### Mark Your Calendar

Depending on location: year-round, winter only, spring through fall, or migration

### Details, Details

- Bigger than a robin; 10¾ inches
- Worth finding in binoculars: Its black feathers have a green sheen, and its red face and deep pink-red belly are beautiful.
- Female looks like male

### Listen Up!

- Harsh *churr, churr, churr*
- Sudden *yick!* alarm call

### Telltale Traits

- Flight almost looks like slow motion
- Glides or soars, without flapping wings
- Often fly-catches from perch, swooping out after passing insects
- Stores acorns and nuts in caches, often in a crevice of a utility pole or a fissure in bark
- May perch on utility wires
- Battles with other woodpeckers over stored food
- Pair remains together year-round

### Look Here

- On a prominent perch in a tree or on a post, flying out to catch insects

### Or Here

- In oaks, collecting acorns
- In flocks in winter, in oak groves or nut tree orchards
- Gliding from perch to ground to catch grasshoppers, crickets, and other insects

*"My acquaintance with this exotically brilliant woodpecker began in the mountains of Colorado"*

—Johnson Neff, *A Study of the Economic Status of the Common Woodpeckers* (1928)

**This beautiful bird can be considered a pest in apple orchards. But after analyzing the contents of hundreds of stomachs of these woodpeckers, Neff concluded that the bird actually eats more harmful insects than it does apples.**

**On the Home Front** May accept a nest box if you live near open Ponderosa pine forests, its typical breeding habitat • The male usually does most of the excavating of a nest hole.

**Wild Menu:** Insects; nuts; acorns; fruit

**Plant Picks:** Oaks (*Quercus* spp.), English walnut trees (*Juglans regia*), grapes, apples

### Feeder Pleasers

- Doesn't usually visit feeders; try offering English walnuts in the shell, or whole corn

### Tricks and Treats

- Has been reported to use nest boxes

## Tending the Store

Unlike birds that store their food still in the shell, Lewis's woodpecker cracks open every bit it gets its beak on. Nuts and acorns are shelled before storage, with the ready-to-eat nut meats and acorn pieces tucked into its cache. In winter, the birds visit their larder daily, spending hours turning the pieces so that they get some air and mold doesn't set in.

# White-Headed Woodpecker

## First Impression

**No mistaking that clownish white face on a solid black body**

WEST

### Mark Your Calendar

Year-round, in mountains

### Details, Details

- Almost robin size; 9¼ inches
- Look for a red patch on head.
- White patches in wings add an accent when the wings are folded. They look flashy in flight.
- Female lacks red on head
- Feathers are often smeared with the sticky pitch of the pines the birds forage in.

### Listen Up!

- Sharp, emphatic *chick!* may be repeated rapidly
- A rattling, metallic call that sounds like a chisel dropped on a concrete floor
- Occasionally drums on wood, but not as much as many other woodpecker species

### Telltale Traits

- Frequently fly-catches its food, flying out from perch to snatch passing insects
- Flakes off scales of conifer bark with its bill to get at insects underneath
- Extracts seeds from conifer cones
- Often forages at base of conifers

### Look Here

- At birdbath

### Or Here

- In conifers, especially Ponderosa pine, but also sugar pine, sequoia, and Douglas fir
- When you visit the Sequoia National Forest in northern California

*"A crowbar instead of a hammer"*

—James Merrill, "Notes on the Birds of Fort Klamath, Oregon" (1888)

**Most woodpeckers are "hammerheads"—they get their food by drilling it out of wood with their strong beak and skull. But the white-headed uses finesse instead of brute strength. It slips its beak under flakes of bark and lifts them off, as if prying with a crowbar.**

**On the Home Front** Not a backyard nester
- Nests in dead pine stumps • Often excavates several holes in same stump • Makes its home at varying heights, from about 4 to 25 feet high, but usually about 8 feet aboveground

**Wild Menu:** Conifer seeds, mostly those of Ponderosa pine; bark beetles and other insects

**Plant Picks:** Ponderosa pine (*Pinus ponderosa*), for future supplies of cones and insects

**Feeder Pleasers**
- Not usually a feeder visitor; keep that suet block up, just in case

**Tricks and Treats**
- Water! This woodpecker loves a good drink and frequently visits birdbaths and other water features.

## Clever Camouflage

Pine trees often have broken stubs of branches that can look white from a distance when the light hits them just right. They'll then cast a shadow that makes the area beneath look black. Are you sensing a connection? Yep, despite its dramatic plumage, the white-headed woodpecker is superbly camouflaged. Its head becomes just another branch stub, and its body a shadow. Only those falling flakes of bark give it away.

# Clark's Nutcracker

*First Impression*
**A big, bold, gray bird with black wings**

### Mark Your Calendar

Year-round; generally at higher elevations

### Details, Details

- Significantly bigger than a robin; 12 inches
- Classy color scheme of pale gray body accented with black wings and tail, with white edges
- Female and male look alike

### Listen Up!

- Betrays its connection to the jays as soon as it opens its mouth: harsh squawks, a guttural *charr, char-r-r-r,* and various yelps and rattles
- Also some musical tooting notes
- An unusual noise is made by its wing feathers when the bird checks a deep dive, such as one down into a canyon: The wind creates a sudden roar against them.

### Telltale Traits

- Big and bold; very tame and curious
- Noisy and boisterous
- Often in flocks
- Flies straight or undulating; also prone to sudden deep dives into canyons
- Often hops or walks on ground
- Hammers at trees to extract larvae

### Look Here

- At the feeder

### Or Here

- Near you, hoping for a handout
- Fly-catching from a perch
- In trees, eating conifer cone seeds, acorns, or berries
- Foraging on ground

This big gray bird shares many traits with a similar big gray bird, the gray jay, who also goes by the name "camp robber." Both are clever and daring, and quick to take advantage of any unattended edibles.

*On the Home Front* Not a backyard nester
- Nests high up in mountains, at 6,000 to 8,000 feet elevation • Builds a huge nest of sticks and bark strips, lined with grasses and pine needles • Usually nests in a juniper or pine, often very high up, in dense branches where the nest is sheltered

**Wild Menu:** Insects, including butterflies; fruit; acorns; seeds from pinecones; any scraps it can get its beak around

**Plant Picks:** Just keep that feeder stocked and the nutcracker will be your new best friend.

### Feeder Pleasers

- Sunflower seeds; chick scratch (a crushed grain mixture available at farm feed stores); suet; nuts; any fat-based recipes you can think of or find for sale in bird supply stores; meat scraps

### Tricks and Treats

- Carry a pocketful of nut meats with you; you may be able to tempt these birds to take them from your open palm.

## Building Supply

If you do any snowshoeing or cross-country skiing in the high country in late winter, you may get to see Clark's nutcrackers collecting materials to build their nests. Juniper twigs are a favorite; the birds wrench them off trees with quick jerks and some help from the sharp edges of their beaks. The construction process takes a while, because the nest needs to be big and thick for insulation from the cold.

# Black-Billed Magpie

## First Impression

Big, exotic, black-and-white bird with super-long tail

### Mark Your Calendar

Year-round

### Details, Details

- Almost twice as long as a robin; 19 inches
- Watch for the flash of iridescence on those black feathers in sunlight.
- Shows big white wing patches in flight
- A black bill separates this species from the yellow-billed magpie of California.
- Female and male look alike

### Listen Up!

- Rapid *shack-shack-shack*
- Various nasal notes

### Telltale Traits

- Conspicuous and brash
- Walks about with tail slightly raised
- That extravagant tail seems to be always twitching when the bird is on the ground.
- Hops when in a hurry
- Often in flocks
- Unmistakable in flight (except where range overlaps yellow-billed magpie)

### Look Here

- Strutting about on ground

### Or Here

- At feeder
- Patrolling for leftovers at trash cans and in parking lots

On the Home Front Both male and female work on constructing the 2- to 4-foot durable nest made of heavy, often thorny sticks.
- A canopy of thorny sticks also covers the top.

*"Magpies were very numerous during the buffalo days"*

—Frank Farley, "Changes in the Status of Certain Animals and Birds during the Last Fifty Years in Central Alberta" (1925)

Magpies followed on the heels of the buffalo hunters, waiting around for their share of any leftovers at the kill. Lewis and Clark also noted the birds' voracious appetites, commenting that they snatched the meat even while it was being dressed after a hunt.

**Wild Menu:** Insects, including grasshoppers, beetles, ants, and others; acorns; grain; berries; food scraps; carrion

**Plant Picks:** A grapevine may attract the birds.

**Feeder Pleasers**
- Meat scraps; suet; magpies prefer meat but will also eat bread and other baked goods.

**Tricks and Treats**
- Magpies are intelligent birds who quickly learn your routine. Feed them at the same time every day, and they'll soon be waiting for their treat.
- A sturdy birdbath can be a big hit.

## Who's Inside?

Knock at a magpie's door, and you never know just who might answer. Those giant-size nests, with all their thorny protection, are too good to waste, so other birds often make use of them when the magpie family departs. In Colorado, I came across a nest that had been claimed by a pair of kestrels (small falcons). Sharp-shinned hawks, mourning doves, grackles, and even ducks and herons have also been known to set up housekeeping in magpie nests.

# Scrub Jay

## First Impression

Big, noisy, bluish gray bird with whitish gray belly

## Mark Your Calendar

Year-round; absent from some northern parts of region; mostly at lower elevations

## Details, Details

- Bigger than a robin; 11½ inches
- In the right light, blue can be striking
- Has no crest
- Female and male look alike

## Listen Up!

- A harsh, scolding cry of *cheek-cheek-cheek!*
- Also a rising note that sounds like a question: *quay-feeeee?*
- Other grating calls, including *ker-wheek!*
- A very quiet, private, and decidedly musical "whisper song" sung to its mate

## Telltale Traits

- Loud, bold, and intelligent
- Also can be secretive and quiet
- Often hops about on ground
- Usually in small groups
- Look for it in shrubs (the "scrub" from which it gets its name).

## Look Here

- At your feeder

## Or Here

- In oak trees or nut trees
- On the ground
- In shrubs or hedges
- Burying nuts or acorns
- At the birdbath

*"Nests with white, black, bay, and sorrel linings"*

—**William Dawson**, on colors of horsehair used in scrub jay nests, *The Birds of California* (1923)

**"The lining varies delightfully,"** Dawson noted, **"but is largely dependent upon the breed of horses or cattle on the nearest ranch."** He recounted how one jay **"pitched out"** the existing lining of its nest when coal-black horsehair became available.

### On the Home Front

May nest in backyard
- Makes a well-concealed, bulky nest of twigs, lined with rootlets • Builds low to the ground, from 2 to 12 feet or so

**Wild Menu:** Acorns, nuts, corn, fruit; insects, including wasps and bees; scorpions, snails, mice, snakes, lizards, and frogs

**Plant Picks:** Plant giant sunflowers (*Helianthus annuus* 'Russian Giant') for these jays

### Feeder Pleasers

- Nuts and peanuts, in the shell; sunflower seeds; suet

### Tricks and Treats

- A freshly filled birdbath may be popular.

## Peanut Gallery

Jays bury nuts and acorns, which may be why these birds are much more strongly attracted to nuts in the shell than seeds at the feeder—as long as they're crackable. Peanuts in the shell are such a draw that, with some patience, you can tame the birds to take them from your hand. I've had good luck by first setting a few peanuts about 10 feet away from me, and standing quietly until the birds retrieved them. Then, over several days, I gradually move the nuts nearer to me until the jays will come within arm's length to get their treat. Finally, they'll take them right from my hand. Try this after a snowstorm, when the birds are hungriest.

# Steller's Jay

*First Impression*

**Striking black and blue bird with big crest**

## Mark Your Calendar

Year-round; usually at elevations up to 3,500 feet

## Details, Details

- Bigger than a robin; 11½ inches
- Accent of small, light stripes on forehead.
- Female and male look alike

## Listen Up!

- Like most jays, the Steller's has a repertoire of harsh calls, plus a gentle, musical song
- A loud, harsh *shaack! shaack! shaack!*
- Occasionally chortles *klook, klook, klook*
- May scream shrilly like a red-tailed hawk

## Telltale Traits

- Loud and conspicuous
- May also be quiet and secretive
- Often raises the alarm when it spots a person walking in the woods
- Often visits singly, instead of in a group

## Look Here

- At your feeder

## Or Here

- Hopping or flitting upward around a tree
- Foraging on the ground
- Burying nuts or acorns

*On the Home Front* May nest in backyard
- Builds bulky cup of sticks and leaves, lined with rootlets or evergreen needles

*"Streaks on forehead paler blue or bluish white"*

—Robert Ridgway,
*The Birds of North and Middle America Part III*
(1904)

The Steller's jay of the West is a geographic race that is slightly different in looks from the Steller's jay of the Pacific Coast. Its twin forehead streaks are whitish blue, instead of cobalt blue.

**Wild Menu:** Acorns; nuts; conifer seeds; insects; frogs; small snakes

**Plant Picks:** Plant Douglas firs or other conifers native to your area. Try annual sunflowers with big seed heads (*Helianthus annuus* 'Russian Giant').

**Feeder Pleasers**
- Nuts and peanuts, in the shell; sunflower seeds; suet

**Tricks and Treats**
- In cold weather, chop up a block of suet into half-inch pieces and scatter it in a tray feeder.

## Fruit Eaters?

Have you ever seen Steller's jays eat fruit? I haven't. Not in my yard, which is packed with serviceberries (*Amelanchier* spp.), elderberries (*Sambucus* spp.), cherries, and every other tempting bird fruit or berry I can squeeze in. Not in the wild, either. Bird lover friends who I've checked with say they, too, have never seen a Steller's eat fruit.

Yet "wild or cultivated fruit" often shows up on published lists of this bird's diet. If you've ever witnessed a Steller eating fruit, I'd love to hear about it. Because the only reports I could find, after determined digging, was an anecdotal account of apples damaged by the jays during a severe drought—a possible reason why Steller's jays might peck at fruit.

# Mountain Chickadee

## *First Impression*

Small, lively, acrobatic gray and white bird with black-striped head

### Mark Your Calendar

Year-round; absent in some areas. Lives at high elevations, often 8,000 to 10,000 feet, especially in nesting season; in fall and winter, many move lower

### Details, Details

- Chickadee size! 5¼ inches
- From fall through early spring, shows distinctly striped head
- As feathers become worn, the white stripe is less distinct, and the black stripes may blend to look like the head of the black-capped species, also common in this region.
- Female and male look alike

### Listen Up!

- Says *chick-a* in the familiar way, then adds its own slower, descending tones to the *fee-bee-bay* that follows
- Also high, thin calls, like a black-capped

### Telltale Traits

- The typical chickadee—swinging from branch tips, flitting through foliage
- A great little acrobat, always in motion
- If disturbed at nest or nest box, hisses and flutters its wings to scare away intruder

### Look Here

- At feeder

### Or Here

- Branch tips and among foliage of conifers
- At conifer cones, often high up in lodge-pole pines, spruces, firs, or other trees
- In fall and winter, look in oaks, cotton-woods, and willows as well.

*"They may be met with almost anywhere in the forested mountains."*

—Florence Merriam Bailey, *Birds of New Mexico* (1928)

WEST

And you may have to look way, way up to get a glimpse of these active little guys that often forage high up in the conifers. Listen for their little voices, then be patient as they move to a lower spot.

*On the Home Front* May use a nest box in your backyard, if you live in the mountains
- Usually uses an existing hole in a dead tree

**Wild Menu:** Insects; conifer cone seeds, other seeds

**Plant Picks:** Any native conifer

**Feeder Pleasers**
- Suet; sunflower seeds; peanut butter and other fatty foods; may eat mealworms and other insect foods

**Tricks and Treats**
- Offer nesting materials, such as fur, tufts of natural fleece, snippets of angora wool, or any other soft materials, in a clean wire suet cage.

## Ups and Downs

Tasty insects are everywhere in the mountain forests in summer. Caterpillars munch the conifers, ants work away, and a menagerie of other six-legged meals scurries about. No wonder so many bird species in this region, including the mountain chickadee, take to the mountains to raise their families. In fall, when insects wane and the weather cools, those birds forsake the forests and move to the valleys and foothills, where food is plentiful.

# Plain Titmouse

*First Impression*

**Very plain, small gray bird with crested head**

## Mark Your Calendar

Year-round; only the juniper titmouse is found in this region

## Details, Details

- About sparrow size; 5¾ inches
- Both juniper and oak titmice are plain gray birds; the oak species has a brownish tinge.
- Female looks like male

## Listen Up!

- The juniper titmouse, the bird found in this region, gives a rapid trill, fairly loud.
- The oak titmouse also trills, but has clear, whistled notes in its refrains, too.
- Both species can sound a lot like chickadees, which are close relatives. Listen for their raspy *tschick-a-dee* call.

## Telltale Traits

- Actively in motion in the branches of trees, picking off insects
- Moves from branch to branch
- Flies with shallow undulating dips
- Often sings from a perch

## Look Here

- At feeder

## Or Here

- In junipers
- In pinyon-juniper woods

*On the Home Front* Happily moves into a nest box • The nest box or cavity is lined with soft, cozy grass, moss, fur, and feathers.

*"This is indeed a plain titmouse"*

—A. C. Bent, *Life Histories of North American Jays, Crows, and Titmice* (1946)

Actually it's *two* plain titmice. The species has been recently divided into the oak titmouse and the juniper titmouse. They look almost alike, but live in different habitat and have different voices.

**Wild Menu:** Insects; acorns; pine seeds and other seeds

**Plant Picks:** Oaks (*Quercus* spp. native to your area); pines, especially pinyon (*Pinus edulis*); junipers (*Juniperus scopulorum, J. osteoperma,* and other spp. native to your area)

**Feeder Pleasers**

- Sunflower seeds; suet; chopped nuts

**Tricks and Treats**

- Offer soft materials at nesting time: wool tufts, bits of fuzzy yarn, feathers, and anything else you can round up.

## Together Forever

Wedding anniversary greeting cards could easily feature titmice as a symbol of a long-lasting union. These plain-Jane birds almost always keep the same mate year after year. And they often return to the same place to raise their family. In 1936, John Price, who studied the family relationships of the plain titmouse, noted: "There was only one case of 'divorce' where a bird took a new mate while its former mate was still known to be living." (*Condor*, Vol. 38). Guess that independent thinker must have had a mighty good reason.

# Bushtit

## First Impression

Tiny gray bird flying out of bush with high, thin calls; then another bird, and another, and another, and another . . .

## Mark Your Calendar

Year-round; absent from northern part of this region

## Details, Details

- One of our smallest birds, even smaller than a chickadee; 4½ inches
- Long tail
- Often looks fluffed-up
- One of the most unusual variations of gender: the male has dark eyes, the female, pale eyes

## Listen Up!

- A constant stream of thin, high-pitched, *tsit-tsit-tsit* calls
- The calls are a great clue to the impending arrival of a flock of bushtits. When you hear them, look around for the bitty birds.

## Telltale Traits

- Constantly on the move, foraging rapidly through the foliage of bushes and small trees, then traveling on to the next
- Often travels with mixed group of chickadees and kinglets in winter
- Tame around people and gentle to each other; no sign of squabbling in their flock

## Look Here

- Moving in a flock from one group of bushes in your yard to the next

## Or Here

- At the birdbath
- Flying through or over your yard in a talkative flock

### *"Intensely gregarious disposition"*

—Robert Woods, correspondence quoted in *Life Histories of North American Jays, Crows, and Titmice* (1946)

**You'll never see a bushtit all by its lonesome self. These tiny birds stick together, roaming the bushes in big flocks.**

**On the Home Front** The nest is a long, loose, hanging sack, suspended from a tree or bush. • It may take a month and a half before the nest is built and egg-laying starts. • Builds in deciduous or evergreen trees

**Wild Menu:** Insects, especially scale insects; spiders

**Plant Picks:** Fruits of any kind, particularly sweet or sour cherries, mulberries (*Morus* spp.), grapes

**Feeder Pleasers**
- Suet, especially suet enriched with insects

**Tricks and Treats**
- Bushtits love their baths. Keep a birdbath brimming, and you may see the whole bunch lining up at once.

## Home Helpers

Bushtits are such sociable birds that they even help each other around the nest. Unmated birds or females whose nests have failed may help to raise another pair's brood. More than one of these helpers, which scientists call "supernumeraries," may help out at a single nest—a nest might have as many as six adults caring for the children. Good thing the birds build those hanging "socks" so strong: At night, everybody piles in to sleep together!

# Mountain Bluebird

## First Impression

An incredible turquoise blue bird—or a sky blue bird when not in breeding plumage

### Mark Your Calendar

Spring through fall in northern part of this region; year-round southward

### Details, Details

- Bigger than a sparrow; 7¼ inches
- Female is gray with pale blue wings; may have red tinge on breast, similar to female western bluebird

### Listen Up!

- Sings mostly in early morning
- Clear, short, warbling song, similar to that of its cousin, the American robin
- Also a quiet, conversational warble, and a nasal *pew* call

### Telltale Traits

- More often seen in the air than other bluebird species
- Fluttery flight
- Often hovers while foraging
- Often perches on a post or other lookout

### Look Here

- At the nest box

### Or Here

- In open areas
- On a fence post
- On utility wires

*On the Home Front* Welcomes a nest box; mount it within 6 feet of the ground in an open, grassy area • Often uses same place next year; builds new nest atop old one

*"Ranges up to the highest meadows"*

—Joseph Grinnell and Tracy Storer, *Animal Life in the Yosemite* (1924)

This gorgeous bluebird lives in pristine mountain meadows and clearings at just below timberline—but it also ranges all the way down into the foothills, and is often spotted around ranch buildings.

**Wild Menu:** Mostly insects; some fruit, including mistletoe berries

**Plant Picks:** Try bite-size berries, such as native currants (*Ribes* spp.) and elderberries (*Sambucus* spp.).

**Feeder Pleasers**

- Mealworms; suet in an accessible feeder; commercial or homemade "bluebird food" (mix cornmeal and peanut butter into a crumbly dough)

**Tricks and Treats**

- Invest in a bluebirds-only feeder to keep other birds from gobbling up those mealworms. An outer cage of wire, similar to a suet feeder, keeps out bigger starlings.
- A heated birdbath is a big draw on chilly days.

## Catch the Concert

Folks used to argue over whether the mountain bluebird actually sang or not. I haven't heard its song, but I don't feel too bad: Even one of the most well-versed authorities on birdsong, Aretas A. Saunders, who wrote about birdsong back in the early 20th century, reported, "In all my experience with this species in Montana, I never heard it sing."

If you live in the West, you can find out for yourself. The current consensus is that this species does warble away early in the morning. Listen up, and see if you agree.

# Western Bluebird

*First Impression*

**Gentle blue bird with chestnut-orange breast and back patches**

## Mark Your Calendar

Migration only in some areas; spring through fall in others; year-round in southern part of region

## Details, Details

- The size of a big sparrow; 7 inches
- Female is much paler blue-gray with faded orange; wings flash vivid blue in flight

## Listen Up!

- A low, whistled, *f-few! f-few!*
- Occasionally, a short burst of chattering

## Telltale Traits

- Like other bluebirds, a calm bird that often sits perched
- In pairs during nesting season; in flocks at other times, especially during winter
- Flies out from perch to nab insects in air
- Swoops from perch and flutters over grass when foraging

## Look Here

- At the feeder

## Or Here

- At the nest box
- On a rock or fence post perch
- Fluttering to the ground after an insect
- On wires

*On the Home Front* Another good reason to put up a nest box! • Early nester; begins when nights are still below freezing • Also nests in natural cavities, old woodpecker holes, or a crevice of a building • Usually raises two broods

*"I awoke in the darkness at 4:20 a.m. to find a bluebird already singing"*

—Winton Weydemeyer, "Singing of the Mountain Bluebird and the Western Bluebird" (1934)

**You'll have to be quite an early bird yourself to beat this bluebird to the punch. In late April, when nesting season is in full swing, males begin serenading long before sunrise.**

**Wild Menu:** Mostly insects; fruit in winter, including mistletoe berries

**Plant Picks:** Elderberries (*Sambucus* spp.) are favored; also encourage native junipers (*Juniperus* spp.) for their eventual berries. Butterfly gardens may attract butterfly-eating bluebirds.

## Feeder Pleasers

- Mealworms and other insect foods; accessible suet; commercial or homemade bluebird food (mix cornmeal and peanut butter into a crumbly dough)

## Tricks and Treats

- Get your nest box up early. By the end of winter, the pairs are already house shopping.
- Bluebirds are a great excuse to go ahead and try a heated birdbath. A daily bath is welcome, even in winter.

## Kiss Me Quick

Hang a ball of mistletoe at Christmas, and you continue a long tradition of inviting a romantic kiss. But mistletoe can be a destructive partner to the lodgepole and other native pines (*Pinus* spp.) and other trees upon which it grows. This unusual plant siphons off nutrients from the tree to which it's attached.

Mountain bluebirds play a big role in spreading mistletoe. They feast on the berries, then fly to a nearby perch to sit and digest.

# Western Tanager

*First Impression*

**A brilliant flash of red-orange, yellow, and black in the trees**

**Mark Your Calendar**

Spring through fall

**Details, Details**

- Smaller than a robin; 8 inches
- Fancy wing bars—one yellow, one white—in flight or perched
- Male has black tail
- Male's red almost disappears in fall
- Female is drab gray-green with yellowish head, breast, and belly, and gray wings

**Listen Up!**

- Low, warbling song, somewhat similar to robin, but huskier
- Frequent *pit-ick* call note

**Telltale Traits**

- One of the most vivid birds of the region
- Forages for insects among the foliage
- Often easily visible when it flies from one tree to another, or fly-catches from a tree

**Look Here**

- At feeder

**Or Here**

- Foraging in mature conifers
- At the birdbath

*On the Home Front* May occasionally nest in backyards with conifers • Often nests in trees along an edge—bordering a road, a meadow, or other opening • Usually picks a Douglas fir (*Pseudotsuga menziesii*), western hemlock (*Tsuga heterophylla*), or other conifer as a homesite

*"They were at first found feeding on early cherries"*

—**W. Otto Emerson, "A Remarkable Flight of Louisiana Tanagers" (1903)**

Cherries are still a draw for western tanagers, more than a hundred years after Emerson noticed the "remarkable flight" of what were once called Louisiana tanagers.

**Wild Menu:** Insects; fruit

**Plant Picks:** Try planting a sweet or sour cherry tree to bring tanagers to your own backyard.

**Feeder Pleasers**
- Cracked corn; millet and birdseed mix; suet; dried fruit, plus halved oranges

**Tricks and Treats**
- Keep a birdbath brimming and you may see a tanager take its bath.

## That's Some Flycatcher!

True flycatchers are drab green birds. Not so the western tanager, who adopts the same technique. If the light is right, this bird will look like a living flame as it sallies out from a tree to snatch a termite or other flying insect, then swoops back to its perch.

I've seen tanagers spend hours at this activity. They start in the morning near the top of a tree, because insects are most active higher up early in the day. Then the birds work their way downward, with frequent pauses to perch and sing. By later afternoon, they're fly-catching from the lowest branches.

WEST

# Black-Headed Grosbeak

### First Impression

A small flock of vivid orange-and-black birds at the feeder, tame and chubby, and showing flashy white wing patches when they fly

### Mark Your Calendar

Spring through fall

### Details, Details

- Smaller than a robin; 8¼ inches
- Flashy white wing patches when the male flies
- Strong, conical beak for cracking seeds
- Female is streaky dark brown with buff breast and pale belly
- Striking striped head on females and juvenile birds

### Listen Up!

- A pretty warbled song of clear, whistled notes with trills, similar to a robin
- Also a sharp *spick!* call note

### Telltale Traits

- Very tame; isn't afraid of people
- Often in a small flock, except when nesting
- Shares habits with its eastern counterpart, the rose-breasted grosbeak

### Look Here

- At feeder

### Or Here

- Foraging in shrubs or trees
- Singing from top of tree
- Flying across open space, with those wing patches flashing
- Eating fruit

*"Grosbeaks come back with glorious songs"*

—Joseph Grinnell and Tracy Storer, *Animal Life in the Yosemite* (1924)

**Loud, sweet singing is the main occupation of male grosbeaks when they arrive on nesting grounds. All day long, they sing from tall perches, claiming a territory as their own.**

On the Home Front Often nests in backyards
- Breeds from subalpine mountainsides to desert areas, where it seeks out bushes and trees along rivers • Builds nest in outer branches of small trees or shrubs

**Wild Menu:** Insects; fruit

**Plant Picks:** Elderberries (*Sambucus* spp.), cherries, blackberries, and raspberries

**Feeder Pleasers**
- Sunflower seeds

**Tricks and Treats**
- Fond of taking a bath; adores a sprinkler or mister

## Gentlemen Before Ladies

Ever wonder where the girls are when you look at your feeder in spring? Migrant songbirds, like the black-headed grosbeak, return to nesting grounds on a schedule that depends on their gender. First come the males, resplendent in spring finery. About a week to 10 days later, the females arrive. Juveniles—birds that hatched from last year's nests—are last on the scene.

That extra time gives males the chance to establish territories, so they have a home territory ready and waiting when the ladies arrive. When it's time to leave in fall, the order is reversed: Males go first, females next, and the kids bring up the rear.

# Red Crossbill

## First Impression

Strawberry red, very tame bird—and get a load of that beak!

### Mark Your Calendar

Year-round; in some areas, winter only

### Details, Details

- Sparrow size; 6¼ inches
- Dark wings—but that bill is the only detail you need
- Female is grayish green

### Listen Up!

- Clicking or buzzy phrases, not melodic, sounds like *kimp kimp kimp*

### Telltale Traits

- Contorts itself like a parrot, clinging and twisting to reach pinecones

### Look Here

- At conifer cones

### Or Here

- At your feeder

*On the Home Front* Unlike that of nearly all other birds, the time of nesting is determined by when the conifer crop ripens. The birds begin nesting anytime from December to September! • Well-concealed nest is placed in a spruce, pine, or other conifer • Parents feed nestlings for weeks after they fledge, until their beaks cross into the shape that allows them to efficiently extract seeds from cones.

*"Can be approached with care"*

—**John Terres,** *The Audubon Society Encyclopedia of North American Birds* (1980)

The intriguing crossbills (both red and white-winged) often allow you to sneak up for a closer look. As long as you're quiet and don't make any alarming, sudden moves, you'll be able to stand near enough to watch them use those fantastic bills to extract seeds from pinecones.

**Wild Menu:** Seeds of conifer cones

**Plant Picks:** Pines, spruces, larches, firs, and other conifers

**Feeder Pleasers**
- Sunflower seeds

**Tricks and Treats**
- Greatly fond of salt. Offer a handful of ice cream maker salt in your feeding tray when crossbills arrive.

## Lap It Up

I haven't had many visits from crossbills, but I'll never forget the flock that spent a few weeks at my place, cleaning off every berry from a hedge of Tatarian honeysuckle bushes. The birds were fascinating to watch, especially since they let me stand just 2 feet away.

But the most jaw-dropping moment was when the flock descended to a "bubbling spring" birdbath I'd set up in the yard. Gathering alongside, each bird maneuvered its head so that its bill was sideways to the water. Then it used its tongue to lap up the water, a drop or two at a time.

# Pine Grosbeak

## First Impression
**Very tame, rosy red bird**

### Mark Your Calendar
Year-round or winter only; absent from some areas

### Details, Details
- A little smaller than a robin; 9 inches
- Blackish wings with white bars
- Juvenile birds may be rusty chestnut instead of the color of Hawaiian Punch.
- Female is gray with greenish head

### Listen Up!
- Soft, whistled song
- Quiet call notes keep a flock in touch

### Telltale Traits
- Hangs around in small groups
- Very calm and easily approached

### Look Here
- Eating berries in winter

### Or Here
- Quietly perching
- At feeder
- In spruce, pine, or other conifer

**On the Home Front** Not a backyard nester
- Nest is well-hidden in dense branches of conifers, usually about eye level or lower
- Like many other Northland birds, this one builds its nest out of whatever's close at hand—conifer twigs, rootlets, grasses—and lines it with needles, lichen, and a few feathers.
- Parents feed young birds a yummy regurgitated paste of vegetable matter and insects.

*"Rather stupid and uninteresting"*
—Neltje Blanchan, *Bird Neighbors* (1897)

Pine grosbeaks spend a lot of time just sitting around. Are they lazy? Nope, just digesting. When they find a good source of food—not a sure thing in winter—they take advantage of it, filling their special throat pouch with as much as they can.

**Wild Menu:** Tree seeds, seeds from conifer cones, weed seeds; tree buds; also fruit and insects

**Plant Picks:** Spruces native to your area, including Englemann spruce (*Picea engelmanii*), alpine fir (*Abies lasiocarpa*), mountain ash (*Sorbus* spp.)

**Feeder Pleasers**
- Sunflower seeds

**Tricks and Treats**
- Pine grosbeaks are a great reason to have a reserve bag of sunflower seeds on hand: Winter flocks may number 100 or more birds!

## Lily Lovers

As snows begin to melt, sunny yellow glacier (also called avalanche) lilies (*Erythronium grandiflorum*) come alive, pushing up at the edge of the retreating snow, right through the white stuff. Within a day or two of the snow's retreat, showy colonies of hundreds of these pretty flowers are in full bloom, bordering the snowbanks. The flowers fade quickly, ripening into seed capsules—which pine grosbeaks seek out for food. Talk about a taste of spring!

# Lazuli Bunting

*First Impression*

**A sparrow-size turquoise "bluebird," singing its heart out and shining like a living jewel**

*"A considerable flock of lazuli buntings "*

—**Arthur Fuller and B. P. Bole, "Observations on Some Wyoming Birds" (1931)**

## Mark Your Calendar

Spring through fall

## Details, Details

- Smaller than a sparrow, only a bit bigger than a chickadee; 5½ inches
- Iridescent plumage, like that of the closely related indigo bunting
- Two highly noticeable white wing bars will quickly tell you this isn't a bluebird.
- Female is warm brown, with a buff breast

## Listen Up!

- A fast, clear, high-pitched, warbling, *see-see-see-sweert-sweert-sweert* song that lasts long
- Also a sharp *pick!* call note

## Telltale Traits

- Sings frequently, all day long
- Male moves from one perch to another around his territory to sing
- Males chase each other in spring.
- After nesting, birds congregate in groups.

## Look Here

- At your feeder

## Or Here

- Singing from the highest perches available
- Foraging in brushy corners of the yard
- In thickets, hedges, and clumps of bushes

*On the Home Front* Usually not a backyard nester • Builds nest low to ground, usually within 3 feet • Well-hidden in dense, shady shrubs of many kinds

Once the kids have left home, buntings gather in small groups to flock and forage. Males continue to sing after nesting is finished, long into summer. Watch how the male bunting changes color in the light; as feathers are exposed at various angles, their shades shift from blue to blue-green. The species is named for the gemstone lapis lazuli, but there are a lot more turquoise tones in those feathers than there are deep, clear blue ones.

**Wild Menu:** Seeds; insects

**Plant Picks:** Tolerate some weedy grasses, such as wild oats (*Avena barbata*) or needlegrass (*Stipa* spp.), in your yard, and lazulis may arrive to glean seeds. Native currants (*Ribes* spp.), which soon grow into a thicket, are a favorite hangout.

**Feeder Pleasers**
- Millet

**Tricks and Treats**
- May visit a birdbath

## Keep an Eye on the Sky

A bird perched in plain view at the tippy-top of a tree makes an inviting target for predators, especially those with wings. Singing male lazuli buntings often get dived upon by sharp-shinned and Cooper's hawks. The hawks may spot the singing bird from above, or zero in on its voice from a perch. Either way, the attack seems to come out of nowhere. If the male bunting doesn't have his wits about him, there may be nothing remaining to mark his territory but a sad little puff of blue feathers where he was perched seconds before.

# Rosy Finch

*First Impression*

**A flock of brown and pink sparrows**

### Mark Your Calendar

Winter only, except high in the mountains, where found year-round

### Details, Details

- Sparrow size; 6¼ inches
- Wing feathers are pale or translucent in flight.
- All adults have a sharply conical little black beak, with a pale area where it joins the head; juveniles have a yellow bill.

### Listen Up!

- They have a husky whistled song of a few notes. Mostly, they use a buzzy *chew* call.
- *Chip!* alarm call

### Telltale Traits

- Exceedingly tame
- Very social birds, in flocks except when nesting
- Usually on ground
- Undulating flight, in sweeping curve
- Long wings allow easy flight even in stiff mountain winds.
- When one bird gives the *chip!* call and flies, all the rest take off with it.

### Look Here

- In feeder or on ground beneath it

### Or Here

- Foraging on ground, especially near patches of snow
- Foraging for insects in conifers
- Investigating weeds protruding from snow

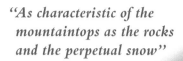

*"As characteristic of the mountaintops as the rocks and the perpetual snow"*

—A. C. Bent, *Life Histories of North American Cardinals, Grosbeaks, Buntings, Towhees, Finches, Sparrows and Allies* (1968)

Rosy finches are part of the winter scene in the West, eagerly visiting feeders and backyards from the mountains to the foothills, lowlands, and even the deserts. But for breeding season, the birds withdraw to the highest mountaintops.

*On the Home Front* Possibly the highest-altitude-nesting bird in North America • Nests on mountaintops in the Rockies and other mountains, in a crevice on a cliff.

**Wild Menu:** Seeds; some insects; some bits of green vegetation

**Plant Picks:** An open area will make these birds of windswept places feel at home. A spread of birdseed is all you need.

**Feeder Pleasers**
- Millet; birdseed mix; sunflower seeds

**Tricks and Treats**
- A birdbath, especially a heated one, may attract several customers.

## Pack Your Bags

A few species of birds in extremely cold conditions feature a unique adaptation that allows them to survive in harsh weather. It's a *gular pouch*, an expandable food storage area off the throat. When rosy finches come across an abundance of food, they can stuff their pouches full to the brim, to be digested later when pickin's aren't as plentiful.

This feature also allows them to carry a generous helping of food from long distances for their nestlings, without having to make exhausting return trips.

# Yellow-Headed Blackbird

### First Impression

**Unmistakable! Big black bird with striking yellow hood**

### Mark Your Calendar

Spring through fall

### Details, Details

- A little smaller than a robin; 9½ inches
- Male flashes big white wing patches in flight
- Female is much less dramatic but still has yellow tinge

### Listen Up!

- Or maybe you should cover your ears—a cacophony of squawks, *squeeps,* rattles, shrieks, and clacks, plus a noise like a chainsaw

### Telltale Traits

- Sight alone is enough to positively ID this dramatic bird.
- Usually in flocks
- Nervous tail flicks

### Look Here

- At feeder

### Or Here

- In flocks on lawn
- In marshes with cattails or other reeds
- In winter, this bird turns to grainfields for food: Huge flocks "roll over" fields, the birds in back moving to the front as they scour the field for wasted grain.

*"Poured out his grotesque love notes"*

—**A. C. Bent,** *Life Histories of North American Blackbirds, Orioles, Tanagers and Allies* **(1958)**

The voice of the yellow-headed blackbird is as attention-getting as its showy colors. You won't have to listen hard to find these birds—their repertoire of weird calls is loud!

**On the Home Front** Not a backyard nester, unless you have a large, reed-fringed pond • Nests in colonies, in a marsh • The male selects a breeding territory, then the females in his harem build nests within it. • Nests are built within a clump of reeds, and woven from reeds.

**Wild Menu:** Weed seeds; grain; aquatic insects

**Plant Picks:** Your feeder will keep these birds content.

### Feeder Pleasers

- Sunflower seed; cracked corn

### Tricks and Treats

- A birdbath or water feature may attract a yellow-headed splasher.

## Social Climbers

Yellow-headed blackbirds nest together in a colony in a marsh. But when it's time for the young to leave the nest, they're on their own. The big, gawky babies can't fly yet, so they take a pragmatic approach—they climb out. Grasping a marsh reed in one foot, then in the other, they make their way upward until it bends under their weight. Then they reach out and make a grab for the next reed. Baby blackbirds look pretty silly climbing around, but it's serious business: One misstep and they can land in the water. At the least, they could get a thorough soaking; at the worst, they could become a mouthful for a hungry fish.

# Broad-Tailed Hummingbird

*First Impression*

**A zippy little green guy with a rosy red throat**

### Mark Your Calendar

Spring through fall; absent from some areas

### Details, Details

- Significantly smaller than a chickadee; 4 inches, and that includes the bill!
- Focus your binoculars to find the white eye ring and the white stripe from eye to chin.
- All-green back
- Rusty chestnut patch on outside tail feathers near body
- Female lacks red throat; hers is grayish

### Listen Up!

- In normal flight, the male's wings make a high trilling sound.
- During a dive, the male's wings buzz loudly.
- Various high-pitched twittering sounds

### Telltale Traits

- Unmistakably a hummingbird: hovers, zips forward, back, up, down
- Often hovers in front of a flower

### Look Here

- At nectar feeder

### Or Here

- At flowers
- Flying through spray of sprinkler
- Perched on a twig

*On the Home Front* May nest in your backyard—but good luck finding that tiny, camouflaged cup! • May freshen up last year's nest by adding new material on top

*"As the country begins to dry up, these Hummingbirds retire to higher altitudes"*

—**Charles Bendire,** *Life Histories of North American Birds* **(1895)**

**Like many birds of the West, hummingbirds spend time at lower altitudes when they return from migration. They follow the bloom of wildflowers up the mountains to their nesting grounds.**

**Wild Menu:** Nectar; small insects; spiders

**Plant Picks:** How about some Rocky Mountain plants for *the* Rocky Mountain hummingbird? Native and cultivated varieties of penstemons (*Penstemon* spp.) are perfect. So are native columbines (*Aquilegia* spp.). Want a little variety? Add salvias (*Salvia* spp.) of any sort.

**Feeder Pleasers**
- Nectar feeder

**Tricks and Treats**
- Attach a mister to your birdbath, or put it on a timer and spray from a tree, shrub, or post.

## *Pretty Chilly*

Western weather is famous for its unpredictability. Hummingbirds wait until the flowers are blooming to begin nesting, but even that may not be long enough. If a cold spell sets in after the eggs are laid, hatching may be delayed because the female may go into a state of torpor, or slowed metabolism, during cold nights. That unique adaptation enables hummingbirds to weather cold temperatures without ill effects. But less body heat from Mom means a slowdown in egg development.

# Birds of the Southwest and California

This region has a beauty all its own. Spectacular rocks and canyons form the backdrop for plants that you'll see nowhere else in the country—stiff-armed saguaro, spiny sticks of brilliant red ocotillo (*Fouquieria splendens*), thorny bushes and trees, and other plants built to survive in this demanding climate.

This is America's desert. Its vast area of land is as lacking in water as other parts of the country are awash in it. Still, plenty of plants and birds have found a niche to thrive in here, and so have people.

## THE LAY OF THE LAND

The desert isn't just one kind of desert. This region features three main types of desert—the Sonoran, the Chihuahuan, and the Mojave—which vary even further within themselves.

Mountain ranges, including the Sierra Madre, the Chisos, the Guadalupe, and others, rise within the deserts in some areas, creating "sky islands" of cooler, slightly wetter microclimates of coniferous forests.

Birds live everywhere in the desert, but

**Vast spreads of fast-growing wildflowers, like these California poppies** (*Eschscholtzia californica*), **color springtime in the arid Southwest.**

people usually stick close to the cities, where the rigorous climate is tempered by creature comforts such as water on demand and air conditioning. That leaves lots of open space for wild things.

## FOOD AND SHELTER

It's 110°F in the shade? Better seek shelter from that brutal sun.

But just what's providing that shade? A rock, a scrubby small tree, a bush—not a shade tree with a dense canopy of big, lush leaves.

Shade trees are rare in this region, except for the cottonwoods along rivers and imported species such as palms and eucalyptus. Instead, you'll find hundreds of native plant species with gray leaves, woolly leaves, tiny leaves, leathery leaves, or other adapta-

tions designed to conserve water in the face of the ferocious summer heat. Thorns are popular, too, to prevent these plants from being eaten by desert animals. Shrubby plants and small trees are widely scattered, with plenty of open space between them, because with less than 10 inches of rain a year, there's not enough water to support dense groves or solid thickets.

Birds of this region know how to make use of any scrap of shade. They select nest sites that provide some relief from the sun, often at the foot of or within the branches or leaves of desert plants. Rocks cast shade, too, so birds often nest or rest beside them.

The particulars of the plants depend on the type of desert. The saguaros of the hot Sonoran yield to yuccas and agave in the Chihuahuan. The extremely dry Mojave, which includes Death Valley, is spotted by

Joshua trees (*Yucca brevifolia*) and other adapted yuccas. The chaparral areas of California are anchored by scrub oaks (*Quercus* spp.) and dense with shrubs adapted to that Mediterranean climate—and to periodic wildfires.

The American deserts are famed for their fantastic sweeps of color when their wildflowers bloom. Most of these are annual species, which can cram their life cycle into a very short span of time—just enough to take advantage of the winter rains. They spring up fast as soon as the rains begin, and blossom in just a matter of weeks. Then they set seed for next year and fade away. Those abundant seeds are a bounty for many desert birds, especially native sparrows and goldfinches.

Insects are just as plentiful in the desert as in more moderate climates, but like the plants, they're adapted to the heat and dryness. Beetles scuttle about, armored scale insects coat the branches, and spiders live in every nook and cranny. All make bountiful bird food!

Yuccas, agaves, and other perennial desert plants and shrubs provide another important food source: nectar. The desert is full of nectar flowers, so no wonder it's also full of hummingbirds. Orioles of this region depend on nectar, too, along with insects and fruit.

Speaking of fruit, that's another important food for birds of this region. Large, juicy fruits of saguaro, prickly pear, and other cactuses are prime bird food. Their high water content gives curve-billed thrashers and other birds a drink whenever they take a bite of pulp.

**The stout arms of saguaro cactus provide a place for nesting cavities and perching spots for owls, woodpeckers, and other birds.**

**The lovely white-winged dove is common in wild brushy areas and in backyards.**

Choose native plants for your yard; you won't have to baby them in this challenging climate. Investigate the possibilities of penstemons (*Penstemon* spp. and cultivars) and salvias (*Salvia* spp. and cultivars); any of them will be a hit with hummingbirds. Grevilleas (*Grevillea* spp. and cultivars), red-hot pokers (*Kniphofia* spp. and hybrids), and other plants from countries of similar climate, especially Africa and Australia, also thrive here; you'll find plenty of them at nurseries.

Most birds in this region are *xerophilous,* adapted to thriving without needing a daily drink of water. Instead, they obtain moisture from cactus fruits, nectar, or other foods they eat. Native plants with fruits and berries are popular with orioles, thrashers, and other fruit eaters; try any offered by your local nursery.

Still, you'll have great results if you put a birdbath in your xeric garden for these xerophilous birds: Most of them are quick to indulge in water if it's offered. Your birdbath may wind up being more popular than your feeding station. Set a basin on the ground, too, for quail and other ground-level birds.

## BIRD LIFE IN THE SOUTHWEST AND CALIFORNIA

Fabulous birds flourish in these conditions of extreme heat and scanty water. Most of them are unique to this region, perfectly adapted to desert life. You'll see an abundance of

**Pines provide tasty seeds for a host of appreciative birds.**

**Prolific flowers provide nectar for butterflies and hummingbirds, plus a banquet of insects and seeds for other birds.**

thrashers, for instance, with extra-long beaks that they use adeptly when foraging among cactus thorns.

Some common American birds also scratch out a living here. The first time I visited the Southwest, I had to check and recheck a field guide before I could convince myself that the robin I saw hopping around in the desert really was a robin. I was sure it had to be some exotic species that had a subtle difference. But nope: It was a plain old robin.

You'll have to look a little harder to see many of the birds of this region. Many species, such as the California towhee, are colored to blend in with the landscape. Other species, though, including the vivid black-and-yellow Scott's oriole, stand out like neon signs against the landscape's subtle hues.

While bird-watchers in wetter regions of the country are straining their eyes to see songbirds far overhead in the foliage, you can enjoy watching birds right at eye level or lower. Most species in this region live at ground level or low to medium heights, because tall trees are scarce, except near water. Irrigated farming areas and riversides attract many birds, which may spill over into nearby backyards.

## Start Here

Even though the Southwest and California region is home to many birds that would never be seen in other regions, it also harbors a lot of familiar friends. Turn to Chapter 6, "Start Here," to find many of your loyal backyard friends, the birds you share with other parts of the country—goldfinches, juncos, cedar waxwings, and many others.

## Regional Specialties

Desert birds are distinctly different from the list of species found in any other region. The acorn woodpecker busies itself stuffing acorns into holes like marbles into a Chinese checkerboard. The tiny pygmy nuthatch roams the pines. Shrubs are decorated with the round, thorny nests of the verdin, a chickadee-like bird with a beautiful yellow head. Cactus wrens and California thrashers duke it out for nesting territories and sitting space at the feeder. Just about everywhere you look, you'll find unique birds that never leave their desert home. Many species native to Mexico or Central America reach the northern extent of their range in this region, including fantastic hummingbird species. That's why southern Arizona, New Mexico, and Texas are famed birding hot spots. Lucky you—you live in the thick of it!

If you live near the borders of this region, be sure to page through the birds of the West, Northwest, and Midwest regions, too. Those regions are your neighbors, and many of their birds may range into your territory.

**This ash-throated flycatcher has recycled a former woodpecker home in a large cactus.**

## Birds of the Southwest and California

Here are the birds profiled in this chapter. Remember to consult the "Start Here" birds, starting on page 79, for other common birds in the Southwest and California.

# Acorn Woodpecker

*First Impression*

**Black woodpecker with clownish pale yellow face and shocking light eyes in black cheeks**

### Mark Your Calendar

Year-round; absent from parts of this region

### Details, Details

- A little smaller than a robin; 9 inches
- Male has a red cap, over onto back of neck
- Flashy white rump and wing patches visible in flight
- Female has a smaller amount of red on head

### Listen Up!

- Highly vocal, with all sorts of raucous sounds
- Often calls *ja-cob, ja-cob* or *whack-up, whack-up*
- Also high, nasal calls
- Drums in short stretches, picking up speed

### Telltale Traits

- Always in a small group, from two or three birds to about 15
- Frequently drills holes for storing acorns and fills them, or is tending its stores

### Look Here

- At suet feeder

### Or Here

- At utility poles or trees, looking after its cache of acorns
- At oak trees, collecting acorns
- At almond or other nut trees
- Fly-catching from a perch

*On the Home Front* Not usually a backyard nester • Excavates nest hole in living or dead cottonwoods or willows, or utility poles

*"A solid 'mass' of acorns, totalling, say, some 20,000"*

—**William Dawson,** *The Birds of California* (1923)

**The acorn woodpecker doesn't seem to have an off switch: The bird drills and stuffs so many holes with acorns that it can't possibly ever eat them all. Many go to waste.**

**Wild Menu:** Acorns; nuts; insects in summer

**Plant Picks:** No surprise here: Plant an oak tree, or an almond, pecan, or English walnut.

### Feeder Pleasers

- Suet; sunflower seeds; nuts; may become a regular at nectar feeder

### Tricks and Treats

- These birds can sure guzzle the sugar water from your hummingbird feeder. Try securing a nectar feeder to a post, so that it doesn't swing under the bird's weight. This convenience may wean it away from your hummingbird feeder. Once the bird is in the habit of using it, gradually switch to a weaker sugar solution (one part sugar to six or eight parts water).

## Skewed Instinct

I first met acorn woodpeckers in Arizona, where a group of these birds was busy tending to its stores. Most of them were inserting acorns—pointy end first—into the perfectly sized holes they'd drilled, but one woodpecker had something else in its beak. I couldn't tell from a distance what it was. Quietly, I moved closer, keeping my binoculars focused on the bird. At last I saw: This guy was storing pebbles! For years I've wondered why.

# Gila Woodpecker

## First Impression

**A "bald" woodpecker with a zebra coat**

### Mark Your Calendar

Year-round, mostly in southern Arizona; absent from much of this region

### Details, Details

- A little smaller than a robin; 9¼ inches
- Finely patterned black-and-white back and wings; soft tan head and belly
- Male has a red crown
- Female looks like male but lacks red crown

### Listen Up!

- Perhaps the noisiest woodpecker, constantly carrying on
- Makes harsh laughing sounds
- Shrill *pit!* calls and rasping *churr*s

### Telltale Traits

- Extremely bold and vocal; you can't miss this bird, because he'll be complaining loudly somewhere nearby
- Highly aggressive
- Threatens and chases others of its kind— and any other bird that comes close; even attacks large thrashers
- Pecks at dead or living trees
- Undulating flight

### Look Here

- At feeder

### Or Here

- In or on saguaro cactus, often pecking at it
- Flying across open space, calling loudly
- Carrying corn or other food to a post or tree to peck at it

*"Afraid neither of being seen nor being heard"*

—M. Gilman, quoted in *Life Histories of North American Woodpeckers* (1939)

Perhaps Gilman had spent a little too much time around the birds, as he continued, "All his talk at us has a distinctly 'colicky' tone and one feels like giving him something to whine about."

**On the Home Front** If you have saguaro in your backyard, you may host a nesting pair.
- May also accept a nest box • Drills a cavity

**Wild Menu:** Ants and other insects; saguaro fruits; mistletoe berries

**Plant Picks:** Saguaro cactus is the first choice for this bird.

**Feeder Pleasers**
- Suet; a quail block—a compressed block of seeds and grain available at feed stores and wild bird supply stores; birdseed mix; dry dog food; nectar; meat scraps and meaty bones

**Tricks and Treats**
- Old books mention this species' fondness for watermelon, so why not give it a try? Cut it into fist-size chunks, with rind intact, and let the birds pick them clean.

## Recycling

Trees are scarce in the Sonoran desert, so woody saguaros are a prime target of Gila and other woodpeckers. Once I saw a female launch itself straight out from a new hole, as if she'd hit the button on an ejector seat.

Woodpecker holes are prime real estate for cavity-nesting birds who can't drill their own. I spotted a cactus wren entering a hole, carrying insects for its babies. A kestrel perched atop another cactus with a nest hole, nervously flicking its tail as it watched me. But the best was last: A tiny elf owl, like a cute little stuffed toy, peered out of a hole, its big yellow eyes glaring fiercely at me. It was so utterly adorable, I wanted to slip it into my pocket.

# Vermilion Flycatcher

*First Impression*

**Small, glowing red bird with grayish black wings and tail**

### Mark Your Calendar

Spring to fall in the southern part of this region; absent or an occasional stray in other areas

### Details, Details

- Sparrow size; 6 inches
- Notice how its red body shows when the bird lifts its wings in flight—beautiful!
- Dark stripe extends backyard from eye
- Take a close look at that tiny thin beak.
- Female is light gray with a streaky white breast and lovely salmon-pink on lower belly to tail

### Listen Up!

- Male sings an ecstatic courtship song, *pit-pit-pit-pit pit-a-see!,* while rising in flight
- A sharp *peet!* call note

### Telltale Traits

- Relatively tame
- Like tanagers, this bright bird can be surprisingly hard to see in trees.
- Spends much of time perched, often conspicuously
- Flies out from a perch after insects

### Look Here

- Flying from one perch to another, often from the tip of a tall stem to a shrub or tree

### Or Here

- Perched at tip of plant or weed stem
- Fly-catching from perch

*"Butterfly-like"*

—Edward Gifford, on the courtship flight of the vermilion flycatcher, *Proceedings of the California Academy of Science* (1919)

**The vermilion flycatcher sings ecstatically during his slow, fluttery courtship flight. At times he hovers like a floating ball of vermilion, with breast and head feathers fluffed to show their blinding red color.**

*On the Home Front* Not usually a backyard nester • Usually nests near a stream or other water • Builds a soft little nest deep in a forked branch of a willow, cottonwood, or other tree

**Wild Menu:** Insects, including many bees

**Plant Picks:** Scattered shrubs, small trees, and flowers with tall stems that make good perches

### Feeder Pleasers

- Not a feeder visitor

### Tricks and Treats

- Feed this flycatcher's predilection for bees by planting flowers such as agastache (*Agastache* spp.), lupines, sunflowers, chamise (*Adenostoma fasciculatum*), and phacelia (*Phacelia* spp.).

## Missed Opportunity

I always wondered why I saw so many excellent photographs of vermilion flycatchers, until I went hunting the bird myself. This species usually sticks to the trees along irrigation ditches or roadsides, so I thought I'd have to search there. But as soon as I walked behind my motel outside of Tucson, I spotted a flicker of burning red. Soon the flycatcher perched on a slim, bare branch, just above eye level.

I was stunned to see that it stayed put as I sneakily approached. In fact, I felt kind of silly taking one baby step after another, because the bird seemed totally undisturbed by my presence. If only I'd had a camera, I, too, could've taken one of those jaw-dropping shots.

# Ash-Throated Flycatcher

*First Impression*

**An alertly perched taupe bird that flashes a startling cinnamon tail in flight**

### Mark Your Calendar

Spring through fall; year-round in extreme southern parts of range

### Details, Details

- Bigger than a sparrow but smaller than a robin; 8½ inches
- Resembles great crested flycatcher of eastern half of United States
- Wings as well as tail show cinnamon color in flight
- Pale yellow belly
- Female looks like male

### Listen Up!

- A vocal bird whose frequent, distinctive calls quickly become familiar
- Loud *quirrr, quirrp* calls, similar to the great crested flycatcher
- Also loud *hip, hip, ha-wheer* or *che-hoo! che-hoo!*
- Often makes soft, low *ha-whip* calls

### Telltale Traits

- Flicks tail up and down and sometimes sideways
- Usually engaged in fly-catching

### Look Here

- Perched conspicuously on a low tree or bush to nab passing insects

### Or Here

- At nest box
- Fly-catching over a flower garden or flowering shrub
- Flying across open space

*"In the boom of a gasolene engine shovel"*

**—Wilson Hanna, describing a nest that moved up and down, "Odd Nesting Site of Ash-Throated Flycatcher" (1931)**

**Like the house wren, the ash-throated flycatcher has a penchant for choosing unusual nesting sites—exhaust pipes, the legs of pants on a clothesline, an empty mailbox, and other cavities.**

*On the Home Front* Often accepts a nest box mounted about 4 to 10 feet high in quiet area
- Nests in woodpecker holes and other natural cavities, as well as in oddball sites

**Wild Menu:** Insects, including bees, wasps, dragonflies, mantids, and cicadas; cactus fruit

**Plant Picks:** Flower gardens are popular hangouts for this bird because of all the insects they attract. Flowering shrubs, such as woolly butterfly bush (*Buddleia marrubifolia*), as well as the fruits of saguaro, cardon, and organ-pipe cactuses are favored; or try elderberries.

### Feeder Pleasers

- Not a feeder visitor

### Tricks and Treats

- Offer a wire basket stuffed with nesting materials, including tufts of sheep's wool; 4-inch pieces of string or yarn; and short, narrow strips of cloth.

## Not a Drop to Drink

Even in the heat of summer in its arid range, the ash-throated flycatcher ignores a tempting birdbath. Juicy fruit, swallowed whole, seems to supply the moisture the bird needs.

In a study in 1977, at a spring in an oak-madrona woodland in California, out of 45 species of birds observed, 21 never came for a drink—and the ash-throated flycatcher was one.

# Pinyon Jay

*First Impression*

**A noisy flock of big, plain, light blue birds**

*"Our most gregarious bird"*

—A. C. Bent, *Life Histories of North American Jays, Crows, and Titmice* (1946)

### Mark Your Calendar

Year-round, although flocks may come and go as they move about in search of food

### Details, Details:

* About the size of a robin; 10½ inches
* Looks squat and chubby compared to longer-tailed jays
* Crestless
* Female and male look alike
* The similar scrub jay, also in this region, has a much longer tail and a pale belly.

### Listen Up!

* Constantly calls in flight, a soft *hoy-hoy-hoy*
* Harsh *karee-karee-karee* or *kree-kree-kree* calls, rising in pitch
* Also various buzzy, trilling, rattling calls

### Telltale Traits

* Usually in a flock, sometimes very large
* Several birds may act as sentries, while the rest of the flock feeds.
* Spends a lot of time on the ground, foraging for food and caching seeds
* Unearths its cached seeds even when buried under snow

### Look Here

* At the feeder

### Or Here

* On the ground
* Foraging in pine trees
* Perched in other trees
* At the birdbath

Noisy and restless, pinyon jays roam about the foothills in flocks. In the wild, flocks can build to 100 or more birds, but much smaller groups visit backyards.

*On the Home Front* May nest in backyards

* Builds a bulky nest in pinyon pines (*Pinus edulis*), junipers, and oaks, usually from 3 to 20 feet aboveground

**Wild Menu:** Pinyon pine seeds and other seeds; juniper and other berries; acorns; plus lizards, snakes, insects, and small mammals

**Plant Picks:** Pines, especially pinyon (*Pinus edulis*), ponderosa (*Pinus ponderosa*), and Jeffrey (*Pinus jeffreyi*); also oaks. For a faster food crop, try planting tall annual sunflowers.

### Feeder Pleasers

* Sunflower seeds; pine nuts in the shell

### Tricks and Treats

* Pinyon jays will drink from a birdbath, but they're not fond of bathing there.
* Provide a bare, dusty area in your yard and you may see these birds, and others, take dust baths.

## Nuts about Pine Nuts

Pinyon pines have big, meaty seeds that are a hit with wildlife and people alike. They're still a staple for native Americans, as they've been for thousands of years. In years when the cones yield a bumper crop, Navajos may collect a million pounds. The nuts are high in fat, protein, and carbohydrates—a single nut supplies about 20 calories! Collecting nuts isn't easy, because they have to be pried out of the cones. Shelling them is even harder. Many folks use a rolling pin to crack the hard brown hulls without smashing the delectable nut meat inside.

# Plain Titmouse

*First Impression*

**Very plain-colored, small gray bird with crested head**

### Mark Your Calendar

Year-round; oak titmouse along coast; juniper titmouse in most of rest of region

### Details, Details

- About small sparrow size; 5¾ inches
- The oak titmouse and the juniper titmouse live in different habitats and have different voices.
- Both juniper and oak titmice are plain gray birds; the oak species has a brownish tinge.
- Female looks like male

### Listen Up!

- Juniper titmouse gives a rapid loud trill
- Oak titmouse also does a trill, but has clear, whistled notes in its refrains, too
- Both species can sound a lot like chickadees. Listen for the raspy *tschick-a-dee* call.

### Telltale Traits

- Actively in motion in the branches of trees, picking off insects
- Moves from branch to branch
- Flies to the next tree with shallow undulating dips
- Often sings from a perch

### Look Here

- At feeder

### Or Here

- In junipers
- In pinyon–juniper woods

*"A high, clear whistle"*
—Ralph Hoffmann, *Birds of the Pacific States* (1927)

**The trademark *Peter, Peter* whistle of the tufted titmouse is echoed by this western counterpart. Taxonomists recently separated the plain titmouse into two species, oak and juniper, partly because the juniper titmouse doesn't have the whistle in its vocal repertoire.**

*On the Home Front* Happily moves into a nest box • The juniper species nests in stumps or crevices of old, gnarled junipers; the oak titmouse seeks out an existing cavity or digs its own hole in soft, decayed wood, usually in— guess what?—oaks.

**Wild Menu:** Insects; acorns; pine seeds and other seeds

**Plant Picks:** Oaks (native to your area); pines, especially pinyon (*Pinus edulis*); junipers (native to your area)

**Feeder Pleasers**

- Sunflower seeds; suet; chopped nuts

**Tricks and Treats**

- Offer soft materials at nesting time: wool tufts, bits of fuzzy yarn, feathers, and anything else.

Like crows and jays, the plain titmouse, which looks like a miniature crested jay, shares the habit of serving as the alarmist when danger is near. It raises an outcry when it spots an owl or hawk, a wandering cat, or sometimes a person walking in its territory.

One year, when I was traveling with our cats (in travel crates), I found out how insistent this small bird can be. We were stopped at a campground, with our caged kitties temporarily set on the picnic table. The cats were justifiably complaining, and a pair of curious plain titmice came to investigate. Perched overhead, they kept up a chatter that drew other birds to see what was going on. Thanks to our felines, we enjoyed some great bird-watching!

# Verdin

*First Impression*

**Little gray bird with yellow face at the nectar feeder**

### Mark Your Calendar

Year-round; absent from some of this region

### Details, Details:

- Smaller than a chickadee; 4½ inches
- Upper parts are ashy or brownish gray; pale below
- Warm chestnut shoulder patch

### Listen Up!

- A whistling *tseet-tsoor-tsoor*
- Several variations of loud call notes, including a rapid *chip chip chip*

### Telltale Traits

- A busy and active little bird
- Behavior similar to a chickadee, but it doesn't hang upside down
- Highly vocal
- Joins mixed flocks of sparrows, juncos, gnatcatchers, and warblers

### Look Here

- At the nectar feeder

### Or Here

- At flowers, searching for insects
- Often in trees or bushes; rarely on ground
- At clumps of mistletoe
- Prefers desert scrub and brushy areas with thorny trees or bushes

*On the Home Front* May nest in a large, naturalistic backyard that opens to wild space, in acacias (*Acacia* spp.), paloverde (*Cercidium floridum*), or mesquite (*Prosopis* spp.) • Nest is often at end of a low branch

*"So strongly is it built that it is difficult to tear one apart"*

—Herbert Brandt, *Texas Bird Adventures in the Chisos Mountains and on the Northern Plains* (1940)

**The ball-shape nests of verdins are a familiar sight throughout their range. The determined Brandt noted that heavy gloves were necessary to handle the nests because "the multitude of thorns will effectively repel bare hands."**

**Wild Menu:** Insects; nectar; and a sampling of small fruits

**Plant Picks:** A flower garden may be a popular foraging place. Thorny native shrubs such as mesquite (*Prosopis velutina* and other spp.) and small trees will also welcome this bird.

### Feeder Pleasers

- Nectar

### Tricks and Treats

- Gather as many kinds of soft materials as you can to offer for nesting in early spring. Feathers are always popular.

## Sleeping Spaces

Once you start looking for verdin nests, you'll see lots of them dotting the small trees and bushes. Are there that many brooding birds in such a small area? Nope. Many of those nests are roosting nests built for sleeping.

The tiny birds use the same strong nest construction to create a safe space to spend the night. Those thorny twigs help keep out snakes and other bird-eating predators.

# Bushtit

## First Impression

Tiny gray bird flying out of a bush with high, thin calls; then another bird, and another, and another, and another . . .

## Mark Your Calendar

Year-round; absent from a few small parts of this region

## Details, Details

- One of our smallest birds, even smaller than a chickadee; 4½ inches
- Long tail
- Often looks fluffed-up
- An unusual variation of gender: males have dark eyes, females have pale eyes

## Listen Up!

- A constant stream of thin, high-pitched *tsit-tsit-tsit* calls
- The calls are a great clue to the impending arrival of a flock of bushtits. When you hear them, look around for the bitty birds.

## Telltale Traits

- Intensely gregarious; always in a flock
- Constantly on the move, foraging rapidly in bushes and small trees
- Often travels with mixed group of chickadees and kinglets in winter
- Tame around people and gentle to each other; no sign of squabbling in flock

## Look Here

- Moving in a flock from one group of bushes in your yard to the next

## Or Here

- At the birdbath
- Flying in a talkative flock
- At the suet feeder

*"An individual bird ... takes temporary leadership, and is followed to a new location"*

—Robert Miller, "The Flock Behavior of the Coast Bush-Tit" (1921)

Miller surmised that it was "the hunger instinct" that caused one bird of the flock to suddenly take off for a new foraging place. No one really knows. Maybe these tiny birds just have wanderlust?

On the Home Front The nest is a long, loose, hanging sack, suspended from a tree or bush.
- Builds in deciduous or evergreen trees

**Wild Menu:** Insects, especially scale insects; spiders

**Plant Picks:** Unsprayed shrubs and trees of any kind

**Feeder Pleasers**
- Suet, especially suet enriched with insects

**Tricks and Treats**
- Bushtits love their baths. Keep a birdbath brimming, and you may see the whole bunch lining up at once.

## Disappearing Act

Bushtits occur in the Northwest and West regions, too. Every few days, a flock of about 40 of these tiny gray mites sweeps into my yard in Washington State. The entire flock plays follow the leader from one shrub to another, then stops off at the suet feeder to fill their beaks. A few minutes later, perhaps with a last pit stop at the birdbath, they're gone again. All told, they may spend 10 minutes, tops, in my acre yard. With these fast-action birds, you'll want to "Catch 'em while you can!"

# Curve-Billed Thrasher

*First Impression*

**Big, drab, grayish tan bird with an outrageous downward curved beak**

## Mark Your Calendar

Year-round; absent from parts of this region

## Details, Details

- Larger than a robin; 11 inches
- Focus your binoculars on that orange eye.
- Faintly speckled breast
- Female looks like male

## Listen Up!

- You'll often hear a sharp, two-note, *whit-wheet!* whistle, given by both sexes. It's loud and startling!
- The male's warbled song of musical phrases sounds a lot like the brown thrasher's. Each phrase is repeated two or three times, then there's a short pause before it's on to the next paired phrases. The song itself is very varied, but usually includes *quit-quit* and *weet-weet* phrases.

## Telltale Traits

- Runs rapidly or hops across the ground
- Flies low and fast from one bush to another
- Tosses aside leaves and debris with its bill
- Digs holes a few inches deep with that beak
- Often hides in shrubbery

## Look Here

- Perched on a cholla cactus

## Or Here

- On the ground
- Beneath shrubs
- At the feeder or the birdbath

*"Like water running through a sieve"*

—Herbert Brown, "The Habits and Nesting of Palmer's Thrasher" (1888)

Watching a curve-billed thrasher (once called Palmer's thrasher) slip smoothly through the branches and among the spines of a cholla cactus is amazing. The viciously spiny cactus is usually so quick to jab its barbed spines into any passerby that it's called "jumping cactus."

*On the Home Front* May nest in backyards
- Usually nests in cholla cactus, 3 to 5 feet aboveground • Builds nest of thorny twigs lined with grass • Competes with cactus wren for nest sites and territory

**Wild Menu:** Insects; cactus fruit

**Plant Picks:** Fruits of any kind, particularly sweet or sour cherries, mulberries (*Morus* spp. and cvs.), and grapes

**Feeder Pleasers**
- Mealworms; suet; millet, milo, and birdseed mix; nuts

**Tricks and Treats**
- Keep a birdbath brimming for this bird.

## Thrashers Galore

Thrashers are hard to identify. Six species of similar thrashers, including Bendire's, curve-billed, California, Crissal, LeConte's, and possibly the long-billed, plus the thrush-like sage thrasher, occur in the Southwest. It takes practice to sort them out where ranges overlap. That's if you get to see them at all—most species are notorious skulkers. They stay in dense brush, coming out to forage on the ground, where their drab colors blend right into the background.

One good way to track down thrashers is to listen for a singing bird. They may sing from within a tangle of branches, but often they move to a conspicuous perch to pour out their long and varied songs. Check the details to figure out which species is doing the singing.

# Hepatic Tanager

*First Impression*

**A soft red, slinky bird in the treetops**

### Mark Your Calendar

Spring through fall in mountain forests; migration only in some areas; absent in some parts of region

### Details, Details

- Smaller than a robin; 8 inches
- Note the brightness of the red (sometimes red-orange) on the bird's crown and throat, compared to the dull red body.
- Female is grayish with yellow-orange forehead and breast

### Listen Up!

- A slow melodic song, full of pauses
- Also a low *chup* call note
- A rising *tweet* in flight

### Telltale Traits

- Slow and deliberate
- Fairly tame birds

### Look Here

- Foraging in pines or oaks

### Or Here

- At feeder
- Fly-catching after passing insects
- At birdbath

*On the Home Front* Not usually a backyard nester, unless your backyard is in or very near a pine-oak forest • Builds a loose, open saucer of stems, grasses, and—for a unique and charming touch—flower stems with flowers still on them • Nests in branch fork in pines and oaks

*"Slow and deliberate in their movements"*

—A. C. Bent, *Life Histories of North American Blackbirds, Orioles, Tanagers, and Allies* (1958)

These beautiful tanagers move slowly and quietly through the treetops and branches of pines and oaks, gleaning insects. The only way to find them there is to look up!

**Wild Menu:** Insects; some fruit

**Plant Picks:** Pines native to your area, such as pinyon (*Pinus edulis*) or Jeffrey (*P. jeffreyi*); grapes or cherries

**Feeder Pleasers**

- Mealworms and other insect foods; halved papaya and other fruits

**Tricks and Treats**

- Provide a pedestal-type birdbath or other water source.
- Hepatic tanagers are fond of butterflies and moths, just in case you need another reason to plant a butterfly-attracting garden.

## A Step Ahead of Science

Official data about the hepatic tanager shows a lot of gaps, including its diet and bathing habits. Yet backyard bird-watchers have snapped photos of this bird at their feeders. And I saw one take a bath when my family was camping in the Chiricahua Mountains of Arizona. As soon as we pulled into the campsite, birds were already gathering. When I filled a frying pan with water, we suddenly drew a crowd. A bright yellow-and-black Scott's oriole alighted on the pan while I was carrying it. I can take a hint—I filled the skillet and set it nearby. Our next customer was a hepatic tanager, who exuberantly splashed nearly all the water out of the pan. Finally, he yielded to the oriole and went off to fluff and preen.

# California Towhee

*First Impression*

**Drab grayish brown bird scratching on ground**

### Mark Your Calendar

Year-round in western California

### Details, Details

- About robin size; 9 inches
- Use binoculars to see orangish eye color.
- Look for the pretty orangish color where the tail joins the body.
- Short, sparrowlike bill
- Female looks like male
- Similar canyon towhee has a reddish cap and a necklace of short, dark streaks and spots; Abert's towhee of Southwest is another look-alike, with dark face

### Listen Up!

- A series of sharp, metallic clinks, *chink-chink-chink-ink-ink-ink,* picking up speed into almost a trill, and often ending with a drawn out, lower *chinnnnk*
- Also a sharp, high *chink* call note

### Telltale Traits

- One of the most common backyard birds
- Tame around people in backyards; much shier in the wild
- Almost always on the ground, either in the open or under a bush or parked car
- Reminiscent of a big sparrow
- Scratches at ground with feet, hopping forward and dragging back

### Look Here

- At feeder

### Or Here

- Foraging on ground or under shrubs

*"Striking together two silver dollars"*

—Richard Hunt, on metallic sound of California towhee, "Evidence of Musical Taste in the Brown Towhee" (1922)

**Short on silver dollars? Then try to imagine the rhythm of this towhee's song: Hunt said it's like a golf ball dropped on a hard surface and "allowed to bounce itself motionless."**

*On the Home Front* May nest in backyards
- Builds a bulky nest in a dense shrub or tree

**Wild Menu:** Seeds, especially weeds; some insects

**Plant Picks:** Scatter a few handfuls of birdseed mix; towhees will forage among the plants' standing stems all fall and winter.

### Feeder Pleasers

- Millet; birdseed mix

### Tricks and Treats

- Rein in your weeding habit, and you'll make towhees happy. They eagerly seek out seeds of pigweeds (*Amaranthus* spp.), knotweeds (*Polygonum* spp.), filaree (*Erodium cicutarium*), and others.

## Home-Court Advantage

Without flashy colors or bold markings, the many species of drab-colored southwestern birds can be tough to identify—for visitors, that is. When you live with these birds, you get to know their voices and habits, which are major clues to sorting out the species.

Geography factors in, too: If you live in L.A., you're not likely to have an Abert's towhee scratching in your backyard. Visitors, though, will have to constantly consult their field guides, to see when they're leaving one species' stomping ground and moving into another's territory.

# Lesser Goldfinch

*First Impression*

**A smaller, darker goldfinch**

### Mark Your Calendar

Year-round in southern and coastal parts of region; spring through fall in rest

### Details, Details

- Smaller than a chickadee; 4½ inches
- Smaller than American goldfinch
- Big white patches show in wings and tail in flight.
- Unlike American goldfinch, doesn't change plumage colors for winter
- Male's black cap extends farther back than that of American goldfinch
- Female is duller and lacks the black cap
- Lawrence's goldfinch also shows up in some parts of this region, usually foraging in weeds under oaks. It's a gray bird with a black face and yellow splashes on breast, wings, and tail.

### Listen Up!

- Canarylike song of varied, rising notes
- A plaintive, high, clear, *te-yeee* or *tee-ee* call

### Telltale Traits

- Gregarious birds, usually in flocks except in nesting season
- Undulating flight
- Often sing and call on the wing

### Look Here

- At the birdbath

### Or Here

- At the feeder
- In gardens or weedy corners, eating seeds
- Perched with the flock in a treetop
- Flying with the flock in dipping, rising flight

*"Especially fond of the seeds of the wild sunflower"*

—**Alfred Gross**, in A. C. Bent's *Life Histories of North American Cardinals, Grosbeaks, Buntings, Towhees, Finches, Sparrows, and Allies* (1968)

**Sunflowers grow wild in this region, reverting to a shorter, widely branching form with seed heads just a couple of inches across. Goldfinches visit the plants as soon as the seeds start to ripen.**

*On the Home Front* May nest in backyard
- Female builds a dainty cup of plant fibers and grasses, lined with thistledown and feathers

**Wild Menu:** Weed seeds, especially thistle

**Plant Picks:** Weed seeds are dear to this bird's heart, so tolerate a few if you can. Or plant a meadow garden with native grasses and flowers.

**Feeder Pleasers**
- Niger seed; millet and finch mix

**Tricks and Treats**
- Water draws this species like a magnet. Any birdbath may attract them
- They're fond of salt; offer a scant handful of table salt in an open tray feeder.

## The Indiana Connection

New Harmony, Indiana, where I used to live, was once a Utopian community full of scientists and freethinkers, including Thomas Say, a 19th-century American naturalist responsible for describing many species of wildlife for the first time—including the coyote and a firefly.

On an 1819 expedition to the Rocky Mountains, Say and companions collected a specimen of the lesser goldfinch. His description was published and made official in 1923.

# Lark Bunting

*First Impression*

**A dramatic black-and-white sparrow**

### Mark Your Calendar

Year-round in southern part of region; spring through fall in eastern and northern parts; migration only or occasional stray in other areas; absent in some parts

### Details, Details

- The size of a big sparrow; 7 inches
- When it's in breeding plumage, look for the male's white wing patches and white tail tip.
- Outside of breeding season, the male is heavily streaked with black face and pale blue beak.
- Female is grayish brown with streaky white breast and dark stripe on throat

### Listen Up!

- A rich, pretty, warbled song of musical trills, interspersed with high, metallic rattling noises
- Low, soft, *hoo-ee* call note

### Telltale Traits

- Not usually a backyard bird, but a vivid presence in surrounding open land
- In huge flocks, from hundreds to thousands of birds, except during nesting season
- The flock moves like a rolling wheel, with birds at the rear continuously fluttering to the front. When they find food, the wheel stops and the birds eat their fill.

### Look Here

- In open areas

### Or Here

- In arid land, grassy areas, or brushy places
- Singing from a fence post

*"Habitat loss due to urbanization"*

—**Diane Neudorf**, on threats to species, *Lark Bunting (Calamospiza melanocorys): A Technical Conservation Assessment* (2006)

**City sprawl can cause more than traffic jams. Although there are plenty of lark buntings, scientists are watching the species for the impact human activities have upon it.**

*On the Home Front* Not a backyard nester
- Builds nest on ground, at foot of sagebrush (*Artemisia* spp.), shrubs, or clump of weeds

**Wild Menu:** Seeds, especially weed seeds; in summer, grasshoppers and other insects

**Plant Picks:** If you have a backyard big enough to suit this freewheeling species—and that means many acres—you won't have to plant anything to draw it in.

### Feeder Pleasers

- Not usually a feeder visitor

### Tricks and Treats

- Spring migration is the best time to observe a flock with males in full breeding plumage.

## Living Up to the Lark

In March or April, the male lark buntings leave the massive wintering flock and move northward to nesting grounds. On this trek, the male birds—in beautiful, fresh breeding plumage—are suddenly gripped by the urge to sing, and what a show they put on! One by one, male birds suddenly rise up from the ground into the air, pouring out an ecstatic song. Because they're still in a flock, there may be dozens to hundreds of males doing the same thing at once. It's an incredible spectacle, both to see and to hear.

# Scott's Oriole

*First Impression*

**A beautiful song coming from a big, slim, striking yellow-and-black bird**

### Mark Your Calendar

Spring through fall; absent in a few areas

### Details, Details

- About the size of a robin; 9 inches
- Male has dramatic black hood, with bright yellow belly and shoulders
- Female is much paler, has dull greenish head, and variable amounts of black on head or breast

### Listen Up!

- Rich, musical song of whistled notes
- Female sings softly near the nest
- Also a quick, harsh *jerk!*

### Telltale Traits

- Usually seen singly or in pairs
- Constantly singing
- Cling to stems of flowers to get nectar

### Look Here

- At nectar feeder

### Or Here

- At fruit feeder
- At flowers
- Climbing quietly along branches through foliage, peering for prey
- At birdbath

*On the Home Front* May nest in backyards
- Often attaches its nest to the drooping, dead leaves of *yuccas*, near where they join the plant
- Builds a cup-shape nest; not as pendulous as those of other oriole species

*"Few birds sing more incessantly"*

**—William Scott, "On the Breeding Habits of Some Arizona Birds" (1885)**

**You'll probably hear this bird before you see it. Scott noted, "At the earliest daybreak, even when the sun is at its highest, and during the great heat of the afternoon, its very musical whistle is one of the few bird songs that are ever present."**

**Wild Menu:** Insects, especially butterflies; fruit; nectar from flowers

**Plant Picks:** Aloes (*Aloe* spp.), ocotillo (*Fouquieria splendens*), red-hot pokers (*Kniphofia* spp.), yuccas (*Yucca* spp.); figs, peaches, apricots, or cactuses.

**Feeder Pleasers**
- Nectar feeder; halved oranges or grapefruits; mealworms; suet, especially with insects

**Tricks and Treats**
- Flowers are key to the heart of Scott's oriole—and not just because of their nectar. The bird may visit your blooms to pluck butterflies.

## Mastering Monarchs

Everyone knows that monarch butterflies are poisonous. Everyone but Scott's orioles, that is: On their wintering grounds in Mexico, the birds eat plenty of them. The secret? Not all monarchs have the same concentration of toxins. In 1979, monarch experts William Calvert, Lee Hedrick, and Lincoln Brower (*Science*) found that Scott's orioles flew repeatedly into the colonies to peck at the butterflies. Often, an oriole would release a butterfly without eating it—probably because its bad taste indicated a higher level of toxins.

# Hummingbirds

*First Impression*

**Tiny, zippy, unmistakable birds with brilliant iridescent color**

### Mark Your Calendar

Spring through fall, migration, or year-round, depending on where you live and on the species of hummingbird

### Details, Details

- Itty-bitty birds, from 3¼ inches to about 5 inches, including the long bill
- This region is hummingbird heaven. Depending on where you live, you might spot Allen's, Anna's, black-chinned, broad-billed, broad-tailed *(shown above)*, calliope, Costa's, magnificent, rufous, or white-eared hummingbirds, plus a selection of Mexican species that occasionally stray northward.

### Listen Up!

- Various twitterings, chips, and high, thin, squeaky calls

### Telltale Traits

- Unique ability to fly frontward, backward, up, or down, or to hover
- So fast you may only hear the buzz as one goes by
- Hover at flowers
- Often perch on slim twigs or other places where takeoff is unimpeded by vegetation

### Look Here

- At nectar feeder

### Or Here

- At flowers
- Perched in shrubs or small trees, or on garden ornaments

*"By the first of July . . . the Hummingbirds are found in countless thousands at higher elevations"*

—**Joseph Grinnell,** *Birds of the Pacific Slope of Los Angeles County* **(1898)**

**Hummingbirds follow the flowers. Many species leave lower elevations by late June, when flowers stop blooming, and head for the mountains, where flowers are then in full glory.**

*On the Home Front* May nest in backyards
- Hummingbird nests are tiny cups built of spider silk, plant down, lichens, and other bits of materials.

**Wild Menu:** Nectar; insects

**Plant Picks:** Hummingbird flowers! Check your local nursery for native perennials, annuals, and shrubs.

### Feeder Pleasers

- Nectar feeder

### Tricks and Treats

- Supply a garden ornament at least 5 feet tall—such as a trellis or hanging basket holder—made of metal less than ½ inch in diameter. If the very top is slender enough for their tiny feet, your backyard hummingbirds may make it a prime perching spot.
- Misters and sprinklers are popular with hummingbirds, who bathe in the spray.

*Green Flowers* _____

Red and red-orange flowers are tops for hummingbirds, bringing in the birds like a beacon. But in the dry-as-a-bone desert, a flower of another color is also a standout: tree tobacco (*Nicotiana glauca*). This greenish-yellow flowered South American perennial blooms from April to September, providing a feast to hummingbirds. It's easy for the birds to zero in on the plant because it stays green in the dry season. The plant sticks out like a green thumb.

# White-Winged Dove

*First Impression*

**A soft taupe-gray dove with a black "pen mark" on the side of its face and a long white crescent along the edge of its folded wings**

## Mark Your Calendar

Spring through fall in southern parts of this region; year-round in a few small extreme southern areas; absent in other parts

## Details, Details

- Bigger than a robin; 11½ inches
- In flight, look for bold white wing patches separating the dark wing feathers from the pale body.
- Use binoculars to admire the blue ring around the orange-red eye.
- Tail has white band at tip
- Female and male look alike

## Listen Up!

- Monotonous, repeated hooting call, with the same rhythm as that of barred owl: *who cooks for you*
- Other slow, deep, cooing sounds

## Telltale Traits

- Usually on ground
- Fast, direct flier; wings make clapping sound on takeoff
- Gather together in large flocks after nesting

## Look Here

- On the ground in open areas

## Or Here

- At the feeder or birdbath
- In gardens, eating weed seeds

*"At times, 3,000 to 4,000 visible in flight"*

—**John K. Terres,** *The Audubon Encyclopedia of North American Birds* **(1980)**

**A gregarious bird, this dove often feeds and travels in huge flocks. Watch for groups of a few thousand during spring migration, as the birds move northward from wintering grounds in the tropics.**

*On the Home Front* May nest in backyards
- Nests in various trees and shrubs, including citrus, mesquite (*Prosopis* spp.), and tamarisk or salt cedar (*Tamarix aphylla*), and in cactus

**Wild Menu:** Seeds, especially wild sunflowers and grain, plus weed seeds, especially dove-weed (*Murdannia nudiflora*); cactus fruit

**Plant Picks:** Scatter a handful of black oil sunflower seed or milo among garden beds.

**Feeder Pleasers**
- Sunflower seeds; birdseed mix; cracked corn; millet and milo

**Tricks and Treats**
- Water is a big draw. A ground-level basin or saucer is best.

## Decimating Doves

The passenger pigeon, now extinct, garners all the publicity when it comes to having been hunted to extermination. But other species of doves and pigeons, including this one, were killed off by the tens of thousands in the old days. From the early 1870s to the 1920s, settlers saw millions of white-winged doves; by 1930, the species was declining fast. Hunting continued, though, and as recently as 1968, three-quarters of a million doves were harvested in Arizona alone. Today, the daily hunting limit for these doves is much less than the 50 birds it was just a few decades ago, and the population is stable.

# California Quail

*First Impression*

**A flock of grayish brown "footballs" with bobbing black topknots**

### Mark Your Calendar

Year-round; the similar Gambel's quail is found year-round elsewhere in this region

### Details, Details

- Robin length but much plumper; 10 inches
- Feather patterns are striking and elegant.
- Black face boldly marked with white
- Breast feathers have a distinctive thin, dark rim, creating an effect like overlapping scales.
- Female has a grayish face lacking bold pattern, and an abbreviated topknot
- Gambel's quail, also in this region, is a similar species but has a plain tan breast

### Listen Up!

- Repeated calls of *whee-hee-hoo*
- Also various other calls, including gurgling noises and a single crowlike *caw*

### Telltale Traits

- Almost always in a flock, except during nesting season
- Follows a regular schedule, showing up at about the same time each day
- Usually walks from place to place
- Only flies if forced by being chased

### Look Here

- At feeder

### Or Here

- At birdbath
- On ground

*"A very perfect model of a husband and father"*

—W. Leon Dawson, on the monogamous California quail, *The Birds of California* (1923)

Was it the "loose" attitudes of the Roaring Twenties that caused Dawson to expand on his theme? "Even in domestication, with evil examples all about and temptresses in abundance, the male quail is declared to be devoted to a single mate."

*On the Home Front* Frequent backyard nester
- Ground-level nests are well-hidden under a shrub or hedge or beside a rock.

**Wild Menu:** Seeds; insects; small green leaves

**Plant Picks:** Try buckwheat for a quail-attracting crop. These birds will also find plenty to eat naturally in your yard.

**Feeder Pleasers**
- Birdseed or cracked corn; a quail block, a compressed block of seeds sold at wild bird supply stores

**Tricks and Treats**
- Give quail a ground-level basin or pool.

## Set Your Watches

I was visiting a friend in southern California one afternoon, when she stood up and said, "Let's take our iced tea and go out to the garden. The quail should be here any minute." "How do you know?" I asked. "Easy," she said. "The covey always comes to feed an hour after sunrise and an hour before sunset." We had just settled ourselves onto her garden bench when there was a sudden movement under the hedge. Like clockwork, there they came, one bird scuttling along after the other in single file. They headed for her garden pool first, where they drank as if they hadn't seen water in weeks. Then they ambled over to the feeding station and settled in for supper.

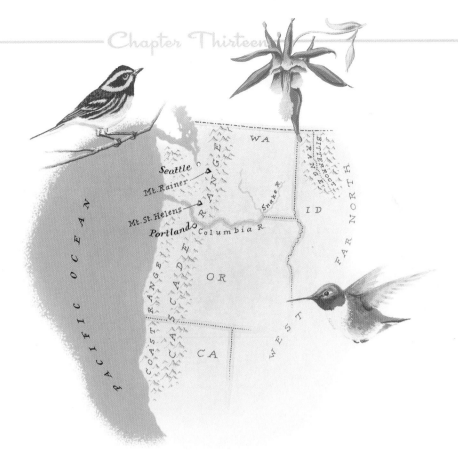

# Chapter Thirteen

# Birds of the Northwest

The Northwest is marked by mountain ranges that run north and south through the region. Major cities, including Seattle, Spokane, and Portland, are located here, but there's still plenty of wild land. Small towns, originally built around local logging or mining companies, dot the landscape. Orchards, wineries, and cattle pastures are common sights in some places. There's a diversity of landscape, from desert sagebrush to deep, dark, moss-draped forests, from mountain forests and alpine meadows to wild, crashing ocean waves pounding the rocky coastline.

## MOUNTAINS ARE THE BACKBONE

Mountain ranges are the defining factor of the Northwest. Their effect on the weather greatly determines the climate and character of each part of this region, because mountains can block rain or channel winds and snow.

Look on a topographical map, and you'll see that the illustration above is just the beginning of the story. On a topo map, the Northwest looks like a piece of badly crumpled

**Steller's jay is at home in higher elevations.**

Along the Northwest coast, where moisture rolls off the ocean unimpeded, the climate is mild and wet. Flowers bloom all winter, and hummingbirds are an everyday sight. Summers can be cool and foggy, and winters are rainy much of the time.

On the east side of the Coast Range, between it and the Cascade Mountains, wide, fertile valleys are home to plenty of people and a thriving agricultural industry. Grass seed, peppermint, raspberries, and other fruit are the mainstay crops. As you leave the valley and move into the foothills, moss-covered big-leaf maples, Douglas firs, and western red cedars dominate the scene, with a tangled understory of evergreen salal (*Gaultheria shallon*) and waist-high sword ferns. Bird life changes gradually as treetop species take over from the blackbirds and sparrows of the lowlands.

East of the Cascades and Rockies, where the mountains have blocked the rainfall coming from the coast, the climate is much drier. Sagebrush and desert plants flourish, trees are shorter and of different species, and rocky outcrops break through the dry grasslands. Birds are almost entirely different here, with dryland and grassland species suddenly replacing the tanagers and grosbeaks of the wet forests.

The mountains themselves add even more variety to the natural life of this region. Conifers dominate their forested slopes until high altitude thins the trees. Some peaks, including the volcanoes Mount Rainier, Mount Saint Helens, and Mount Hood, offer their own kind of very-high-altitude habitat. Mountain goats cling to rocky precipices, golden eagles cruise the heights, and alpine meadows are ablaze with flowers and butterflies during short summers.

paper that's been roughly smoothed out again. These mountains are rugged, with steep slopes and deep, forested canyons.

## Meet the Mountains

In the north are the Olympic Mountains—tall, jagged peaks that form an unbroken sweep against the sky where Puget Sound cuts far inland from the Pacific Ocean. Some areas, including Tacoma and Seattle, are dripping wet. Other places that fall in the "rain shadow" of mountain ranges that block moisture, such as the town of Sequim on the Olympic Peninsula, receive such a diminished amount of rain that lavender farms are big business.

Birding is big in this region, because there's so much variety. A day trip can quickly take you to entirely different surroundings than you have at home.

## LEGENDARY RAIN

Living with the Northwest's rain is a point of pride for many northwesterners. Others become seasonally depressed when the gloom rolls in during fall, and some move here only to leave again after a few years of what seemed like never-ending rain.

The big secret, though, is that the rain only lasts part of the year. In summer, the climate is about as good as it gets. One pleas-

**Thick moss covers trees and forest floor.**

ant, sunny day follows another, with barely a sprinkle or even a cloud.

## Rain, Rain, Come to Stay

Those mountains, plus its proximity to the Pacific Ocean, make much of the Northwest a mighty rainy place. Lush green forests carpeted in moss so thick you can't hear your own footsteps are nature's reward for the months of rain that soak the region each year.

West of the Cascades, the climate has two main seasons: rainy and dry. (East of the Cascades is a different story, which we'll get to a bit farther on in this chapter.)

The rainy season usually begins in earnest in late October. Look at the 5-day forecast now and you'll see there's a rain cloud for almost every day, with only an occasional picture of the sun; just a couple of weeks before, the opposite was true.

By the time November gets a good start, the sun is a rare sight. I often joke with friends that the forecasters put a picture of the sun in their weekly predictions just to keep us all sane. As long as there's some hope of sunshine, the rain seems to be more easily endured.

Most of the time, the rain is light. You soon get used to going about any outdoor activities you choose, even if it's raining. Besides, those hundred-foot trees in the forests do an excellent job of catching most of the falling droplets while you walk under them. Only once in a while do you get a cold trickle down your neck when you nudge a branch!

The first time we cut a Christmas tree in the national forest—a ritual for many folks in this region—I was stunned by how heavy the 6-foot tree was. A few good shakes dislodged most of that weight: It was water collected among the needles of the sweet little fir.

As for boots, I generally don't bother. The thick layer of conifer needles and decomposing logs underfoot, blanketed with moss, soaks up water like a sponge. In fact, if you break off a piece from a rotting log in the rainy season, you can squeeze clear, cold water out of it.

I do miss the sunshine in the Northwest, but I also love a dim, rainy day in the woods. Winter wrens burst into song on all sides, tiny kinglets and chickadees forage through the trees overhead, and if I'm lucky, I'll catch a glimpse of a lovely varied thrush.

## Rain, Rain, Go Away

By April, rain is usually beginning to dwindle in the Northwest, and by May, the skies are mostly sunny. Because the winters are mild west of the Cascades, flowers bloom earlier. That means that your bed of beautiful bearded iris or even roses is likely to be turned into mushy petals by rain. As for daffodils, I quickly learned to plant only single, strong-stemmed varieties: The fluffy types end up on the ground, thanks to the weight of spring rains.

Some years have rainy springs, others dry. But by June, it's sunny almost every day. Temperatures are moderate, and gardens grow like crazy. Don't be too envious, though, because by July, plants are starting to look like they could use a drink. Backyard grass, velvety green right through winter, goes dormant in summer. Now the birdbath becomes the hot spot in the yard, as chickadees, finches, buntings, and black-headed grosbeaks take turns at the water.

Summer is also the time when the snow melts in the mountains, and hundreds of subalpine wildflowers flood the meadows with color. It's my favorite time of year—a feast of flowers! I always see plenty of birds then, too, including nesting juncos, warblers, and thrushes in the mountains.

## DIFFERENT ON THE DRY SIDE

Northwest rain doesn't accurately depict the climate once you venture east of the mountains. In the "rain shadow" areas, moisture is scarce, so plant life and bird life are totally different. So is the climate. Instead of a wet and dry season, the central and eastern parts of the Northwest have four distinct seasons: cold, often snowy winters; brief springs; hot, parched summers; and autumns that can change to winter in a heartbeat.

Thunderstorms, a rare event on the west-

**On the dry side of the mountains, pines and grasslands replace lush, mossy forests.**

ern side of the mountains, are taken in stride here. And wind is a fact of life. In winter, it sweeps down from Canada; in summer, it sweeps up from the Southwest deserts with a desiccating effect.

Instead of the lush, easy life of the western-side birds, where food is plentiful year-round, birds in the eastern parts of the Northwest have to work hard for a living. In this area a well-stocked feeder and a reliably filled bird-bath are great inducements for lazuli buntings, lesser goldfinches, and other birds to visit your yard.

## THE LAY OF THE LAND

Towering firs, spruces, hemlocks, and cedars create forests big and small in the western part of this region. Alders spring up in any patch of open ground. East of the mountains, pines and junipers take over, and the trees become sparser and finally give way to sagebrush and shrubs.

Tree seeds—including a bounty from conifer cones—provide meals for chickadees, nuthatches, and other northwestern birds. Insects abound, too, nourishing orioles, tanagers, and hunting hordes of tiny bushtits.

A myriad of streams, rivers, and waterfalls in the western part of the region provide a bounty of other insects. In the grasslands, there's even more on the menu, including grasshoppers, ants, and plenty of other delectable critters. Plus the bark and dead wood of all those northwestern trees supply more feeding places for woodpeckers, nuthatches, brown creepers, and other birds adapted to gleaning bark or pecking into wood.

Fruit eaters such as cedar waxwings and tanagers find plenty to sing about here. Along with miles of cherry orchards and vineyards, the Northwest is filled with berry-bearing shrubs and wild fruit trees. Blackberries are the most common, and most notorious: They fill many an opening, gone wild from an introduced species. There's such a huge crop of blackberries that many go uneaten, even those berries that linger into the depths of winter. At higher elevations, huckleberries (*Vaccinium* spp.) and currants (*Ribes* spp.) provide abundant fruit for varied thrushes and hermit thrushes.

## BIRD LIFE IN THE NORTHWEST

Birding is a popular pastime in this region, but it often isn't easy. Many species are hard to find in the dense vegetation. And many spend most of their lives high in the treetops. I soon learned their songs and calls, so that I wouldn't have to spend so much time craning my neck trying to get a bead on whoever was singing far above me. When I returned to the East for a visit, I was surprised by how easy the birding seemed to me. Finding a scarlet tanager in an oak tree—which for me was once a frustrating challenge—was now much easier, compared to finding a singing Townsend's warbler in the dark branches of a 150-foot fir.

Many birds occur singly in the Northwest, and roam relatively large territories. It often takes some looking to spot even a single individual. The number of songbird species isn't as great as I was accustomed to in other places: There are no thrashers, mockingbirds, or catbirds at every corner. Instead of dozens of warbler and vireo species, there's only a scant handful. Did I mention there are no blue jays? Well, maybe a rare stray now and then.

But I'm not complaining. There are fabulous Steller's jays and engaging scrub jays. Enough sparrows to keep you busy with binoculars year-round. And I still get shivers every time I hear a varied thrush's eerie whistle at twilight, or listen to the liquid trill of a winter wren. Whatever Northwest habitat you live in, you'll find plenty of birds to make life interesting.

## Start Here

The Northwest shares many of the birds in Chapter 6, "Start Here," with other regions.

Familiarize yourself with those common and abundant "Start Here" birds to get to know your most familiar backyard friends. These are the birds you share with other parts of the country—chickadees, white-breasted nuthatches, American goldfinches, juncos, cedar waxwings, and many others. Then get to know the regional specialties here.

## Regional Specialties

You'll find other favorite friends spotlighted in this regional section. Some of these birds also occur in other regions. But every single one of them may turn up in your northwestern backyard.

Be sure to page through the birds of the Far North, Midwest, and Southwest, too. Many of them also range across the border into northwestern backyards.

## Birds of the Northwest

Here are the birds profiled in this chapter. Remember to consult the "Start Here" birds, starting on page 79, for many other common birds in the Northwest.

# Pileated Woodpecker

*"The large red-crested woodpecker"*

—Mark Catesby,
*The Natural History of Carolina, Florida, and the Bahama Islands* (1731)

**First Impression**

Humongous cartoon character Woody Woodpecker

### Mark Your Calendar

Year-round in some parts of this region; absent from some areas

### Details, Details

- As big as a crow; 16½ inches
- Big, strong beak
- Watch for big white patches in the wings, and even bigger white patches underneath when the bird flies.
- A pointy tuft of feathers on the head
- Female is similar to male but lacks the red forehead and red mustache

### Listen Up!

- Hollers *awoik! awoik!* in a ringing voice
- Sounds very similar to the flicker, but louder and slower
- Drums on resonant surfaces, long and loud

### Telltale Traits

- Often pecks at logs as well as dead trees
- Pries off long strips of dead wood to get at carpenter ants
- Often flakes off bark
- Flies like a crow, with deep wing beats
- Noisy; can be heard from far away
- Can raise and lower that incredible red crest

### Look Here

- At your suet feeder

### Or Here

- Clinging to tree trunk
- Pecking at dead trees or dead limbs
- Flying or swooping from tree to tree

You can pronounce "pileated" as either "pie-lee-ated" or "pill-ee-ated." It simply means crested—and what a crest this big bird has!

**On the Home Front** Not usually a backyard nester • Pair shares territory all year

**Wild Menu:** Insects, mostly carpenter ants and wood-boring beetle larvae, with a sampling of spruce budworm and other delicacies; nuts; small amount of berries

**Plant Picks:** None

**Feeder Pleasers**

- Suet, served in a stationary feeder

**Tricks and Treats**

- In this region, carpenter ants and termites are abundant, thanks to all that decaying wood.

## The Postman Rings Twice

For all their size, pileateds are easy to overlook. Watch for a pile of wood chips at the base of a tree, then look up. If you're lucky enough to discover a current nest cavity, watch for the parents' "shift change." Both birds take turns keeping their young ones cozy. When the relief parent is arriving, it calls on its way to the nest to alert the sitting bird, who will often peek out and give a soft *chuck*. When the returning bird comes in for its landing, the one in the hole often gives a few soft tap-tap-taps before flying out.

# Lewis's Woodpecker

## First Impression

A large black woodpecker with a pale collar, gliding across an open area between trees

### Mark Your Calendar

Varies depending on specific location; might be year-round, winter only, spring through fall, or migration only

### Details, Details

- Bigger than a robin; 10¾ inches
- Its black feathers have a green sheen, and its red face and deep pink-red belly are beautiful.
- Female looks like male

### Listen Up!

- Harsh *churr, churr, churr*
- Sudden *yick!* alarm call

### Telltale Traits

- Unusually slow flight, almost looks like slow motion
- Glides or soars at times, without flapping
- Often fly-catches from perch, swooping out after passing insects
- Stores acorns and nuts in caches, often in crevice of utility pole or fissure in cottonwood bark, for winter feeding
- May perch on utility wires
- Battles with other woodpeckers over stored food
- Pair remains together year-round

### Look Here

- On a perch in a tree, especially a pine; or on a post, flying out to catch insects

*"Such enormous appetites I was glad to give them their liberty"*

—Charles Bendire, who kept a few young woodpeckers captive, *Life Histories of North American Birds* (1895)

Grasshoppers were a favorite of his captives, reported Bendire, noting that his charges "climbed everywhere over the rough walls of my house."

### Or Here

- In oaks, collecting acorns
- In flocks in winter, in oak groves or nut tree orchards
- Gliding from a perch to the ground to catch grasshoppers, crickets, and other insects

### On the Home Front

May accept a nest box if you live near open Ponderosa pine forests, its typical breeding habitat

**Wild Menu:** Insects; nuts; acorns; fruit

**Plant Picks:** Oaks (*Quercus* spp.), English walnut trees (*Juglans regia*); grapes and apples

### Feeder Pleasers

- Doesn't usually visit feeders, but offer it English walnuts in the shell or whole corn

### Tricks and Treats

- Has been reported to use nest boxes

## "Utility" Poles

Not quite what their makers had in mind, but poles with utility indeed! Those tall wood poles are a utilitarian favorite of Lewis's woodpeckers. The poles often split open some shallow cracks as they age, creating inviting fissures that are just the right size for stuffing full of acorns. One summer, when grasshoppers were extra plentiful, I spotted one of these woodpeckers parking its extra insects in a utility pole. The pretty bird crammed dozens of grasshoppers into the cracks, securing them with well-placed beak taps.

# Red-Breasted Sapsucker

*First Impression*

**Odd calls that lead to a blackish woodpecker with a red head and breast**

### Mark Your Calendar

Year-round

### Details, Details

- A little smaller than a robin; 8½ inches
- The only woodpecker in this region with a red head and breast
- The red is not as flashy as that of many woodpeckers.
- Watch for the white wing patches and white rump, especially in flight.
- Male and female look alike

### Listen Up!

- A grab bag of odd, nasal calls: most often, a mewing or squealing *neeah*
- To keep in touch, a pair of birds gives hoarse *wik-a wik-a* calls.
- May also make a *geert* sound
- Much less vocal in winter

### Telltale Traits

- Tapping and drumming sounds are a surefire sign that a woodpecker is nearby.
- Moves up and down tree trunks in herky-jerky movements on short legs
- Often stays on same tree for hours

### Look Here

- On the trunk or limbs of living trees, sometimes not far from ground

### Or Here

- Tapping or drumming on stumps or dead trees, sometimes at very top of tree

> *"67 species of fruit, forest, and ornamental trees"*
>
> —Johnson Neff, tallying the targets of this species, in "A Study of the Common Woodpeckers in Relation to Oregon Horticulture" (1928)

**With that kind of variety, your backyard may have trees that red-breasted sapsuckers will investigate for sap potential.**

*On the Home Front* Digs out a cavity in a dead tree or in a dead snag of a living tree

**Wild Menu:** Sap; ants and other insects; tree fruit, seeds, and inner bark

**Plant Picks:** May sample elderberries (*Sambucus* spp.) and huckleberries or blueberries

**Feeder Pleasers**
- Not usually a feeder visitor

**Tricks and Treats**
- Apple trees are favorites of this sap-seeking bird.

## Going Down?

It gets cold in them thar hills, so in fall, many sapsuckers move down from their summer homes at high elevations in the mountains. If you live in lower areas, especially near a river or other water, winter will be your prime time for hosting these red-tinged birds.

Keep an eye out for their calling card: rows of small, closely spaced holes drilled into the trunks of trees in your yard. Scan those trees every time you're outside. These birds can be mighty quiet when they're on a tree, and it's surprisingly easy to overlook them entirely. On a rainy winter day, they blend right into the mossy bark.

# Scrub Jay

## *First Impression*

Big, noisy, bluish gray bird with whitish gray belly

### Mark Your Calendar

Year-round; mostly at lower elevations; absent from some northern parts of this region; Steller's jay usually at higher elevations than scrub, but often overlap

### Details, Details

- Bigger than a robin; 11½ inches
- The Pacific race has a distinct blue necklace across its breast and whiter underparts than the interior race.
- Female and male look alike

### Listen Up!

- A harsh, scolding cry of *cheek-cheek-cheek!*
- A questioning: *quay-feeeee?*
- Other grating calls, including *ker-wheek!*
- A very quiet, private, and decidedly musical "whisper song," sung to its mate

### Telltale Traits

- Loud, bold, and intelligent
- Also can be secretive and quiet
- Often hops about on ground
- Usually in small groups
- Look for it in shrubs (the "shrub" from which it gets its name)

### Look Here

- At your feeder

### Or Here

- In oak trees or nut trees
- On the ground beneath shrubs
- In shrubs or hedges
- Burying nuts or acorns

*"The flat-headed jays"*

—Harry Swarth, *The Pacific Coast Jays of the Genus* Aphelocoma (1918)

In the eastern United States, where the only jay species wears a jaunty crest, a "flat head" would look odd. In the West, jays come in crested and crestless species.

*On the Home Front* Nests in trees, sometimes in blue elder (*Sambucus caerulea*) and other shrubs, sometimes in dense vines, such as wild grape

**Wild Menu:** Huge variety: nuts, fruit, insects, snails, mice, snakes, frogs

**Plant Picks:** Plant giant sunflowers for seeds.

**Feeder Pleasers**
- Nuts and peanuts, in the shell; sunflowers; suet

**Tricks and Treats**
- A freshly filled birdbath may attract jays.

## *The Peanut Gallery*

Scrub jays quickly learned that my appearance in the yard means one very important thing: the possibility of a treat. Like a cat hearing a can opener, they fly in from blocks away as soon as I come outside. The tamest among them swoop within a few feet to watch me with bright black eyes. Easy to grasp what they're thinking: "Peanuts! We want peanuts!" How do they know what's in my lumpy pocket? I trained them, by tossing them the treats every time I came outside. And they trained me, to always bring peanuts in the shell along.

# Chestnut-Backed Chickadee

## First Impression

Little brown, black, and white bird, never sitting still

### Mark Your Calendar

Year-round in some parts of this region; absent from others

### Details, Details

- Small chickadee size, of course; 4¾ inches
- The only chickadee with a chestnut-colored back
- Black cap and throat
- Male and female look alike

### Listen Up!

- These little cuties don't sing a whistled song but they are fairly vocal.
- Listen for a higher, thinner variation of the classic call, sounding like *kiss-a-dee*.
- Also a buzzy trill similar to the chipping sparrow's and a *tsidi-tsidi-cheer-cheer*

### Telltale Traits

- More common in rural or forested areas
- Often upside down on branches
- Always on the move, searching leaves and branches for caterpillars and other insects
- In winter, often part of a flock of nuthatches, kinglets, and other chickadee species

### Look Here

- At the feeder

### Or Here

- In conifer trees; possibly deciduous trees
- In shrubs and hedges

*"Old familiar friends in more richly colored garments"*

—A. C. Bent, *Life Histories of North American Jays, Crows and Titmice* (1946)

**Gray and white with a black-trimmed head is the typical garb of most chickadee species. This one takes it up a notch with a pretty, rusty brown back and sides.**

**On the Home Front** Nests in cavities—including, maybe, that nest box in your backyard
- Prefers nest boxes that face east to southeast, probably because they warm up faster

**Wild Menu:** Insects; seeds; buds

**Plant Picks:** Native conifers in your yard will make these little guys feel at home.

**Feeder Pleasers**
- Suet; sunflower seeds; nuts

**Tricks and Treats**
- If you live within nesting territory, a wire suet cage stuffed with wool, feathers, and other soft materials may draw nest-building birds.

## Variations on a Theme

With some practice, it's pretty easy to peg a birdcall as that of a chickadee. But figuring out which species is which is for the advanced class! These birds sound very similar, even when they're saying *chick-a-dee*. Some species are more sibilant, others change the tempo, others say more *dee-dees*, and this one raises the pitch. Still, no matter how tricky they can be to sort out, the same suet and sunflowers will satisfy all species—and bring them in where you can identify them by color instead of calls.

# Bushtit

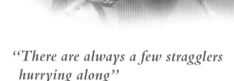

## First Impression

Tiny gray bird flying out of bush with high, thin calls; then another bird, and another, and another, and another . . .

## Mark Your Calendar

Year-round; absent from northern part of this region

## Details, Details

• Even smaller than a chickadee; 4½ inches
• Long tail
• Often looks fluffed-up
• An unusual variation of gender: The male has dark eyes, the female, pale

## Listen Up!

• A constant stream of thin, high-pitched *tsit-tsit-tsit* calls
• When you hear their calls, look around for a flock of the bitty birds.

## Telltale Traits

• Intensely gregarious; always in a flock
• Constantly on the move, foraging rapidly through the foliage of bushes and small trees, then traveling on to the next
• Often travels with mixed group of chickadees and kinglets in winter
• Tame around people and gentle to each other; no sign of squabbling in flock

## Look Here

• Moving in a flock from one group of bushes to the next in your yard

## Or Here

• At the birdbath
• Flying through or over your yard in a talkative flock

*"There are always a few stragglers hurrying along"*

—A. C. Bent, *Life Histories of North American Jays, Crows and Titmice* (1946)

**Gregarious bushtits travel in a flock that moves, mostly as one, from one bush or tree to the next. But there always seem to be a few who aren't paying attention and must rush to catch up.**

On the Home Front The nest is a long, loose, hanging sack, suspended from a tree or bush.
• The birds are strongly attached to their flock.

**Wild Menu:** Insects, especially scale insects; spiders

**Plant Picks:** Unsprayed shrubs and trees

**Feeder Pleasers**
• Suet, especially suet enriched with insects

**Tricks and Treats**
• Keep a birdbath brimming, and you may see the whole bunch lining up at once.

## It's a Marvel

Orioles are famous for their fabulous hanging nests, but the little bushtit does an even more marvelous job. The pair actually makes its fabric out of spider silk with some pieces of vegetation. The birds add to it until it stretches across a branch fork or other gap. Then the female sits in it, causing it to stretch downward. While the male adds bits of moss, lichens, and other material to the outside, the female keeps stretching the nest until it forms a long, loose sack, shaped like a gourd—but looking more like a mossy green sock!

# Varied Thrush

*First Impression*

**A fancy robin with a dark necklace**

### Mark Your Calendar

Year-round; many move to higher altitudes for nesting, lower elevations for winter

### Details, Details

- About the same size as a robin; 9½ inches
- Long-necked, short-tailed, with a plump tummy
- Back may appear grayish, black, or deep blue
- Use binoculars to admire the orange trim on head, throat, belly, and wings.
- Female is paler and has gray breast band

### Listen Up!

- An extended, single-note, buzzy whistle
- Also a short *vree* trill, or a harsh *churr* note

### Telltale Traits

- Very shy and usually difficult to approach
- Spends a lot of time on ground or near it
- Usually moves a short distance at a time, either by hopping or flying
- Rarely seen far from cover
- May be aggressive at feeder, driving off other birds

### Look Here

- At the feeder

### Or Here

- In shady, dark areas, in, under, or near shrubs and trees
- Often associates with robins, so take a good look at those birds in your backyard
- At the edge of a forested area

*"Where spruce trees and alders and crowding ferns contend for a footing"*

—**William Dawson, on where varied thrushes are found,** *The Birds of California* **(1923)**

**Apparently Dawson must've spent at least one winter in the famously rainy Northwest. His description continues: ". . . and where a dank mist drenches the whole with a fructifying moisture."**

*On the Home Front* Not usually a backyard nester • Usually nests in mature forests

**Wild Menu:** Worms; berries; seeds; slugs; snails; fruit; insects; nuts, especially acorns

**Plant Picks:** Blueberries, blackberries; manzanita and bearberry (*Arctopstaphlyos* spp.); toyon (*Heteromeles arbutifolia*)

### Feeder Pleasers

- Millet and birdseed mix; accessible suet

### Tricks and Treats

- May use a birdbath, if it's near shelter

## Not Quite Harmony

The eerie and strangely beautiful song of the varied thrush is as unique as its plumage. Unlike other thrushes, which sing complicated melodies, this songbird has an exceedingly simple song. It's a slightly buzzy whistle on one pitch, held for about 2 seconds. After a long pause, it whistles again—but on a different pitch. Pause, then another whistle, again on a different pitch, and so on for the entire concert. Because the notes sound similar yet are different tones, you could easily be fooled into thinking there's more than one varied thrush in the vicinity.

# Swainson's Thrush

*First Impression*

**Quiet olive-brown robinlike bird with speckled breast, on ground**

## Mark Your Calendar

Spring through fall in some areas; migration only in others

## Details, Details

- Smaller than a robin; 7 inches
- In the western part of this region, this thrush shows more russet than olive coloring on its back and head; that russet-backed race gives way to the interior race, a drab olive-brown bird.
- Look for its "spectacles": the pale eye rings with pale lines from eyes to beak, to distinguish it from the similar hermit thrush.
- Female and male look alike

## Listen Up!

- A long song of repeated phrases, in typical fluting thrush style; one transcriber suggests *whip-poor-will-a-will-e-zee-zee-zee,* going up at end
- Piping call note sounds like spring peeper

## Telltale Traits

- Often on ground, but also in shrubs and treetops
- Gets around on ground in long, bouncy hops
- May sing at night

## Look Here

- At berry bushes

## Or Here

- On ground

*"They sang almost continuously through the night"*

—Wilfred Osgood, "Biological Investigations in Alaska and Yukon Territory" (1909)

Many thrush species are famed for occasionally singing at night, but usually you'll hear only a few phrases, not an hours-long concert. Osgood's observations were made in summer in Alaska, where "nights" are light enough for walking, fishing—or birds singing.

*On the Home Front* Nests in many different trees and shrubs • The female builds a cup of grasses, stems, and twigs.

**Wild Menu:** Berries; insects; snails

**Plant Picks:** Blackberries and raspberries, twinberry (*Lonicera involucrata*)

**Feeder Pleasers**

- Doesn't usually visit feeders, but it might like mealworms and other insect foods

**Tricks and Treats**

- Offer moss for nest building.
- May visit a birdbath, particularly one near to ground

## *Twice as Nice*

Wild cherries and chokecherries (*Prunus* spp.) in the Northwest are a favorite food of the Swainson's thrush. The bird nibbles off the flesh of the small fruit, then drops the pit to the ground. Each visit may result in dozens of dropped pits—a bonanza to some creatures below.

I once came across an old bird nest being used as a pantry by one of those creatures. When I peered into the pretty, mossy nest to see how it was constructed, a bright-eyed deer mouse looked up at me from atop its treasure trove of cherry pits.

# Townsend's Warbler

## First Impression

Black and yellow on a small, fast-moving bird

### Mark Your Calendar

Spring through fall in some parts of this region; winter only along much of coast; migration only in some areas

### Details, Details

- Chickadee size; 5 inches
- Bold black markings on head and throat
- Back is olive green
- Two white wing bars
- Female is paler version of male

### Listen Up!

- A persistent singer; listen for *weez weez weez zeee* or *swe swe swe zee*
- A sharp *chip!*

### Telltale Traits

- Highly energetic
- Very territorial; male aggressively chases other males during nesting season
- May join a mixed flock of chickadees, nuthatches, and kinglets in winter

### Look Here

- At suet feeder

### Or Here

- Quickly moving through foliage of trees or shrubs during migration
- Singing while foraging or from perch in tall conifer
- At birdbath

**On the Home Front** May be a backyard nester if you have large spruce or fir trees • Can be hard to observe because it nests at 60 feet or higher

*"Incessantly repeated ... comes the song of the Townsend warbler"*

—Walter Taylor and William Shaw, *Mammals and Birds of Mount Rainier National Park* (1927)

This wood warbler's song is one of the signature sounds of the great Pacific Northwest forests. It filters downward from the tops of the immensely tall trees, where the little birds flit amid the foliage.

**Wild Menu:** Insects

**Plant Picks:** Douglas fir (*Pseudotsuga menziesii*)

**Feeder Pleasers**

- Suet; peanut butter; mealworms; possibly nectar

**Tricks and Treats**

- Try a trickling, naturalistic birdbath to tempt this pretty little bird.

## Sweet Stuff

Got a hummingbird feeder? Some house finches, woodpeckers, and several species of wood warblers, among others, have learned to help themselves to a sip of sugar water.

This warbler already has a predilection for sweet stuff. On wintering grounds in Mexico and Central America, Townsend's warblers are often seen visiting trees that are infested with colonies of scale insects. Like aphids, scale insects excrete a sticky-sweet substance known as honeydew. It's so desirable that the warblers fight over it.

# Wilson's Warbler

## First Impression

Tiny, active yellowish green bird with black beret

### Mark Your Calendar

Spring through fall in forested areas; anywhere in this region during migration

### Details, Details

- Smaller than a chickadee; 4¾ inches
- Even without binoculars, you can catch the black button eye and black cap on that yellow face.
- Female has duller, browner cap than male

### Listen Up!

- A bright, hurried, staccato twitter rising in pitch
- Also a *chip* call note

### Telltale Traits

- Restless and quick-moving
- Often jerks its tail
- Flutters, almost hovering in midair, when chasing insects

### Look Here

- Foraging in shrubs or hedges

### Or Here

- In willows and other trees, usually within about 15 feet from ground
- Often near water
- In rhododendrons or blackberry thickets

### On the Home Front

Usually nests in forests or swamps, but may nest in wooded backyard
- Builds nest on or near ground

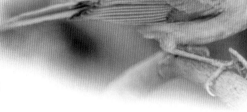

*"A flash of sunny gold"*

—A. C. Bent, *Life Histories of North American Wood Warblers* (1953)

The Wilson's warbler has an olive green back, tail, and wings, but it's that flash of bright yellow underparts that you'll notice as the bird moves quickly through the bushes.

**Wild Menu:** Insects

**Plant Picks:** Blackberry patch; also shade gardens with sword ferns (*Polystichum munitum*) and rhododendrons (*Rhododendron* spp.)

**Feeder Pleasers**
- Not usually a feeder visitor, but you can try offering mealworms

**Tricks and Treats**
- Warblers are a great reason to invest in a recirculating pump for your birdbath; a gentle liquid gurgling may entice them.

## Sit Tight

Like many warblers, the female Wilson's often stays on the nest when a human approaches. Since the nest is well-hidden by foliage, the chances are better you'll overlook it if she just sits tight. Ornithologists call a bird like this a "close sitter"; it's a trait shared by many species of wood warblers.

If you're lucky enough to notice a nest, that sit-tight habit will give you a good opportunity to get a close look at Mama. If you blunder into a nest by accident, the female bird may flutter pitifully on the ground, pretending she has a broken wing. It's all an act to distract you from that precious cup of eggs or babies. Back off a few paces and stand quietly, and she'll soon return to her nest.

# Yellow Warbler

*First Impression*

**A vivid dash of yellow among the willows**

**Mark Your Calendar**

Spring through summer; one of the earliest fall migrants

**Details, Details**

- Chickadee size; 5 inches
- Vivid rusty red streaks on breast
- Female is duller colored, with muted olive-streaked breast

**Listen Up!**

- Bright, high-pitched *sweet sweet sweet sweeter than sweet* or s*weet sweet sweet I'm so sweet*
- Also *chip* call

**Telltale Traits**

- Forages in shrubs and plants relatively close to ground
- Like most warblers, a fast, restless little bird
- Males are very territorial and chase and fight with other males in breeding season.

**Look Here**

- Got any willows? They're magnets for this bird.

**Or Here**

- Foraging in gardens, hedges, or shrubs
- In brush along fences
- At the birdbath

*On the Home Front* May nest in backyards, but usually nests in wild places with thickets and trees • Generally builds nest on ground or from about 3 to 7 feet up, though some may be higher • Makes beautiful, deep cup of fibers with many soft materials

**"Nor does it mind our company in the least"**

—**A. C. Bent,** *Life Histories of North American Wood Warblers* (1953)

It's tricky to get close enough to most wood warblers to snap a picture, but yellow warblers are a much easier subject. They seem to have no fear of people, and will allow you to approach closely.

**Wild Menu:** Insects

**Plant Picks:** Willows, including pussy willows (*Salix* spp.); also substantial bushy plants, such as hibiscus (*Hibiscus moscheutos* and other spp.) and elderberries (*Sambucus* spp.)

**Feeder Pleasers**

- May visit for mealworms

**Tricks and Treats**

- Consider a naturalistic ground-level birdbath, with a trickling dripper to catch this bird's attention.

*Cover Up* _____

This tiny, pretty bird is a frequent target of the parasitic brown-headed cowbird, which lays its eggs in the warbler's nest. One of the few birds that seems to recognize the difference between the cowbird's much larger, brown-speckled white eggs and its own small, pale bluish, spotted eggs, this warbler often cuts its losses. When it spots cowbird eggs, it covers up the cowbird eggs and its own eggs by building another nest bottom over them. Then it begins its egg-laying process all over again.

# Black-Headed Grosbeak

*First Impression*

**A small flock of vivid orange-and-black birds at the feeder, tame and chubby, and showing flashy white wing patches when they fly**

## Mark Your Calendar

Spring through fall

## Details, Details

- Smaller than a robin; 8¼ inches
- Male flashes eye-catching white wing patches in flight
- Note the strong, conical beak, built for cracking seeds.
- Female is streaky dark brown with buff-colored breast and pale belly
- Striking striped head on females and juvenile birds

## Listen Up!

- A pretty warbled song of clear, whistled notes with trills, similar to a robin's
- Also a sharp *spick!* call note

## Telltale Traits

- Very tame; isn't afraid of people
- Often in a small flock, except when nesting
- Shares many habits with its eastern counterpart, the rose-breasted grosbeak

## Look Here

- At feeder

## Or Here

- Foraging in shrubs or trees
- Singing from top of tree
- Flying across open space, with those wing patches flashing
- Eating fruit

*"It eats a considerable quantity of orchard fruit"*

—**Foster Beal, "Birds of California in Relation to the Fruit Industry" (1910)**

Birds were once classed as either friend or foe by weighing the cultivated crops they ate against the pest insects in their diet. Beal recommended that the black-headed grosbeak not be killed despite its taste for fruit, because it is "an active enemy of insect pests."

*On the Home Front* Nests low, from as little as 3 feet aboveground to about 20 feet
- Usually makes home near creek or river

**Wild Menu:** Insects; fruit

**Plant Picks:** Elderberries (*Sambucus* spp.), cherries, blackberries, raspberries

**Feeder Pleasers**
- Sunflower seeds

**Tricks and Treats**
- Fond of taking a bath; adores a sprinkler

## A Cup of Moss

As a born-and-bred easterner, I had quite an adjustment period before the dim, damp conifer forests of the Northwest felt like home. After a few years, though, I found it perfectly normal that every surface in a Northwest forest is swathed in moss. In fact, I've become a fan of it.

When I spy an unusually lush ball of moss within arm's length, I can't resist touching it. Sometimes, instead of inches of springy moss, I discover a surprise beneath the green carpet: an old bird nest, often that of a black-headed grosbeak. Like any other stationary object in these wet woods, an unused nest soon is covered by luxuriant moss.

# Lazuli Bunting

## First Impression

A sparrow size, turquoise "bluebird," singing its heart out and shining like a living jewel

*"Lively and pleasing"*

—John James Audubon, on the lazuli bunting's song, *The Birds of America* (1841)

## Mark Your Calendar

Spring through fall

## Details, Details

- Smaller than a sparrow, only a bit bigger than a chickadee; 5½ inches
- Iridescent plumage, like that of the closely related indigo bunting
- Two highly noticeable white wing bars will quickly tell you that this isn't a bluebird.
- Female is soft, warm brown, with a buff-colored breast

## Listen Up!

- A fast, clear, high-pitched warbling *see-see-see-sweert-sweert-sweert* song that lasts long
- Also a sharp *pick!* call note

## Telltale Traits

- Sings frequently, all day long
- Male moves from one perch to another around his territory to sing
- Males chase each other in spring.
- After nesting, birds congregate in groups.

## Look Here

- At your feeder

## Or Here

- Singing from the highest perches available
- Foraging in brushy corners of the yard
- In thickets, hedges, and clumps of bushes

Buntings are indefatigable singers. The male lazuli bursts into song frequently, all day long, except when he's caring for the fledglings of the first brood while his mate is sitting on the second nest.

On the Home Front May nest in backyards that open to wild places • Builds nest close to ground, within 3 feet • Just about any shrub will do.

Wild Menu: Insects; seeds, especially grass seeds

Plant Picks: Sow a patch of bluegrass seed or lettuce seed in an open area near a shrub. Let it go to seed, and you may see a flash of lapis blue in your own yard.

### Feeder Pleasers

- Millet; finch mix

### Tricks and Treats

- A well-stocked feeder is the best temptation.
- May visit a birdbath

## A Bit of a Stretch

The invasive reed canary grass (*Phalaris arundinacea*) is highly unpopular with people, but a big hit with the avian population. The grass stems are long and flexible, so it takes ingenuity for the birds to bring those seeds to their beaks. I once watched lazuli buntings cling to a stronger weed nearby, then s-t-r-e-t-c-h to reach the grass seeds. As soon as they pulled out a seed, though, the stem moved out of reach again. Finally one bird wised up: He inched his way up the stem, bending it as he went. By the time he reached the seed head, it was touching the ground. He pinned it down with one foot and ate at lesiure.

# Purple Finch

*First Impression*

**Small raspberry-red bird with alert look**

### Mark Your Calendar

Year-round along coast; winter only farther inland; absent from part of this region

### Details, Details

- The size of a sparrow; 6 inches
- More intense all-over color and stouter than a house finch
- Look for the raised feathers on the head, which give the bird an alert look that's different from a house finch.
- Female is streaky brown with light eye stripe; muddier facial pattern in this region than in purple finches elsewhere

### Listen Up!

- Fast, rising and falling, warbled song
- Call note is a sharp metallic *tick!*

### Telltale Traits

- Can raise head feathers for an almost crested effect
- An erratic wanderer; some years may bring many, other years only a few

### Look Here

- At tray or tube feeder

### Or Here

- In trees
- At fruit trees, eating buds or blossoms

*On the Home Front* Nests may be at just about any height, all the way to 50 feet aboveground.
• Usually tucked among the dense branches of a conifer • The dense cup of twigs and roots has a fine lining of grasses, plant fibers, and hair.

*"They bathe in brooks with the temperature below freezing point"*

—**Edward Forbush,** *Birds of Massachusetts and Other New England States* **(1919)**

**Purple finches are water lovers, whether they show up in the Northwest or in New England. Supply a birdbath in winter and you're likely to see these pretty birds reveling in the bath.**

**Wild Menu:** Seeds of trees and weeds; occasionally tree buds or flowers; some berries

**Plant Picks:** Conifers; raspberries or blackberries; ash trees (*Fraxinus* spp.) for seeds

**Feeder Pleasers**
- Sunflower seeds; finch mix

**Tricks and Treats**
- Put a small handful of rock salt into an open tray feeder, or set up a salt block.
- If your yard is near a forest or has large conifers that might be considered for nest sites, try offering soft materials, such as tufts of natural wool, for lining.
- Birdbaths are popular year-round with purple finches.

## Savoring Seeds

Ash tree seeds are held in small, elongated, flat pods that grow in dangling clusters. When I was a kid, we called the pods "bananas," and served them at our dolls' tea parties.

I haven't had a doll tea party in ages, but I do enjoy watching purple finches eat their share of these seeds right in the trees. Oregon white ash (*Fraxinus latifolia*) is common along the mighty Columbia River in my part of the Northwest. In spring, cedar waxwings gather in the trees to eat the pollen-dusted flowers. In winter, I search the bare silhouettes of the trees to spot small flocks of purple finches, busily working at the persistent dangling seeds.

# Lesser Goldfinch

*First Impression*
**A smaller, darker goldfinch**

### Mark Your Calendar

Year-round in some areas, mostly along coast; spring through fall in other areas; absent in some parts of this region

### Details, Details

- Smaller than a chickadee; 4½ inches
- Smaller than American goldfinch
- Big white patches show in wings and tail in flight.
- Unlike the American goldfinch, this species doesn't change plumage colors for winter.
- Male's black cap extends farther back than American goldfinch, which has only black forehead
- Female is duller version and lacks black cap

### Listen Up!

- Canary-like song of varied, usually rising notes
- A plaintive, high, clear *te-yeee* or *tee-ee* call

### Telltale Traits

- Gregarious birds, usually in flocks except in nesting season
- Undulating flight
- Often sing and call on the wing

### Look Here

- At the birdbath

### Or Here

- At the feeder
- In gardens or weedy corners, eating seeds
- Perched with flock in treetop
- Flying with flock in dipping, rising flight

*"Captured only by using water as bait"*

—**Ernest Clabaugh, on catching this species for banding, "Methods of Trapping Birds" (1930)**

**Lesser goldfinches live in arid areas as well as more moderate climes, but all find water irresistible. A birdbath is an even bigger attraction than a feeder, in all seasons.**

*On the Home Front* May nest in backyard
- Female builds dainty cup of plant fibers and grasses, lined with soft stuff such as thistledown and feathers

**Wild Menu:** Weed seeds, especially thistle

**Plant Picks:** Weed seeds are dear to this bird's heart, so tolerate a few if you can. Or plant a meadow garden with native grasses and flowers.

### Feeder Pleasers

- Niger seed; millet and finch mix

### Tricks and Treats

- Water draws this species like a magnet. Any birdbath may attract them, but they'll find it faster if you add a dripper they can hear.
- Like other finches, they're fond of salt; try a scant handful of ordinary table salt in an open tray feeder.

## A Little Off

You'll probably do a double take when you spot your first lesser goldfinch. The birds look and act a lot like their bigger cousin, the American goldfinch, and even their voices have a similar querying quality. But something is just a little off.

When I saw my first birds of this species at my birdbath, it was the small, almost flattened-looking head of the male that first caught my eye. Then I noticed the dark back that gave the bird its old name of "green-backed goldfinch." Since the American goldfinches were still in sunny yellow, it was easy to figure out that this bird was something else.

# Golden-Crowned Sparrow

*First Impression*

**A bunch of streaky brown birds with striped heads topped with yellow, busily feeding on ground**

### Mark Your Calendar

Winter only from coast to east of mountains; absent in some parts of this region

### Details, Details

- A big sparrow; 7¼ inches
- During breeding season, males and females sport a bright yellow crown bordered by dramatic black stripes.
- Head markings are less distinct when not nesting

### Listen Up!

- Sweet, whistled notes in a minor key, to the tune of *"Three Blind Mice"*

### Telltale Traits

- Almost always in loose flocks
- Sings frequently, even in winter
- Picks up seeds from ground
- Raises head feathers when excited
- Unlike many sparrows, golden-crowneds often fly up into tree when disturbed, instead of diving for bushes

### Look Here

- In or below feeders

### Or Here

- In trees, shrubs, and hedges
- In flower gardens
- Eating seedlings and new grass sprouts

*On the Home Front* Not a backyard nester
- Nests from British Columbia to Bering Sea

*"Young birds are particularly tame and unsuspicious"*

—Harry Swarth, "Birds and Mammals of the Skeena River Region of Northern British Columbia" (1924)

**The same trait holds true in the Lower 48. In fall, when golden-crowned sparrows flock to feeders within their range, it's easy to approach them quietly without causing alarm. Got your camera ready?**

**Wild Menu:** Seeds, insects, buds, flowers, and young seedlings

**Plant Picks:** It may eat buds and flowers of calendula (*Calendula officinalis*), or pansies (*Viola × wittrockiana*); also eagerly eats newly planted lawn grass and sprouts of fall-planted garden peas.

**Feeder Pleasers**
- Millet; birdseed mix

**Tricks and Treats**
- Let some birdseed sprout beneath your feeder; golden-crowned sparrows may nibble on it.

## What's That You Say?

It's easier to remember a bird's song if you can translate it into English. The cardinal's *what cheer,* the brown thrasher's *hoe it hoe it, cover it up, cover it up,* and the white-throated sparrow's *old Sam Peabiddy* are quick clues to remember when you hear the actual bird. They can also give you a fun peek into the past.

Looking for the mother lode in Alaska a century ago was exhausting work with pick and shovel. Maybe that's why to the ears of goldminers, the golden-crowned sparrow seemed to be singing *I'm so weary.* Discouraged miners suggested another variation: *no gold here.*

# Lincoln's Sparrow

*First Impression*
**A song sparrow that looks different**

**Mark Your Calendar**

Winter only along the coast; spring through fall in most other parts of this region

**Details, Details**

- Small sparrow size; 5¾ inches
- Smaller than the similar song sparrow
- Black streaking on buff-colored breast may merge into a spot, like on the song sparrow
- Use binoculars to look for the buff-colored cheeks, breast, and sides.
- Male and female look alike

**Listen Up!**

- A musical, bubbly song that bursts forth like that of a wren
- A *chip* call of communication or alarm
- Buzzy *zeet* or *zrr-zrr-zrr* notes during breeding season

**Telltale Traits**

- A skulker; very secretive
- Usually stays low to ground in heavy cover; rarely far from shrubs or trees
- Chases moths and plucks their wings before eating
- Often scratches on ground, kicking both feet backward, to uncover insects and seeds
- Sometimes with flocks of other sparrows

**Look Here**

- On the ground under your feeder among other sparrows

**Or Here**

- Beneath or in dense shrubs or hedges
- In trees
- In bramble patches

*"Tom's Finch"*

—Name bestowed by John James Audubon, in honor of his companion, young Tom Lincoln, who shot the specimen, "Macgillivray's Finch," *Ornithological Biography* (1834)

To get a close-up look at birds, early naturalists depended on guns rather than binoculars. "Tom's Finch" (name later changed to Lincoln's sparrow) is an elusive bird that flits from one bush to another.

*On the Home Front* Not a backyard nester, unless your backyard is many acres in size; seeks undisturbed location • Nests on ground

**Wild Menu:** Seeds; insects
**Plant Picks:** Think thick cover for this bird: dense hedges, groups of tight-knit shrubs, and patches of blackberries and raspberries.

**Feeder Pleasers**
- Millet; birdseed mix

**Tricks and Treats**
- A well-stocked feeder near sheltering bushes will help this shy bird feel at home.

## Check and Double-Check

Like the lesser goldfinch and other more unusual backyard visitors, Lincoln's sparrow can be easily overlooked. A lone bird often joins a flock of mixed sparrows to scratch for seeds. Sad but true, sparrows are one of the regular visitors that we often take for granted. Take a few minutes to look carefully at each bird in a bunch under the feeder—with binoculars. You may be surprised at who's dining.

NORTHWEST

# Dark-Eyed Junco (Oregon Race)

## First Impression

**A striking black hood and a flash of white tail feathers**

### Mark Your Calendar

Year-round; absent from some areas in nesting season

### Details, Details

- Sparrow size; 6¼ inches
- Rust-tinged brown back and cinnamon sides
- Male and female have white belly and white outer tail feathers
- Female is paler version of male

### Listen Up!

- Both male and female sing
- Song is a short trill; you'll often hear it in feeder birds in early spring
- Sharp *chip!* or buzzy *tzeet* calls

### Telltale Traits

- Usually on or near ground
- Often in flocks
- Often scratches at leaf litter to uncover seeds and bugs

### Look Here

- Under or in the feeder

### Or Here

- Beneath shrubs
- In winter, on the lawn or in flower or vegetable gardens
- Singing from a tree in spring

**On the Home Front** Retreats to conifer forests in mountains in nesting season; may be a backyard nester in those areas • Usually builds nest on ground, in natural cavity near rock or tree, or sometimes among roots of a wind-fallen tree

*"There is not an individual in the Union who does not know the little Snow-bird"*

—John James Audubon, *The Birds of America* (1831)

Juncos, or snowbirds as many folks still call them, are common across the country. In the Northwest, the most familiar race is the Oregon junco, which sports a dramatic black hood.

**Wild Menu:** Seeds; in nesting season, insects; may eat snow for moisture in winter

**Plant Picks:** Juncos are prone to panic attacks: They dive for the nearest bush when they get scared. Scattered shrubs and hedges of any kind will give them safe hiding places. Tolerate a few weeds in your yard if you can, too; juncos eagerly eat weed seeds.

**Feeder Pleasers**

- Millet; birdseed mix

**Tricks and Treats**

- Supply a birdbath, and juncos will visit frequently.
- Wait until spring to cut back the dead stems in your gardens, so juncos can forage there all winter.

## Going Up

Oregon juncos leave my lowland yard in April. I generally forget all about them until my first foray into the mountains to see the wildflowers at higher altitudes. As soon as the road starts to seriously climb, I see juncos flitting about along the edges or twittering from the bushes.

It always takes me a second to say, "Oh, right, juncos!" Then I start watching for singing males and nesting pairs—maybe the same birds that will flock to my yard again in fall.

# Western Tanager

*First Impression*
> A brilliant flash of red-orange, yellow, and black in the trees

### Mark Your Calendar
Spring through fall

### Details, Details
- Smaller than a robin; 8 inches
- Use binoculars to admire those fancy wing bars when birds are in flight or perched.
- Male has black tail
- Male's red almost disappears in fall
- Female is drab gray-green with yellowish head, breast, and belly, and gray wings

### Listen Up!
- Low, warbling song, somewhat similar to robin's, but huskier
- Frequent *pit-ick* call note

### Telltale Traits
- A visual standout: one of the most vivid birds of this region
- Forages for insects among the foliage
- Often easily visible when it flies from one tree to another, or fly-catches from a tree or other perch

### Look Here
- At feeder

### Or Here
- Foraging in mature conifers
- At the birdbath

*On the Home Front* May occasionally nest in backyards with conifers, if you live near forest

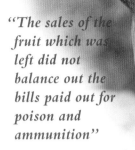

*"The sales of the fruit which was left did not balance out the bills paid out for poison and ammunition"*

—W. Otto Emerson, quoting correspondence from H. A. Gaylord, "A Remarkable Flight of Louisiana [now western] Tanagers" (1903)

Early orchardists despised these beautiful birds because they gobbled the cherries from their trees. Growers killed the birds by the hundreds when they descended on their orchards. I often wonder how many of these birds we'd see today if they hadn't been killed wholesale back in the old days.

**Wild Menu:** Insects; fruit

**Plant Picks:** Plant a sweet or sour cherry tree to attract tanagers—and be prepared to share the crop!

**Feeder Pleasers**
- Cracked corn; millet and birdseed mix; suet; dried fruit, plus halved oranges

**Tricks and Treats**
- Keep a birdbath brimming and you may get to see a tanager take its bath.

## Living Flames

Seeing a tanager makes it a red-letter day in my book because the birds aren't plentiful. One glorious May day, I was visiting Catherine Creek, a wildflower area on the dry side of the mountains in Washington. I was studying a purple flower when a sudden flicker of yellow and red caught my eye.

Coming up the hill through the gnarled oaks was a flock of western tanagers. Not the hundreds I've read about in the old days, but at least a dozen. They moved rapidly through the oak branches over my head, picking off insects at the flowering oak catkins. Occasionally, one of the birds would dart out into the air after a flying insect, its vivid colors flashing like flames. It took just seconds for the birds to pass, but it was a sight I'll remember forever.

# Rufous Hummingbird

*First Impression*

**A flash of iridescent copper and orange**

**Mark Your Calendar**

Spring through fall

**Details, Details**

- Tiny! 3¾ inches, and a good part is beak
- Female is iridescent green with a dab of orange-red on throat

**Listen Up!**

- Buzzy sounds and variations of *zee-chew-chew-chew*
- Male dives from a great height, producing a stuttering *v-v-v-vroooom*

**Telltale Traits**

- Unmistakable: He hovers! He buzzes! He goes backward, forward, sideways!
- Pugnacious personality

**Look Here**

- At nectar feeder

**Or Here**

- At flowers, especially red or red-orange blossoms or tubular-shaped blossoms
- Perched on slender twig or other raised spot, often at top of young tree or shrub

*On the Home Front* Often nests in backyards, but nest is almost impossibly hard to find • Makes tiny and well-camouflaged nest that looks exactly like knobby bit of lichen-covered branch • The tiny cup, about the size of a Ping-Pong ball cut in half, is made of plant down and bits of bark and moss, held together with spiderwebs and lichens.

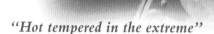

*"Hot tempered in the extreme"*

**—Henry Henshaw, "List of Birds Observed in Summer and Fall on the Upper Pecos River, New Mexico" (1886)**

**You'll see vicious battles when rufous hummingbirds seek the same nectar feeder or flower. The males will often perch nearby even when they're not drinking, so they can zoom out and drive away any competition.**

**Wild Menu:** Nectar; insects

**Plant Picks:** "Hummingbird flowers," which have tubular blossoms, especially in red or orange-red: Start with red-flowering currant (*Ribes sanguineum*) and salmonberry (*Rubus spectabilis*) to catch the attention of spring migrants. Columbines (*Aquilegia formosa* and other spp.) and penstemons (*Penstemon* spp.) are popular; so are salvias (*Salvia* spp.), red-hot pokers (*Kniphofia* spp.), and honeysuckles (*Lonicera* spp.).

**Feeder Pleasers**

- Nectar feeder

**Tricks and Treats**

- A mister or garden sprinkler may attract bathing hummers.

## *Can't We Just Get Along?*

Every time I see a photo of several hummingbirds sharing a feeder, I wonder if there's something I'm doing wrong. That's just not the scene at *my* feeder. Once in a while a male and female will dine side by side. But two males? Or a crowd? Never.

Turns out it isn't my behavior, but the habits of the hummingbird species I've hosted that make the difference. Some species are just more willing to share than others. And my usual birds, the rufous hummingbirds, are the most temperamental of the bunch.

# Anna's Hummingbird

*First Impression*

**Tiny, zippy bird with neon pink head and throat**

## Mark Your Calendar

Year-round within about 100 miles of the coast; spring through fall only in inland northern California; absent elsewhere in this region. Eastward in this region, watch for the smaller, purple-throated calliope hummingbird, from spring through fall.

## Details, Details

- Smaller than a chickadee, but one of the larger hummingbirds: 4 inches
- Female has small iridescent pink-red patch in center of throat

## Listen Up!

- Rapid twittering when chasing another hummer
- Thin, high, squeaky *screetch screetch screetch*
- Listen for explosive, single *TEWK!* at the bottom of a male's courtship dive: The sound is so loud and so odd it may take you a while to believe it came from that tiny hummer.

## Telltale Traits

- A typical hummingbird, with all the incredible flying skills of its family
- Often perches on thin tip of tree, skinny branch, or garden ornament

## Look Here

- At nectar feeder

## Or Here

- At flowers
- On a slender perch, often singing
- Up in the air overhead during courtship
- At a mister or sprinkler

*"He will use the same perch almost constantly"*

—**A. C. Bent,** *Life Histories of North American Cuckoos, Goatsuckers, Hummingbirds and Their Allies* (1940)

**Keep an eye out for perched hummingbirds when you're out in the yard. The male often chooses a perch where he's silhouetted against the sky.**

*On the Home Front* Often a backyard nester, but tiny nest easy to entirely overlook • Builds very small cup of lichens, plant down, and spider silk on branch

**Wild Menu:** Nectar; plus a bigger proportion of insects than most hummingbirds

**Plant Picks:** Tubular "hummingbird flowers," especially in red or orange-red: red-flowering currant (*Ribes sanguineum*), salmonberry (*Rubus spectabilis*), columbines (*Aquilegia* spp.), penstemons, salvias, honeysuckles (*Lonicera* spp.), and many others

**Feeder Pleasers**
- Nectar

**Tricks and Treats**
- Water, especially a mister or sprinkler that the bird can fly through, are a hit in all seasons. If you use a handheld nozzle, hummers in your yard may show up to flit through the spray.

## Thanks for the Flowers!

Old field guides on my shelf show I have no chance of seeing an Anna's hummingbird in my backyard, yet the birds are here year-round. Because of global warming? Nope. Because of gardens. Anna's hummingbird once lived only in parts of California. As civilization spread, and people's backyards sprouted flowers, Anna's changed their ways. When bird lovers added nectar feeders, these hummers became even more widespread.

# Band-Tailed Pigeon

## First Impression

**What are those pigeons doing way out here in the forest?**

*"Recovered from former decimation"*

—John Terres, *Encyclopedia of North American Birds* (1980)

### Mark Your Calendar

Year-round; absent from some areas in this region; usually above 2,000 feet elevation except in some coastal areas

### Details, Details

- Bigger than a regular pigeon; 14½ inches
- Male and female look alike
- Subtly colored in shades of gray and rosy gray, with white crescent on back of neck
- Eyes are dark; bill and legs are yellow
- Wide band at tip of tail is much paler gray than rest of tail, easily visible in flight

### Listen Up!

- Similar to other pigeons and some owls, a deep, mellow *who-whoo who-whoo who-whoo*
- Also guttural and nasal calls
- Their wings make a loud flapping noise when the birds take off.

### Telltale Traits

- Usually in small flocks
- Fast, direct flight
- Perches and feeds in trees and on ground
- Sometimes hangs upside down while feeding in trees

### Look Here

- Feeding on fruit in your yard

### Or Here

- May visit feeders

**On the Home Front** Not usually a backyard nester • Typically nests in heavily forested areas • Makes a loose platform of twigs and sticks

Like the passenger pigeon of the eastern half of the country, the band-tailed was once hunted excessively in the West. Luckily, the slaughter stopped before these birds were completely wiped out.

**Wild Menu:** Grain; seeds; fruit; acorns and other nuts; flowers of trees; occasionally insects

**Plant Picks:** Native red or blue elderberries (*Sambucus callicarpa, S. racemosa, S. caerulea*). Manzanita (*Arctostaphylos columbiana*), salal (*Gaultheria shallon*), and junipers may attract a feeding flock.

**Feeder Pleasers**

- Hazelnuts in the shell; corn; birdseed mix

**Tricks and Treats**

- If you see band-tails nearby, scatter a few handfuls of rock salt and birdcage grit in a tray feeder.
- When acorns are abundant, collect some for the feeder; these pigeons swallow them whole.

## Picture Window

My son got to know a small flock of band-tailed pigeons quite well one summer. Outside his bedroom window of our house on the coast of Oregon grew several big bushes of native red elderberries, and a single bush of later-ripening blue elder. Once the pigeons had spotted them, the birds were daily visitors. Though bulky, they were remarkably agile as they climbed around on the twigs. When a branch bent beneath their weight, they moved down it like tightrope walkers to reach the berries at the tip. They drove our indoor cats crazy!

# Mountain Quail

*First Impression*

**Tiny chickens with topknots, running through the brush**

### Mark Your Calendar

Year-round; at high altitudes during summer nesting season; descend lower in winter

### Details, Details

- Larger and plumper than a robin; 11 inches
- Sides are striped with vertical white bars
- Head plume is long and straight, not curled like other quail
- Male and female look alike
- California quail, also in this region, have curled topknots and different markings.

### Listen Up!

- Male and female make soft clucking, wheezing, and whistled calls
- Male also gives a loud, crowing *QUEEark!*

### Telltale Traits

- Very secretive and elusive, always in or near dense shrubs
- Usually walks or runs
- When startled, may explode into flight
- Likes to dust bathe

### Look Here

- Scuttling across open space between bushes or hedges

### Or Here

- In nearby brushy areas
- In a variety of wild habitats, from fir forests to sagebrush stands near aspens

*On the Home Front* The mountain quail is so elusive that its home life hasn't been extensively studied. • Nests on ground, often on steep hillsides, against log or beneath bush

*"As a lonely mountaineer he is not half known"*

—John Muir, on this "very handsomest and most interesting of all American partridges," *The Yosemite* (1920)

The mountain quail is a secretive bird that usually sticks to the mountains. If your yard borders a wild habitat and your style is naturalistic, you may see them occasionally.

**Wild Menu:** Fruits; seeds; acorns; seeds from conifers; leaves; buds; flowers

**Plant Picks:** A dense cover of shrubs is a must. If your yard is part of a quail's territory, smooth sumac berries (*Rhus glabra*) may help coax the bird into view.

**Feeder Pleasers**

- If you see a quail at your feeder, it's most likely a California quail scarfing down the cracked corn. Mountain quail aren't feeder visitors.

**Tricks and Treats**

- If you have a natural or naturalistic creek on your property, watch for a covey drinking.

*Grazers*

Mountain quail sample any vegetable matter in their path. As the covey moves like a flock of grazing animals, the birds nibble along the way. A nip of a leaf there, a bite of seeds here, a few buds from that bush, some fallen conifer seeds, the seed heads of flowers. Bulbs of wildflowers are scratched up, and even mushrooms may be fair game. It's a varied diet that changes according to the kind of habitat a particular flock adopts.

# RECOMMENDED READING

Thousands of books about birds have been published over the years, so choosing those you like best is a matter of personal taste. Most of the books and publications I cited in this book are from my personal collection of field guides, old books, and journals. I've found them at used-book shops, library sales, flea markets, yard sales, and on the Internet. They still turn up, more often than you might expect, and usually at reasonable prices. The hunt is part of the fun!

## Traditional Field Guides

Visit a bookstore to see the many comprehensive field guides that are available. These chunky, pocket-size books (okay, big pockets!) are made to take along on outings; most have sturdy bindings and wipe-clean covers. Choosing a field guide is a matter of personal preference; some have photos, others have illustrations; some are limited to particular areas, others cover the entire country. I like field guides that include a range map next to each species' picture, rather than maps grouped at the back of the book; that way, I can tell instantly whether that bird is likely in my area.

These traditional field guides are highly popular with bird lovers.

Sibley, David Allen. *The Sibley Guide to Birds.* New York, NY: Knopf, 2000.

Robbins, Chandler S., Bertel Brun, Herbert S. Zim, and Arthur Singer. *Birds of North America: A Guide To Field Identification, Revised and Updated* (Golden Field Guide from St. Martin's Press). New York: St. Martin's Press, 2001.

Peterson, Roger Tory. *A Field Guide to Eastern Birds.* 5th edition. Boston: Houghton Mifflin, 2002

Peterson, Roger Tory. *A Field Guide to Western Birds.* 3rd edition. Boston: Houghton Mifflin, 1998

## The Bent Books

The "Bent books" are my favorite series about birds. I first encountered this 20-volume series (published between 1919 and 1968) in the Kutztown State College library, in eastern Pennsylvania, when I was 16; they formed the basis of my education in bird life and lore, and I still draw from them today. Just last spring, while watching a pair of courting and nesting Virginia rails in a swamp, I thought, "Wonder what Bent has to say about this?" and pulled out his book when I reached home. Reading a Bent book is almost as good as sharing stories with a fellow bird-watcher.

Arthur Cleveland Bent collected hundreds of anecdotes and sifted through published material to fill each volume with a lifetime of learning about the bird species of

North America. The many volumes were published by the Smithsonian Institution; most were reprinted by Dover. They are out of print, but you can still find many reasonably priced copies on the Internet or at used-book shops and other sources.

Look for A. C. Bent, *Life Histories of North American Woodpeckers*, and other "*Life Histories of . . .*" books (Smithsonian Institution or Dover reprint; various publication dates).

You can also find some Bent books online at www.birdsbybent.com/; excerpts appear on Web sites (search for the name of the bird you're interested in, plus the name "Bent").

## The Treasure Hunt for Old Books

Back in the dark ages before the Internet, the only way you could track down an old book was by asking a bookshop to send out postcards to other shops, expressing interest. It was often a months-long process with disappointing results. Today, you can simply go online and track down a copy of just about any book you might be looking for in a matter of minutes.

My favorite book finder is AbeBooks, www.abebooks.com, a clearinghouse Web site that lists tens of thousands of books and other publications offered by booksellers around the world, any of which you can purchase. You can browse by category (Warning: Can be addictive!) or search for a specific book. Each seller describes the condition of its book or publication and lists its price, so you can choose a volume that enhances your library and fits your budget. Back issues of ornithological journals, such as the *Auk*, are available for as little as $1 apiece, plus shipping.

The auction site www.ebay.com also includes listings for interesting old bird books and journals.

Booksellers often list out of print books on www.amazon.com; just search for the book by name, then click on "Used & New."

If you do an online search for the title you're looking for, you're likely to find other sources that offer the book. Happy hunting!

## Scientific Journals

The *Auk* is the journal of the American Ornithologists' Union (AOU). Founded in 1883, the AOU is devoted to the scientific study of birds, although many of the earlier issues of the journal include anecdotes contributed by amateur bird-watchers. The first issue of the *Auk* was published in 1884, and it's still being published today. Anyone who likes birds can join the AOU; an annual membership costs $80 (student rate, $26).

www.aou.org
American Ornithologists' Union
1313 Dolley Madison Blvd.
Suite 402
McLean, VA 22101
(703) 790-1745

The *Condor* is the journal of the Cooper Ornithological Society (COS), founded in 1893; the *Condor* has been published since 1899 and is still going strong today. COS is dedicated to the scientific study of birds and their conservation, and encourages membership for anyone who enjoys birds. Fees are similar to those of the AOU. You can join the COS via its Web site or through the Ornithological Societies of North America (OSNA; see opposite page).

www.cooper.org
Cooper Ornithological Society

Joining the Ornithological Societies of North America (OSNA) opens the door into the world of serious birders. This umbrella organization gathers together various bird-focused organizations to make it easier to manage memberships and publications. It was founded in 1979 by the AOU, the COS, and the Wilson Ornithological Society. Today it also handles membership services for the Association of Field Ornithologists, the Raptor Research Foundation, and the Waterbird Society, along with its original three. Join any of these organizations through OSNA, and you'll receive the *Ornithological Newsletter,* published six times a year. It's chock-full of news and opportunities for bird-watchers who want to, or already have, made birding part of their life's work. You'll find info about volunteer and paid field assistant positions, for which helpers are needed outdoors ("in the field"), plus news about research grants, scientific meetings, and other members.

www.osnabirds.org
OSNA Business Office
5400 Bosque Blvd., Ste. 680
Waco, TX 76710
(254) 399-9636

# SOURCES

I often say I wish I could meet each one of you because I have a feeling we're kindred spirits. Since there's nothing I like more than talking with friends about birds, plants, and nature, I've created a place where we can do just that. Just stop in at my Web site, www.sallyroth.com. You'll find pictures from my own backyard, stories that I couldn't squeeze into this book, news about upcoming projects, and plenty of ideas for making your own place a real haven for birds, butterflies, and other wild creatures. You'll also find a place on the Web site where you can ask questions, share your own discoveries, or just enjoy talking to like-minded folks about birds, gardening, and nature. See you there!

Also, check out the sources below for bird supplies and plants for all regions of the country.

## Supplies

Look for bird feeders, nest boxes, and bird-seed at nearby wild bird supply stores. Discount stores and even supermarkets also carry a selection of products. Craft sales and bazaars often have handmade feeders and houses.

Online, try these Web sites. All offer a wide variety of supplies and temptations for the backyard bird lover.

Duncraft
102 Fisherville Rd.
Concord, NH 03303
(888) 879-5095
www.duncraft.com
*Online, phone, mail order, printed catalog also available free upon request*

BestNest
4750 Lake Forest Drive, Suite 132
Cincinnati, OH 45242
(877) 562-1818 or (513) 232-4225
www.bestnest.com
*Online catalog only; online or phone orders*

Wild Birding World
The Kayes Group, Inc.
PO Box 3326
Mesquite, NV 89027
(845) 834-3215
www.wildbirdingworld.com
*Online catalog only; online or phone orders*

www.abirdsworld.com
(877) 725-1965
*Online catalog only; online or phone orders*

www.Amazon.com
*Online only*

**Plants**

All of the plants I've recommended in this book's regional bird profiles are widely available in those regions. If you're hunting for bird-approved plants, start with your local nurseries and garden centers. Independently owned nurseries usually have staff members who know plants and can help you find what you need. Many stock a selection of native species. Prices may be lower at garden centers, but the selection is usually not as good and the staff not as knowledgeable. Don't see what you're looking for? Just ask; they may be able to order it for you. You can also order plants online; just search for the plant by name.

You can find an excellent selection of native plants and other bird-appealing plants, including wildflowers, grasses, shrubs, trees, and vines, at trustworthy mail-order suppliers, too. Here's a very small sampling to whet your appetite.

### Northeast

Tripple Brook Farm
37 Middle Rd.
Southampton, MA 01073
(413) 527-4626
www.tripplebrookfarm.com
*Hundreds of fabulous plants—I need a bigger yard!—including native viburnums and many, many other natives*

### North and Midwest

Hamilton's Native Nursery & Seed Farm
16786 Brown Rd.
Elk Creek, MO 65464
(417) 967-2190
www.hamiltonseed.com
*Seeds and plants of native grasses, prairie flowers, shrubs, and trees, plus other great finds*

### Southeast and South

Woodlanders, Inc.
Bob McCartney
1128 Colleton Avenue
Aiken, SC 29801
(803) 648-7522
www.woodlanders.net
*One of the older native plant specialists (since 1979), Woodlanders offers bird-attracting natives for Southern regions. Call for a catalog; no online shopping—yet.*

### West

Blake Nursery
316 Otter Creek Rd.
Big Timber, MT 59011
(406) 932-4195
www.blakenursery.com
*Specializes in plants for western gardens, including a terrific selection of hardy Montana natives that will thrive elsewhere in the West, too—or give that western touch to an eastern garden.*

### Northwest, West, and Southwest

Forestfarm
990 Tetherow Rd.
Williams, OR 97544-9599
(541) 846-7269
www.forestfarm.com
*Plant addicts, beware: One look at this chunky, jam-packed catalog and you're sunk. An unbelievably vast selection of thousands of plants, including natives from across America. Lots of favorite plants in my gardens have come from Forestfarm—even when I lived in Pennsylvania.*

# PHOTO CREDITS

© Wally Bauman/Alamy: page 239

© Mark Belko/Alamy: page 42 *(top)*

© Blickwinkel/Alamy: page 268

© Rick and Nora Bowers/Alamy: page 290

© Gay Bumgarner/Alamy: page 2

© Gary W. Carter/Alamy: pages vii, 83 *(blue jay)*, 112

© Chao-Yang Chan/Alamy: page 26

© Jim Cole/Alamy: page 52

© Bruce Coleman Inc./Alamy: page 275

© Corbis Premium Collection/Alamy: pages 85, 224

© Danita Delimont/Alamy: pages 34, 101 *(Eastern)*, 109, 301

© Peter Forsberg/Alamy: page 25

© franzfoto.com/Alamy: page 296

© William Leaman/Alamy: pages 36, 43, 53 *(top)*, 183, 210, 221, 267, 298

© Clive Limpkin/Alamy: page 46 (left)

© Oyvind Martinsen/Alamy: page 48

© Mike Mckavett/Alamy: page 247

© Mira/Alamy: page 10

© David Osborn/Alamy: page 24

© Malcolm Schuyl/Alamy: page 259

© Stock Connection Distribution/Alamy: page 209

© SuperStock/Alamy: page 101 *(inset)*

© Terry Wall/Alamy: page 227

© Chris Wallace/Alamy: page 244

© Deborah Allen: page 186

© David Boyle/Animals Animals: pages 8, 238

© Mark Chappell/Animals Animals: pages 214, 271

© Alan G. Nelson/Animals Animals: page 4

© Marie Read/Animals Animals: pages 212, 215, 222

© AP Images: page 29

© Linda Freshwaters Arndt: page 140

© Ron Austing: pages 83 *(inset)*, 84, 89, 92, 98 *(myrtle)*, 130, 135, 164, 171

© Cliff Beittel: page 87

Courtesy of Kevin Burke/Earlham College: page 33

© Mark Bolton/Corbis: page xvi

© Joe McDonald/Corbis: page 18

© Norbert Schaefer/Corbis: page 7

© Tom Stewart/Corbis: page 3

© Richard Day/Daybreak Imagery: pages viii, 21, 81, 91, 95, 96, 103, 106 *(dark-eyed)*, 127, 128,

© Barbara Gerlach/DRK Photo: page 305

© Donald M. Jones/DRK Photo: page 246

© Tom and Pat Leeson/DRK Photo: page 22

© Digital Vision/Getty Images: page 16

© Image Source/Getty Images: page 13

© Photographer's Choice/Getty Images: page 38

© Steve Greer Photography: page 86

© Russell C. Hansen: page 118 *(ruby-throated)*

© Janet Horton: pages 45 *(right)*, 80, 111, 250

© Bill Leaman/The Image Finders: page 126

© Peter LaTourrette: front cover, page iii

© Tom and Pat Leeson: pages ix, 82, 97, 99, 102, 106 *(top inset)*, 117 *(Baltimore)*, 161, 179, 181, 187, 226, 236, 237, 243, 265, 285, 304

© Kitchin and Hurst/Leeson Photo: pages 131, 245

© Steve Maslowski: pages 6, 180

© Charles W. Melton: page 248

© Jerry Mercier: page 110

© Matthias Breiter/Minden Pictures: page 153

© Tim Fitzharris/Minden Pictures: pages 134, 288

© Christo Baars/Foto Natura/Minden Pictures: page 234

© Dietmar Nill/Foto Natura/Minden Pictures: page 166

© Thomas Mangelsen/Minden Pictures: page 159

© Michael Quinton/Minden Pictures: pages 155, 169

© Tom Vezo/Minden Pictures: pages 165, 190, 233, 286, 292, 295

© Aflo/Nature Picture Library: page 197

© Wegner/ARCO/Nature Picture Library: page 23

© Niall Benvie/Nature Picture Library: page 28

# INDEX

**Boldface** page numbers indicate illustrations. <u>Underscored</u> references indicate boxed text.

# USDA PLANT HARDINESS ZONE MAP

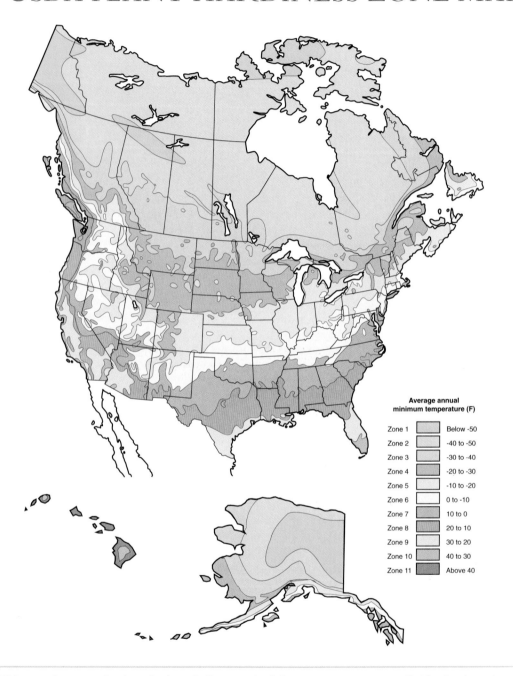

**Average annual minimum temperature (F)**

|  |  |
|------|-------------|
| Zone 1 | Below -50 |
| Zone 2 | -40 to -50 |
| Zone 3 | -30 to -40 |
| Zone 4 | -20 to -30 |
| Zone 5 | -10 to -20 |
| Zone 6 | 0 to -10 |
| Zone 7 | 10 to 0 |
| Zone 8 | 20 to 10 |
| Zone 9 | 30 to 20 |
| Zone 10 | 40 to 30 |
| Zone 11 | Above 40 |

This map is recognized as the best indicator of minimum temperatures available. Look at the map to find your area, then match its pattern to the key at right. When you've found your pattern, the key will tell you what hardiness zone you live in. Remember that the map is a general guide; your particular conditions may vary.